P

Captain
James Cook

Rob Mundle

ABC
Books

The ABC 'Wave' device is a trademark of the Australian Broadcasting Corporation and is used under licence by HarperCollins*Publishers* Australia.

First published in Australia in 2013
This edition published in 2017
by HarperCollins*Publishers* Australia Pty Limited
ABN 36 009 913 517
harpercollins.com.au

HarperCollins*Publishers*
Level 13, 201 Elizabeth Street, Sydney, NSW 2000, Australia
Unit D1, 63 Apollo Drive, Rosedale, Auckland 0632, New Zealand
A 53, Sector 57, Noida, UP, India
77–85 Fulham Palace Road, London W6 8JB, United Kingdom
2 Bloor Street East, 20th floor, Toronto, Ontario M4W 1A8, Canada
195 Broadway, New York NY 10007, USA

National Library of Australia Cataloguing-in-Publication data:

Mundle, Rob, author.
Captain James Cook / Rob Mundle.
ISBN: 978 0 7333 3543 3 (paperback)
ISBN: 978 1 4607 0061 7 (ebook : epub)
Includes index.
Cook, James, 1728-1779
Explorers – England – Biography.
Voyages around the world.
Pacific Ocean – Discovery and exploration.
Other Authors/Contributors: Australian Broadcasting Corporation
910.92

Cover design by Matt Stanton and Daniel Valenzuela, HarperCollins Design Studio
Cover image: *Endeavour Leaving Plymouth*, Painting by Geoff Hunt RSMA represented by Artist Partners
Typeset in Bembo by Kirby Jones
Maps by Map Illustrations www.mapillustrations.com.au
Index by Olive Grove Indexing Services
Printed and bound in Australia by McPhersons Printing Group
The papers used by HarperCollins in the manufacture of this book are a natural, recyclable product made from wood grown in sustainable plantation forests. The fibre source and manufacturing processes meet recognised international environmental standards, and carry certification.

In memory of President John F. Kennedy,
who reminded us:

*All of us have in our veins the exact same percentage of
salt in our blood that exists in the ocean, and, therefore,
we have salt in our blood, in our sweat, in our tears.
We are tied to the ocean. And when we go back to the sea,
whether it is to sail or to watch it, we are going back from
whence we came.*

HM Bark *Endeavour.*
(Artist David Hobbs; reproduced courtesy of the Australian National Maritime Museum, owner of the *Endeavour* replica.)

1. fore topgallant
2. mainmast
3. yard
4. main topgallant
5. fore topsail
6. main topsail
7. bowsprit
8. mizzen topsail
9. spritsail topsail
10. block
11. foresail
12. mizzen
13. cathead
14. spritsail course

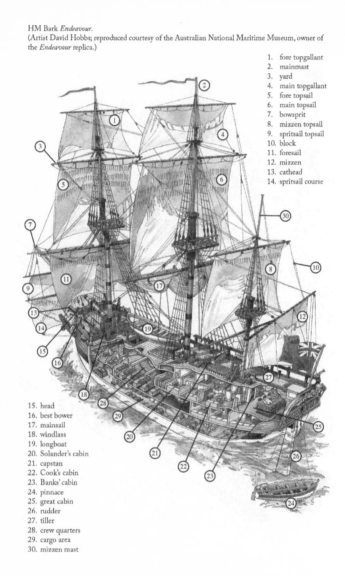

15. head
16. best bower
17. mainsail
18. windlass
19. longboat
20. Solander's cabin
21. capstan
22. Cook's cabin
23. Banks' cabin
24. pinnace
25. great cabin
26. rudder
27. tiller
28. crew quarters
29. cargo area
30. mizzen mast

HM Bark *Endeavour.* Artist David Hobbs; reproduced courtesy of the Australian National Maritime Museum, owner of the *Endeavour* replica.

Contents

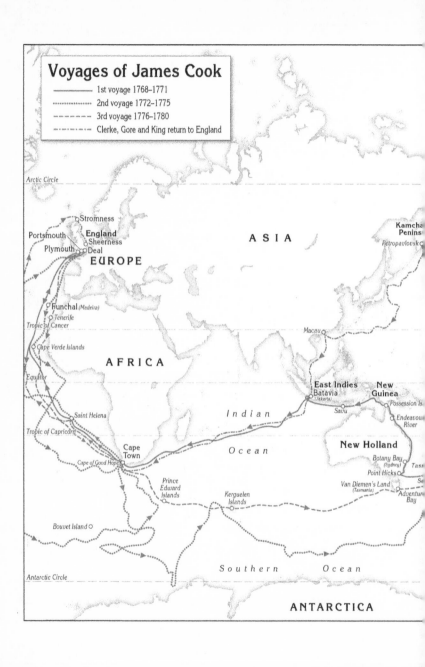

Voyages of James Cook

- —————— 1st voyage 1768–1771
- ···················· 2nd voyage 1772–1775
- — — — — 3rd voyage 1776–1780
- —··—··—·· Clerke, Gore and King return to England

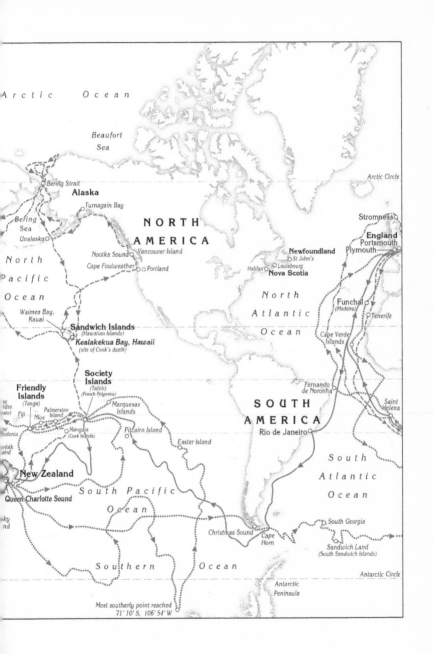

Arctic Ocean

Beaufort Sea

Arctic Circle

Bering Strait
Alaska
Turnagain Bay

Bering Sea
Unalaska

Stromness

England
Portsmouth
Plymouth

NORTH AMERICA

North Pacific Ocean

Nootka Sound
Cape Foulweather
Vancouver Island
Portland

Newfoundland
St John's
Louisbourg
Halifax
Nova Scotia

North Atlantic Ocean

Funchal
(Madeira)
Tenerife

Waimea Bay, Kauai

Sandwich Islands
(Hawaiian Islands)
Kealakekua Bay, Hawaii
(site of Cook's death)

Cape Verde Islands

Society Islands
(Tahiti)
(French Polynesia)

Fernando de Noronha

Saint Helena

Friendly Islands
(Tonga)
w ides atu)
Fiji
Palmerston Island
Niue
edonia
Mangaia
(Cook Islands)

Marquesas Islands

SOUTH AMERICA
Rio de Janeiro

rfolk and

Pitcairn Island

Easter Island

South Atlantic Ocean

New Zealand

South Pacific Ocean

sky nd

Queen Charlotte Sound

South Georgia

Christmas Sound
Cape Horn

Sandwich Land
(South Sandwich Islands)

Southern Ocean

Antarctic Circle

Antarctic Peninsula

Most southerly point reached
71° 10′ S, 106° 54′ W

Escape from the Great Barrier Reef.

Captain James Cook

A Wisp of Wind

A board His Majesty's Bark *Endeavour*, the ship's bell, which was mounted in its belfry on the foredeck above the anchor windlass, had just tolled twice. It was the signal for the near 100 men on board that it was five o'clock in the morning, the completion of the first hour of the morning watch.

For the previous four months, *Endeavour* and her crew had travelled more than 1700 nautical miles along a coastline to the north of a headland that had appeared off the ship's bow on 19 April 1770. In history, that date is recognised as the day the great seafarer James Cook first sighted the east coast of New Holland. In doing so he contributed significantly to solving a maritime mystery that had been debated for centuries.

At this very moment, though, things had gone awry: it was looking increasingly likely that the ship and everyone on board would be lost, probably without trace. *Endeavour*, now situated beside New Holland's reef-strewn northern coastline, was becalmed and drifting towards annihilation.

Windless as it was in the early hours, it was not a flat calm. The ship was slowly heaving from side to side in response to powerful ocean swells that were rolling in from the south-east like liquid mountain ranges in perpetual motion – the remnants of a mid-ocean storm that had its core somewhere out in the Pacific. The crests of these monsters were only seconds apart, and as each one loomed and surged against *Endeavour*'s hull it would pitch her massive bulk towards the heavens and roll her to starboard then to port in a slow, pendulum-like motion. And with every lurch came an ugly discord of sound from aloft as the heavy canvas sails slatted inside-out, and the solid timber yards, from which they were set, groaned in protest.

There was another haunting noise, however – like rolling thunder – that was originating from a source away from the ship, and it was causing escalating concern for all on board. The men knew what it was, so well that everyone, from the captain to the lowliest able seaman and servant boy, was constantly peering through the darkness and watching in dread at the dim scene that was slowly becoming defined off *Endeavour*'s starboard side. As their ship drifted closer to it, they saw wave after monstrous wave being compressed into a horribly powerful peak before exploding and collapsing with a booming roar into a seething mass of ghostly white water – thousands of tons of it – onto the coral reef that had so abruptly impeded its progress. The wall of water would then cascade across the reef like an unstoppable tsunami.

The motion that came from each wave as it approached the reef, and the sweep of a current being generated by a tide that was on the flood, were combining to move *Endeavour* at an alarming rate towards the boiling white water. And there was nothing that could be done to prevent it.

By this time, Cook and his crew had been away from their home port in England for almost two years to the day, on a voyage that initially took them to Tahiti to observe the transit of Venus across the sun. The Royal Society had commissioned that part of the expedition, in the hope that data recorded from sights taken during this rare astronomical phenomenon in June 1769 would provide the most accurate figure yet on the distance between Venus and the sun. Such information would enable scientists to more precisely calculate the size of the solar system.

With that undertaking completed, Cook had followed his instructions from the Admiralty, which, in taking the opportunity that came with one of their ships being in this newly discovered part of the world, directed him to take a sweep into the Southern Ocean in search of *Terra Australis Incognita* – the Great South Land. Should nothing be found, he was to continue west, towards where, on 13 December 1642, Dutchman Abel Tasman had discovered 'a large land, uplifted high' – the west coast of the southern island of New Zealand. By sailing towards that point, Cook would inevitably make landfall. Once there, he would be able to explore the largely unknown coastline and fill in the extensive gaps left by Tasman.

Cook's instructions from the Lords of the Admiralty for this part of the voyage were deemed to be secret, as they did not want to alert other European maritime nations to the exploratory nature of the mission. Britain wanted to keep any success to itself.

There was another important element relating to this voyage. Any discoveries that might be made would present a unique opportunity to expand the world's knowledge of the flora and fauna of this part of the world. As a result, there was on board a special group whose task it was, following their observation of the transit of Venus, to seek all possible samples of the previously unknown native plants and wildlife they would almost certainly find on land and sea. Leading this group was a member of the august Royal Society – more formally known as the Royal Society of London for Improving Natural Knowledge – wealthy 27-year-old naturalist Joseph Banks; he came with eight assistants, including a natural scientist, two artists and servants, as well as his two dogs.

Eton- and Oxford-educated Banks, who would later in life become one of the world's most prominent patrons of natural science, was so enthusiastic about this venture with Cook that he had invested around £10,000 of his personal wealth to support it. That figure converts to more than £10 million ($17 million) today. Needless to say, Banks was given the best sleeping quarters on the ship, on a par with the captain's.

*

Once New Zealand had been reached, and whatever possible exploration of that region completed, Cook had been given the option of returning home via Cape Horn or the Cape of Good Hope. He chose the latter, primarily for the safety of his ship and his men. It would be a longer but less dangerous passage that way, for *Endeavour* was by then showing signs of structural fatigue, and they would thereby avoid the perils that came with rounding the notorious, storm-lashed Cape Horn.

Cook resumed a passage to the west until, on that historic day of 19 April 1770, a lookout stationed near the masthead shouted in high excitement: '*Land ho!*' There was a coastline off to the north-west and, soon after it was sighted, the most obvious landmark would go onto Cook's chart with the name Point Hicks: a tribute to that man who first saw it, 31-year-old Second Lieutenant Zachary Hickes.

As *Endeavour* closed in on the land, the coast was seen to disappear over the horizon to the north-east, and on considering this, Cook called for a change of course in that direction so it could be traced. But to where, no one knew.

During the following four months, as his ship weaved her way north, this remarkable seafarer explored and mapped every possible detail of the coastline – sometimes by going ashore for a more accurate view of his surroundings.

Now, though, he was experiencing the worst part of a nightmare that had haunted him for weeks, one caused mainly by sailing almost blindly through the hundreds upon hundreds of threatening coral cays and reefs making up what we know today as the Great Barrier Reef. It had been a harrowing passage, and Cook would later note: 'we have sailed 360 leagues without ever having a man out of the chains heaving the lead [to measure the depth] when the ship was underway, a circumstance that I dare say never happened to any ship before and yet here it was absolutely necessary.'

The captain had known from the moment his ship became imprisoned in the coral maze that the odds were stacked in favour of high drama. He had also known he had no alternative but to continue sailing downwind to the north, and to explore this coast to the best of his ability.

In the middle of the night on 11 June, Cook's fears were realised: *Endeavour* ploughed into an unseen reef that was lurking just below the sea surface. The ever-articulate Banks put that dramatic scene into words in his journal:

> ... the tide ebbed so much that we found it impossible to attempt to get her off till next high water ... Anchors were however got out and laid ready for heaving ... The tide began to rise and as it rose the ship worked violently upon the rocks so that by 2 she began to make water and increased very fast ... Now in my own opinion I entirely gave up the ship and packing up what I thought I might save prepared myself for the worst.

Through great seamanship, determination and the good fortune that came with the weather being relatively benign, *Endeavour* was re-floated and the necessary repairs completed over a seven-week period, in a sheltered river mouth on the mainland. During that time, Cook convinced himself it was imperative to find a channel through the outer reef that was wide enough and deep enough for the ship to make good her escape to the open sea. Ironically, it was because Cook accepted that the dangers of sailing within the confines of the reef were too great that he found himself in this latest, far more perilous situation.

Five days after *Endeavour* resumed her voyage, escape from inside the reef was achieved via a channel to the east of Lizard Island. Initially, all was well. The ship made good speed north, her sails billowing on the face of a strong south-east trade wind as she pursued a course well wide of the reef. This was the first time in three months that all aboard could enjoy the relief that came from having safe and deep water under the keel. It was especially the case for those with the responsibility of being a lookout – usually one or more of the mates, if not the captain or officers. Their task was now casual, not constant.

There was one problem emerging which had to be confronted, however. Every time *Endeavour* surged down one of the large, deep-blue rolling seas and gouged out a white bow wave more than a metre high, a torrent of water would spew into the bilge. The carpenters were sent below and forward to find the cause, and they soon reported to the captain that the repairs made to the bow after the grounding on the reef had obviously not extended high enough above the waterline. Water was pouring in through damaged planks and open seams, filling the bilge along the entire length of the ship at the disconcerting rate of 9 inches an hour. With there being no way to make repairs, the only solution was for one of the pumps to be manned around the clock until conditions eased. Cook would later note that 'this was looked upon as trifling to the danger we had lately made our escape from'.

For Cook, the mental reprieve that came with being rid of the reef would be brief. By not having the coast in sight, he was now decreasing his chance of successfully completing the next stage of his mission. Having confirmed the existence of the east coast of New Holland, he still needed to discover if a channel or strait existed between wherever this new-found coast terminated and the land to the north known as New Guinea, the southern coast of which had been charted by Spain's Luís Vaez de Torres more than 160 years earlier. So, after enjoying some forty-eight hours away from danger, the captain, 'fearful of over shooting the passage supposing there to be one between this land and New Guinea', issued the order to wear ship and hold a course to the west until the outer edge of the reef, or the coast, became apparent.

The reef that threatened their very existence right now was sighted just before sunset on 15 August, about 2 leagues – 6 nautical miles – to the west, off *Endeavour*'s port side. Cook elected to continue sailing north and into the night on a course he hoped would parallel this considerable navigational hazard, but around midnight, when the wind suddenly changed direction from east-south-east to east-by-north – turning the reef into an intimidating lee shore – he quickly realised he must adopt a more cautious course. His well-calculated call was for the ship to be tacked immediately and sailed on a near reciprocal track back to the south and away from the danger. Soon afterwards, though, with the reef a mere 2 nautical miles to leeward, the wind faded to nothing and the sea surface went glassy.

A shouted enquiry from the deck to the lookout aloft had him confirm that, in the dim light of the waning moon, he could still see the large surf breaking onto the reef: a long, shadowy streak of grey that was unmistakable against the blackness of the sea. Over the next hour or so, bearings were taken and calculations made, causing the captain to declare with some level of concern that *Endeavour* was 'nearing the reef fast by means of a flood tide and S.E. swell'.

The destruction of the ship became more likely with the wash from each wave, and as this occurred, so the haunting sound of the pounding seas grew proportionately louder. They were nature's death knell. 'A little after 4 o'clock the roaring of the surf was plainly heard,' Cook would later write in his journal, 'and at day break the vast foaming breakers were too plainly to be seen not a mile from us towards which we found the ship was carried by the waves surprisingly fast ...'.

With no breath of breeze, it was impossible to sail away from the danger, so Cook had to consider all other options. He immediately ordered that two of *Endeavour*'s three boats – the 10-foot-long yawl and 18-foot longboat – be hoisted out and manned in an attempt to tow the ship away from the threat. At the same time, even though it was still dark, he had the carpenters set about making hasty repairs to the damaged pinnace (similar in length to the longboat), so that it, too, could lend assistance in the towing operation. But even with all three boats in the water and eighteen men hauling their hearts out on the oars, this desperate effort proved near futile. All they could achieve – while assisted by some of the ship's crew manning sweep oars set from *Endeavour*'s two stern ports – was to get 'the ship's head round to the northward', Cook noted, 'which seemed to be the only way to keep her off the reef or at least to delay time'.

Cook then had to accept that nature held the advantage – they were still being swept towards the reef: 'We had at this time not an air of wind and the depth of water was unfathomable, so there was not a possibility of anchoring, in this distressed situation we had nothing but providence and the small assistance our boats could give us to trust to.'

All the while, the crewman in the chains at the side of the ship, adjacent to the helm position on the quarterdeck, continued to heave the lead in the hope of finding the bottom. Should he make that call then the anchor, the best bower, which was at the ready, could be lowered the instant an order was shouted from the quarterdeck. But each time the leadsman deftly swung the 14-pound weight, which was attached to a long line, and looped it into the sea, the call he made for the captain's benefit simply added to the magnitude of the looming disaster: '100 fathoms. No ground Sir … 120 fathoms. No ground Sir … 150 fathoms. No ground Sir.'

In layman's parlance, the reef edge that appeared about to become the ship's nemesis was the summit of a vertical coral cliff-face that descended some 300 metres to the ocean floor – the height of the Eiffel Tower in Paris!

The leadsman's proclamations only fed the fear that was then tearing at the minds of all on board: it would be impossible for any man to survive the incredible force the roaring seas would exert on the ship the moment it was smashed to pieces on the reef by the giant waves. In such a catastrophic maelstrom, every crew-member would either be killed by the impact or drown. The point had been reached where only a miracle could save the sailors and their ship from this terminal situation.

Incredibly, though, while *Endeavour* was trapped by the calm and being drawn towards the reef as if responding to a powerful natural magnetic force, the men on board showed no evidence of panic. Every one of them who was required to sail the vessel stood at his position – most at the ready on the braces and sheets that controlled the sails to respond immediately and trim the sails to suit any puff of wind that might miraculously appear. With it still being dark – sunrise was not until 6.35 am – this task was doubly daunting, as it was all about the senses. In daylight, the sailors would be able to see any small dark patches of ripple generated by a slight breeze on an otherwise glassy sea. At this time, though, all around them was black.

The dedication of his men was not lost on the captain:

> It was six o'clock and we were not above 80 or 100 yards
> from the breakers, the same sea that washed the sides of
> the ship rose in a breaker prodigiously high the very next
> time it did rise so that between us and destruction was
> only a dismal valley the breadth of one wave … we had
> hardly any hopes of saving the ship … yet in this truly
> terrible situation not one man ceased to do his utmost
> and that with as much calmness as if no danger had been
> near. All the dangers we had escaped [previously] were
> little in comparison of being thrown upon this reef
> where the ship must be dashed to pieces in a moment.

Banks wrote of their wretched predicament: 'our case was truly desperate, no man I believe but who gave himself entirely over, a speedy death was all we had to hope for and that from the vastness of the breakers which must quickly dash the ship all to pieces was scarce to be doubted. Other hopes we had none.'

But suddenly, silent prayers were being answered …

'There's a breeze,' one of the anxious tars would almost certainly have shouted as he felt it waft across his craggy, weather-beaten face.

Others would have agreed in unison, at the same time sensing that its direction meant they just might be able to avoid catastrophe. They looked aloft – yes, the sails were stirring – and with that a sense of urgency took over.

Orders shouted from the quarterdeck called for the braces and sheets to be quickly trimmed, so that the ship's canvas wings could capture every ounce of force from this faint breeze that was fanning through the rig. The morsel of relief that came when the sails began to fill was magnified considerably when it was realised that *Endeavour* was responding to the helm. The helmsman had steerage – she was ever so slowly making headway, and that would enable her to be guided away from the menacing white water thundering onto the coral a stone's throw away.

Even so, the captain and his most experienced seamen knew they were far from being out of the reef's grasp, simply because it was impossible to say how long the gentle breeze would prevail. Was this puff their lifesaver, or simply the Sirens tormenting them like a cat pawing at a half-dead bird?

Whichever scenario proved to be true, at this moment it was taken for the desperately needed miracle they had prayed for, and the fact that it came from a desirable direction made the moment even more remarkable.

Minutes later, *Endeavour*, still rolling in response to the large swells, was one boat-length away from the reef ... then two ... then three ... That was until, within ten minutes the torture returned: the benevolent breath disappeared as quickly as it had appeared.

Anxiety returned to the heart of every man.

Pages of scrunched-up paper were thrown over the side and into the water to check on the ship's rate and direction of drift. They confirmed the worst. The threat was re-emerging.

But again a miracle: the slightest of breezes prevailed and moved them to a safer distance. As the sea now became illuminated by the rising sun, the lookout shouted out that there was a channel ahead. Soon another development assisted them, in the form of a change in the tide.

And so, on Thursday, 16 August 1770, a twist of fate – a quirk of nature in the form of an ever-so-gentle and unexpected puff of wind – had changed the course of history. Cook and his men were spared from the fatal consequences of a horrendous shipwreck, one that might have remained a maritime mystery forever; one that would have deprived the world too soon of the greatest maritime navigator, explorer and cartographer of all time.

CHAPTER ONE

From Farm Boy to Seafarer

It was 1745, and James Cook – a strapping, brown-haired, brown-eyed Yorkshire lad more than 6 foot tall – had not long been in the coastal village of Staithes, in England's north-east, when he began to realise that the sea would be his destiny. For the seventeen-year-old, it was a slow transition initially, from fascination, to obsession, and then fact.

First settled by the Vikings around 900 AD, Staithes is a tiny fishing village compressed into a gorge, with a winding, ribbon-like stream, the Roxby Beck, meandering through its midst. During Cook's short time there, the village comprised irregular-sized stone and brick residences of one or two levels, squeezed together along narrow thoroughfares, and most with their front doors opening out onto the street. All the houses had steeply sloping chimney-topped roofs of terracotta or slate. What legitimate wealth there was in the town came from the sea – Staithes boasted one of the largest fishing fleets in England – and the mining of alum and other minerals from the cliffs surrounding the village. Additional, illegitimate wealth resulted from the place being a haven for smugglers and their vessels.

Cook had gone to Staithes to start his working life as a junior assistant to a merchant, haberdasher and grocer named William Sanderson. As he had wandered along the cobblestoned High Street back on that first day, looking for Mr Sanderson's shopfront, his height and strong build would have made him conspicuous among the locals. At the same time, he no doubt sensed he was negotiating a somewhat claustrophobic, man-made cavern, thanks to the proximity of the residences to the street. It was an environment that was totally foreign to his upbringing amid the rolling green hills about 20 miles inland. And life in Staithes appeared to be far more exciting than what he had known in the country, where he had often helped his father, a farm worker, toil in the wide open fields. Here the air was filled with the smell of the sea and seaweed, and the waterfront was a mass of fishing boats, fishing nets and fishermen who had returned from the sea, or were preparing to head out.

Young Cook had come to work for Sanderson in the hope that one day he himself might become a merchant. He was already well qualified for such an occupation, having demonstrated a considerable aptitude in arithmetic at school, and Mr Sanderson, as a 'grocer' – a merchant who traded in 'gross quantities' of a remarkably wide range of products, including foodstuffs and household goods – needed someone who had aptitude for numbers.

Apart from the experience of being employed in the shop, where he slept under the counter each night – a practice not uncommon for apprentices of the day – the young farm boy became intrigued by the vibrancy of life in the busy little seaport. The harbour at Staithes opens onto the North Sea (which in that era was commonly referred to as the German Sea or Oceanus Germanicus), a location that led to many a well-travelled sailor patronising Sanderson's waterfront premises. Inevitably during these visits, Cook's fertile mind would be filled to overflowing – regaled and liberally nourished by colourful stories of adventure on the high seas and the excitement that came through visiting ports near and far.

The impact of such stories was so profound on Cook that after only a few months in Staithes, his thoughts about the future were soon turning away from being a merchant and towards adventure at sea: seafaring was, for him, far more appealing than the world of commerce where he would be doing little more than selling uninspiring essentials of everyday life.

Legend has it that the tipping point came when a well-weathered sailor strolled into the store and used a one-shilling piece minted to Britain's South American trading organisation, the South Sea Company, to pay for his purchase. Young James is said to have looked at the coin as if it were an omen guiding him to his future: as though it held magical powers – conjuring up a thousand stories of distant lands.

Within eighteen months of arriving in Staithes, Cook had, with the full support of his employer, decided to move on from working the shop floor to walking the deck. So the tall young Yorkshireman packed his bags, bade Mr Sanderson farewell, and travelled 10 miles south to another seaport, Whitby, on the River Esk.

A clue to Whitby's place in English history is seen atop one of the high hills surrounding the town, where the ruins of Whitby Abbey, founded by St Hilda in 658 AD, stand in defiance of time. In 1746, the town was about to add to its impressive history: it was from here that the remarkable seafaring life of Captain James Cook, the great master mariner, navigator, explorer and cartographer, evolved.

With a population of more than 10,000, Whitby was considerably larger than Staithes, and far more active as a seaport. Around 250 ships, the majority owned by local businessmen, sailed out of the Esk each year and traded with ports across the known world. Cook's new hometown was 25 miles directly east of his birthplace, Marton-in-Cleveland, yet the two were like comparing wheat and weeds with kippers and kelp.

Cook was born on 27 October 1728, the second child of 34-year-old Scotsman James Cook, and his wife, Grace (née Pace), in a humble and extremely small mud-walled cottage, known locally as a 'biggin'. It would have comprised two rooms, at most, and is thought to have had a dirt floor and thatched roof. There were no more than three tiny windows, bringing a minimal amount of light into the dim interior.

The family home would have been a damp, dank and bleak introduction to the world for baby James. The roof and walls of such a basic abode almost always leaked, causing the floor to be constantly wet. There was no sanitation and, with soap a highly priced luxury, personal hygiene was almost nonexistent for most families of this low social strata. To counter the inevitable pungent smells that were part of such a clammy circumstance, and to make the house more habitable, fragrant herbs – more than likely meadowsweet – as well as straw, were strewn throughout the cottage. Meadowsweet was the preferred choice of all classes of the Georgian era, having been the favourite strewing herb of Queen Elizabeth I more than a century before.

On 3 November 1728, an entry in the register at the village church, St Cuthbert's, told of the newborn's baptism: 'James, the son of a day labourer'. He had a brother, John, who was one year older, and by the time James was seventeen, five sisters and another brother had been born. Sadly, four of those siblings did not live beyond four years, while John passed away aged twenty-two. Only his sisters, Christiana and Margaret, enjoyed longevity, both living beyond sixty.

James Cook senior was recognised locally as a diligent farm worker who demonstrated an intelligent approach to his tasks. He was employed by an estate owner, George Mewburn, until 1736, when he accepted the full-time position as foreman, a 'hind', on the stately and historic Aireyholme Farm, near Great Ayton, 6 miles to the south of Marton-in-Cleveland. The property, which has its origins dating back more than 1000 years to the time of the Saxons, and remains a fully operational farm to this day, is located on the lower slopes of Roseberry Topping – an impressive, Matterhorn-like peak standing 1049 feet above sea level. When James Cook senior took up his employment, the farm was owned by Thomas Skottowe, Lord of the Manor of Great Ayton.

James junior, then eight years old, is believed to have attended the local school, which had been established by a farm owner in the district, Michael Postgate. It has been suggested that Skottowe paid for James's schooling as part of an incentive for James senior to remain in his employ, and because he was impressed by the young lad's dedication to learning. As many as thirty children attended the school, the curriculum of which comprised four main subjects: reading, arithmetic, writing and religion. Cook remained there until just before he took up his apprenticeship in Staithes, by which point his academic achievements had led to the Lord of the Manor eagerly recommending him to his friend William Sanderson.

Similarly impressed with the teenager's intelligence and work ethic, it was Sanderson who now provided Cook with an introduction to Whitby-based shipowners John and Henry Walker. The Walker brothers had a fleet of commercial vessels operating primarily in the coal trade, working the lucrative passage that took coal from Newcastle-on-Tyne, north of Whitby, down south to London. Other ships in their fleet made cargo runs to ports around the North Sea and in the Baltic.

Before taking up his position with the Walkers, Cook was obliged to sign a 478-word indenture Agreement which outlined his obligations to his 'master', whom he was required to 'faithfully serve' throughout the three-year apprenticeship. Among many conditions, the document stipulated that the apprentice 'shall not commit fornication, or contract matrimony within the said term', nor would he 'haunt taverns or playhouses'.

In return, the master was obliged to teach him 'the trade, mystery and occupation of the mariner' and provide him with 'meat and drink, washing and lodging'. The latter point meant that Cook, along with up to fifteen other apprentice sailors, was accommodated in the fourth-level attic of John Walker's riverfront home in Grape Lane, near the centre of town. In keeping with their life at sea, these apprentices slept in hammocks suspended from the rafters. When it came to work, they didn't have far to go to board their ships – Walker had the vessels that were in port docked at his residence.

The Walkers were highly respected in Whitby. They were Quakers, a religion based on high morals, integrity and a solid work ethic. John Walker, who had been impressed by Cook's approach to work right from the outset, would go on to become the young lad's lifetime friend and mentor.

While visions of the South Seas and dreams of ocean adventures propelled Cook's life on its new journey like a warm trade wind filling a ship's sails, there was nothing glamorous or romantic about this initiation. His ship, *Freelove* – a name meaning 'divine grace' – was a solidly built 341-ton three-masted collier (often referred to as a bark or a cat), about 100 feet in overall length and with a broad beam. Having been purpose-designed to carry coal, internal volume was of great importance. This meant she was relatively slab-sided and flat-bottomed. The latter feature brought a number of advantages: *Freelove* was shallow draft, so she could navigate river entrances and waterways where there was little depth of water. It also allowed her to 'take the ground' – that is, sit safely on a mudflat or sandbank when the tide had ebbed. These far-from-pretty ships were functional but not fast; however, they could handle the heavy weather that the North Sea delivered all too often.

Having served out a suitable period of training, Cook first sailed aboard *Freelove* in the depth of winter in February 1747. Now aged eighteen, he was posted as a 'servant': a junior position where he would 'learn the ropes' when it came to actually sailing the vessel, and assist with loading and unloading the coal. He and other young apprentices, usually fifteen in the crew of twenty-five, would scurry aloft to set, reef or furl sails as dictated by the wind and demanded by the master. In reality, though, this role was hardly different from a young lad starting work in a coal pit, except that Cook was aboard a lumbering collier where, in good times, he could enjoy the open sea and wide horizons. At other times, his lot was similar to that of the young mine-worker: it was a dirty, grubby, grimy and laborious existence, one in which it often seemed there was more coal dust on the decks than sea mist in the air. Each round voyage from Whitby to Newcastle, then London and back to Whitby, was about 600 nautical miles. Some 400 vessels plied this route annually, the majority completing at least six voyages in that time.

The 50-nautical-mile passage from Whitby to Newcastle would have taken around ten hours to complete. Once *Freelove* entered Newcastle's Tyne River, the hard yards began. The crew, assisted by local keelmen (waterfront coal loaders) used buckets, skips and slings to first unload the ballast the ship had carried to provide stability when under sail, then load the coal into the empty hold – usually between 300 and 400 tons of it, depending on the size of the vessel. This procedure was then reversed in London: the coal would be discharged at docks on the north bank of the River Thames, about a mile downstream from London Bridge, which at the time was the only structure spanning the river.

Every round trip aboard *Freelove* took about four weeks to complete, depending on the weather. One can only imagine the physical appearance of Cook and his crewmates after being exposed to so much coal dust during that time. Yet none of this toil deterred Cook from holding course when it came to his career path. Most importantly, he was gaining experience under sail on the notorious North Sea, which, because it was so shallow and strewn with sandbanks, could be one of the roughest and toughest expanses of ocean known to man. In many places in the south, where the water was less than 20 fathoms, wicked storms, accompanied by huge breaking waves, were commonplace. Little wonder these waters were the graveyard for countless ships and men over the centuries.

Each time Cook returned to Whitby, he would apply himself to his studies, all of which were aimed at qualifying him for a future as a seafarer, and hopefully, one day, as the master of his own vessel. This dedication would lead to him being self-taught in the important areas of algebra, trigonometry, geometry, astronomy and navigation, the latter being a subject urged upon him by John Walker.

After completing three coal runs aboard *Freelove*, Cook was brought ashore temporarily to work on the rigging and fitting-out of the Walkers' newest ship, *Three Brothers*. The maintenance, repairing and re-rigging of vessels were familiar tasks for Cook and his fellow apprentices, particularly during wintertime, when most of the ships remained in port. Once Cook had finished his three-year apprenticeship, the Walkers transferred him to *Three Brothers*, and he remained part of her crew until 1752. He was then promoted to the position of mate aboard another new vessel in the fleet, *Friendship*.

It is interesting to note that 1752 was the year of calendar reform in England – when the *Calendar Act of 1751* took effect. This was 'an Act for regulating the commencement of the year; and for correcting the calendar now in use'. The legislation was enacted to coincide with Britain changing from the Julian calendar to the Gregorian calendar in September that year. Simply put, it meant that eleven days were removed from the month of September, so the day after 2 September 1752 became 14 September 1752. Also, until this change, each year was deemed to start on 25 March, but the legislation decreed that in future it would begin on 1 January. The consequence of this has led to considerable confusion on many occasions over actual dates relating to this period, and debates that continue to this day. For example, when Cook was born on 27 October 1728, England was using the Julian calendar, but after 1752, when the Gregorian calendar was introduced, his birth date, strictly speaking, would be 7 November.

As the years progressed, so Cook's horizons expanded. At one stage he joined the crew of *Mary*, another in the Walkers' fleet, and sailed to the Baltic and St Petersburg. He also crewed on a ship transporting troops to Ireland. On each voyage he applied himself assiduously to developing his sailing and navigation skills under the guidance of the master.

Fully supportive of Cook's emerging talent, John and Henry Walker offered the 26-year-old the position of master aboard *Friendship* in the summer of 1755. However, his mind was by then focused on a world that extended way beyond coal runs across the North Sea. He had decided to move on, to 'take his future fortune' in a different direction – namely, with the Royal Navy – so he politely declined the Walkers' offer, and with it a virtual guarantee of a secure career in the merchant marine.

Cook surprised many by choosing to enlist. He would have to start in the service's lower ranks, and it was rare for a man from the merchant marine to make that choice. Should someone in his position have wanted to escape the mundaneness of working aboard a coastal collier on short voyages, he always had the option of joining another company and crossing the Atlantic or sailing to the Far East and beyond. In fact, by opting for the navy in 1755, Cook chose a career path that entailed everything most men would want to avoid.

One of Britain's most acclaimed writers of the eighteenth century – and the man who gave the country its first dictionary – Dr Samuel Johnson, best explained a seafarer's life in this era when he wrote: 'No man will be a sailor who has contrivance enough to get himself into jail; for being in a ship is being in a jail, with the chance of being drowned.' More than two centuries later, highly respected Cook biographer John Cawte Beaglehole, OM CMG, reflected on this quote of Johnson's when comparing life in the Royal Navy with that in the merchant marine:

> Men enough went to sea to give the lie to that remark;
> the merchant service at least was adequately manned.
> The navy was a different matter. Its physical conditions
> were worse; its pay was worse; its food was worse, its
> discipline was harsh, its record of sickness was appalling.
> To the chance of being drowned could be added the
> chance of being flogged, hanged or being shot, though it

> was true that deaths in battle were infinitely fewer than
> deaths from disease. The enemy might kill in tens,
> scurvy and typhus killed in tens of hundreds.

Sailor that he was, Cook would have contemplated all these things when considering his future. If he felt any apprehension about advising the Walkers of his decision, it would have been quickly erased when John Walker assured him he had no hesitation in writing a positive reference recommending him for the service. This was yet another example of the rapport and mutual respect the two men grew to enjoy. Cook was forever grateful for Walker's support and guidance during their nine years together at Whitby. He wrote to him regularly, and on the rare occasions when he visited his family in Great Ayton, he always tried to see Walker as well.

Around this time, Cook's father retired from his role as foreman at Aireyholme Farm, and he and Grace subsequently either built or renovated a two-storey residence nearby. Later, when fame came to James Cook junior through his exploits as a navigator and explorer, this cottage became recognised as 'Cook's Cottage', due to a misguided belief that the seafarer had spent his younger years there. In 1933, by which time the residence was a derelict structure, it was purchased by Sir Russell Grimwade of Melbourne, who subsequently gifted it to the people of Victoria as part of the state's centenary celebrations the following year. Grimwade had the cottage transported – brick by brick, tile by tile, with even the attached ivy included – to Melbourne, where it was carefully rebuilt in the city's Fitzroy Gardens as a tribute to the great explorer.

The cottage stands today as the oldest building in Australia, and the original English ivy continues to grow on its walls. While the residence has been billed as having been Captain Cook's home, history suggests that he did not live in this house for any period of time, if at all. Furthermore, it's about half the size it was in Cook's day: a section was demolished, apparently to make way for a roadway in Great Ayton.

CHAPTER TWO

Life on the Lower Deck

Cook signed up with the Royal Navy on 17 June 1755, in Wapping, close to Execution Dock on the north bank of the Thames. While this dock was a point of arrival and departure for navy and merchant ships, its macabre name was most appropriate: it was the site for public hangings of felons and Royal Navy offenders. One of the most gruesome, and famous, executions occurred more than fifty years prior to Cook's enlistment. On 23 May 1701, the legendary British pirate Captain Kidd was hung at Execution Dock (it took two attempts because the noose broke on the first occasion), then his body was gibbeted (hung on public display) for years thereafter as a deterrent to others.

Cook's decision as a 26-year-old to volunteer as an able seaman for naval service was both bold and well calculated. Most men looking for a life on the quarterdeck had been enlisted during their early to mid teens by their father or a family friend with ties to the navy. Cook was not concerned by this. The Royal Navy was where he wanted to be; it promised the life and opportunities he desired, so, if in the early stages it meant he played a subordinate role to men many years his junior, then so be it. It was the future that mattered. Even so, there was nothing pleasant about being on the lower deck of any ship of that era: the calibre of men making up the crew left a lot to be desired. Cook's early years in the navy would later be seen as a valuable time in his career, since, unlike so many officers, he experienced first-hand the bottom rung – the tough side – of shipboard life. There is no doubt this contributed to him being a great leader of men in the years to come.

At the time when Cook presented his papers to the navy, England was involved in what was referred to as the 'Phoney War' with France – a chest-beating period of confrontation between the two nations that served as a build-up to history's first global conflict, the Seven Years War. Hostilities would be formalised once Great Britain, under King George II, officially declared war on the French in May 1756, and Louis XV of France made a counter declaration a month later. As was always the case, the threat of impending war meant that the navy was desperate for recruits: men skilled or unskilled who could man the ships. The number required was quite astonishing – an expansion from 16,000 to 80,000 was needed, and as quickly as possible if Britain was to go onto a full war footing. With insufficient volunteers to fill the quota, the Royal Navy's infamous press gangs took over the recruitment drive – by coercing, or simply forcing, men into the service. The majority of their hapless victims came from the merchant marine, but sometimes they were just ragamuffins and ruffians from the streets.

This being the case, one can only imagine the look of surprise on the face of the lieutenant who received Cook, on that day in June 1755. Here was a fit and healthy, nine-year veteran of the merchant marine, with excellent qualifications – sufficient to be a master, no less – who was abandoning all that to become an underling in the Royal Navy: an able seaman with a monthly wage of just £1 4 shillings. For the under-manned Royal Navy, it was almost too good to be true. So little wonder that, after the lieutenant checked the new recruit's credentials, plans were swiftly made for Cook to go to Spithead, the anchorage off the south coast at Portsmouth, where he would board HMS *Eagle*, a 58-gun 147-foot fourth-rate ship with a complement of 400 men.

Eight days later, on 25 June, Able Seaman Cook was rowed in a navy longboat across the Solent from Portsmouth and out to *Eagle*. Once there he clambered up the side of the ship, stepped onto the deck and reported for duty.

While everything about *Eagle* was considerably larger, and cleaner, than the likes of *Freelove*, he could not have been overly impressed by what he saw. The ten-year-old ship had come out of dry dock in Portsmouth on 8 May, following a refit and completion of repairs after she was damaged by a storm while in the dock. It was now some six weeks later, and despite the entire ship being abuzz with the frenetic activity of shipwrights, riggers and crew going about their tasks, *Eagle* was still a long way from being ready to put to sea – another six weeks in fact. It would have been a lot easier to have this work carried out while the ship was in the dry dock, but with crew at such a premium and often difficult to retain, ships were usually moved out to the anchorage in the Solent whenever possible to stop would-be deserters from getting ashore.

Eagle had a new commander, Joseph Hamar, a captain with no glorious past and, it would soon transpire, an inglorious future. Hamar's initial orders required him to sail *Eagle* to the south-west coast of Ireland and undertake a lone patrol, intercepting and inspecting any suspicious-looking vessel that came within sight – all part of the overall plan to frustrate any attempts by the French to transport cargo or military men between foreign ports. The first contact came off the southernmost point of the British mainland, The Lizard, only four days after the ship had weighed anchor at Spithead and headed west on the English Channel. Cook, who was keeping a journal detailing the voyage, recorded the moment: 'Friday 8 August. Fired a shot and brought to and examined a ship from Antigua bound to London out of which we impressed 3 men ...'

Cook's lowly rank ensured he had little, if any, contact with the captain. However, his considerable sailing experience with the Walkers obviously brought him to the attention of *Eagle*'s sailing master, Thomas Bisset, because a month after joining the ship he was promoted to master's mate. His new role was to report to Bisset on everything that related to the actual sailing of the ship – rigging, equipment, anchoring and sails. Most importantly for Cook, the promotion meant that Bisset would help him to better understand the operation of this Royal Navy vessel, which was around four times the tonnage of a Whitby collier, with a ship's complement some twenty times the size of anything the Yorkshireman had previously experienced.

Eagle reached the coast of Ireland a few days after the initial intercept and commenced her patrol. It proceeded without incident until 3 September, when a storm intervened, carrying winds so powerful that Hamar became convinced that the mainmast had been overloaded to the point where it had 'sprung' – fractured – between the decks. Cook's journal entry for that Monday morning reads: '6AM A very hard gale. Lost the driver boom overboard. 7AM Reefed the fore sail and balanced the mizzen. 9AM Brailed up the main sail ... 10AM Found the main mast to be sprung in the lower partner ...'

The captain decided that the damage was sufficiently serious for *Eagle* to head to the Devonshire port of Plymouth for repairs. Once there and the anchor was set, the Royal Navy's local master mast-maker inspected the structure and declared it to be sound. Hamar would now have been expected to return to his patrol immediately, but for some inexplicable reason, he showed a distinct reluctance to do so. Instead, he elected to dock the ship so that the bottom could be cleaned and tallowed. It was an action that did not impress the hierarchy of the Admiralty, and their response was swift. Within a few days Hamar was declared to be an 'incompetent officer' and was relieved of his duties. This proved to be his last posting as a sea-going captain, and, as fate would have it, his demise greatly benefited Cook's career.

Eagle's new commander, 32-year-old Yorkshireman Hugh Palliser, was one of the Admiralty's preferred people; an officer who was rising impressively through the ranks and destined for far greater things. He had just returned from escorting a convoy of transport ships across the Atlantic to the British colony of Virginia, so the posting to *Eagle* was a logical progression for him. Palliser's naval career had started at age twelve, when he first went to sea in the company of an uncle. By the time he was eighteen, he had passed his qualifying exam to become a lieutenant, but he had to wait for the actual promotion because he was too young.

Palliser's presence on the ship reminded new recruit Cook just how far down the ranks he was within the service. Palliser was only five years his senior, yet he had twenty years' more naval experience. He took up his first command on a Royal Navy vessel in the same year as Cook joined the Walkers in Whitby.

It is not known when the new captain and the master's mate first met, but the evidence suggests that there was a solid bond from the outset. Palliser realised he had a talented man of considerable seafaring experience in Cook, and before long the foundation of what would become a lifelong friendship had been established. In particular, he taught Cook much about navigation and mapping. This relationship saw Palliser mentor Cook, much like the championing that the younger Yorkshireman had enjoyed from Great Ayton's Lord of the Manor, Thomas Skottowe, more than a decade earlier.

Captain Palliser had the sails set and *Eagle* leaving Plymouth in her wake on 8 October. She sailed under orders to join a large squadron patrolling the western approaches of the Channel, where the British were desperate to apply a stranglehold to French maritime activities – naval and merchant. Any ship they captured was to be sailed back to England as a prize. For much of this time, the Channel was in a foul mood, making everything about the deployment unpleasant. Adding to the wretchedness, the majority of vessels that Palliser and his crew hunted down, stopped and searched turned out to be friend, not French.

Eagle's first success came with the interception and detention of a French fishing vessel, which was returning home laden with a catch taken off the coast of Newfoundland. Some

150 French prisoners were transferred to *Eagle* before a small crew were sent aboard the French prize to sail her back to England. She certainly wasn't the most exciting catch, but it was a start. Further success came a week later with the capture of a more valuable prize: a French snow – a two-masted merchant vessel similar to a brig.

Soon afterwards, Cook had his first exposure to the full force of a naval battle, albeit as an observer. *Eagle* stood by on 15 November, as ordered, while other RN ships blasted the French 50-gun *Espérance* into submission before she sank. 'Received on Board from the Esperance 26 Prisoners at 4 o'clock,' Cook wrote that day. 'The Esperance on fire there being no possibility of keeping her above water ...'

By now, with winter approaching, the storms became more frequent and severe. The cold was taking a toll on the men and the punishing conditions were damaging the ships, including *Eagle*. At times the combination of a howling wind, flogging canvas and a pounding sea sent earthquake-like shudders through the entire vessel. *Eagle* had already suffered mast failure during this patrol, and now the power of the storms was causing structural problems as well.

Palliser and his men were no doubt pleased, therefore, when *Eagle* and five other ships were ordered by the patrol commander, Vice-Admiral John Byng, to return to Plymouth for repairs and a refit. *Eagle* arrived there on 23 November and, after off-loading more than 200 French prisoners, she went into dry dock. She remained in port for the entire winter, not returning to active service until 13 March the following year.

While the patrol was considered successful, Palliser went ashore in Plymouth a frustrated man. Four days later, he fired off a missive to the Admiralty in London complaining most strongly about the standard of his crewmen: 'When their Lordships shall think proper to Complete this Ship's Complement I hope they'll be pleased to Order her a few good Men, for I assure you I have been much distressed this last Cruise having so very few Seamen on board ...'

Master's Mate Cook was obviously one of those 'very few', because on 22 January he was advised by the captain that he was to be promoted. Cook's reference to this in his log was simple: 'AM had a Survey on Boatswain's [bosun's] Stores, when [I] Succeeded the Former Boatswain ...' This new supervisory position brought him a salary of £4 per month and made him responsible for the maintenance and repair of all parts of the ship, on deck and aloft, plus the boats.

When *Eagle* returned to patrol duties in the Channel and off the coast of France in March 1756, she was under orders very similar to those of the previous operation. Initially there was little success, except for the interception of two very small sloops that were smuggling tea and brandy from Guernsey to England.

Sunday 4 April marked another important first in the seafaring life of James Cook, when he was directed by Palliser to go aboard a British cutter that was part of their squadron and take command. The following day, while on patrol, Cook took time to make a small sketch of the features, man-made and natural, of the coastline around Morlaix in Brittany, in the north-west of France. It is believed that this was the first time that he revealed his impressive talent, one that was essential for explorers of that era.

Cook remained as master of this vessel for some weeks, no doubt revelling in the responsibility that came with being independent and in command. The experience ended when he and his crew were transferred to the commodore's ship, HMS *Falmouth*, and returned to Plymouth. They were then put aboard the 60-gun HMS *St Albans* for more patrol work on the Channel.

Shortly before Britain's declaration of war against the French on 18 May, Cook was transferred back to *Eagle*. From the moment he went aboard, he was shocked to see so many members of her crew either extremely ill or dying, primarily because of exposure to the elements. It was an image that became so firmly embedded in his mind that it would influence his later life as a ship's commander.

Fortunately, then, Cook's return to *Eagle* was a brief episode. Soon he was directed to take command of a French prize, *Triton*, and sail her with an English crew back to Plymouth. On reaching port, he was then ordered to sail *Triton* on to London, which he reached without incident at the end of June. Six weeks later, though, Cook was back aboard *Eagle* in Plymouth and faced with distressing news. Illness was again sweeping through the ship and had taken a terrible toll: twenty-six of the crew, including the ship's surgeon, had died, and 130 others were in hospital.

There was an obvious solution to this unacceptable situation, and Palliser made sure that the Admiralty knew it. Most of his crew were 'landsmen', who came aboard without clothing suitable for seafaring, and the navy's allowance for slops did nothing to help. Palliser wrote: 'Naked when they came on board being for the most part Vagabonds not one in Twenty of them that had more than a Shirt and one ragged Coat ...' The Admiralty took note and ordered Palliser to 'let the men be supplied with what they absolutely want and no more, and take care they do not sell any part thereof'.

Eagle departed from Plymouth in early August, and for the next four months played a role in blockades and the pursuit of French ships. With winter approaching and crewmen again falling ill, she returned to Plymouth in early November and remained there for a month before resuming normal duties.

Cook's first direct involvement in battlefront action came six months later when, on 31 May 1757, *Eagle*, in company with the similar-sized HMS *Medway*, pursued and engaged the 1500-ton 64-gun French East Indiaman *Duc d'Aquitaine*. The action took place in the Atlantic Ocean, about 180 nautical miles south-west of Ushant, the island that today marks the north-westernmost point of metropolitan France.

The pursuit commenced at one o'clock in the morning in driving rain, with *Eagle* leading the way under a press of sail. In his own words, Palliser 'let out the Reef, & set Studding Sails & Cleared Ship for Action' to ensure maximum speed.

This would prove to be an abrupt introduction to the brutality of maritime warfare for Cook, as the French defended their ship with every ounce of force available to them. Palliser's log entry after the engagement provided a summary:

> At 1/4 before 4 Came alongside & Engaged at about Two Ships lengths from her the Fire was very brisk on both Sides for near an hour, she then Struck to us, She proved to be the Duc d'Aquitaine last from Lisbon, mounting 50 Guns all 18 Pounders, 493 Men ... Our Sails & Rigging cut almost all to Pieces. Soon after She Struck her Main & Mizzen Masts went by the Board. Employed the Boats fetching the Prisoners & carrying [our] Men on board the Prize. Our Cutter was lost alongside the Prize by the going away of her Main Mast ...

Eagle had three men killed during the action, and another two died within forty-eight hours. Eighty others were wounded either on deck or when cannonballs fired from the French ship smashed into her topsides and tore her innards apart. The French paid a much higher price in defeat: of *Duc d'Aquitaine*'s crew, fifty were killed and thirty wounded.

Although not terminally damaged, *Eagle* was badly smashed. Palliser's report to the Admiralty detailed the condition of his ship: 'Twenty shot holes through her sides. Three lower deck ports shot away ... The bowsprit much wounded. The foremast, a shot through the middle of it ... Two anchor-stocks shot away ... almost all the running rigging shot away. Sails rent almost to rags ...' In short, there was hardly anything aloft that *wasn't* damaged – masts, spars and yards, sails and rigging all reflected the intensity of the close-quarters encounter.

Consequently, it would have been Cook, as bosun, who led the way when it came to *Eagle*'s crew doing everything possible to secure the ship and repair essential rigging just so the few undamaged sails they had left could be set and sheeted home. Once that was achieved, *Eagle* was turned to the north-east, and began an arduous and slow passage back to the Devonshire coast, 300 nautical miles away.

Medway had remained on the fringe of the battle and, apart from an accidental explosion of gunpowder on board that injured ten crewmen, was unscathed. She took the wreck of *Duc d'Aquitaine* in tow and headed for Plymouth in company with *Eagle*.

Even though *Duc d'Aquitaine* was in ruins – *Eagle* had made the topsides look like Swiss cheese by blasting ninety-seven holes in her – naval officers in Plymouth believed that the French ship could be a valuable prize, a theory that was soon confirmed by naval surveyors, who advised that she could be repaired. It was good news for the Lords of the Admiralty, who saw an opportunity to rub salt into the enemy's wounds. They wanted her sailing as HMS *Duc d'Aquitaine* under the Union flag and defending England as quickly as possible. The French East Indiaman was immediately placed into dry dock for a rebuild.

The Admiralty took time to congratulate Palliser on his efforts, declaring: 'Captain Palliser should be informed that their Lordships were highly pleased with his success and gallant conduct on this occasion ...'

The pressure of war also made repairs to *Eagle* a high priority. Within a month of arriving back in port, she had been re-rigged and the hull repaired – an impressive effort. On 12 July 1757, she sailed out into the Atlantic, bound for Halifax, Nova Scotia, again with Palliser as captain, but the bosun, James Cook, was not on board.

Cook's absence was due to the intervention of two of his mentors, Palliser and John Walker. The latter had been following Cook's naval career with interest, and believed most firmly that a mariner of his ability should be higher up the ranks. Walker duly contacted his local parliamentarian, the member for Scarborough,

William Osbaldestone, with a request that he do what he could to see Cook become a commissioned officer. Osbaldestone subsequently wrote to Palliser regarding the issue.

It was a difficult situation for Palliser. Like Walker, he was impressed by Cook and in no doubt that, had he joined the navy as a teenager, this 28-year-old man would now have been well advanced in the service. However, there was little he could do, especially in light of a recent edict reminding officers that no midshipman or mate could sit for his lieutenant's examination unless he had six years' naval service. Cook had been in the RN only two years.

Palliser's reply to Osbaldestone explained the strict limitations, but he also suggested that there was an opportunity for promotion via a 'master's warrant ... by which he would be raised to a station that he was well qualified to discharge with ability and credit'.

So, through Walker's encouragement and Palliser's suggestion, Bosun James Cook attended Trinity House, at Deptford Wharf in south London, on 29 June that year. There, he sat for, and passed, an examination qualifying him to 'take charge as Master of any of His Majesty's Ships from the Downs thro' the Channel to the Westward and to Lisbon'. As if that wasn't pleasing enough, he was discharged from *Eagle* the following day and immediately appointed master aboard HMS *Solebay* – a three-masted 24-gun single-deck frigate used primarily for convoy escort and patrols. The captain was Robert Craig.

Cook was well aware of the considerable responsibilities that came with being a ship's master, having turned down such a position aboard one of the Walkers' colliers. But the difference between being a master on a 'cat' and his duties aboard *Solebay* was enormous: the frigate was around four times the displacement, had a crew of 200-plus compared with the collier's twenty-five, while her rig and general equipment were inordinately more complex. As master, he was essentially the manager of the ship. He answered directly to the captain, was at all times responsible for the navigation, and, through the bosun, was responsible for all repairs and maintenance of the standing and running rigging, plus the sails, masts, yards and spars.

In short, if anything went wrong with the general operation of the ship, the master was answerable directly to the captain.

Cook did not join *Solebay* for a full month after his discharge from *Eagle*. It is easy to speculate that during this time he probably visited his family in Yorkshire, as well as the Walkers, having possibly spent some time in London before then. When he finally went aboard on 30 July, *Solebay* was at anchor in Leith Road on the Firth of Forth, a huge bay on the east coast of Scotland. She was based there because, being a frigate, she had the speed needed to pursue and intercept vessels that were smuggling goods between this region and France.

Yet this new posting proved to be short-lived – lasting little more than a month. Five weeks after discharge from Craig's vessel on 7 September, Cook was appointed master of the newly launched fourth-rate ship-of-the-line HMS *Pembroke*.

Cook travelled south to Portsmouth to join the new ship, and went aboard as master on 27 October, his twenty-ninth birthday. As a 64-gunner, *Pembroke* carried almost three times the firepower of *Solebay*, so Cook's latest appointment represented an important step forward in the Royal Navy. As before, it is distinctly possible that he was nominated for the position from within. His predecessor on *Pembroke* was none other than Thomas Bisset, who, as master aboard *Eagle*, had supported Cook's promotion to master's mate.

Under the command of the much-admired Captain John Simcoe, *Pembroke* was in Portsmouth Harbour being provisioned for a patrol off the coast of France when Cook stepped onto her heavy timber deck and presented himself to the captain. Once ready for sea, she was moved out 6 nautical miles to the anchorage off St Helens on the Isle of Wight, where she underwent final preparations.

Two weeks later, on 8 December, she and the other ships in the patrol were signalled to unfurl their sails, weigh anchor and head into the Channel, their eventual destination Cape Finistère, on the northern coast of the Bay of Biscay. It was the start of winter, a bleak time to be on these waters, but the seasons are of no consequence when there's a war to be fought. For the next two months, the fleet carried out their orders to arrest or harass any French ships they might intercept, and any other vessels thought to be loyal to Louis XV.

While the English Channel was the primary battleground between the British and the French at this stage of the Seven Years War, there was an equally acrimonious confrontation developing on the opposite side of the Atlantic between the same two adversaries. And both *Pembroke* and James Cook were soon to play important roles there.

A few months prior to the ship's completion of the winter patrol mission and her arrival in Plymouth in February 1758, the British Cabinet had decided to accelerate its attempts to overrun French colonies in North America. After all, the French were leaving no doubt about their intention to take all of Britain's holdings in that part of the world, starting with 'New Scotland' – Nova Scotia. The two key French strongholds in the colony of New France (now the eastern portion of Canada) were Québec and Louisbourg, the latter being the fortress town that controlled the entrance to both the world's largest estuary, the Gulf of St Lawrence, and the St Lawrence River, which duly gave important access to Québec and therefore the interior. Initial plans for a British land assault on Louisbourg were abandoned due to the prevailing weather, and this decision led to Britain's new prime minister, William Pitt, ordering that Louisbourg, followed by Québec, be taken via a combined naval and army attack. It was a plan of immense proportions, so much so that every available British ship would be needed on that side of the Atlantic to carry the flag.

Just twelve days after *Pembroke* returned home and dropped anchor, she was fully reprovisioned and heading across the Atlantic Ocean as part of a fleet comprising eight line-of-battle ships, three frigates, two transports and two fire-ships. This was an immensely proud moment for Ship's Master James Cook. He fully expected to be put to the test on what was his first crossing of the Atlantic. The experiences that lay ahead, however, might even have excelled the wildest dreams of that young farm boy from the fields of Marton-in-Cleveland.

The bark *Earl of Pembroke*, later HM Bark *Endeavour*, leaving Whitby Harbour in 1768, as painted by Thomas Luny (1759–1837). National Library of Australia, nla.pic-an2280897

CHAPTER THREE

The Taking of Québec

Within two days of departing from Plymouth on 22 February 1758, the Royal Navy taskforce had cleared The Lizard and was sailing south into the vast wilderness of the Atlantic. Ahead lay a challenging 4700-nautical-mile passage via Teneriffe and Bermuda to the British-held port of Halifax, Nova Scotia. This circuitous route was chosen so that the fleet had the best chance of sailing in favourable following winds for the majority of the voyage. Even so, it was quite possible that they would experience a widely varying weather pattern that only a salty seafarer's experienced eye could decipher. Being late winter, an icy blast out of the north was not improbable.

A careful lookout was also being kept for any sign of billowing sails on the horizon. The French were forever lurking on these waters, hunting for any British prize, and this flotilla would be a valuable one.

Because of this threat, it was important for the British ships to get as deep into the Atlantic, and south towards Teneriffe, as quickly as possible. Yet with it being essential that the lighter displacement and efficiently rigged frigates remain in visual contact with – and thereby serve as armed escorts to – the valuable but more vulnerable transports, the crews aboard the frigates were constantly furling and unfurling sails to control the speed of their ships. This was all done at the behest of the fleet commander, the battle-hardened Admiral Edward Boscawen, known affectionately as 'Old Dreadnought', but often referred to as 'Wry-Necked-Dick', because of the way he canted his head to one side.

It was obvious to both warring nations that the key to holding control of New France was to keep both Louisbourg, on the south-east corner of Cape Breton Island, and Québec under the same flag. Atlantic-facing Louisbourg was the more important of the two places, being the gateway to the region. By controlling that town, it was not difficult to defend the Gulf of St Lawrence and therefore protect Québec, located upstream at the St Lawrence River narrows and one of the oldest towns in North America, having been founded in 1608.

Not surprisingly, since gaining control of Louisbourg in 1745, the French had spent considerable manpower and money turning the settlement into one massive fortress. For the British, their recently founded capital of Nova Scotia, Halifax, 200 nautical miles south-west of Louisbourg, was the ideal place from which to mount an assault on the French territories. Halifax's long, narrow and deep harbour extended 13 nautical miles directly inland, making it a safe anchorage for a large fleet of ships, and, most importantly, it did not become icebound in winter.

The crossing of the Atlantic by the British fleet took just over ten weeks, and while it was a relatively uneventful passage, there was considerable concern aboard *Pembroke* when she arrived. Twenty-six crewmen had died en route, most of them falling victim to scurvy, and many more had to be hospitalised. As with the suffering he'd witnessed aboard *Eagle*, this was a situation that would have a profound influence on Cook's later life as an expedition commander. In addition to these losses, another five of *Pembroke*'s crew decided to steal the small yawl and desert. They were never seen again.

Following the aborted first attempt to take the fortress town, Prime Minister Pitt left no doubt that he wanted both Louisbourg and Québec in British hands. To achieve this,

Admiral Boscawen had assembled a fleet of mammoth proportions; the recently arrived taskforce combined to form a veritable armada totalling 157 warships manned by some 40,000 crew and carrying 14,000 soldiers, led by General James Wolfe of the British Army. On 28 May 1758, the fleet departed from Halifax and began closing on Louisbourg. *Pembroke* was not part of the initial wave, however, having been forced to stay in port because too many of her crew were still immobilised. It was not until 7 June that she sailed in convoy with three transports, two schooners and a cattle sloop.

When *Pembroke* anchored off Louisbourg five days later, word came that Wolfe had led a large army of men ashore on 8 June and forced the French to retreat inside the giant fortress. It wasn't without incident, thanks to the surge of the sea breaking on the beach and rocky shore in Kennington Cove (located on the north side of Gabarus Bay), plus the initial French resistance. The casualty list recorded more than sixty men killed and 146 wounded – and at least 100 of the small boats ferrying soldiers ashore were wrecked in the surf. Even so, Wolfe would later describe the landing as 'next to miraculous'.

From the time *Pembroke* arrived at the cove, Cook, as master, coordinated the transport of troops, weapons and supplies to shore whenever conditions allowed. Once the men were on the beach, they faced a trek of about 4 miles north, first over rough terrain then marshland, before reaching a point where they could position themselves for an effective assault on the French stronghold, which was located on the southern side of the large bay. The fortress was initially designed by the French to defend Louisbourg from attacks by the British from the sea, so it was poorly prepared for a land-based attack such as this. The British soldiers were therefore able to locate their guns on the marshland and nearby hills with virtually no challenge from the French.

While these preparations were underway, Wolfe received an intelligence report that reinforced his belief that his men would be able to take the fort. The report confirmed that the number of French defenders was considerably fewer than expected – 7000 soldiers, sailors and marines. Ironically, this shortage of manpower stemmed from Britain's abandoned attempt to take Louisbourg the previous year. When the French fleet returned home across the Atlantic in October 1757, many of their soldiers and crewmen were struck down by 'ship fever', or typhus. More than 2000 died while at sea, and another 10,000 after the fleet had arrived in Brest. The resulting shortage of available fighting men, plus a misguided belief that the British were planning to sail across the Channel in 1758 and mount major attacks on the French coast, led to most of King Louis' ships remaining in home waters when they would otherwise have been in Louisbourg for this latest confrontation. That year, a support squadron did depart from Toulon, in the south of France, bound for Louisbourg, but it was intercepted by the British off Cartagena, Spain, and blasted to the point of surrender.

During the Siege of Louisbourg, the weather played into French hands at least – albeit briefly. In the middle of June, a powerful Atlantic gale, with near hurricane-force winds, hit the British fleet hard and fast. It was so strong that every RN ship anchored off the coast could easily have been driven ashore and wrecked. The only option was to retreat to sea, but the wind was so powerful that the men manning the windlass on each vessel were not able to raise the anchor: the force of the wind on the hull and rig was too great. Instead, masters of almost every vessel, including Cook on *Pembroke*, had to get the bower cable – made of some 1000 strands of triple-laid tarred hemp – hacked through as quickly as possible so that the ship could escape. Meanwhile, other crew-members were frantically going about the task of hoisting a minimum number of heavy-weather fore-and-aft sails to ensure that the vessel had the speed and manoeuvrability needed to sail away from the shore and get the necessary sea-room. For the French, this break in hostilities presented the opportunity for them to sink four of their own ships at the harbour entrance, to the east of the fortress town, in the hope that they could blockade the port. It was to no avail.

The marshland had made it extremely difficult for the British to move their heavy guns and equipment into advantageous positions for an all-out attack, and it was not until 26 June that the cannons boomed into action. The French withstood the barrage for a month – until the night of 25 July. That was when Admiral Boscawen, using the cover that came from a thick fog, sent small boats from as many British ships as possible, into the port in order to take off with the two French men-of-war that remained. Some 600 men were involved, and they were able to successfully tow one of the large ships, *Bienfaisant*, away from the dock, while the other, *Prudent*, ran aground and was torched by British sailors.

This attack, which Boscawen described as 'a very brilliant affair, well carried out', was the breaking point for the French, as they then had no means of escape from Louisbourg. Their commander, Chevalier de Drucour, surrendered the following day, with Cook logging the time as 11 am. Soon afterwards, the Union flag was flying over Louisbourg.

The British victory would later be recognised as a major turning point in the Seven Years War. It was the first powerful step by Britain towards ending French domination in North America.

With that battle decided, one could easily have expected the British to base a force of considerable size in the fortress, but Mr Pitt had other ideas. Having seen England forced to surrender the same fort as part of the peace negotiations with France in 1745, following what was known in the British colonies as King George's War, Pitt resolved for it never to happen again. To that end, in 1760 the prime minister would instruct sappers and engineers to tunnel under the fortifications and destroy the town and port using explosives. That way, there was nothing left to trade with the French in any further peace negotiations.

After the guns fell silent following the siege, the British moved in and took control of Louisbourg. Cook took the opportunity to go ashore from *Pembroke*, landing on the sandy beach in Kennington Cove at the same spot where General Wolfe had established his beachhead seven weeks earlier.

As he wandered along the beach among the wreckage of small boats, abandoned cannons and other military equipment, he became intrigued by the activities of a man who was working quietly and methodically nearby. What especially drew Cook's attention was an odd-looking piece of equipment this fellow had with him – a long-legged tripod of about chest height, topped by a small flat board, approximately 2 foot square. Each time the man stopped somewhere, he would set up the tripod, level the little tabletop and place a few instruments on its surface, before apparently taking some sights on the surrounding topographical features and jotting down notes. He'd then move on to another location and repeat the procedure.

Cook's intrigue soon had the better of him. He approached the man, introduced himself, and asked the obvious questions. The tripod, he learned, was called a plane table and it was used as a tool for collecting data when surveying.

The conversation continued and before long Cook became aware that he was speaking with Samuel Holland, Royal Engineer and first Surveyor-General of British North America. As a member of the British Army, Holland had been commissioned by the government to survey and map a large part of the east coast of North America.

Prior to the recent offensive, Wolfe had tapped the Dutch-born surveyor's exceptional skills, by requesting he go into enemy territory around Louisbourg and study the terrain. After carrying out his surveys, Holland would send the information back to Halifax so that the general could formulate the most effective plan of attack. And his contribution had been extensive: Holland surveyed most of the land around the fort's perimeter – more than 2½ miles of high stone block walls. There were times when he had to duck for cover, as French soldiers in the fort spotted him and fired their muskets in his direction. He also sounded water depths in and around the harbour and surveyed some of the nearby coastline. Once they had all of Holland's information at their disposal, Wolfe and his fellow commanders were able to decide that Kennington Cove was where the British forces should land. Now, with the battle won, Holland was spending the remainder of the summer completing the work he had started.

The surveyor and *Pembroke*'s master quickly struck up a rapport, so much so that Holland, realising that Cook held a genuine interest in the science, offered to teach him the skills needed to be a surveyor. Cook's ship lay at anchor in Louisbourg Harbour until 28 August. It was a month that would prove to be of significant assistance to the Yorkshireman's career in the long term.

During that same period, the possibility of an immediate attack on Québec was discussed by the military hierarchy – Royal Navy and British Army. It was the prime minister's wish, and Wolfe and Simcoe, *Pembroke*'s captain, both supported the idea. The navy's admirals overruled them, however, arguing that it was late in the summer season, and if winter snow and ice arrived early, all would be lost.

An alternative form of immediate action against the French was authorised, however. In early September 1758, Sir Charles Hardy led a small squadron of ten ships, including *Pembroke* – carrying between them three battalions of soldiers led by Wolfe – to the Bay of Gaspé and the Gulf of St Lawrence. Their orders were to harass and destroy as many French settlements as possible and leave the inhabitants in no doubt as to what was to come the following summer: an uncompromising British attack on Québec. Hardy's mission was not as successful as had been hoped, but at least the French knew the British were on their way.

The ships were back at anchor in Louisbourg on 2 October, and during the six weeks they lay there, what would later become an important artefact in British maritime history came into existence. With the encouragement of John Simcoe, and through the application of what he had learned from Samuel Holland, Cook had taken the time during the 'harass and destroy' operation to carry out a survey of Gaspé Bay and its harbour. During the following year, this would become the first published chart created by Cook. It was credited to 'James Cook Master of his Majesty's Ship the Pembroke', and its creator dedicated the work to the master and wardens of Trinity House, Deptford, where he had successfully sat for his Master's Certificate.

As a break from his role as master aboard *Pembroke* while in Louisbourg, Cook was given a task that was a throwback to his early days aboard the Whitby colliers. He was appointed to the command of a small schooner and directed to sail to a port in Nova Scotia – probably Sydney, which was 60 nautical miles away on the northern coast – to take on a cargo of coal.

Louisbourg was destined to be icebound during winter. While it was still necessary to maintain a presence there, the fleet commander, Rear-Admiral Philip Durell, ordered his ships, *Pembroke* among them, to head for Halifax, where they would spend the season. After a five-day passage south, the fleet arrived there on 19 November.

Although Halifax was considered the best place to ride out the winter, it still proved to be a frigidly cold, wet and windy season. During January, conditions worsened, with the arrival of huge snowfalls and frosts. This was a particularly tough time for the men of the lower deck, primarily because their clothing was inadequate for such bitterly cold weather. Light pants, a shirt, vest and light jacket were all that most of them had for protection and bodily warmth. Some didn't even have shoes. Still, they worked as demanded, cleaning and maintaining their ship so that she would be ready to sail come spring. Living in such a claustrophobic, harsh environment meant misdemeanours were not uncommon among the men, but the cat-o'-nine-tails and detentions kept indiscretions to a minimum.

As bad as this North American winter was, it soon became apparent that being in Halifax, and not Louisbourg, was the right decision. This point was not lost in a letter that Durell sent to the Secretary of the Admiralty:

> This winter of 1759 has proved the severest that has
> been known since the settling of the place. For these
> two months past I have not heard from Louisbourg.
> Many vessels have attempted to go there, but have met
> with ice eighteen and twenty leagues [60 nautical miles]
> from the land; so were obliged to return, after having
> had some of their people froze to death, and others frost-
> bitten to that degree as to lose legs and arms …

During these bitterly cold months, Cook was far from idle. He and Holland, working alongside Simcoe, spent a considerable amount of time in the great cabin aboard *Pembroke*. There, using the limited information available, they created charts of the Gulf of St Lawrence and its river, which led to Québec – all part of the preparation for the British attack there. Holland expressed admiration for his protégé's ability to learn and for the surveying skills that he was already demonstrating. In a letter sent later to Captain Simcoe's son, the Dutchman wrote: 'Mr Cook could not fail to improve and thoroughly brought in his hand as well in drawing as in protracting, etc.'

Simcoe, whom Holland recognised as a 'truly scientific' man, urged Cook to learn spherical trigonometry and the practical part of astronomy – the primary elements in celestial navigation. Cook took up the challenge, and very much lived up to his captain's expectations. Through Simcoe's encouragement, *Pembroke*'s master was on his way to becoming one of the first men to comprehend and apply the 'new' form of navigation – celestial navigation – using a sextant. The first example of such an instrument had been created by Englishman John Bird just two years earlier.

It is probable that these chart-making sessions also resulted in the creation of the first known 'sailing directions' for seafarers, titled as directions for the 'Harbour of Louisbourg in Cape

Breton'. And all the signs are that most, if not all, of the documents, were created by Cook's hand. This material was designed to provide ships' captains and navigators with as much detail as possible relating to known navigational hazards in the region, together with information on the location of safe channels and the flow of currents. The work is undated, but the documents must have been created soon after the British attack on Louisbourg, as the wreck of the French ship *Prudent* is shown near the harbour entrance as a point of reference for navigators.

One of the major benefits that came from wintering in Halifax rather than returning to England was that the British fleet was spared a time-consuming return voyage across the Atlantic before making the move to take Québec. The entrance to the St Lawrence River was only 450 nautical miles away – perhaps twelve days' sailing time – and from there it was another 400 miles upstream to Québec. An added bonus was that the French were denied three additional months to prepare their defences. It also greatly decreased the possibility of there being any significant relief or reinforcements coming from France.

The water-borne attack on Québec was to be, like that seen in Louisbourg, a combined army and navy operation that included 9000 'redcoats' under Wolfe's command, and 13,500 sailors. The naval element, led by the highly regarded Admiral Sir Charles Saunders, later appointed First Lord of the Admiralty, would transport Wolfe and his battalions up the St Lawrence to the point of engagement at Québec, while at the same time securing control of the gulf and the river. As an additional tactical ploy, an army of foot-soldiers, commanded by General Jeffrey Amherst, and comprising British troops and American rangers, would move on Québec overland from the west.

Amherst knew all too well that his would not be an easy undertaking: his army had to contend with challenging terrain and well-defended French forts that they needed to overrun along the way. The navy's role was equally demanding, as the large fleet, ranging from ships-of-the-line to small support vessels, would surely struggle when it came to navigating the river as they closed in on Québec.

What few details that were available on navigating the St Lawrence River originated from earlier British attempts to take the clifftop settlement, during the reigns of King William III and Queen Anne. But the fact that Saunders and his fellow strategists had no reliable charts of the gulf or the river – even the chart that Cook and Holland had drawn was based on scant information – was only part of the problem. Of major concern was that the larger and lumbering ships-of-sail, which were extremely difficult to manoeuvre in tight quarters, would have to contend with unseen sandbanks, rocky shoals and unpredictable eddies as they moved up what was known to be a hazard-strewn waterway. Most of the time, there was likely to be insufficient wind for them to counter the fast-flowing ebb tide, which meant that their progress would be staggered: they could only ride the flood tide for its duration, usually between five and six hours, before they would be forced to stop again and hold their ground at anchor.

The move came on 5 May 1759, when the flag signal went aloft aboard Durell's flagship, signalling that the quest for Québec was about to start. It was time for the fleet to depart the port.

Crews of the thirteen ships-of-the-line rushed up the ratlines for the first time in months and manned the yards, ensuring that the sails unfurled in the appropriate succession while orders were barked their way, and elsewhere, from the quarterdeck. When everything was prepared, other crewmen manned the windlass on the foredeck, inserting the heavy wooden bars in their slots, then, when ready, they began heaving down on those bars, hauling in the bower cable and raising the bower to the constant rhythm of the large ratchet pawls clacking away.

Soon enough, the ships of this fleet, which had been at anchor in Halifax for almost six months, were easing their way out of the harbour, nudging their respective bows into Atlantic Ocean swells before turning north for the looping course to Louisbourg, then to the west and the Gulf of St Lawrence.

Before long, though, captains and crews alike were starting to think they might have departed too soon. Their ships were surrounded by fields of large and loose ice – a significant threat to any vessel. Cook, who was probably experiencing such an event for the first time in his maritime career, registered his impressions in his log: 'at 7 [am] tacked Close along Side the Ice which Stretched away to the ESE as far as Could be distinguished from the Mast Head.'

With the ice came a fog so thick that the lookouts on each ship had soon lost sight of the other vessels. Over the following days, to ensure they stayed in contact and did not collide, cannons and small arms were fired at regular intervals, so that positions of ships in close proximity could be recognised.

Ten days out from Halifax, deep grief descended on *Pembroke* and across the fleet. Captain Simcoe, who had been ailing for some time and confined to his cabin since the fleet was off Louisbourg, died as the result of a severe bout of pneumonia. It was a profoundly sad time for Cook. He had lost a good captain and close friend; one of the cherished few who'd had a substantial influence on his career. The following day, 16 May, Simcoe was buried at sea off Anticosti Island, at the entrance to the St Lawrence River. Cook logged brief details: 'at 6 Buried the Corpse of Captain John Simcoe & fired 20 Guns half a Minute between Each Gun.'

Adding to the challenge for the British fleet, as the ships made their long, south-westerly passage up the St Lawrence, was the lack of buoys in the river marking the channel. This was only to be expected: the French, knowing that an attack would be coming in the spring, had no doubt removed them late the previous year as part of their defence strategy. However, as the British had hoped, any plan by the French to establish gun batteries on the riverbanks and on islands in the river, and of scuttling ships in the narrows to create a blockade, had been rendered impossible. The defenders had had no time to implement their desired level of resistance before the warmer weather made its first appearance.

By 20 May, the fleet was anchored off the small, cigar-shaped Barnaby Island, 150 nautical miles downstream from Québec. From that moment, word spread rapidly upriver to the capital that the British were advancing. Admiral Saunders directed a small number of ships to remain at the island for protection purposes; then, on the next flood tide, the bulk of the fleet, including *Pembroke*, moved another 100 nautical miles upstream to Île aux Coudres, just 50 nautical miles from the target. By this time, Cook's vessel had a new captain, John Wheelock, who had been promoted to the position from the 20-gunner HMS *Squirrel*.

The most formidable threat to the progress of the British fleet towards Québec came on 8 June, when a section of the river known as The Traverse was reached. The British knew this stretch of the river was notorious for its shallows, its proliferation of shifting sandbanks, and its churning currents – hazards again made much worse for their ships by the absence of channel markers. For two days after the fleet arrived there and anchors had been set, Cook and the masters of a number of other ships were aboard small boats taking soundings and mapping a way through the maze. His log, written as tersely as ever, noted: '9th June, the boats of the fleet engaged sounding the channel of The Traverse ... returned satisfied with being acquainted with the channel ...'

Occasionally, a few French soldiers, as well as members of the local indigenous population, would fire on the British ships after they began moving through The Traverse, but they caused little trouble.

By 27 June, the French were left in no doubt as to the magnitude of the threat their town was facing. There, on their doorstep to the north-east, was an armada of vessels – near 150 of them – all flying the Union flag and most anchored in the river basin between Point Lévis and Île d'Orléans. The ships were within a 3-mile radius of the town, which sat atop Cap Diamant, a 300-foot-high promontory along the northern side of the river as the St Lawrence stretched downstream to the north-east. In his clifftop fortress, the French commander, Lieutenant-General Louis-Joseph de Montcalm, had rallied some 15,000 troops with which to defend Québec and New France.

Within twenty-four hours the pendulum had swung dramatically in France's favour. A powerful storm whipped up and rolled across Québec, causing many of the British ships to drag anchor, some of them running aground, while several small boats were lost. Fast and responsible action by the crews minimised the problems for the invaders, only for the fleet to then be confronted by an even greater danger.

Seizing the opportunity that came with the wind direction and a favourable tide on a dark, moonless night, Montcalm had set his fire-ships adrift and ablaze. His intention was for them to float downstream and create havoc among the enemy – the naval version of an archer's flaming arrow. Unfortunately for the defenders, most of these combustible vessels had been set alight too soon, so by the time they reached the anchored British ships, they were merely smouldering hulks. Two that were still blazing ran aground, while those that reached the fleet were towed clear of their intended targets by British sailors before they caused any damage.

Wolfe established a land base for his men at the western end of Île d'Orléans, and then in early July a major battery, made up of hundreds of cannons, was put in place across the river from Québec. With the town now well within British sights, Wolfe initiated the first stage of his grand attack by commencing an incessant shelling of the fortress. For two months, cannonballs rained down on the Frenchmen, and twice the lower part of the town – that closest to the river – was set ablaze.

Cook, like the masters of all vessels, was busy ensuring that every manoeuvre, order and activity was carried out smoothly and efficiently aboard his ship. At one stage, *Pembroke* was directed into a rapid-response action to save HMS *Richmond* and *Diana*, his log recording:

> Cut and Slipped per order of the admiral and ran up the
> river in order to cover the Richmond and Diana which
> was Attacked by a Number of the Enemy's Row boats,
> which Rowed off as Soon as we got up … Sent the
> Long boats and 30 Men on Board the Diana to assist in
> getting her guns out, at 4 fired a 24 pound Shot at the
> Enemy's Row boats going down the River …

Around this time, Wolfe decided to avoid the ongoing minor skirmishes with the French and go to the second stage of his plan: mounting a full-scale assault on the fortress by putting his troops ashore on the north side of the St Lawrence. But first he needed an accurate chart of river depths along the chosen shoreline.

Cook became an integral part of this project. He and others spent days taking soundings along the north shore, immediately below the fortress and on the upstream side, hoping they could find a location offering deep water and little current, so that the two primary vessels for landing troops could be secured as close to shore as possible. This is where Saunders and Wolfe drew on Cook's previous experience, because the hulls of these landing vessels were similar in shape and proportion to the cats that the Yorkshireman had sailed out of Whitby for the Walkers. As a result of discussions with Cook, Wolfe wrote the following to his brigadier, Robert Monckton, on 28 July: 'The Master of the Pembroke assures the Admiral that a Cat, can go within less than 100 yards of the Redoubt [stronghold] – if so, it will be a short affair …'

The location decided on by Wolfe for what would become the Battle of Beauport was immediately downstream of the fortress at an area known as the Shoals of Beauport. This part of the attack on Québec, which came on 31 July, turned into a disaster for the British. Despite *Pembroke* and HMS *Centurion* using their carronades to lob the heaviest possible ammunition onto the defenders, both cats carrying the troops were hammered by French cannon-fire, resulting in a total toll of 500 dead or wounded. The only option left for the British was to set fire to the two landing vessels, abandon the attack and retreat.

The major shortcoming in this attack was that the cats ran aground well away from the riverbank, so the majority of the troops could not get to the shore. Unfortunately for Cook, he was deemed by many to be wrong in his suggestion that the vessels could achieve their goal. He was eventually vindicated when it was shown that most of the soundings were taken at high tide, and the attack happened when the tide was on the ebb.

By early September 1759, there was still no sign of General Amherst and his ground troops moving towards Québec from the west. So, with autumn approaching and time running out, Wolfe decided he must go it alone.

Preparations were rapid and intense. Cook's role in helping set up a decoy downriver from the main attack was revealed by Captain Wheelock in his log: 'At 10 [am] our Master went and laid Several Buoys on the Shoals of Beauport ... at noon the Enemy attempted to cut away the Buoys our Master laid, but was [driven] off by the fire of the Richmond ...' While a force led by Saunders would provide 'a feint to Land at Beauport in order to Draw the Enemy's Attention', as Cook later put it, Wolfe's plan was to land his troops upstream – 1½ miles south-west of Québec town, in a cove known as Anse-au-Foulon. To create added confusion for the French, another decoy landing using some of the warships was planned for Cap-Rouge, 6 nautical miles upstream.

Under the cover of darkness on 12 September – and with the decoys working to full effect – every available small boat in the fleet was used to transport 4500 British redcoats to the shore. Simultaneously, the cannons at Point Lévis provided 'Continual fire against the Town all night' from across the river. The soldiers were then able to land at their secluded cove, and from there they scaled the sloping cliffs of Cap Diamant, and at dawn surprised the French with their presence.

The final showdown came later that morning in the Battle of the Plains of Abraham, named after the plateau just south-west of the fortress overlooking the river. There, the two sides lined up facing each other on the open field with just 35 yards separating them. Once in place, they started blazing away with their muskets and a few cannons. There was frenzied activity on both sides, as the muskets of the day took between fifteen and thirty seconds to reload.

In a battle that lasted little more than fifteen minutes, it was the British who, from the outset, showed they were faster and more capable with their weapons, and as a result, the French line was quick to collapse. From that moment, those French troops still standing made a hasty retreat to the fort. Yet even with the benefit of the security provided by the compound, the defenders were unable to gain the upper hand. Five days later, they realised that surrender was inevitable. It had been a bloody battle with a terrible toll: around 650 soldiers were killed or wounded on each side. Among the dead were the two army generals, James Wolfe and Louis-Joseph de Montcalm.

The British, with both Louisbourg and Québec now under the Union flag, were well on their way to changing North American history forever.

CHAPTER FOUR

Canadian Winters

Less than a week after the victory at Québec, it was time for Cook to pack his uniform and slops. He was being transferred under an order from Admiral Saunders to HMS *Northumberland*, a promotion of some importance. Captained by Alexander, Lord Colville, his new ship was a third-rate 70-gunner manned by 500 men, and not dissimilar to *Pembroke*. As it turned out, Colville was also destined for greater things, because within a month he too was promoted by Saunders – to the position of Commander-in-Chief in North America, with the rank of commodore.

With William Adams as the newly appointed captain, *Northumberland* was one of a small fleet of ships directed to return to Halifax for the winter. They arrived there on 27 October 1759 – the day that Cook turned thirty-one. He and all those who had wintered aboard their ships at Halifax the previous year knew what to expect. Some days were sunny and still, but most delivered bone-chillingly cold temperatures, boredom and the monotonous, often incessant sound of storm winds howling through the rigging.

With so many men on board, there was no pleasure for those in the cramped accommodation below deck. It was like a rabbit warren for humans, and much of it didn't offer standing headroom. Worse still, the 'head' – the toilet – was located in the open air on deck, right at the bow. Cabin fever was rife in what Cook biographer John Cawte Beaglehole has described as these 'between deck dungeons', while suggesting: 'A great many more men would have run away from the British navy, one fancies, winter or summer, if they had known where to run to …'

Their primary duty was to ensure that the ship would be ready to sail back to Québec as early as possible during the following spring. Ship's Master Cook was no doubt overseeing the maintenance aboard *Northumberland*. He also spent a considerable amount of time embracing his studies and developing his cartographical skills.

The latter was evident through his creation of a more precise chart of Halifax Harbour. Despite the winter weather, Cook took an extensive number of soundings across the waterway, and, thanks to his new-found talents as a surveyor, established a more accurate picture of the shoreline and its surrounds. A reference to his studies at this time comes from a young lieutenant named King, who greatly admired the Yorkshireman and wrote: 'I have often heard him say, that, during a hard winter, he first read Euclid, and applied himself to the study of mathematics and astronomy, without any other assistance, than what a few books, and his own industry, afforded him.' It was the late Captain Simcoe and Samuel Holland who had encouraged Cook to read the works of Euclid, the Greek mathematician from around 300 BC, considered the 'Father of Geometry'.

It seems that while Cook was collecting data for his charts of Halifax Harbour, Admiral Saunders was, on the other side of the Atlantic, collating all the data taken from the surveys of 'the River St Lawrence, with the Harbours, bays and Islands in that river'. He had gathered this information from numerous sources, including Cook, in response to special orders from the Admiralty, which required that observations, soundings and bearings be carefully carried out wherever possible 'so that all existing charts may be corrected and improved'. After collating the results, Saunders then forwarded his report to the Lords of the Admiralty. Suitably impressed, their direction was that it be published.

The duty for such an undertaking fell to the most prominent and successful cartographical engraver in London at that time, Thomas Jefferys, of Charing Cross. There would have been little out of the ordinary for Jeffrys when it came to carrying out the Admiralty's instructions, except for the considerable size of the publication – twelve sheets measuring some 7 feet by 3 feet, containing maps, charts and highly detailed sailing directions. With regard to its place in James Cook's story, the published work owed much to his involvement. A considerable amount of the detail clearly came from his participation in surveys made while Saunders' fleet was moving upriver towards Québec. Other details originated from the chart that he and Holland had created, with the assistance of Captain Simcoe, aboard *Pembroke* over the winter of 1758–59. So, while there was, quite understandably, no direct recognition of either Cook or Holland, because they were simply carrying out the tasks they had been ordered to do, this can be seen as the first major survey work to be published in which Cook made a substantial contribution. Of equal importance, the quality of the work left no doubt that he was emerging as the maritime equivalent of what Samuel Holland had proved to be on land.

Captain Adams consistently used two words in his journal – 'nothing remarkable' – to describe his impression of the days as they dragged on while *Northumberland* lay idly at anchor in Halifax. Meanwhile, Cook often busied himself with his ongoing survey of the harbour using one of the ship's small boats.

It was 22 April 1760 when Colville decided that conditions were suitable for his fleet to set sail for Québec, where their role would be to help consolidate the British hold on the town. Their departure proved to be a premature one, however. Two days out of Halifax, progress was halted when the fleet encountered a dense fog and then became stuck in a field of ice for twenty-four hours. Life for those standing watch on deck was almost unbearable: ice was hanging off the rigging, while damp sheets, lines and ropes became frozen, making them near impossible to handle. Once free, the ships sailed through fields of ice until 12 May.

Four days later they reached Île du Bic, in the St Lawrence River. There, the captain of a British sloop that was already at anchor delivered news to Colville that caused considerable anxiety: the British hold on Québec was being challenged by the French, and help was needed immediately.

Weeks before, a French battalion under the command of General de Lévis had made a move to retake the town, and it was only through clever tactics and good fortune that the outnumbered British defenders had been able to catch the enemy unawares, strike a heavy blow and hinder the advance. Eventually, though, the numerical advantage held by the French became a telling factor in what became known as the Battle of Sainte-Foy. The British lost a considerable number of men while continuing their defence and, on 28 April, were forced to retreat behind the city wall, which they were still bravely defending.

Colville wasted no time in having his fleet weigh anchor and head for Québec. Just forty-eight hours later, his ships were anchored in the basin adjacent to the town. Once there they received some welcome news: three other British ships, including HMS *Vanguard* and HMS *Diamond*, had arrived a day earlier and were already fighting the French attackers, but it was not until Lévis saw Colville's fleet arrive that he realised all was lost, and he made a rapid retreat.

It then became a relatively uneventful summer in Québec for the British, especially after Montréal and other provinces surrendered to General Amherst on 8 September. He had started his move north from what was the province of New York, up the Mohawk River, across Lake Ontario, then on to the St Lawrence River – a strategy that gave his army the easiest access to Montréal.

News of the French capitulation reached Colville four days later and rapidly spread to French and British ears across the provinces. When the French governor-general, Pierre, Marquis de Vaudreuil-Cavagnial, signed the surrender document, the British assured the near 70,000 former residents of New France that they would not be deported, their property would not be confiscated, and that they had freedom of religion, the right to migrate to France, and equal treatment in the fur trade. New France and its surrounding territories subsequently became a single British colony: Canada.

This news was soon being celebrated in the British territories to the south. The Old Church in Boston declared: 'Grateful reflexions on the signal appearances of divine providence for Great Britain and its colonies in America, which diffuse a general joy …' In the same announcement, the occasion was described as 'the thanksgiving-day, on occasion of the surrender of Montreal, and the complete conquest of Canada, by the blessing of heaven on his Britannic Majesty's brave troops, under the auspicious conduct of that truly great and amiable commander, General Amherst'.

With the cessation of hostilities, the lot of the sailors in Colville's squadron was considerably easier. The ships remained at anchor in the river basin immediately below the town, and in clear sight of the large Union flag that was flying proudly over the fortress. They would remain there for a month following the 8 September surrender, with the majority of men being assigned to maintaining their ships. A few, including Cook, worked on further improving the existing charts of the St Lawrence River in that region, taking additional soundings in the waterway and surveying the shoreline.

Despite being able to stand down from their previous war footing, the sailors found that any breach of discipline would not be tolerated. Hardly a day went by when the lash did not come out to punish a man for insubordination, as decreed under the Royal Navy's Articles of War, and at one stage an execution was carried out for all in the fleet to observe. This occurred after three men had deserted by stealing a canoe, and were subsequently caught, court-martialled and sentenced to death.

Colville then decided that he should be more lenient – so only one man would die. As Adams recorded in his log: 'The Commodore, having pardoned two of them, they Cast Lots who should die. He whose Lot it was, was Executed Accordingly …' The unfortunate individual was hanged from one of *Vanguard*'s yardarms.

Cook was called on to apply his expertise to an unusual circumstance when he had to supervise the salvage of *Northumberland*'s longboat. It was a four-day exercise which started when the bower cable on *Vanguard* parted and the ship was carried by the current through the anchored fleet. Unfortunately, *Vanguard* fouled *Northumberland*, and as a result the heavily laden longboat capsized and sank.

The onset of winter meant it was time for Colville's fleet to take on board the departing British troops and head back to Halifax for yet another layover. During these preparations, Captain Adams was transferred to the 32-gun *Diana* and Nathaniel Bateman left HMS *Eurus* and joined *Northumberland* as captain. It appears that Cook was not overly concerned by Adams' departure: there is no strong evidence of them striking any level of rapport.

After waiting for the start of the ebb tide, the fleet weighed anchor on 10 October, farewelled Québec and sailed for Halifax. Fifteen days later, the crew of *Northumberland* and those of all other ships in Colville's fleet guided their vessels towards their designated anchorages, the men applying their long-learned seafaring skills.

As each ship approached that point, speed was reduced according to distance off through the progressive furling of the square sails, while fore and aft sails were either trimmed on or off to increase or decrease speed, or lowered completely. At the same time, the anchor on the starboard bow – the 'best bower' – was released from its stowage position and suspended from a solid piece of timber known as a cathead, which extended out over the water near the bowsprit. When the call came from the master for the bower to be released, a crewman would uncleat the line supporting the anchor on the cathead, and with that there would be a mighty splash as the anchor, weighing more than a ton, hit the water and descended to the bottom. Simultaneously, the heavy bower cable that was attached to it would slither rapidly off the foredeck, out through the deck-level hawsehole and into the water like a giant snake.

At the appropriate time, after the leadsman had declared the depth and enough cable had been let run out, the call would come from the foredeck, for the benefit of the senior officers on the quarterdeck, that the bower cable had been made fast. All was secure.

It was not until August 1762 that *Northumberland* ventured from her anchorage. And that was only to the harbour's careening wharf, where she was hove down on the ebbing tide so that her underbelly could be cleaned of goose barnacles, weed and other small shell-like crustaceans. Up until then, the same routine that was experienced during the previous winters was resumed, and once again it was a repeat of the same miserable winter experience. Their food was the same too – apart from some much-savoured frozen beef from Boston, their diet comprised primarily pork, peas, oatmeal and vinegar (usually boiled up into some form of stodge), plus beer.

If there was a brief moment of excitement during their hibernation in Halifax, it would have been the time when there was a fire in the town, and sailors rushed ashore to help douse the flames. There was also a moment of drama when *Charming Nancy*, a merchant ship from London, sailed into port, struck an uncharted rock at the harbour entrance and sank.

Cook's personal highlight during that 1760–61 winter was quite different. On 19 January, Lord Colville made a decision that was obviously high recognition of Cook's contribution to the surveys undertaken while the fleet was bound for Québec. According to his own report, the commodore 'directed the storekeeper to pay the Master of the Northumberland, fifty pounds in consideration of his indefatigable industry in making himself master of the pilotage of the River St Lawrence'.

While it was well known that Cook, like many other masters in the fleet, had been involved in the desperately needed survey, this was the first clear indication that he had led the way. And he had excelled at his task – one that helped ensure that the ships made a safe passage upriver towards their anchorage off Québec.

This could well have been a special thank-you from Colville simply because his own superiors had acknowledged that, as admiral of the fleet, he had done a remarkable job in getting his ships through to Québec virtually without incident, and in a very short time. This achievement was seen as being a key element in the conquest of New France and the creation of Canada: the rapid approach had eliminated any chance of a French fleet trying to regain control of the town.

If the officers and men of *Northumberland* had assumed that they would be in Halifax for just one winter following the French capitulation, it was wide of the mark. They were, in fact, there for two, and almost two full years – a security force that was on stand-by on that side of the Atlantic, just in case France tried to regain its lost territory.

The French, still stung by their recent defeats, lay low through the summer of 1761, and continued to do so until the middle of the following year. Then they made the decision to take St John's, on the island of Newfoundland, a 500-nautical-mile sail to the north-east of Halifax. It was a small fishing port that the British held but had neglected – something all too apparent, as they had only sixty-three men defending the town's garrison. This made for an easy target for the French, who wanted to take it as small compensation for their losses in territory to the British during the past four years, and also to give them valuable access to cod-fishing in the region. It's also quite possible that the French saw St John's becoming a bargaining chip in peace negotiations, but they would soon realise that there was no peace to negotiate.

They made their move by sending 800 elite troops, led by Chevalier de Ternay, aboard five ships from Brest, breaking the British blockade of the French coast in the process. The force sailed directly to St John's, which surrendered without incident on 27 June 1762. Two weeks later, a local brig, which had escaped capture, sailed into Halifax and raised the alarm for the British.

A strategy for the retaking of St John's soon evolved, and within four weeks the British move on the little town was underway. *Northumberland* was one of the many ships that became part of the rapid response, an effort that included a large number of ground troops. The strategy came into full effect on 12 September, when the British landed on Avalon Peninsula at Torbay, just 10 miles north of the town. The French defenders soon realised that they were about to be out-gunned and out-manoeuvred, even though they had established fortifications around much of St John's perimeter. The French ships in port left with such haste they didn't even wait to take on board the troops they had delivered – or pick up their own crewmen who were aboard the longboats that had towed the ships clear of the harbour. In what Lord Colville would later describe as a shameful flight, the French vessels made good their escape under the cover of fog.

After six days of trying to hold the town, the French troops finally surrendered. From that day, France would no longer hold any territorial claim in North America – having also ceded New Orleans and the Mississippi Valley to Spain about this same time – although French would remain the language spoken across much of Québec.

On 20 September, a small British squadron – which had been sent from England the moment the news arrived there about the French occupation – sailed into St John's Harbour. Much to Cook's delight, he soon realised that the leader of this fleet was none other than his mentor Captain Hugh Palliser.

Cook's time in St John's was brief, however. He was directed to join Captain J.F.W. DesBarres, a highly respected member of General Amherst's battalion, based in recent times in New York. Like Samuel Holland, DesBarres was a military surveyor. The pair were sent to bays and settlements along the coastline of the Avalon Peninsula, in order to conduct extensive surveys of the surrounding waters and other towns.

After arriving back in England a few weeks later, Colville took time to write to the Admiralty regarding the retaking of St John's and to also explain what had subsequently taken place. His letter said in part:

> I have mentioned in another Letter that the Fortifications on the Island of Carbonera, were entirely destroyed by the Enemy. Colonel Amherst sent thither Mr DesBarres an Engineer, who surveyed the Island and drew a Plan for fortifying it with new Works: when these are finished, the Enterprise's six guns will be ready to mount on them ... Mr Cook, master of the Northumberland, accompanied Mr DesBarres. He has made a Draught of Harbour Grace, and the Bay of Carbonera; both which are in a great measure commanded by the Island, which lies off a Point of Land between them. Hitherto we have had a very imperfect Knowledge of these Places; but Mr Cook who was particularly careful in sounding them, has discovered that Ships of any size may lie in safety both in Harbour Grace and the Bay of Carbonera ...

While these comments by Colville would have shown Cook in a favourable light at the Admiralty, he actually contributed considerably more to surveying coastlines in the region, including the harbour at St John's. In the weeks after that town was secured, *Northumberland* visited Placentia and the Bay Bulls, where Cook carried out extensive surveys and created charts. These experiences, together with his previous work, led to him writing highly detailed notes on what he had observed, all of which were incorporated in a notebook later published as *Description of the Sea Coast of Nova Scotia, Cape Breton Island and Newfoundland.*

After carrying out its survey work, *Northumberland* returned to St John's. Once there, the crew received the news they had been waiting to hear for a considerable time: they were homeward bound!

On 7 October 1762, *Northumberland* weighed anchor while a crew laden with eager anticipation set and trimmed the sails with new-found vigour. The ship cleared the entrance to St John's in company with the three vessels that Palliser had brought with him from England a few weeks earlier.

The ships made good time across the Atlantic, for after just nineteen days at sea they were lying at anchor at Spithead, off Portsmouth. Cook and many of his shipmates had been away from home for four years and eight months.

The Battle of Signal Hill at St John's had marked the final North American battle of the Seven Years War. With that conflict now nearing its end, there was no longer a requirement, in the foreseeable future, for *Northumberland* to remain a fighting ship. By 8 December that year, the entire ship's company had been stood down, and on departing, Cook collected £291, 19 shillings and three-pence in pay owing to him.

While he had been away from England for so long, every experience he had enjoyed would, in some form, contribute significantly to his future in the Royal Navy. This future was assisted in no small way by further acknowledgement from Lord Colville, now promoted to Rear-Admiral of the White. On 30 December, Colville wrote to the Secretary of the Admiralty and tendered a glowing report regarding Cook and his contribution to the British campaign in Canada:

> Mr Cook late Master of the Northumberland acquaints
> me that he has laid before their Lordships all his
> Draughts and Observations, relating to the River

St Lawrence, Part of the Coast of Nova Scotia, and of
Newfoundland

On this Occasion, I beg leave to inform their
Lordships, that from my Experience of Mr Cook's
Genius and Capacity, I think him well qualified for the
Work he has performed, and for greater Undertakings of
the same kind. These Draughts being made under my
own Eye I can venture to say, they may be the means of
directing many in the right way, but cannot mislead
any ...

Colville's highly favourable opinion of Cook's dedication and
talents was not lost on the Admiralty. Cook would never step
aboard a large ship-of-war again. Instead, fate would carry him
to then inconceivable heights within the Royal Navy.

CHAPTER FIVE

A Bride – Post-haste

After being rowed ashore in one of *Northumberland*'s boats, Cook stepped onto English home soil for the first time since departing for Nova Scotia with Boscawen's taskforce in February 1758. With him now on the dockside at Portsmouth was a trunk filled with all the survey material he had gathered while serving in North America. Charts, soundings, sailing directions, descriptions and surveys – the same material that Colville commended him for when he wrote to the Lords of the Admiralty later that month.

Cook was keen to get his works to the Admiralty as soon as possible. To that end, he climbed aboard a horse-drawn carriage and was soon enduring the bone-jarring 100-mile ride up the rutted dirt, sometimes cobblestoned, road that meandered through the villages, forests and rolling countryside between Portsmouth and London. One would have expected that this energetic Royal Navy seafarer would have had his meeting with the Admiralty foremost in his mind, yet that was probably not the case. It appears that an even more significant event lay ahead – one that has baffled biographers and historians, and brought an element of intrigue to his life story.

It occurred a fortnight later, on 21 December, when Cook married Elizabeth Batts, a 'highly personable' young lady who, being twenty years old, was fourteen years his junior. The ceremony took place at St Margaret's Church in Barking – a busy fishing village 20 miles east of London, sited on the banks of a tributary of the Thames. This is the first record of any association between the young Miss Batts and James Cook, yet it is extremely unlikely that they met, committed to each other and married within the two weeks of his return. The more probable scenario is that this marriage came about through an enduring friendship, the origins of which dated back perhaps fifteen years – to when, as an apprentice seafarer, Cook was sailing into London aboard the Walkers' collier *Freelove*.

Elizabeth's parents, Samuel and Mary Batts, ran the Bell Alehouse on Wapping High Street, close to Execution Dock. Theirs was one of the few respectable dockland establishments in London's seamy waterfront district, less than a mile downstream from today's Tower Bridge. This area, which was at the eastern end of the commercial docks, and known as the Pool of London, was where *Freelove* is believed to have docked each time she brought her cargo of coal to the town from Newcastle-upon-Tyne. The congested waterfront scene that *Freelove* and all other ships in port created was one of a logjam of vessels, which in turn created a dense forest of masts and yards; hundreds of them, seemingly strung together by a vast web of rigging. Those same ships disgorged thousands of seafarers, merchant and navy men, the majority of whom were, by day and by night, boozing, brawling and buying women. Fortunately for those men wanting to avoid such depravity, establishments like the Bell Alehouse provided decency and sanctuary amid an otherwise unsavoury environment, but they were few.

Like John and Henry Walker, Elizabeth's parents were Quakers, and it appears that the Whitby-based shipowners established a friendship with the couple. As a result, well before Cook's time with the company, the Bell Alehouse became the place where the Walkers' crews were fed and lodged while in port. Sadly, baby Elizabeth never knew her father, who died the year she was born. Three years later, however, her mother married John Blackburn, and they continued to operate the inn. Blackburn is said to have supported Elizabeth as if she were his own child.

Elizabeth Batts would have been just four or five years old when Cook first visited the Bell, during one of his early voyages to London. If he had been unaware of his hosts' only child then, he and Elizabeth might have met during one of his visits to the alehouse while he was in town as a member of the Royal Navy, possibly when he spent near a week there in 1755 during his sign-up procedure. Elizabeth would have been thirteen at the time. Another possibility was two years later, between his sitting for the Master's Certificate at Deptford and joining the *Solebay* in Scotland, by which point Elizabeth was apparently living with family or friends in Barking. Had that been the case, then she might have either met Cook, or renewed their acquaintance, when visiting her mother at the alehouse.

The surprising fact is that there is no known evidence of communication or courtship between the pair, and no written reference to their relationship on his part, or from any of his associates in the merchant marine or Royal Navy. Any correspondence between the couple that might have existed before the wedding, and certainly all letters and notes they exchanged during their life together, were burnt to ash by Elizabeth prior to her death. As disappointing as this act is for historians delving into Cook's life, her reasons were understandable: they were too personal, too sanctified, to be shared with others.

Amid all the speculation on the background to their relationship, the only known fact is that the couple were wed that December day at the grey-stone, square-towered St Margaret's, set among the meadows beside Barking Creek. The local vicar performed the service under an Archbishop of Canterbury licence, a document that allowed the couple to be married without the issuing of formal banns publicly announcing the pending nuptial. The church register reads:

> James Cook of the Parish of St Paul, Shadwell, in the
> County of Middlesex, Bachelor, and Elizabeth Batts, of
> the Parish of Barking in the County of Essex, Spinster,
> were married in this church by the Archbishop of
> Canterbury's licence, this 21st day of December, one
> thousand seven hundred and sixty-two, by George
> Downing, Vicar of Little Barking, Essex.

It is not known which family members attended the ceremony. Once the formalities were completed, the newlyweds took a carriage ride back to town where they set up their home in Shadwell, a short way east of the alehouse. No doubt the motivation behind the couple deciding to marry so soon after Cook's return to England was due to the likelihood of him being sent back to sea at short notice. On this occasion, at least he and Elizabeth were able to enjoy three months together before that was the case.

In March 1763, Cook learned that he was heading back to Canada, or more specifically, Newfoundland. With the Treaty of Paris having been signed on 10 February, the extent of the British holding in North America had increased enormously. As a consequence, much of the territory and its coastline needed to be surveyed accurately for military and commercial reasons, as well as for the planning of settlements: borders, boundaries and shorelines needed to be defined.

The two surveyors with whom Cook was most familiar, Holland and DesBarres, were dealing primarily with surveying the landmass. With regard to the vast range of maritime projects resulting from acquisitions under the treaty, Cook had already proved his worth as a surveyor to the Governor of Newfoundland, Captain Thomas Graves (later Lord Graves). Not only had the captain's appointment as governor just been extended, but his territorial purview was now expanded to include much of Labrador, Anticosti Island and other islands in the Gulf of St Lawrence.

Graves had no hesitation in recommending Cook for this latest task. The Admiralty, however – as aware of the quality of Cook's work as the Lords were, via references from Palliser and Colville – was slow to commit. This procrastination prompted Graves to write to the Secretary of the Admiralty, Mr Philip Stephens, in early April 1763, requesting 'to know what final answer he shall give to Mr Cook, late Master of Northumberland, who is very willing to go out to survey the Harbours and Coasts of Labrador and the Draughtsman he was to get from the Tower [of London], as they both wait to know their Lordships' resolution and the footing they are to be upon'.

Soon after this communication, on 6 April, an increasingly frustrated Graves again wrote to the Admiralty, asking the board to formally advise Cook of his latest mission, since: 'I have this moment seen Mr Cook and acquainted him he was to get himself ready to depart, the moment the Board was pleased to order him ...' His recent change of marital status aside, the Yorkshireman was certainly keen to go – not least because, at a promised 10 shillings a day, his pay would equal what Palliser was receiving as captain of *Eagle*.

When contemplating the job that lay ahead, Cook recognised the magnitude of the task. The accuracy of his work would be crucial for the safety of ships entering and departing the Gulf of St Lawrence and the river, as well as vessels sailing the coast of Newfoundland. He was also pleased to know that Graves had been granted permission to purchase two vessels, of about 60 tons burthen, once the ship transporting the surveying party across the Atlantic, HMS *Antelope*, had reached Newfoundland. One would be specifically for Cook's use while conducting his coastal surveys.

Having been made aware, unofficially, that he was to go to Newfoundland, Cook and his wife were, like Graves, anxiously awaiting confirmation of his appointment, and details of his departure. It was not until the middle of April that the desired communication from the Secretary of the Admiralty was received:

Sir,

My Lords Commissioners of the Admiralty, having
directed Captain Graves, of His Majesty's Ship, the
Antelope, at Portsmouth, to receive you on board and
carry you to Newfoundland in order to your taking a
Survey of Part of the Coast and Harbours of that Island.
I am commanded by their Lordships to acquaint you
therewith: that you must repair immediately on board
the said ship, she being under sailing orders, that you are
to follow such orders as you shall receive from Cap T
Graves relative to the said service and that you will be
allowed Ten shillings a day during the time you are
employed therein …

Graves' frustration with the Admiralty continued – this time
because of the tardy despatch detailing his orders to sail. The
document finally arrived on 19 April. With the orders in hand
and his impatience suitably extinguished, Graves would have
hoped for *Antelope* to be underway in a matter of days, sailing
west out of the English Channel and into the North Atlantic.
Unfortunately, more delays plagued his plans.

First, he had to cut short a visit to London and rush back to
the ship, which was then anchored at Spithead, after news
reached him that some of the crew were on the verge of
mutiny – a reflection of a tide of discontent among the men of
the lower deck that was spreading across the Royal Navy fleet
at the time. Fortunately, his prompt response to the problem,
the promise of reforms, and the dismissal of the principal
troublemakers among *Antelope*'s crew steadied the situation.
From that moment, his men continued to work as expected
towards preparing to go to sea.

Then, there was a problem relating to Cook. Despite
receiving his orders on 19 April to travel to the port and go
aboard the ship, he did not present himself to Graves for another
fifteen days. This was due, in part, to Cook deciding to visit the
Tower of London and meet with the military's surveying and

mapping experts in the Ordnance Office. He wanted to discuss with them the task to which he had been assigned, and the fact that he needed an assistant – someone with knowledge of the very latest surveying techniques and equipment, including the use of a theodolite. No doubt Cook's experiences with his scholarly associates Holland and DesBarres caused him to make this approach.

As if that delay was not enough to contend with, Graves then learned that a muster of the ship's men revealed that fifty-five had 'ran' – deserted – even though *Antelope* was at anchor offshore. To make matters even worse, there was also one noted absentee among the names on the ship's manifest: William Test, the draughtsman whom the Ordnance Office had directed to travel with Cook and assist him with his work. He simply failed to show up.

Captain Graves was then obliged to advise the Admiralty of his dilemmas via another letter, which read in part: 'Mr Cook arrived here yesterday but without an Assistant, which defect I will endeavour to replace here if possible, under an expectation of the same encouragement their Lordships were to give Mr Test ...' By 'encouragement', Graves was no doubt referring to the 6 shillings per day that the Admiralty had granted Test 'in addition to what he receives from the Board of Ordnance'. It was soon learned that William Test had an understandable reason not to join the ship: the Ordnance Office had agreed to give him leave so that he could join Cook, but without pay!

After some considerable effort over the following days, Graves found a suitably qualified replacement in Edward Smart, a resident of Lambeth, in South London, who was an ordnance draughtsman. Unfortunately, there was too little time for him to be aboard *Antelope* before her departure. Instead, he sailed aboard HMS *Spy* a short time later and joined Cook in Newfoundland.

Early on 15 May 1763, Graves strode along the deck of his ship, cast a weather eye towards the heavens, noted the direction of the wind and the state of the tide, and then declared it was time to sail. With that, the master ordered the crew into action. What followed was the time-honoured and complicated procedure for an eighteenth century square-rigged ship to get underway – one that needed to be orchestrated perfectly from start to finish.

It began while *Antelope* lay at anchor head-to-wind. On the call from the bosun, the hands manning the windlass began hauling away on the bars they used for leverage, bringing in the bower cable and raising the anchor. At the same time, some crew-members were called on to hoist the jib, while others were on stand-by to set and trim the sails as required. Those men took to their tasks after the shrill of the bosun's whistle confirmed 'anchor's aweigh' – the bower was clear of the bottom.

Meantime, there was action at the starboard side of the vessel amidships: men were working on bringing aboard the brig, which had been launched to assist with the raising of the bower and the recovery of the anchor buoy. Once most of the crew aboard the small boat had clambered up the side of *Antelope* and onto the deck, the brig was then hoisted from the water and onto the main deck using a block-and-tackle system set from the outboard end of the yardarms.

The majority of the responsibility then went to the men tending the sails. At the desired moment, they were ordered to ease out the buntlines on the sails that needed to be set so that they unfurled; then the sheets and tacks of those sails were hauled on. With that done, there came the critical move whereby the fore and main courses (the lower square sails set on the foremast and mainmast, respectively) were back-winded – set so they blew inside out (back against the masts) – in order that the ship's bow would be blown away from the direction of the wind, that is, downwind.

For the next few minutes, *Antelope* continued to make no headway; instead, her bow was driven off to leeward by the powerful force that came from the sails being back-winded. She was held this way until she lay six points – almost beam on (side on) – to the direction of the wind. Once that point was reached,

Antelope was in a position whereby the sails could be set properly and forward progress achieved: the leeward braces on the yards, and the rope sheets attached to the sails, were trimmed accordingly, and very soon the hiss of a bow wave was being heard by the men on the foredeck. *Antelope* was safely underway.

In its entirety, this was a time-consuming operation. From the moment that the bosun confirmed 'anchor's aweigh' to when the ship was on course and making headway, the process could span thirty minutes or more.

For Cook, everything about this particular departure was a new experience. Never in his career as a seafarer had he not been actively engaged in some way in the manoeuvring and sailing of the vessel, especially when it was time to weigh anchor. This time, though, he was not 'Master Cook', but 'Surveyor Cook'. His role was passenger and interested observer on a voyage of more than 2000 nautical miles across the North Atlantic.

Newfoundland is an island sufficiently large to be conspicuous on world maps. It sits like a bastion guarding the Gulf of St Lawrence from the Atlantic, and while roughly triangular in shape, is so irregular in its form that it could be said to resemble a large blotch sitting off mainland Canada's north-east coast.

For Cook, the rugged nature of the coastline was symbolic of the complexity and extent of the work he would undertake. While the distance between the island's extremities is around 300 miles, it lays claim to 6000 miles of coastline because of its natural features: long peninsulas and myriad harbours, inlets, bays and coves. The climate is perennially cold and foggy, and the rain falls like frozen bullets. The wicked Arctic storms that blast in from the north are legendary, and for the wrong reasons. This fact was all too evident in September 1775 when an almost inconceivable 4000-plus men, primarily British sailors, perished as a consequence of 'Independence Hurricane' hammering Newfoundland's east coast.

In addition, there are the icebergs that drift south from Greenland year-round and contribute to a very long winter. These challenges combined to give Cook just five months – between early June and late October – to carry out his surveys. And it was already the middle of June when *Antelope* reached Newfoundland.

Captain Graves directed that the ship anchor in Trepassey Harbour, on the south-east corner of the island, 70 miles to the south of St John's on Avalon Peninsula. Once there, five additional ships came under his command for the purpose of covering as much of the region as possible that summer. Not surprisingly, Cook was assigned the most difficult of the surveys to be carried out: to chart and detail the sometimes inhospitable, rugged and barren (yet spectacular) shoreline from Cape Race, near where they were anchored, to Cape Ray, on the island's south-west corner. It was a distance of 250 nautical miles in a direct line, but probably twice that for Cook should his ship trace its every cranny. For this, he was directed to board the 25-gun HMS *Tweed*, which was under the captaincy of Charles Douglas.

Prior to being transferred, Cook handed Captain Douglas the orders that Graves had drafted for the captain's benefit, relating to the survey work. For Cook, there came a surprise at the outset, concerning a goodwill provision under the Treaty of Paris. The relevant part of Douglas' orders gave a hint of what was to come:

> ... you are to proceed without a moment's loss of
> time ... to the Island of St Peter where you are to afford
> him [Cook] all the assistance in your power by boats or
> otherways in taking an accurate survey of the Island[s] of
> St Peter and Miquelon with all the Expedition possible,
> that no Delay be thereby given to the Delivering [of]
> these Islands up to the French ...

Britain had ceded control of St Pierre and Miquelon to allow the French access to the fishing grounds they would otherwise struggle to work had the British laid claim to every particle of New France. The dilemma for Cook was that the two islands – 12 miles off Newfoundland's southern coast, and 100 miles to the west of Trepassey Bay – were to be officially handed over on 10 June, yet it was not until three days later that he stepped aboard *Tweed*. And he still had an entire survey of the 93-square-mile islands to complete before the transfer could take place.

When *Tweed* finally sailed into the harbour at St Pierre, a French frigate was already there in anticipation of the handover. A matter of hours later, the governor-designate, François-Gabriel d'Angeac, supported by fifty soldiers, arrived aboard the French ship *Garonne* to take formal possession. Also on board were the first French residents for the islands: 150 men, women and children, the men being either fishermen or merchants.

D'Angeac was indignant when he realised that the islands were not ready for occupation, and that the British residents – who, under the terms of the agreement, would go aboard *Tweed* and depart the islands – were still there. Cook all but ignored the presence of the governor-designate and immediately commenced surveying the shorelines of the mountainous and desolate islands. It was Douglas' job to deal with d'Angeac. In his report on the handover, Douglas wrote that the Frenchman 'was (you may believe with some difficulty) persuaded to remain on board with his troops, until the fourth day of July when (the survey of St Peter's being completed) that Island was delivered to him in form: and our Surveyor began with the other [Miquelon] …'

This was a diplomatically sensitive time for Douglas – who became a master of procrastination when dealing with d'Angeac – and a difficult survey for Cook. Nonetheless, Graves' orders were completed by the end of July, at which point the French took full control. Cook and the British residents of the islands then sailed back to St John's, where he was disappointed to learn that *Spy*, carrying his assistant, Edward Smart, had not yet arrived. More to his liking was Graves' advice that he had purchased a 68-ton gaff-rigged schooner named *Sally* for Cook to use as a full-time survey vessel.

After being renamed HMS *Grenville*, apparently in honour of Britain's new prime minister, her first assignment saw her depart St John's, turn to port, and sail a course towards the north-western tip of Newfoundland. From there, she sailed south, in close proximity to the western coast, where Cook surveyed, mapped and detailed as many of the major harbours and islands as possible. It is probable that Cook completed an entire circumnavigation of Newfoundland on this particular expedition.

When he returned to St John's, he was pleased to see *Spy* in port: Smart had arrived. In a matter of days the two men were aboard *Grenville* and heading to sea, this time to survey the coastal regions around St John's. They did this for almost two months – right up until the first signs of the bleak Newfoundland winter appeared, in the form of falling temperatures and biting winds. There was nothing more they could do until the following year, so on 5 November, Cook and Smart were aboard *Tweed* and sailing to the east: homeward bound towards England.

Tweed averaged 5 knots – around 100 miles a day – for the crossing of the Atlantic, and was at anchor at Spithead, on the Solent, on 29 November. Understandably, Cook made haste for London and a much-desired reunion with Elizabeth. Within minutes of arriving home, he was proudly cradling in his arms his first-born child: a son named James, who had been born seven weeks earlier, on 13 October 1763.

Cook spent the next five months in London. Much of that time was assigned to expanding all the information he had gathered in Newfoundland into a more presentable and readable form, with Smart's assistance. He also decided to purchase a new family home, a place where Elizabeth could enjoy more green space; a residence where a growing family would be more comfortable. The move was only a mile to the north of where they were then living in Shadwell – to the small village of Mile

End Old Town – but the difference in lifestyle was considerable. The new Cook family residence was a small terrace: number 7, Assembly Row, on Mile End Road.

Cook's reputation within the Royal Navy, and with the Admiralty, continued to be bolstered by what was seen as his dedication to duty, attention to detail and ability as a mariner. He was increasingly recognised as a man of considerable value to the service, someone they could not afford to lose – and they didn't. Cook would spend all the northern hemisphere summers through to 1767 on the waters around Newfoundland continuing his surveying activities. Meanwhile, on a personal front, there were two developments that made this demanding task more pleasurable.

In early 1764, Captain Hugh Palliser, a man he much admired, was appointed successor to Captain Graves as Governor of Newfoundland. Then, on 18 April, the Navy Board, acting on the advice of the Admiralty, formally appointed Cook master of *Grenville*, which was at the time still lying in St John's Harbour. Additionally, he was to sail the vessel back to England at the end of the summer that year.

There was sad news also during this period. Apart from having to find a crew for his latest commission, he needed to appoint another assistant: Edward Smart died just eight weeks before he was due to join Cook aboard HMS *Lark*. The ship duly departed from Portsmouth on 7 May.

Over the following four, all-too-often foggy and cool summer seasons in Newfoundland, Cook's remarkable work as a maritime surveyor was unmatched within the Royal Navy, but while his endeavours also brought considerable personal satisfaction, the desired results did not always come without incident. The first of these unfortunate moments – and potentially the most lethal – happened on 6 August 1764, just three weeks after *Lark* arrived in St John's. *Grenville* had sailed to the northernmost point of Newfoundland and was anchored near Cape Norman, so that Cook and some of his men could board the cutter, go to the shore and set up the theodolite for survey purposes. To those who had remained on *Grenville*, the first indication of anything untoward was the sight of the cutter being rowed back towards the ship at a rapid rate, amid anxious shouts from the men in it. *Grenville*'s log broadly detailed the incident: '2pm – Came on board the Cutter with the Master who unfortunately had a Large Powder Horn blown up & Burst in his hand which shattered it in a Terrible manner, and one of the people that stood hard by suffered greatly by the same accident ...'

How the horn-shaped container came to explode is not known – it could have happened while Cook was filling it with gunpowder. There was considerable concern for the injured Cook and the crewman, as no one aboard *Grenville* had any medical expertise. Some members of the crew recalled seeing a large French ship anchored in nearby Noddy Harbour, less than 10 miles away – she was more than likely, surely, to have a doctor on board. Consequently, there was an immediate response from the crew: the anchor was weighed, all possible sail was crammed on, and *Grenville* headed for Noddy Harbour as fast as she could sail.

Fortunately, the French ship was still there, and her complement did indeed include a doctor, so both Cook and the injured crewman received treatment. Cook had a gaping wound between his thumb and forefinger, and another deep wound on his wrist. Although he would have been tended to in the best possible way, any painkiller could only have come in the form of a large and swift swig of spirits, while to stop any major bleeding, the wounds would have been either heavily bandaged or covered with boiling pitch.

Grenville stayed in Noddy Harbour for almost three weeks, until 25 August, to allow Cook and the other injured man to recuperate. While some crew continued survey work from there, others took the opportunity to push the boundaries of discipline aboard the ship: they brewed spruce beer and consumed it in copious quantities, which led to many of the tars becoming extremely drunk. When he became aware of this, Cook made sure that discipline was restored as quickly as it had departed. Several of the crew, including his senior hand, Peter Flower, were 'Confined to the Deck for Drunkness and Mutiny', while the instigator was also forced to 'run the Gantlope [gauntlet]' – a physical punishment in which an offender was forced to run between two rows of crewmen who were ordered to repeatedly beat him.

Cook resumed his survey activities as soon as he was well enough, and stayed with them until the end of October, when he returned to St John's. He was there for only a few days, because on 1 November *Grenville* was back at sea, heading for England. Captain Palliser forwarded a letter to the Lords of the Admiralty, advising them of the incident in which Cook had been injured. The contents of Palliser's letter led to them writing to the First Lord, Lord Halifax, on 14 November:

> Mr. Cook, the surveyor, has returned. The accident to
> him was not so bad as it was represented. Nor had it
> interrupted his survey so much as he [Captain Palliser]
> expected. He continued on the coast as long as the
> season would permit, and has executed his survey in a
> manner which, he has no doubt, will be satisfactory to
> their Lordships. I have ordered him to proceed to
> Woolwich to refit his vessel for the next season, and to
> lay before the Board, Draughts of his surveys with all his
> remarks and observations that may be useful to Trade
> and Navigation in those parts …

Grenville duly docked at Woolwich, to the east of London, on 12 December, although the actual overhaul was done at Deptford. Cook was able to make his eagerly awaited return to his family two days later. It would be a far happier reunion than he could ever have anticipated. For, on that very same day, Elizabeth gave birth to their second son, Nathaniel.

As usual, Cook spent much of the winter preparing charts and details of his observations ready for publication by the

Admiralty. He was also in contact with the Lords regarding a more pressing problem: the condition of *Grenville*. Her hull below the waterline was 'Very much eat with worms', he advised their Lordships, and a survey had condemned most of the sails and the rig. The latter point presented an opportunity to make her a considerably better, and more manageable, vessel, Cook told them, adding that the rig should be changed from that of a schooner, which featured only fore-and-aft sails, to one that also carried square sails. On this last issue, he reasoned as follows:

> Permit me to set forth the utility of having her rigged into a Brig, as I presume it may now be Done without much additional expense to the Crown, for Schooners are the worst of vessels to go upon any Discovery, for in meeting with any unexpected Danger their staying [tacking] cannot be Depended upon, and for want of sail to Lay a Back they run themselves ashore before they wear [go onto the opposite tack] … [I] pray you will be pleased to take these [reasons] into your Consideration, and if they appear reasonable, to order her to be rigged into a Brig, as I Cannot help thinking but that it will enable me to Carry on the Survey with greater Dispatch, and Less Danger of Losing the Vessel …

The Lords agreed, and the new-look *Grenville* was relaunched for the 1765 survey expedition rigged as a brig. In December that year, eight months after departing from England, Cook returned home bearing a considerable amount of highly valuable survey data and reports, all of which brought well-deserved accolades, especially after they had been published and brought to the attention of fellow mariners. At the same time, he was happy to report to the Admiralty, the new rig configuration made *Grenville* a far better ship.

*

Cook was headed back to what was, by then, very familiar territory on the opposite side of the Atlantic for the summer of 1766. This time, though, there was an additional objective. He had been commissioned to observe a natural phenomenon, one that appealed to him immensely: an eclipse of the sun.

It was 20 April when *Grenville* sailed down the Thames on the ebb tide and headed for the open sea. She arrived at the incredibly beautiful and mountainous Bonne Bay, on Newfoundland's west coast, on 1 June. After a few days there, Cook set a course for the Burgeo Islands, just off the southern coast, the place he decided was most suitable for observing the eclipse and accurately recording the duration of the transit. That might have been the case in a perfect world, but it was an anxious wait leading up to the event, as the region was shrouded in fog, thick cloud and misty rain. Fortunately, clear weather reappeared and the job was done. While there is no direct reference from him about this undertaking, he was no doubt pleased with the success that was achieved, which would later be recognised by the Royal Society.

It was somewhat ironic that a person he was yet to meet, and who would play a most influential role in the next period of his career, happened to be in St John's when Cook returned there from the Burgeo Islands on what was his thirty-eighth birthday, 27 October 1766. Joseph Banks, an emerging light within the Royal Society in England, was in Newfoundland aboard HMS *Niger* to sate his scientific interests in the region. It is unlikely that the two men met at this time, however, as their overlap in the port was brief. *Niger* sailed for England the following day, while *Grenville* departed six days after that – with an Indian canoe that Banks had collected, strapped onto her deck. It was a relatively fast and comfortable passage for the small brig, as favourable westerly winds prevailed for the majority of the passage. Nineteen days after leaving St John's, *Grenville* was abeam of Beachy Head, on England's southern coast, and making good speed up the English Channel towards the entrance to the Thames, and home.

On his return to England, Cook delivered details of his observations to Dr John Bevis, a dedicated astronomer and highly respected Fellow of the Royal Society of London for Improving Natural Knowledge. Although a modest man, Cook was no doubt pleased to hear himself later described as 'a good mathematician, and very expert in his business'. The detail that Cook presented to the Royal Society provided its members with the opportunity to accurately calculate the difference in longitude between the Burgeo Islands and the English town of Oxford – a valuable exercise, as the calculation of longitude, which involved lunar distances, still frustrated navigators of this era. The British were acutely aware of the consequences of navigational error, particularly relating to longitude. Fifty-nine years earlier, in what became known as the Scilly Naval Disaster, four large British ships in a naval fleet of twenty-one were driven ashore onto the Scilly Isles, 25 miles south-west of Land's End, at the height of a storm, resulting in the loss of 1400 sailors. It was later accepted that the inability of the navigators to calculate longitude was the reason for the tragedy. This ongoing problem for navigators caused the British Government, in 1714, to offer £20,000 to anyone who could provide a 'generally practicable and useful method' of establishing longitude within an acceptable level of accuracy.

There is little doubt that Cook's highly detailed report on the eclipse brought him into favour with influential members of the Royal Society. Such notability would have enhanced his chances of being selected for a project that became the next chapter in his remarkable life: namely, sailing to the South Pacific for observation of the transit of Venus across the sun in 1769.

Happy to be back in his warm family environment, Cook set about his now usual routine of preparing all the survey information he had collected over the previous summer in Newfoundland in readiness for presentation to the Admiralty and, ultimately, publication. This included the details he had gathered from the observation of the solar eclipse, and it was from this particular part of his presentation that a new interest was roused for him: that of the calculation of longitude using lunar observations. Because of this, he suggested to the Admiralty, in a letter dated 11 March 1767, that the most valuable piece of new equipment they could provide him with, for what would be his fifth and final season in Newfoundland, was a reflecting telescope. The Secretary of the Admiralty agreed and passed on a recommendation to the Lords.

While Cook's activities in Newfoundland in 1767 were relatively straightforward, both his departure from England and the end of the return voyage were not uneventful. The 1st of April was a miserable day, with fog and rain. After the pilot came aboard, the ship was warped away from the dock on the Thames and anchored so that she could lie in wait for the ebb tide to flow and carry her downstream. Suddenly, as *Grenville*'s log reveals, another ship emerged through the murk: 'at 8 am a Collier Named the Three Sisters ... of Sunderland in Coming Down the River fell athwart our hause [anchor cable] & carried away our Bowsprit, Cap & Jib Boom.'

Cook was most unimpressed, as were his crew, who delivered a tirade of abuse towards those aboard the offending vessel. His eyes scanned the deck of *Three Sisters* in search of the master, so he could vent his anger in that direction. But the moment he sighted his target, Cook recognised him – it was Thomas Bloyd, a former schoolmate from back in Great Ayton. With that, Cook's anger abated, apologies were delivered and accepted, and his crew then set about repairing the damage.

Months later, when *Grenville* sailed back to St John's at the conclusion of that year's survey work, she was minus her topmast. It had been lost during a gale while working the west coast in late September. The broken spar was quickly replaced and on 23 October, *Grenville*'s bow was once again pointing towards home.

This passage across the Atlantic was nothing out of the ordinary, but on reaching the English Channel, the ship paused off Deal to take on board a pilot before sailing on past Dover and into the Thames Estuary on 10 November. They were then on the home stretch, but that didn't stop a vile storm from descending on the waters that *Grenville* was traversing.

What was logged as 'a hard Storm of Wind & Excessive heavy Squalls and showers of Rain' struck with such violence that the crew struggled from the outset to keep the ship under control. They took in sails at a frantic rate and lowered the yards and topmast to reduce windage, while the helmsman tried desperately to hold a course that would keep them clear of the threatening shore around Sheerness, off to leeward. Despite these determined efforts, they were losing the battle against an extremely powerful wind and roaring seas, so their only option was to drop anchor and hope it held – but it did not. *Grenville*'s log related the story: 'let go Best Bower and Veered away ... Struck yards & Topmasts. At 6 the Best Bower parted & we trailed into shoal water & at 7 She Struck very hard ...'

The shuddering thump that came as 'she struck very hard' reverberated through every one of *Grenville*'s planks, and simultaneously delivered a frightening message for the captain and his crew: they were aground on a lee shore and instantly in grave danger. There was every chance they could lose the ship, and with that, their lives would be in peril.

Nothing more could be done. The crew could only hang on and hope that the storm would soon abate, but that was not the case. When the tide turned and began to flood, their predicament worsened, as Cook recalled: 'She lay pretty Easy until the flood made when the Gale still continuing she ... lay down upon her Larboard [port] bilge; hoisted out the Boats & hove everything overboard from off the Decks [including, apparently, Banks' Indian canoe] & Secured all the Hatchways ...'

At midnight, when there was still no sign that their situation would improve any time soon, and there being every chance that the vessel would break up, Cook ordered his men to abandon ship. Some were directed to make for the shore in one of the boats, while those aboard the ship's small cutter were to head for the Royal Navy yard at Sheerness and raise the alarm. There was no guarantee that either of these efforts would succeed – these boats could easily have been swamped and the men drowned – but it was the only chance they had if they were to survive.

By next morning, the weather had moderated, and at 10 am Cook and his crew, along with men from the Sheerness yard, made their way out to the ship, which was still lying on her side. Once aboard, all were delighted to find that she had sustained little damage. A salvage effort commenced immediately. Anchors were carried by some of the boats out to deeper water, while other men on board *Grenville* began to lighten her load, jettisoning everything possible – including the pig iron and shingle ballast – so that she would have the best chance of being re-floated on the incoming tide. Their efforts were suitably rewarded: 'At high water, the Vessel floated, hove her off & made Sail for Sheerness. At 5 anchored between Sheerness & the Nore light, Employed Clearing the Decks & putting the Hold to rights ...'

Repairs to the rigging were also made there, before *Grenville* headed for home. On 15 November, a very relieved crew were no doubt pleased to see the smooth waters of the Thames. Then their anchorage at Deptford hove into view. Finally: 'At 9am lashed alongside the William & Mary Yacht off Deptford Yard ...' It had been a dramatic homecoming for everyone, but for Cook, it turned from dramatic to something very special. The moment he walked through the front door of his home on Mile End Road, Elizabeth greeted him with yet another child – their first daughter, also named Elizabeth.

While he settled back into home life and worked on translating his surveys into charts, other forces were working in his favour behind the scenes within the Royal Navy. His work to date had left only the best impressions with his superiors. So much so that when Captain Palliser met with the French Ambassador in London later that year, and produced a chart drawn by Cook while they were discussing fishing grounds around Newfoundland, Palliser described his fellow Yorkshireman as 'the King's Surveyor'.

Palliser's proclamation was not premature: it was recognition that had been hard earned, and, accordingly, it was well deserved. Cook was a pioneer; a man who, primarily through self-education, developed and applied techniques not previously considered for the science of maritime surveying. As a consequence, throughout his life and to this day, it is universally accepted that the remarkably detailed and accurate charts and documents he created from his time in Newfoundland set new standards.

His high standing among maritime surveyors was made most apparent some 120 years later, when Admiral William James Lloyd Wharton, hydrographer to the Admiralty between 1884 and 1904, wrote of Cook's works:

> The Charts he made during these years in the schooner
> *Grenville* were admirable. The best proof of their
> excellence is that they are not yet wholly superseded by
> the more detailed surveys of modern times. Like all first
> surveys of a practically unknown shore, and especially
> when that shore abounds in rocks and shoals, and is
> much indented with bays and creeks, they are imperfect
> in the sense of having many omissions; but when the
> amount of the ground covered, and the impediments of
> fogs and bad weather on that coast is considered, and
> that Cook had at the most only one assistant, their
> accuracy is truly astonishing …

CHAPTER SIX

The Captain and His Ship

During the brisk English winter of 1767–68, Cook spent much of his time at his desk at home dedicated to his cartographic work, compiling data from the surveys he had completed during the previous season in Newfoundland and applying it to highly detailed charts. He also wrote the instructions, notes and explanations needed to accompany those charts. Each document was crafted with deft and delicate strokes from an ink-laden quill, a writing implement that had been part of everyday communications for the preceding 1200 years. Occasionally he would pick up a small knife – a pen knife – and sharpen the nib of the quill to a finer point so he could create more intricate detail.

While absorbed in this task, Cook had no reason to think that 1768 would be any different from the previous five years: he would be spending another summer season in Canadian waters under orders from the Admiralty. Yet behind the scenes within that upper echelon of the Royal Navy, fate was shaping a dramatic change of course for James Cook.

The first indication that new horizons were emerging came at the time his latest works were ready for publication. On 12 April 1768, the Admiralty announced that Michael Lane, who had been Cook's assistant aboard *Grenville* the previous year, had been appointed 'to act as Master of the brig Grenville and surveyor of the coasts of Newfoundland and Labrador in the absence of Mr Cook, who is to be employed elsewhere'. There was no hint as to the meaning of 'elsewhere'. For Lane, the appointment led to him spending the next seven summers charting the waters around Newfoundland and along adjacent coastlines.

As history would subsequently reveal, the Admiralty's move had been influenced by a meeting of the Royal Society on 12 November 1767, three days before Cook's return from St John's. The meeting was called at the Society's headquarters in Crane Court, off Fleet Street, to discuss the fact that the orbit of the brightest planet in the night sky, Venus, was due to reach a point where it would transit the face of the sun on 3 June 1769 – little more than eighteen months hence. In the world of science and astronomy, such an event was considered to be of immense significance. This was especially true of the century-old Royal Society, which viewed the transit as a scientific project that formed part of the foundation for its very existence.

The scale of the solar system posed one of the great conundrums of the eighteenth century. It was a puzzle that, if it could be solved, would bring an entirely new and far more accurate dimension to navigation, and a far greater understanding of the solar system itself. At that time in history, scientists knew of only six planets orbiting the sun – Uranus was not discovered until 1781, Neptune in 1846, and Pluto as late as 1930. But the distance of each of the identified half-dozen planets from the sun was unknown, as was that of the Earth from the sun.

The opportunity to solve such a celestial puzzle lay with the transit of Venus, and as this particular event was to be the last one for more than a century, its importance for the future of scientific endeavour was immeasurable. Transits of Venus come in a dramatically irregular pattern: two happen just eight years apart, after which there is a span of around 120 years before the next occurrence. The upcoming transit was the second within this eight-year cycle, and the observations taken in 1761 had failed to provide accurate data. After 1769, it would be well beyond a lifetime before this planetary phenomenon could again be observed.

When gliding across the face of the sun, Venus would appear, through a telescope, as a small but easily identifiable black speck. The key to being able to calculate the approximate distance of Venus from Earth, and the sun, on its elliptical orbit was to observe the transit from at least three different places on Earth, and the further apart those sites were the better. The reason for this was that the information gathered from each of these points – the duration of the transit at that site and the angle of the sun from Earth at that time – would differ considerably. Once the Royal Society's mathematicians in London had this data, they could, by applying the principles of parallax, come up with the answer: a 'eureka' moment that scientists and astronomers rarely get to celebrate. Using this information, the previously unknown distances between planets in the solar system could then be calculated. In addition, the same knowledge would greatly assist those eighteenth-century navigators who used celestial navigation to calculate the position of their ships while at sea, particularly when it came to the vexing issue of longitude. There would be a similar benefit for explorers mapping new territories, as they would now be able to pinpoint topographical features more accurately.

With Great Britain being a world leader in astronomy at this time, it was no surprise that, during their 12 November meeting, members of the Royal Society agreed that everything possible should be done to most effectively observe the transit. It was decided that a committee would be appointed to select the most suitable observation sites around the world, nominate the people best qualified to act as observers, and select what equipment should be used. Not unfortuitously for Cook, one of the members of this committee was Dr John Bevis, the man who first brought Cook's name to the attention of the Society, following his report on the eclipse over Newfoundland in August 1766.

At their first meeting, Bevis and his fellow Transit Committee members agreed that of all the places being considered for observing the transit, the one farthest from England – a location somewhere in the South Seas – would provide the most important reading. This was because of the prolonged trajectory that Venus would be taking across the face of the sun when seen from that part of the world. Amsterdam and Rotterdam islands, both in what is now the Kingdom of Tonga, were among the sites suggested. The two other locations in the northern hemisphere were Norway's North Cape and Hudson Bay in Canada.

The emphasis placed on the South Seas data meant that a suitable ship had to be readied as soon as possible to ensure that the observers would be at their destination well before the transit occurred. Equally importantly, the expedition required substantial funding to cover the costs of men and equipment. With the limited time available before the ship would need to sail, the committee elected to ask the government to provide a vessel, and make a direct approach to King George III, requesting £4000 to cover the expedition's costs. This letter, written in February 1768, was fulsome in its content.

In establishing the crucial nature of the venture, the members reminded His Majesty that a successful mission would 'contribute greatly to the improvement of Astronomy, on which Navigation so much depends', and that 'the British Nation has been justly celebrated in the learned world, for their knowledge of Astronomy, in which they are inferior to no Nation upon Earth, Ancient or Modern'. The letter warned that this status could be under threat, however – as 'several of the Great Powers in Europe, particularly the French, Spaniards, Danes and Swedes are making the proper dispositions for the Observation thereof'. Therefore, the reasoning continued, it would 'cast dishonour' upon Britain should it 'neglect to have correct observations made of this important phenomenon'.

Much to the delight of the Royal Society, the King agreed to the request within two weeks of having received it.

When considering potential candidates to serve as observers on the Society's behalf, the Astronomer Royal, Reverend Nevil Maskelyne, proposed that thirty-year-old Alexander Dalrymple would be 'a proper person to send to the South Seas having a particular Turn for Discoveries, and being an able navigator, and well skilled in observation'. It was also proposed at the meeting that Captain John Campbell – 'if he pleases to go' – would be an able commander of the ship. Campbell, himself a member of the Transit Committee, was a seafarer of considerable ability who, like Cook, had his origins in the English coastal coal trade. The Society then wrote to all those whom they considered to be suitable candidates and asked if they would take up the position nominated for them.

To the great surprise of many, Campbell declined the offer, while Dalrymple, who accepted, clearly defined in his response to the Society's president, the Earl of Morton, the parameters of his involvement. 'I shall most certainly not let slip an opportunity of making an Observation so Important to Science as that of the Transit of Venus,' he declared, before adding: 'However, it may be necessary to observe that I can have no thought of undertaking the Voyage as a Passenger going out to make the Observations, or on any other footing than that of having the management of the Ship intended for the service.' The committee did not immediately reject this condition, so it was assumed by all – including Dalrymple – that he would be the commander of the South Seas expedition, as well as an observer.

Within the Royal Society, Alexander Dalrymple was known for being a man of self-promotion. The Scotsman first came to the attention of its members through the publication of pamphlets and a booklet dealing with discoveries in the South Pacific. He was always a noticeable presence at Society dinners and other gatherings, all the while using his persuasive manner to have members believe that he was an able navigator.

However, while he could not be described as a fraud, the distance between reality and fantasy appeared to be broad.

At the age of fifteen, Dalrymple sailed to Madras, in India, where he became an employee of the East India Company. He was an avid reader, something that fostered a spirit of adventure and a desire to explore the East Indies. He eventually became deputy secretary of the company's Madras operation and later, very briefly, the deputy governor of Manila, which was under British occupation at the time. When it came to his professed ability as a seafarer, though, there was no evidence to suggest that he had achieved anything of note under sail, nor served an apprenticeship, let alone acted as commander of a ship ... But that didn't matter to him; he wanted to command this voyage to the South Seas. Truth be known, Dalrymple held an underlying desire to explore what he could of the region and thus claim full recognition for anything he might discover.

While making the proud announcement to the Transit Committee that King George had agreed to support the expedition, the Earl of Morton confirmed that he had recommended to the Lords of the Admiralty that Dalrymple command the vessel, which the Royal Navy would supply. However, the response from their Lordships regarding this recommendation was far from positive. The Admiralty advised that it saw such an appointment as being 'entirely repugnant to the regulations of the Navy'. The First Lord, Sir Edward Hawke, mindful of previous failures under similar circumstances, is reputed to have declared that he would rather cut off his right hand than permit anyone but a 'King's Officer' to command one of His Majesty's naval vessels. From that point, there was only one solution: the voyage to the South Seas would become a project for the Royal Navy.

The first step in that direction came on 5 March when the Admiralty directed the Navy Board to nominate a vessel from within the fleet that would best suit the demands of the expedition. It soon became apparent that there was nothing immediately available, so, at the end of the month, they adopted the only alternative: to purchase a ship.

Two colliers of similar design were chosen, *Valentine* and *Earl of Pembroke*, of which, following comparative surveys at Deptford, *Earl of Pembroke* was found to be in better condition. The selection of this vessel was confirmed in a letter to the Secretary of the Admiralty on 29 March:

> ... we desire you will acquaint their Lordships that we
> have purchased a cat-built Bark, in Burthen 368 Tons
> and of the age of three years and nine months, for
> conveying such persons as shall be thought proper, to
> the Southward for making observations of the passage
> of the planet Venus over the Disk of the Sun, and pray
> to be favoured with their Lordships' directions for
> fitting her for the service accordingly, in which we
> presume it may be necessary to sheath and fill her
> bottom, and prepare her for carrying six or eight light
> carriage guns of Four pounds and eight swivels ... and
> in other respects as the nature of the voyage may
> require ... And that we may also receive their
> commands by what name she shall be Registered on
> the list of the Navy.

The purchase price was £2800 and the ship was renamed His Majesty's Bark *Endeavour*. (While the common belief is that 'bark' referred to the ship's rig, it actually defined the build of her hull.)

With Campbell and Dalrymple out of the running for the role of leader, the Admiralty had numerous contenders from which to choose a master for *Endeavour*, including Samuel Wallis and John Byron. Both of these men had recently explored areas of the Pacific on expeditions that were symbolic of a shift in focus by the Admiralty and the Royal Society towards the South Seas, following Britain's victory in the Seven Years War. The First Lord of the Admiralty at that time, the

Earl of Egmont, initially sent Byron aboard HMS *Dolphin* in 1764, then Wallis as captain of the same ship in 1766. In doing so, he signalled the start of a long period of British interest in the region.

Both Byron and Wallis were well qualified to command the Society's upcoming mission. Their past explorations contrasted favourably with Cook's complete lack of experience in this field, an issue that left the acclaimed maritime surveyor seemingly outside the list of contenders for the role. Despite being a highly capable seafarer, Cook could only lay claim to having been the master of *Grenville* – a 68-ton schooner, some 60 feet in length, with a crew of just twenty. Somehow though, possibly because of the pressure of time, his name started to surface in conversations, both at the Royal Society and within the Admiralty. As those discussions progressed, and expertise was being considered, Cook's lack of comparable experience began to be outweighed by strong references in his favour from two of his champions: Hugh Palliser and Secretary of the Admiralty Sir Philip Stephens. The Lords listened and were soon won over by this strong belief in Cook. He would be the commander.

The minutes of the Royal Society's meeting on 5 May formally acknowledged that Cook would be appointed as master of the ship and leader of the expedition, on behalf of both the Royal Society of London for Improving Natural Knowledge and the Royal Navy, and that he would be one of the designated observers of the celestial event, along with Charles Green, former assistant to the Astronomer Royal. Cook attended this meeting, the minutes of which noted too that he 'accepted the employment in consideration of such gratuity as the Society shall think proper, and an allowance of £12 a year for victualling himself and the other observer in every particular'. He also accepted the offer of 100 guineas from the Society for his work as an observer.

Twenty days later, Cook received a letter from the Admiralty confirming the appointment – and a promotion:

> Whereas we have appointed you First Lieutenant of His
> Majesty's Bark, the Endeavour, now at Deptford, and
> intend that you shall command her during her present
> intended voyage; and, whereas, we have ordered the said
> Bark to be fitted out and stored at that place for Foreign
> Service, manned with seventy men ... and victualled to
> Twelve months of all species of Provisions ... except
> Beer, of which she is to have only a proportion for one
> month and to be supplied with Brandy in lieu of the
> remainder: you are hereby required and directed to use
> the utmost despatch in getting her ready for the sea
> accordingly, and then falling down to Galleons Reach,
> take in her guns and gunners' stores at that place and
> proceed to the Nore for further orders ...

As a lieutenant, Cook was one rank below that of a captain in
the Royal Navy, but by being commander of *Endeavour*, he was
recognised as 'captain'. His rate of pay was 5 shillings per day.

When all elements were taken into consideration, his
appointment could be seen as nothing short of remarkable in
the annals of the Royal Navy. Nevertheless, the decision-
makers were confident they had the right man – one of high
character and few words who bore the preferred traits of a
seafarer, commander, navigator and leader of men.

While he was absorbing the pleasing, and very unexpected,
opportunities that were unfolding for him, one can only
wonder if Cook's mind ever flashed back to that day in
Mr Sanderson's store in Staithes. The day when he held a
seemingly magical South Sea Company shilling in his hand –
the coin that conjured magnificent visions of ocean adventures
and new frontiers, and altered the course of his life.

The parameters of the *Endeavour* expedition changed quite
considerably with the return to England of Captain Samuel
Wallis aboard HMS *Dolphin*, just five days before the Admiralty
penned the letter of appointment to Cook. When Wallis

departed in 1766, his orders were to sail on an east–west circumnavigation of the world, first through the spectacular but treacherous Straits of Magellan, near Cape Horn, then into the South Seas. The expedition was designated as a voyage of discovery that, it was hoped, would finally prove the existence or otherwise of *Terra Australis Incognita* – the Great South Land – the theoretical landmass in the mostly unexplored South Seas region of the southern hemisphere. The same region constituted a huge part of the Pacific Ocean.

Unfortunately for Wallis, his exploration efforts were curtailed by a severe southern hemisphere winter, a damaged rudder, and a leaky ship – the latter problem possibly caused in part by an activity in Otaheite (Tahiti), the mountainous and supremely beautiful tropical island he had just discovered. This 'activity' involved the removal of many of the ship's iron hull nails, iron being a material previously unknown to the islanders, and so immediately highly prized. Crewmen were said to have bartered the nails for 'love' – as explained most succinctly by Cook biographer Beaglehole: 'welcoming and tender were the brown beautiful girls, with tattooed thighs and chaplets [garlands] of sweet-smelling flowers, though a little mercenary it is true – so that the ship almost fell to pieces as ardent spirits in her company wrenched out the nails that were the price of love ...'

All three factors combined to make it impossible for Wallis to comply with his orders to conduct an extensive search for undiscovered lands. Instead, the only way he could keep his ship afloat with any level of confidence, and keep his men safe, was to promptly set a course for Batavia (only for many of his crew to die there due to dysentery), then the Cape of Good Hope, before turning north for home. When *Dolphin* finally reached England in May 1768, Wallis delivered to the Admiralty and the Royal Society news of his important discovery – Tahiti. It was, he explained, a place in the South Seas that was 'one of the most healthy as well as delightful spots in the world'. He named this place 'King George the Third's Island' in honour of the British monarch.

The discovery of King George's Island, as Cook and others would soon refer to it, meant that there was now another location to be considered by the Transit Committee. Three months remained before *Endeavour* was due to sail, a reality that led to Wallis suggesting most strongly that his discovery was the ideal place, mainly because it offered easy access to the shore and a safe anchorage. Society members respected his judgement: King George's Island it was. Via a subsequent letter to the Admiralty, this new discovery became *Endeavour*'s destination.

There was a second request of note to the Lords from the Society, regarding the inclusion of a research group aboard the ship:

> ... Joseph Banks, Esq., Fellow of this Society, a
> Gentlemen of large fortune, who is well versed in
> Natural History, being desirous of undertaking the same
> voyage, the council very earnestly request their
> Lordships that in regard to Mr Banks's great personal
> merit and for the advancement of useful knowledge, he
> also, together with his suite, being seven persons more
> (that is eight persons in all) together with their baggage,
> be received on board of the ship under the command of
> Capt. Cook ...

Banks' closest associate among the supernumeraries was the naturalist Dr Daniel Solander, a man who would contribute much to the research that would come from the expedition. There were also two artists in the group, Sydney Parkinson and Alexander Buchan; and, as assistant naturalist and personal secretary to Banks, Herman Diedrich Spöring – a man with a leaning towards the study of history and, like Solander, a Swede. Of the four servants accompanying this group (their inclusion took the number in the party to nine), James Roberts and Peter Briscoe were from Banks' Lincolnshire estate; the other two (described as 'negroes') were Thomas Richmond and George Dorlton.

What the Royal Society didn't mention was that 25-year-old Banks would also be taking his two dogs – a greyhound named Lady, and a spaniel. They were to be used for hunting and retrieving wildlife specimens.

In a letter written at the time to legendary Swedish botanist Carl Nilsson Linnaeus, Royal Society Fellow John Ellis said that Banks was expected to invest an incredible £10,000 of his own wealth in the project. He also explained the role that Banks, Solander (a former student of Linnaeus) and their entourage would play on the voyage:

> No people ever went to sea better fitted out for the purpose of Natural History, nor more elegantly ... they have all sorts of machines for catching and preserving insects; all kinds of nets, trawls, drags, and hooks for coral fishing; they have even a curious contrivance of a telescope, by which, put into the water, you can see the bottom at a great depth, where it is clear ...

London-born Banks was a close friend of Lord Sandwich, who was First Lord of the Admiralty on three occasions during this era, so there was little surprise when the Admiralty approved this request in late July. It is highly likely that the decision was made even easier with the knowledge that Banks intended to contribute such a large amount of money to the expedition. Regardless, it was a resolution that placed even greater pressure on the already tight schedule to have *Endeavour* refitted and ready to sail, as considerably more would need to be done to accommodate the independent group. Time was already running short, and Venus would wait for no man.

No doubt Cook would have met Banks at Crane Court, while attending the meeting to discuss his appointment as commander and an observer for the expedition. There are reports that the two men showed considerable respect for each other from the outset, but, of course, it would have been impossible for any third party to imagine what it was they were witnessing with this initial encounter. It was the start of a friendship that grew to become the most powerful and successful union in the history of exploration on earth.

The bond between Banks and Cook spanned the three remarkable 'voyages of discovery' into the Pacific and subsequently led to the creation of that great triumvirate of seafarers and explorers: Cook, Bligh and Flinders. Bligh sailed with Cook, and Flinders sailed with Bligh – and Banks was the catalyst bonding all three. It was Cook who imparted much of his hard-earned knowledge of seafaring, exploration, cartography and caring for crew on to Bligh, who in turn conveyed it to Flinders.

In the spring of 1768, though, all that lay way beyond perception and over history's misty horizon.

From the moment his appointment became official on 25 May, Cook's immediate task was to oversee the final preparation of *Endeavour* at the Royal Navy Dockyards at Deptford. The yard, which was established on the south bank of the Thames some 250 years earlier, under orders from King Henry VIII, comprised a large ship basin, dry docks, and solid stone buildings that housed many of the operations needed for shipbuilding and maintenance. As close as Deptford was to London – just 5 miles downstream as the ebb tide flowed – this extremely busy facility was in direct contrast to the tranquil environment that surrounded it: wide green fields, where cattle grazed lazily and little else happened. In the distance, though, about a mile away across the fields to the south-east, Flamsteed House could be seen. This was the original structure of what is now the Royal Greenwich Observatory, the home of Greenwich Mean Time and the world's prime meridian – the two principal elements of navigation.

On the same day that the Admiralty announced his appointment, word reached Cook from the dockyard officers that work on the ship would be sufficiently advanced the following week for the crew – many of whom he had hand-picked because of their considerable seafaring experience – to be able to go aboard. He then arranged to be transported to Deptford two days later so that he could see his new command for the first time and become acquainted with her. To get there, he would almost certainly have been rowed downriver from London aboard a small naval launch or cutter, with him sitting at the stern. When he arrived at Deptford, *Endeavour* was afloat in the basin and the centre of much activity. Shipwrights, riggers and general labourers were toiling at their assigned jobs, across her length and breadth.

As he stepped onto the deck for the first time, Cook would have stood out among all others present, not simply because of his height, but also because of his impressive lieutenant's uniform – an open-faced blue jacket with large, boldly embroidered gold cuffs, collar and front, as well as gold-laced buttons. The waistcoat, which also featured gold buttons, was, like his breeches and stockings, white. His shoes were black leather and had ornate pinchbeck buckles. To cap it all off, he would have been wearing a tricorn hat.

Once aboard, Cook presented his ribbon-like red, white and blue Commissioning Pendant to the most senior officer on duty, and this was then hoisted to the top of the mainmast. Once the 10-yard-long pendant had reached full hoist and begun its swirling dance in the breeze, the message was there for all to see: Lieutenant Cook was on board *Endeavour* and in charge as captain. Cook recorded of his first weeks as commander: 'From this day to the 21st of July we were constantly employed in fitting the Ship taking on board stores and Provisions ...'

Fortunately, the fact that *Endeavour* had previously been a coastal collier – which, ironically, operated out of Whitby for some time – meant that the new captain was familiar with her primary features and her proportions. But that same awareness left Cook in no doubt as to the magnitude of the task that confronted him. The transformation of this ship from collier to expedition vessel impacted on almost every part of her. From gunwale to gunwale, stem to stern and bilge to masthead. This refit was the top-priority project at Deptford, not least because three valuable weeks had already been lost due to worker unrest.

No sooner had Cook taken up his command than he was pleased to learn that while in dry dock, the bottom of *Endeavour*'s hull had been sheathed – not in copper sheeting, which was the emerging trend, but in the traditional manner, using timber boards, his preferred method. The hull planks had first been covered with a mixture of tar and felt, before the almost inch-thick boards were laid over the top as an outer skin and fastened to the hull using thousands of galvanised nails.

Cook was convinced that this was the best way to prevent his ship being attacked by the ocean's version of termites, the teredo worm, on such a long voyage into tropical waters: the boards used for the sheathing were sacrificial, not structural. Also, should the ship ever run aground and need repairing, the repairs would be easier to complete without copper sheathing.

It must be asked if there was also an element of intuition associated with Cook's preference for timber over copper: did this highly experienced seafarer think that the supposed benefits that came from copper sheathing might, in time, be outweighed by new and as yet unforeseen problems? If this was the case, then Cook could well have saved his ship, and the lives of his entire crew. The most catastrophic example of such copper-related problems occurred in 1780, when the Royal Navy's 100-gun, three-decker HMS *Royal George* suddenly sank in calm waters off Spithead, taking around 900 crewmen to a watery grave. The cause was an electrolytic action between the ship's copper hull sheathing and the iron fastenings in the hull planks. *Royal George* literally fell apart: the fastenings failed, the planks sprang open and the ship took on a torrent of water. Other ships suffered a similar fate just two years after being copper-sheathed – and Cook's voyage was destined to be at least that long.

One feature that Cook insisted on for the expedition was that era's version of a lightning conductor – an 'electric chain', which was rigged from the masthead to a point below the waterline. It was an addition that came as a consequence of that historic event in 1752 when Benjamin Franklin flew a kite in an electrical storm in the hope that it would be struck by lightning, which it was. From this experiment, electricity was better understood, and the importance of creating a way of 'earthing' a lightning strike became obvious.

On a ship, the solution was a lightning chain, and it turned out that Cook's decision to install such a device on *Endeavour* was a wise one. She was spared serious damage during a savage thunderstorm while at anchor in Batavia. A Dutch ship, which was anchored nearby, was partially dismasted by a lightning strike in the storm, while aboard *Endeavour*, when she too was struck, the only incident of note was when the shockwave associated with the powerful thunderbolt caused a marine sentry to drop his musket.

No doubt Cook would have familiarised himself with every detail of the marine survey that had been carried out on *Earl of Pembroke* at the time of purchase, and from that he would have been left in no doubt that she was robustly built. The majority of the ship was constructed of oak – a hard and very strong timber which had been used in shipbuilding as far back as the days of the Viking longships, in the ninth and tenth centuries. Moreover, he would have noted with approval that much of the hull had been secured using treenails: oaken dowels up to 3½ feet long, hammered into holes bored through planks, frames, beams and the vessel's spine. Once the ship was launched, these dowels would swell as a result of absorbing moisture, and this would stop the timbers from pulling apart. Iron bolts were also used in the construction, a feature that would have alerted Cook to a problem that might emerge during the voyage, namely 'iron sickness'. Iron fastenings tended to rust over a period of time and cause the timber around them to rot, to the point where the fastenings became loose and the structure was weakened. Being aware of the potential for this to happen, Cook would have insisted that the fastenings were checked regularly.

The job list for the conversion of a coal carrier to an expedition ship being prepared for a circumnavigation – one that would eventually prove to be almost 40,000 nautical miles in total distance sailed – was, by any standards, daunting. For a start, the accommodation plan for this ship of just 106 feet in overall length, 29 feet 3 inches beam and 14 feet draught, had to be increased from twenty berths to near 100, something that called for an entire new lower deck to be built along *Endeavour*'s full length. The creation of this new deck made it necessary to modify the main deck so that the amount of internal volume below was appropriate for the men. Even so, much of that space did not offer full headroom; there were places where they needed to be on hands and knees to move around safely.

The necessity to change the layout was further compounded by the inclusion of Banks' party on the voyage. The ship's officers, who otherwise would have been accommodated near the great cabin, aft on the main deck, had to be moved to the new lower deck. Banks was set up in a small athwartships cabin at the forward end of the great cabin, while Cook's cabin, which was smaller and not as well appointed, was on the port side of the great cabin.

Apart from the modifications to the hull at Deptford, *Endeavour*'s masts were replaced and re-rigged. She also took on the bulk of the stores and provisions while there. This included a load of coal, which would be used for warming and drying the ship, particularly in cold weather. Coal was preferred over wood, as it took up considerably less space in the bilge and, by being heavier, contributed to the stability of the vessel. More than 8 tons of iron ingots were also placed in *Endeavour*'s bilge as ballast. Deckhands and dock workers toiled tirelessly filling *Endeavour*'s voluminous hold with provisions and equipment. Among further items were a large quantity of salt, 100 gallons of spirits – this time arrack, the world's only naturally fermented alcoholic beverage – plus additional hogsheads, puncheons and barrels for both wine and water. There were also medical supplies for the ship's surgeon, and all the equipment needed for the observation of Venus.

Of high priority were the ship's three new boats. They came as the result of a naval warrant issued on 12 April stating: 'Long boat, pinnace and yawl to be built by Mr Burr for the Endeavour Bark.' This was obviously an order to an outside supplier, who was probably based in the south-coast boatbuilding town of Deal. No details exist on the design or construction of these boats, but Deal was recognised for its clinker-built (with overlapping planks) small boats: so, if they came from there they would almost certainly have been built using that form of construction. Clinker-built boats have a better strength-to-weight ratio over carvel (smooth plank) construction, making a clinker boat a far better option for such a gruelling voyage. The longest of these tenders was probably 18 feet overall.

Seven weeks after Cook took command, the refit was complete, at a cost of £5394, 15 shillings and four-pence. *Endeavour* was finally ready to leave Deptford, and did so on 21 July. She made her way downriver to Galleons Reach and remained there until the end of the month. In that time, the majority of her armaments were put aboard: six 4-pounder carriage guns, each weighing about 1300 pounds, and twelve blunderbusses, which were mounted on swivels. Four of these were fitted to the ship's boats, so that they could be used for protection in foreign waters.

With everything in readiness for putting to sea, a pilot went aboard *Endeavour* on the morning of 30 July. Soon afterwards, the ship was riding an ebb tide and a favourable light westerly breeze down the Thames on her way to The Downs, an anchorage off the coast of Kent, about 10 miles north of Dover.

On 7 August, four days after her arrival there, Lieutenant Cook joined his ship at the Channel anchorage. He had been in London, farewelling his wife and young family, and receiving his orders from the Admiralty.

His instructions came in two packets, both marked 'Secret'. The first, which he was to open at the time of departure, directed him to sail *Endeavour* to Tahiti on a west-about course that would take the ship around the world's most ill-famed point of land, Cape Horn, at the southern tip of South America. The second packet was not to be opened until after he had completed his observations of the transit of Venus. The instructions relating to this packet were very much to the point: 'When this Service [the observation of Venus] is performed you are to put to Sea without Loss of Time, and carry into execution the Additional Instructions contained in the enclosed Sealed Packet.'

The initial orders were for Cook to first sail *Endeavour* to Madeira to take on wine, then to 'proceed round Cape Horn to Port Royal Harbour in King Georges Island'. It was suggested that along the way he might stop somewhere in Brazil or the Falkland Islands, for fresh water and provisions.

Just twenty-four hours after rejoining the ship, Cook called for the anchor to be weighed and sails to be set in what was the faintest of breezes. Before long, *Endeavour* was sailing the English Channel for the first time in her new form, and under her new name, but she was barely making progress towards Plymouth. It took six tormenting days to cover the 200 nautical miles to that destination. That equated to just 36 miles a day at an average speed of 1.5 knots.

As soon as she achieved her anchorage off Plymouth and the best bower was dropped, Cook ordered a boat to go ashore and arrange for an express horse-drawn carriage to make a 400-mile return trip to London so that Banks and Solander could be transferred to the ship. The pair had remained in London to make final preparations. The other members of the Royal Society entourage were already aboard *Endeavour*, as was their luggage.

There was a never-ending stream of activity taking place aboard the ship in the lead-up to departure from English waters. This included the arrival of a complement of twelve marines – a sergeant, corporal, drummer, and nine privates. The final stores and equipment were also being ferried to the ship from shore, including four additional carriage guns and twelve barrels of gunpowder.

Back in London, the Admiralty had made a late decision to increase the complement of active sailors for this voyage to seventy, which was a significantly greater number than would normally have been required to sail a ship of *Endeavour*'s size. The decision came as a result of a belief manifested by the Lords that on a two-year expedition, as they knew this was likely to be, there was a high probability of death among the men as a consequence of accidents and disease. In fact, even before departure, there had been problems, when five of the original crew had to be discharged due to sickness or for personal reasons; another eighteen had decided they simply didn't want to go, and so became 'run men' – deserters. All were replaced.

While *Endeavour*'s captain remained in the dark regarding the contents of his secret instructions, there was growing speculation in London, particularly in the press, as to what Cook's complete orders entailed. A speculative report in *The Gazetteer* in August 1768 read: 'The gentlemen, who are to sail in a few days for George's Land, the new discovered island in the Pacific Ocean, with an intention to observe the Transit of Venus, are likewise, we are credibly informed, to attempt some new discoveries in that vast unknown tract, above the latitude 40.'

Cook was pleased that five of his shipmates from *Grenville* had agreed to join him aboard *Endeavour*, as well as his wife's cousin, sixteen-year-old Isaac Smith, who would go on to become a master's mate. Supporting the captain as senior officers were three seafarers of high repute: Second Lieutenant Zachary Hickes, Third Lieutenant John Gore, and the master, Robert Molyneux. The latter two men, and six other members of *Endeavour*'s complement, had returned to England only three months earlier after being aboard *Dolphin* for her most recent circumnavigation. Probably the most popular man by reputation of all on board was the incredibly competent John Thompson.

It was his role to be cook for the working crew, while the captain had his own cook, as did the lieutenants. Despite having only one hand, Thompson would make sure the crew was well fed, no matter how rough the weather.

There was one other significant addition to *Endeavour*'s company: a well-travelled nanny goat. This animal had already completed one circumnavigation, with Wallis aboard *Dolphin*. Now, she was destined for a second. While her role was simply to provide milk for the officers, she had earned a reputation for being cantankerous and for standing her ground. One day in Tahiti during the Wallis expedition, she apparently took umbrage to a number of islanders who had come on board, and decided to clear the decks. It took the nanny one short burst of speed, ending in a solid head-butt into the rear end of one of the visitors before the whole mob took fright and bolted for their canoes.

A week before *Endeavour* departed from her berth off the Devonshire coast, Cook mustered his crew for two important matters. The first was to read to them the Articles of War – a 3475-word Royal Navy document detailing the laws of the ship when it came to discipline, conduct and the punishment for any misdemeanours. These regulations were to be implemented by the dozen marines on board. It was also their role to protect the captain.

Cook's other duty of the day was one the men found to be rather more gratifying. He gave each one of them two months' pay in advance. He later noted: 'they were well satisfied and expressed great cheerfulness and readiness to prosecute the voyage.'

Over the next few days, the heavily laden *Endeavour* rode quietly at anchor, responding on the odd occasion to a change in the direction of the wind, or the set of the tide. There was one last call to be made – to set sail and weigh anchor – and this was where the captain and his men had to be patient. They had to wait until the wind was from a suitable direction and of sufficient strength for the ship to depart in safety.

The moment that Cook was able to make that call, the first chapter of what history would recognise as one of the three most important voyages of discovery ever undertaken would be underway.

An imagining by John Mortimer (1740–79) of some of the main participants in Cook's first voyage to observe the transit of Venus; from left to right Dr. Daniel Solander, Joseph Banks, Cook, Dr John Hawkesworth (who earned Cook's disapprobation for his edited account of Cook's first voyage), and Lord Sandwich, First Lord of the Admiralty and another of Cook's patrons. Banks' two dogs are also shown.
National Library of Australia, nla.pic-an7351768

CHAPTER SEVEN

Cape Horn and the South Pacific

It was 26 August 1768 – late summer in the northern hemisphere, when the sun heads south for the equinox and one of its biannual interludes with the Equator. Each morning for the previous six days, Cook had been on deck early, first to check the direction and strength of the wind, and then to scan the skies, looking for any sign of a change in the weather. On each occasion he had reached the same conclusion: not today.

However, the morning of the 26th was different. Cloudy as it was, there was an encouraging north-westerly component to the breeze, and it looked like it would hold, if not strengthen. The captain discussed the situation with his senior officers and decided that the day had arrived.

With that, the master ordered a small complement to take the pinnace – the captain's official boat – into the port to collect Messrs Banks and Solander, who had opted to stay onshore after their carriage had rattled along the cobblestoned streets and into Plymouth from London ten days earlier. At the same time, the master ordered the crew on deck to ready the ship for sailing, and in an instant, men went up the ratlines on all three masts, heading for the yards, while others tended the lines at the mast base. Those aloft quickly released the sails, which had been firmly lashed to the yards, and they were then ready to be hauled down and set.

As the ship's bell was rung four times to signal that it was 2 pm, the anchor was being weighed and calls were coming from the quarterdeck for the sequential setting of the sails – some set aback and others trimmed normally, as small gangs of tars hauled away in unison on the sheets and braces, so *Endeavour* would fall away from the wind, then onto the chosen southerly course towards the wide open waters of the English Channel. Before long, the burble of the bow and quarter waves was confirming that the ship was making headway: she was on her way to King George's Island, some 13,000 nautical miles distant – and beyond.

As everyone on deck watched the coastline around Plymouth gradually fade into *Endeavour*'s meandering white wake, the feeling was of excitement, suspense and speculation on just how many years they might be away from home and what might occur along the way. They were destined to be sailing unknown seas and possibly towards lands that had been waiting to be discovered by the outside world since the beginning of time.

Soon after departure, the captain made the first entry in his journal relating to the voyage: 'At 2pm got under sail and put to sea having on board 94 persons including Officers, Seamen, Gentlemen and their servants, near 18 months provisions, 10 carriage guns, 12 Swivels with a good store of Ammunition and stores of all kinds ...'

As was the case in this era, the times Cook entered in his journal throughout the voyage were 'ship time'. A ship's calendar day started at midday: twelve hours before 'civil time' – the time on land. So, at 2 pm aboard ship, which was two hours after the new day became the 26th, it was two o'clock in the afternoon of the 25th on land. Ship time was a custom of captains during the eighteenth and early nineteenth centuries, based around sun observations for navigation. When the sun was at its zenith, it was midday on the meridian where they were located – and that was deemed to be the start of a new day.

The wind remained light overnight, so *Endeavour* moved at a crawl – only around 3 knots. Then, soon after first light, the lookout reported the faint outline of The Lizard, the southernmost point of England, around 15 miles to the north-west. This sighting meant that the ship had sailed about 50 nautical miles since departure. Six days later, the situation was very different: *Endeavour* was near 400 nautical miles west of south from The Lizard, and well into the Bay of Biscay, which was living up to its reputation as a cauldron for savage storms. All on board were getting their first taste of a howling and harrowing Atlantic tempest, where the decks were constantly awash as seas broke across the heavily rolling ship.

As the weather deteriorated and the wind increased in velocity, so men went aloft to secure the sails that had been furled, and to lash down the reef points on those few sails still being carried. While these men were high in the rig, it was realised an iron fitting that supported rigging on the topmast had carried away and needed to be reattached to prevent a possible mast breakage. There were dilemmas on deck as well:

> Very hard gales with some heavy showers of rain in the most part of these 24 hours, which brought us under our two courses [sails], broke one of Main topmasts Futtock plates, washed overboard a small boat belonging to the Boatswain and drowned between 3 and 4 dozen of our poultry, which was the worst of all. Towards noon it moderated so that we could bear our Main topsail close reefed …

The worst of the weather lasted for two days. From then, *Endeavour* made relatively good time towards Madeira, where she was to take on supplies of water and wine for the voyage. She anchored off Funchal, on the southern side of the island, in the early evening of 13 September, having sailed 1200 nautical miles in eighteen days.

Twenty-four hours later, while the empty casks were being taken ashore, and the bosun and his men were busy caulking the leaks that had developed in the topsides and deck during the worst of the gale, there was a tragic accident involving the master's mate, 35-year-old Alexander Weir. During the night, the hawser on the small stream anchor had slipped, so the anchor needed to be reset. Once daylight came, the offending anchor was hove up and suspended beneath the longboat in order for it to be relocated further away from the ship.

The men, including Weir, were in the process of releasing the anchor when the buoy-line attached to it wrapped around his leg. In an instant he was ripped over the side of the longboat and dragged down with the heavy load. There was no hope for him. Shouts of distress to those aboard the ship saw crewmen respond immediately, by rushing to the windlass and raising the anchor. When it finally broke the surface, Weir's body was found still tangled in the rope.

Back in London, over the period of this passage from Plymouth to Madeira, emotion had swung from joy to sorrow for Elizabeth Cook. Obviously unbeknown to the captain, she had given birth to their third son, Joseph, on the day that *Endeavour* departed from Plymouth. Eerily, the baby boy died on the day the ship reached Funchal. It was a heartbreaking event that Cook would not learn of until his return home almost three years later.

The success of such a long voyage as this, which was being undertaken through widely varying latitudes and weather conditions, would greatly depend on the health of the crew, so even before *Endeavour* reached Madeira, Cook was implementing his theories on how best this could be achieved. His biggest challenge was to minimise the impact of the dreaded and usually fatal curse of all seafarers – scurvy. Reinforcing this desire was his awareness of the impact that the disease had had on George Anson's expedition of 1740–42, a venture that was not dissimilar to his own. Anson's effort was also an east–west circumnavigation, and by the time he returned to England, scurvy had claimed around 1300 of the 2000 men who were aboard the small flotilla making up the expedition. It was this tragedy that inspired a Royal Navy surgeon, Scotsman James Lind, to study the disease and try to find a cure. Eleven years after Anson returned home, Lind published his findings in a book, *A Treatise of the Scurvy*. He declared his belief that scurvy was a nutritional disease, and that during his research, men who were given oranges and lemons, in particular, recovered. Lind's publication was one of many dealing with scurvy in this era, and this no doubt led to Cook deciding to introduce the most nutritional diet possible for his crew. Most importantly, this involved the inclusion of green vegetables whenever he could. Because of this, Cook is, quite justifiably, credited by many for virtually eliminating scurvy aboard his ship, although it is quite possible that he didn't realise what elements were responsible for this success.

In knowing that he would not be able to supply his men with a regular supply of citrus fruit on this long voyage, Cook looked for an alternative, and this led to him turning to greens. Until now, experienced sailors were used to little more than hard tack like ship's biscuits, salted meats and unappealing soups for their daily diet, so there was no doubt that he would face a challenge when it came to implementing the new dietary regimen.

The captain's plan was to have his crew consuming what he believed to be healthy foods such as wort (a malt extract), cabbage (or sauerkraut), wild celery and scurvy grass (a cress-like plant that is found close to the sea in Europe). He later explained that when any man showed a symptom of scurvy – lethargy, bleeding from the gums, the loss of teeth, or open lesions – the sailor in question was to receive a liberal serving of wort, adding that 'by this Means and the care and Vigilance of Mr M[o]nkhouse, the Surgeon, this disease was prevented from getting a footing in the Ship'.

The resolve to ensure his crew were well fed became apparent in Madeira when, on 16 September, Cook noted in his journal, 'Received on board Beef and Greens for the Ship's Company ...' Then, the following day, his determination to implement discipline among the men when it came to diet led to this note: 'Punished Henry Stevens, Seaman, and Thomas Dunster, Marine, with 12 lashes each, for refusing to take their allowance of Fresh Beef ...' It was a punishment that delivered the appropriate message to the entire crew. They needed very little inducement over the remainder of the voyage to follow the captain's orders on diet.

Cook's journal also revealed that all 'the people' were served potable soup and sauerkraut regularly, but that not all were enthusiastic about the sauerkraut. So here he applied another form of psychology to ensure it was consumed: 'The Sour Krout the Men at first would not eat until I put in practice a Method I never once knew to fail with seamen, and this was to have some of it dressed every Day for the Cabin Table, and permitted all the Officers without exception to make use of it and left it to the option of the Men.' There was one other interesting addition to the diet, which came in Madeira: 'Issued to the whole Ship's Company 20 pounds of Onions per Man.'

Cook was also a great advocate of cleanliness – personal hygiene – during this voyage and those that followed. He insisted that each member of his crew bathe regularly, while it was also everyone's duty to ensure that conditions below deck remained as fresh and hygienic as possible. In fact, his edict on this matter went beyond a Royal Navy regulation that stated: 'The Captain is to be particularly attentive to the cleanliness of the men, who are to be directed to wash themselves frequently ...'

The men bathed, as such, by splashing themselves with cold water from a bucket. They laundered the few clothes they had with them by scrubbing the items on deck before hanging them to dry. Unfortunately, with the air so often laden with salt, these clean clothes could prove to be abrasive to the skin when worn. At times, when any large amount of laundry needed to be done, including linen from the great cabin, it was tied in a bundle, tossed overboard on a line, and towed behind the ship so that the turbulence of the wake could wash it clean.

Regardless of these calls for cleanliness, there was still one problem that plagued every ship on the high seas in this era – rats! They thrived on the provisions that were carried in the hold, and any other morsels of food they could find. The solution came in the form of cats, but unfortunately, on most voyages, the birth rate of the rats exceeded the consumption rate of the cats.

On 18 September, *Endeavour* was ready to continue the voyage, this time with an additional 3032 gallons of wine, 270 pounds of fresh beef and a live bullock on board. At midnight, the sails were set, the anchor weighed and a gentle breeze began propelling her towards Cape Horn – probably via Rio de Janeiro. It was a decision that would depend on the weather they experienced while closing on the coast of South America.

The men were to spend the next fifty-six days at sea, and during that time Banks and others put to good use any time the ship was becalmed by going out in one of the boats and using guns and nets to collect birds and fish samples for research. They also collected barnacles and any shellfish they could find attached to driftwood. Their most intriguing prize during these excursions was Portuguese man-of-war jellyfish.

Back on board, to allow for the stifling heat that came with being in the equatorial regions, Cook decided to make life more tolerable for his men by introducing a new watch system. The crew, which had until then been divided into two watches, was split into three so that each man would have an eight-hour break when not on watch. The captain was also pleased to realise by now that Banks and his 'people' were definitely not passengers: as they sailed deeper into foreign waters, they took their research efforts to new levels. Most satisfying for Cook was that he and Banks greatly respected each other's talents, even though the young naturalist tended to demonstrate an assertive manner at times.

While progress was slow in the generally light breezes, the crew had to be forever vigilant for what they called 'white squalls'. These were savage gusts of wind that would seemingly appear out of nowhere, to the point where, if they were not anticipated with precautionary measures such as easing the sails, the rig could be seriously damaged by the force. Fortunately, when one such squall hammered *Endeavour* on 24 October as she neared the Equator, the men were quick to act and therefore avoid any damage occurring. When it came to navigation, the captain and senior officers spent a considerable amount of time each day taking sun, moon or star sights using a sextant so they could calculate the ship's position. This involved a mathematical procedure based around the time the sight was taken and the angular measurement of the celestial target at that time. The Nautical Almanac, detailing the coordinates of the moon, planets and fifty-seven stars, provided much of the information required in the process. Once the ship's position was placed on the chart, the course could be checked or a new one plotted.

The following day, *Endeavour* crossed the Equator, cruising along at 4 knots on a west-by-south course in what Cook described as 'a Gentle breeze and clear weather, with a moist air'. The 'crossing of the line' into the southern hemisphere on any vessel always demanded an initiation for those on board who had not previously ventured south of the Equator. On this occasion, it included the captain, who recalled:

> Every one that could not prove … that he had before
> Crossed the Line was either to pay a Bottle of Rum or
> be Ducked in the Sea, which former case was the fate of
> by far the Greatest part on board; and as several of the
> Men chose to be Ducked, and the weather was
> favourable for that purpose, this Ceremony was
> performed on about 20 or 30 …

Not surprisingly, Cook willingly paid his ransom in the form of a bottle of rum, and thereby bought exclusion from the more humiliating act of being dunked. Banks did likewise, but he had to pay three times the fare because of the two dogs he had with him. Others in the crew were chosen to pay a sum on behalf of the ship's cats. Those sailors who opted for a dunking over having to part with a bottle of rum were placed in a crude wooden chair, which was attached to a halyard, before being hoisted to the outboard end of a yard and then dropped unceremoniously into the water. With the dunkings completed, the celebration continued until midnight, during which time there was a considerable amount of wine, rum and beer consumed.

On 27 October, Cook had cause for his own celebration as he turned forty. Yet there was no evidence of this in his journal, which simply recorded that a fresh gale was blowing and, in essence, the ship was progressing according to plan.

Five weeks after the Equator was crossed, *Endeavour* was well clear of the exasperating conditions that prevailed in the doldrums. She was then bowling along; churning out a bold bow wave while harnessing a brisk north-easterly trade wind with everything suitable set, including studding sails, spritsails and the mizzen. With the ship making such good speed, it was decision time for the captain: 'I now determined to put into Rio de Janeiro in preference to any other port in Brazil or Falkland Islands, for at this place I knew we could recruit our Stock of Provisions … and from the reception former Ships had met with here I doubted not but we should be well received …'

He could not have been more wrong about the reception. Having sailed down the coast of Brazil for five days, *Endeavour* then inched her way into Rio de Janiero's harbour before anchoring off the Isle of Cobras, adjacent to the town's waterfront. While his ship was gliding towards the anchorage, Cook followed formal procedure by sending two officers ashore in the pinnace to advise the town's viceroy of their arrival and the reasons for their presence. However, when the pinnace returned, neither officer was aboard. When asked the reason, the coxon replied that the men would be detained 'until the captain went ashore'.

Next, a small boat, with twelve armed local soldiers on board, arrived on the scene and started circling the ship. Fifteen minutes later a *desembargador* (judge), together with a colonel from a Portuguese regiment, went aboard *Endeavour*. After initially indicating that the ship wasn't welcome in port, the judge did an about-face and advised that the viceroy, in Banks' words, 'would give us every assistance in his power'. Finally, Cook was told that he was welcome to go ashore if he desired, but everyone else must remain with the vessel.

More confusion came the following day, 14 November, when the visitors were told who among them was permitted onshore. This list did not include Banks and his entourage, 'the passengers'; they were 'particularly objected to' and had to remain on the ship. Banks, who refused to accept this directive, put it to the test – and failed: 'in the Evening [we] dressed ourselves and attempted to go ashore under the pretence of a visit to the Viceroy, but were stopped by the Guard boat whose officer told us that he had particular orders which he could not transgress, to Let no officer or Passenger except the captain pass the boat ...'

The stand-off, which continued for forty-eight hours, deteriorated further when Cook realised that the sentinel who was put aboard his launch, supposedly in recognition of the captain's authority, was actually a guard under orders to control his every movement. Cook tried to remonstrate with the viceroy over the treatment he and his men were receiving, but this went nowhere. In fact, three days after he'd complained about the situation on his launch, he learned that one of his lieutenants and crewmen were taken into custody for refusing to have guards aboard their boat. This crew would later report to Cook that the soldiers had beaten them, according to Banks, and that they were thrown into a dungeon 'where their companions were chiefly Blacks who were chained'.

An additional, unassociated drama came that same evening when, during an 'excessive hard storm of wind and rain', two of the ship's three boats that were tied alongside *Endeavour* – the longboat and the yawl – broke their mooring lines and rapidly disappeared downwind into the darkness. The longboat had no-one aboard, and while the men aboard the yawl did everything possible to save it from being wrecked on rocks, they were quickly fighting to save themselves. It was a tense few hours, for, as well as fearing for the safety of his men, Cook had to accept that two of the ship's assets, both vital to the success of the mission, might well have been lost. Later that night, when the storm eased, it seemed that fortune was on the side of the expedition: the men aboard the yawl made their way back to the ship. The undamaged longboat was recovered the next day.

On 21 November, in a message to Cook, the Portuguese viceroy, who was a soldier and not a sailor, finally revealed why *Endeavour* and her crew were being treated so poorly: he held no comprehension of the transit of Venus, and therefore believed that this expedition was a guise for something more sinister. He compared *Endeavour*'s lines with other ships he had seen, and became convinced she was not a Royal Navy vessel at all. Cook's journal noted that the viceroy 'still keeps up his Doubts that she is not a King's ship, and accuseth my people of Smuggling, a thing I am very Certain they were not guilty of'. Another of the viceroy's theories was that she was a merchant vessel.

Finally, by 1 December, all doubts had cleared and peace was achieved. That done, Cook was able to purchase the fresh provisions he required and put them aboard. At this time, all operations were generally running smoothly, but the 'persuader' – the cat-o'-nine-tails – had to be called on to deal with two wayward crew-members: Robert Anderson, who attempted to desert the ship while on duty ashore, and a marine, William Judge, who used abusive language towards the Officer of the Watch. Both received the maximum twelve lashes at the hand of the bosun's mate, John Reading – but the captain deemed that Reading had been too easy on the men.

The result was that he too received twelve lashes, for 'not doing his Duty in punishing the above two Men'.

It was 2 December when *Endeavour* was moved towards an offshore anchorage as part of her preparation to sail on the next stage of the passage to Cape Horn. While this was happening, Banks made a note in his journal that succinctly expressed the general feeling held by the men when it came to their time in Rio de Janeiro: 'this Morn thank God we have got all we want from these illiterate and impolite gentry, so ... we sailed ...'

As brief as this relocation to the anchorage was, there came another tragedy involving a crewman. It was an incident that reminded all on board how one slip almost always brought fatal consequences on a difficult-to-manoeuvre ship such as this. 'Peter Flower, Seaman, fell overboard,' Cook wrote, 'and before any Assistance could be given him was drowned ...' Despite this note being in his usual succinct form, the loss was particularly poignant for the captain, as Flower was a close associate: Cook had sailed with him since his early days of survey work in Newfoundland.

On 5 December, the final stage of *Endeavour*'s move towards the open sea came to a dramatic halt due to an unanticipated incident that actually threatened the ship. It was flat calm, and as the boats were towing the ship towards a new anchorage near the harbour entrance, they came in close proximity to the town's principal fortification at Santa Cruz. At the moment when the fort was off the starboard beam, two thundering cannon-blasts burst forth, one sending a cannonball hurtling just over the top of the mainmast while the other fell short of the ship. An understandably enraged Cook ordered progress be halted immediately and the anchor dropped, then directed an officer to go ashore to the fort in a boat 'to know the Reason of their firing'.

It was soon apparent that there had been a mistake: each time a ship was departing the harbour, orders were to be sent from the town to the fort declaring that the vessel could depart, but in *Endeavour*'s case this had not happened. Embarrassed officials apologised profusely for the breakdown in communications between the army brigadier in town and the fort. *Endeavour* was then allowed to proceed.

By 3 am on 9 December, Rio de Janeiro was, thankfully, long gone in *Endeavour*'s wake. The atmosphere on board was calm as the ship made her way south through the night on a gentle breeze.

There was, however, a very large swell running, a leftover from a recent Atlantic storm. This was often bringing a sudden, violent motion to the ship, so much so that at one stage, those on deck were alarmed to hear a loud, splintering crack come from above: the whip-like shock-load on the rig from one of these big waves was so strong that it caused the fore topgallant mast (the top one-third of the mast) to snap like a dry twig. Instantly, the shout went out from the quarterdeck for men to get aloft and contain the wildly gyrating section of mast, yard and sail, so that any further damage to the remaining rig and sails was minimised. By dawn, the broken section was on the deck and the ship's carpenter was already shaping a new one from timber that was on board for such an event.

On a number of occasions, *Endeavour*'s efforts to reach Cape Horn were thwarted by brutal storms that swept in from the south. At one point, when it was not possible to make any headway, Cook had to call for only two of the very smallest sails to remain set, and reefed at that, so that his ship could lie-to. Here, for the first time on this voyage, another virtue of her powerful design could be appreciated, even by a non-seafarer like Joseph Banks. He wrote that the ship had 'shown her excellence in laying-to remarkably well, shipping scarce any water though it blew at times vastly strong; the seamen in general say that they never knew a ship lay-to so well as this does, so lively and at the same time so easy'.

Even so, it was the 'liveliness' that, at times, made shipboard life barely tolerable, especially for those men in the cramped quarters below deck who were trying to sleep in their hammocks during their off-watch. The problem was that each time the ship bucked and tossed with some level of severity, those in the hammocks – which were slung closely together between deck beams – continually banged into one another, making sleep next to impossible for the occupants.

It was even uncomfortable in the captain's great cabin. This was an area usually assigned to him exclusively, but in this case, with so many guests aboard, it was crowded every day and night. Banks noted the difficulties he was experiencing: 'Wind foul, blew rather fresh so the ship heeled much which made our affairs go on rather uncomfortably ...'

It was in rough conditions such as these that the use of the ship's latrines – the heads or 'seats of ease' – became both a difficult and dangerous exercise. These facilities were nothing more than two broad planks extending beyond the bow of the ship (one each side of the bowsprit) with an appropriately sized circular hole cut in them, and canvas tubes extending downwards for about 3 feet to reduce the undesirable effect that any updraught of wind or sea spray might have. This feature was of particular importance if the windward-side head had to be used. As the pre-eminent researcher on the design and construction of *Endeavour*, Ray Parkin, explained, safety wasn't completely ignored on these seats of ease: 'There [were] also two spars nailed to the hull at an angle on the forward side of the platforms with a lifeline/guardrail ... for the safety of the occupant during devotions.'

Whenever possible, Cook and the other Royal Society observer, Charles Green, spent much of their time comparing lunar navigation observations each had taken to plot *Endeavour*'s position on the chart. While timepieces in the mid eighteenth century were notoriously unreliable, the accuracy that these two men achieved was quite remarkable, particularly when it came to the very difficult calculation of longitude. Also, through his quest for perfection as a navigator, Cook was continually searching for answers to the problem of variations experienced in the direction of the magnetic compass needle. He recognised that the needle changed direction significantly according to the course being steered, but he was unable to deduce that the compass needle was, in the main, being influenced by the magnetic attraction of metallic objects and fastenings located close to the compass. It was not until 1805 that one of Cook's greatest admirers, Matthew Flinders, discovered the reason for this anomaly and came up with a solution – the Flinders Bar.

Even when *Endeavour* was being slowed by contrary winds, Cook did everything possible to get to Cape Horn as quickly as possible. Once there, he and everyone else aboard fully expected to be met by the worst imaginable conditions, so every preparation that could be made to ensure the safety of the ship was being undertaken, including the re-caulking of the ship's decks to prevent leaks below, and the replacement of any suspect sails with new ones. To increase stability, six of the large and very heavy carriage guns were stowed in the lowest part of the hold, and as each cask of fresh water in the same hold was emptied, it was filled with salt water. Additionally, with the weather getting colder and icy blasts expected, the captain ordered that each man receive a new issue of clothing – Fearnought heavy woollen jackets and trousers – 'after which I never heard one Man Complain of Cold,' Cook said.

Christmas Day 1768 saw *Endeavour* 1000 nautical miles south of Rio and approximately 1200 nautical miles from Cape Horn. Despite their isolation, captain and crew could see no reason not to celebrate, as Banks recalled: 'Christmas Day; all good Christians, that is to say all hands, get abominably drunk so that at night there was scarce a sober man in the ship. Wind, thank God, very moderate or the Lord knows what would have become of us …'

At every possible opportunity since setting sail from Rio, Banks and his associates continued to spend their time collecting samples of the wildlife they were observing, by snaring or shooting birds, catching or netting fish, and even catching butterflies that had been blown offshore by strong winds. There was one particular day when the presence of butterflies was quite amazing: 'the air was crowded in an uncommon manner with Butterflies chiefly of one sort, of which we took as many as we pleased on board the ship, their quantity was so large that ... many thousands were in view at once in almost any direction you could look, the greatest part of them much above our mastheads ...'

Instead of going around Cape Horn, Cook could have sailed through the Straits of Magellan to reach the Pacific, but he decided on the former option after hearing unfavourable reports from captains who had attempted to sail through the straits. This 300-nautical-mile shortcut through the southern regions of South America has its entrance 200 nautical miles to the north of the cape. While the waters there were always smooth, the challenges were great: the wind was renowned for changing direction and strength in an instant, there were fast-flowing foul tides to be faced, and ships attempting the passage needed to anchor regularly to hold ground against wind and tide. This constant call to anchor caused great fatigue for a ship's crew, something that Cook did not want for his own men.

By mid January, though, he could well have been questioning his decision to round the Horn. *Endeavour*, which was then in Le Maire Strait, between the southern point of Argentina and Staten Island, was being hammered by horrible weather – snow, hail, lightning, thunder, strong winds, and a sea so powerful that she was pitching to the point where the bowsprit was being plunged underwater. Each time a thunderstorm approached, there was a call to haul the lightning chain to the top of the mainmast, in a bid to protect the ship should there be a direct hit.

Despite the cold, when Banks and his team went ashore at Success Bay on the southern coast of Tierra del Fuego, they were astonished by how little clothing was worn by the natives, who were 'of a reddish Colour nearly resembling that of rusty iron mixed with oil'. They wore cloaks of seal skin thrown loosely over their shoulders, but the men, in particular, held few inhibitions about concealing their 'privy parts'.

On the morning of 16 January 1769, Banks, Dr Solander, the artist Alexander Buchan, four servants, two seamen, plus Monkhouse and Green, went ashore with the plan to penetrate as far as they could into the hills and investigate the flora and fauna. It was a cool but sunny day and they were making good progress towards the top of one of the summits when Buchan suffered a seizure, probably through fatigue. A fire was lit to create a warm environment for him, and while those who were most tired were directed to stay and comfort him, Solander, Green, Monkhouse and Banks pressed on.

When high on the alp, a snowstorm arrived virtually unannounced, so severe that Banks realised that while they would be able to return to Buchan and the others, there was no hope of getting back to the ship that night. Banks was amazed by the intensity of this summertime snowfall – it was unlike anything he had ever seen or been aware of in Europe. While every effort was being made to keep everyone alive in the bitterly cold conditions, by morning Banks' two 'negro' servants, Thomas Richmond and George Dorlton were dead. The remainder of the party, weak as they were from being exposed to the elements, then battled their way down to the beach before rowing back to the ship.

The surging seas and powerful winds that accompanied the snowstorm caused *Endeavour* to remain holed up in Success Bay for four days. During this time, Cook was anxiously watching for the weather to turn in his favour, and this came at 2 am on 21 January. There was no time to be lost: the call was for all hands to their positions for setting sail and weighing anchor. Cape Horn lay 100 nautical miles to the south-west, and once around the legendary landmark, *Endeavour* would enter the South Pacific and sail north-west to the welcome warmth of King George's Island. With westerly winds certain to prevail for much of the time, the captain's strategy for rounding the Horn was to sail well to the south so that the ship could, when the timing was right, be tacked and sail a safe course towards her destination, well clear of the western coast of South America.

On Thursday, 26 January – a hazy day with 'fresh gales' coming out of the west – the distinct profile of the promontory that was the cape on Hornos Island could be recognised faintly, about 18 miles off the ship's starboard bow. This was the start of *Endeavour*'s planned course towards the high latitudes of the Southern Ocean.

Sometimes the gain over a single day was merely a few miles, as westerly winds forced *Endeavour* onto a course that was little more than due south. This ship, like all other square-riggers, was barely capable of sailing to windward, even in light winds. In those conditions, *Endeavour*'s bluff bow caused her to bullock her way through the Southern Ocean swells that were rolling her way. For Cook, his first rounding of the cape was nowhere near as bad as he expected, but even so, he and every other man on board was experiencing another form of brutality that comes with being in this part of the world: the biting cold, rain, hail, sleet and snow.

Occasionally there was some level of respite when the weather had a complete about-face and the wind went calm; and while the rolling seas remained, this did not deter Banks and his men from seizing the opportunity to launch a small boat and take what samples of nature they could find in close proximity to the ship. While Cook and his seafarers considered these conditions benign, the captain noted that the majority of the 'land men' were incapacitated with what Banks referred to as 'a bilious attack'. Today it is called seasickness.

The push to the west eventually saw *Endeavour* 250 nautical miles to the south of the great cape. Unknown to Cook at the time, another 250 nautical miles to the south of that position was an icy isthmus – part of the yet-to-be-discovered snow-covered land of Antarctica. The world would not know of the existence of this continent for another half-century.

Remarkably, the wind gods continued to look favourably on *Endeavour*: on 1 February they even delivered an east-south-easterly breeze, and this enabled her to achieve a very welcome 106-nautical-mile gain to the west in twenty-four hours. By this time, Cook and his officers were starting to feel comfortable about their rounding of the Horn; the log entry revealed that the ship's course had then been changed dramatically, to west-by-north. This meant that she was virtually aiming at King George's Island, which was still more than 4500 nautical miles ahead. A few more days of this weather pattern would provide certainty that they were well clear of the dangers associated with rounding Cape Horn and on a safe course towards their destination. Still, the motion from the large Southern Ocean swells was doing Banks and his men few favours: 'During all last night the ship has pitched very much so that there has been no sleeping for land men,' Banks wrote.

By 13 February, Cook's lunar observations confirmed that *Endeavour* was north, and well to the east, of the western entrance to the Straits of Magellan. It had been a remarkably easy passage around the much-dreaded cape, one that had taken a surprisingly short period of twenty-three days to execute. The captain wrote in his journal that the most amazing aspect of this particular part of the passage was that the winds never reached a point where he had been forced to call for even the topsails to be reefed – sails that would normally have been the first to be reduced in area in the event of strong winds. Cook continued:

> [This was] a Circumstance that perhaps never happened
> before to any ship in those Seas so much dreaded for
> Hard gales of Wind; in so much that the doubling
> [rounding] of Cape Horn is thought by some to be a
> mighty thing, and others to this day prefer the Straits of
> Magellan … I am firmly persuaded from the Winds we
> have had, that had we come by that Passage we should
> not have been in these Seas [this far advanced], besides
> the fatiguing of our People, the damage we must have
> done to our Anchors, Cables, Sails, and Rigging, none
> of which have suffered in our passage round Cape
> Horn.

Banks was particularly gratified to have disproved the oft-held belief of land-based theorists that the imagined Great South Land existed in this part of the world, some saying that its presence would counterbalance the existence of the great landmasses in the northern hemisphere. He wrote with considerable emphasis: 'It is … some pleasure to be able to disprove that which does not exist but in the opinions of Theoretical writers.'

Cook concurred with Banks' assessment, basing his theory on the existing sea state and noting: 'The south-west swell still keeps up … a proof that there is no land near in that quarter.' He added that *Endeavour*'s impressive run of 660 leagues since rounding Cape Horn confirmed 'that we have had no Current that hath affected the Ship Since we came into these Seas, this must be a great sign that we have been near no land of any extent because near land are generally found Currents.'

As the weather continued to improve and the threat of gales diminished, *Endeavour* was able to remain on a course to the north-west. It was easy going, so Cook took the opportunity to have his men raise from the hold the six carriage guns and position them on the waist of the ship.

On 26 March, a day of squalls and rain, there was another tragedy on board, which Banks recorded with some level of emotion:

> This evening one of our marines [William Greenslade] threw himself overboard and was not missed until it was much too late even to attempt to recover him. He was a very young man, scarce 21 years of age, remarkably quiet and industrious, and to make his exit the more melancholy was driven to this rash resolution by an accident so trifling [petty theft] that it must appear incredible to everybody who is not well acquainted with the powerful effects that shame can work upon young minds.

Greenslade was accused of stealing a small portion of sealskin while on sentry duty. He intended to use this to make a tobacco pouch; however, when some of his fellow marines discovered that he was the perpetrator of the theft, they bullied him to the point where he went to the bow of the ship and disappeared.

By early April, the balmy south-east trade winds of the South Pacific were well established, and in response *Endeavour* was surging along in a delightful breeze that was coming over her port quarter. She had all sails set and was bullocking her way down beautiful, blue South Pacific swells with a bone in her teeth – a surging white bow wave. This was the sort of sailing that led Cook to declare: 'Her best sailing is with the wind a point or two abaft the beam, she will then run 7 or 8 knots and carry weather helm.' (Weather helm is where the ship has a slight desire to turn towards the direction of the wind, being the preferred 'feel' for the timoneer.) However, not every day was truly representative of the imagined temperate tropics. There were numerous occasions when the ship was battered by the pelting rain associated with tropical thunderstorms.

Soon *Endeavour*'s course had her sailing westward along the latitude on which King George's Island was said to lie. By doing this, the chance of missing the target was minimised.

On 4 April, sixty-nine days after rounding the Horn, those on board sighted land for the first time since departing from that cape. Cook diarised his observation: 'an Island of about 2 Leagues in circuit and of an oval form with a Lagoon in the Middle for which I named it Lagoon Island. We saw several of the Inhabitants, the Most of them Men and these Marched along the shore abreast of the Ship with long clubs in their hands as though they meant to oppose our landing.' Judging by this description, they were seeing one of the islands of the Tuamotu Archipelago, 500 nautical miles to the east of their destination.

They continued on without stopping. Light winds sapped *Endeavour*'s average speed, so it wasn't until 6 am on Tuesday, 11 April, that great excitement swept the ship: King George's Island could be seen off the bow. 'It appeared very high and Mountainous,' wrote Cook.

As they continued to close on what was becoming an increasingly beautiful coastline, the captain took the time to contemplate the voyage since leaving England 229 days earlier – the best part of eight months – but it was the condition of his men that impressed him most: 'At this time we had but very few men upon the sick list, and these had but slight complaints. The Ship's company had in general been very healthy, owing in a great measure to the Sauerkraut, Portable Soup and Malt.' Cook was also pleased to note that his theory regarding the medicinal benefits that the malt extract (wort) played in containing scurvy had, thanks to the diligence of the surgeon, Monkhouse, been proved. In time, however, it would be shown that it was the greens that were responsible for the good health of the men.

At the Society Islands. This picture, c1786, attributed to John Cleveley from sketches made by his brother James – a marine painter – show the industry that occurred when Cook's ships landed and underwent repairs. State Library of NSW, Dixson Galleries DGD 27, 6 / a4472006.

CHAPTER EIGHT

Arcadia

After seeing her billowing sails emerge over the eastern horizon and head their way, the islanders were quick to respond to *Endeavour*'s bold approach. They loaded their canoes with all types of tropical foodstuffs and artefacts, then put to sea to greet the visitors, in the hope that they could barter for the most valuable items the strangers might bring, especially those made from iron.

On board *Endeavour*, Banks was awestruck by the welcome. Ever observant, he quickly became aware that there was one highly prized item among everything being offered:

> They had one pig with them which they refused to sell for nails upon any account but repeatedly offered it for a hatchet; of these we had very few on board so thought it better to let the pig go away than to give one of them in exchange, knowing from the authority of those who had been here before that if we once did it, they would never lower their price …

At 7 am on 13 April 1769, *Endeavour* was guided ever so slowly into what Wallis had earlier named Royal Bay (Matavai Bay to the islanders). The moment the man swinging the lead in the chains advised that the water depth was 13 fathoms, a loud order was barked from the quarterdeck for the remaining sails to be hauled up while the best bower was released from the cathead and lowered.

By this time, the ship was like a giant swan surrounded by a flock of cygnets: countless canoes, some of them outriggers and others large catamarans with sails of woven matting. They were all carrying excited men and women eagerly displaying the produce and goods they wanted to trade. In the distance, on the coconut palm-fringed beach of black sand that bordered the bay, hundreds more islanders waited to welcome their visitors. At this point, Lieutenant Gore and the master, Molyneux, both veterans of the Wallis expedition, indicated to Cook a man they recognised as being a leader of the community. As an immediate indication of friendship towards the islanders, the captain then invited this man, and a few others, to join him aboard the ship, so that 'much could be made' of them.

After that, *Endeavour*'s boats were hoisted out, to allow Cook and other senior members of the crew, together with Banks and his colleagues, to be ferried ashore. Banks' journal recorded: 'we were met by some hundreds of the inhabitants whose faces at least gave evident signs that we were not unwelcome guests, though they at first hardly dare approach us, after a little time they became very familiar.'

After two days there, Cook, Banks and the others were convinced that this was the right location for the observation of the transit, which was still seven weeks away, and so 'resolved to pitch upon some spot upon the North-East point of the Bay, properly situated for observing the Transit of Venus, and … there to throw up a small fort for our defence'. This wooden-fenced fortification included a small portable observatory made of canvas, from where they would watch the event; more than fifty tents to house the scientists and members of the crew; plus a kitchen, and facilities for the blacksmith. Logically enough, it became known as Fort Venus, which led to the headland becoming Point Venus today.

On the day the building of the fort began, Cook, Banks and some of his group went a short distance inland, and when they reached a stream, Banks claimed three ducks in a single shot of pellets from his musket. The small band of islanders accompanying them struggled to comprehend the noise and what had caused the ducks to plummet from the sky. It 'surprised them so much that most of them fell down as though they had been shot likewise', was Cook's observation. Whether or not word of this seemingly miraculous event was immediately carried back to other islanders on the beach is unknown, but while Cook and his party were returning to the fort site, they heard a series of musket shots. An islander, who, it could be suggested, was already aware of the potential of the foreigners' odd-looking weapons, had snatched a sentry's musket and run off. Before he could get far, however, he was shot and killed by marines amid a cluster of 100 shocked islanders.

This incident could have ended Cook's mission on King George's Island there and then. It represented a clash of two diametrically opposite cultures, with very different lifestyles, values and understanding. Conciliation suddenly became paramount, although it took considerable appeasement from both sides to re-establish the desired level of relations. Fortunately, through gestures and speech, Cook was able to convince the chief and some of his elders that they should sit down on the beach with him to go over the incident. Banks revealed the outcome:

> ... we got together a few of [the islanders] and
> explaining to them that the man who suffered was guilty
> of a crime deserving of death (for so we were forced to
> make it) we retired to the ship not well pleased with the
> day's expedition, guilty no doubt in some measure of the
> death of a man who the most severe laws of equity
> would not have condemned to so severe a punishment.

The contrast between the two cultures was no better displayed than in their respective attire. Despite being in the tropics, Cook was always resplendent aboard ship and onshore in his officer's uniform, including stockings, leather shoes and tricorn hat, while the islanders wore next to nothing, and were totally uninhibited about it – something the Englishmen struggled to comprehend. Still, they were equally pleased when it came to the svelte, coffee-skinned women. The latter, like the men, wore a knee-length wrap of cloth or matting around their waist, or a shoulder-width woven mat with a hole in the middle through which they put their heads, folded down and tied at the waist.

Within a very short time of arriving, 26-year-old Banks – naturalist and well-educated man of science that he was – had registered in his journal details of the exceptional hospitality afforded the visitors by 'the Indians', before adding a bold statement about this paradise: 'In short, the scene we saw was the truest picture of an arcadia of which we were going to be kings that the imagination can form.'

Apart from the spectacular way that nature had used its colours and forms to create this South Seas paradise, Banks, like every other man, was struck by the beauty of the women and their free-spirited attitude towards sex.

> ... we walked freely about several large houses attended by the ladies who showed us all kind of civilities our situation could admit of, but as there were no places of retirement, the houses being entirely without walls, we had not an opportunity of putting their politeness to every test that maybe some of us would not have failed to have done had circumstances been more favourable; indeed we had no reason to doubt any part of their politeness, as by their frequently pointing to the matts on the ground ... they plainly showed that they were much less jealous of observation than we were.

And later: 'The foremost of the women ... unveiling all her charms gave me a most convenient opportunity of admiring them by turning herself gradually round ... she then once more displayed her naked beauties and immediately marched up to me ...'

Cook, while similarly impressed with the beauty of the land and its people, was appalled to learn of the locals' practice and acceptance of what the outside world knew as infanticide:

> One amusement or custom ... is founded upon a Custom
> so inhuman and contrary to the Principles of human
> nature. It is this: that more than one half of the better sort
> of the inhabitants have entered into a resolution of
> enjoying free liberty in Love, without being Troubled or
> disturbed by its consequences. These mix and Cohabit
> together with the utmost freedom, and the Children who
> are so unfortunate as to be thus begot are smothered at the
> Moment of their Birth ...

Regardless, relationships between *Endeavour*'s crew and the captivating young women of Otaheite – which Cook had ascertained as being the name the natives gave to their land – were as abundant as tropical blooms. And while the captain harboured no objection to this, he reminded his men that the primary reason for their presence on the island was to observe the transit. Little else mattered.

Within days of their arrival, the euphoria associated with being in this nirvana was dealt a blow when a member of Banks' party, artist Alexander Buchan, suffered another seizure and died. It was a loss that greatly affected Banks, who held Buchan in high regard:

> ... his Loss to me is irretrievable, my airy dreams of
> entertaining my friends in England with the scenes that I
> am to see here are vanished. No account of the figures
> and dresses of men can be satisfactory unless illustrated
> with figures: had providence spared him a month longer
> what an advantage would it have been to my
> undertaking'

At all times, the English were keen to show the islanders how they punished men for their misdemeanours. This was a demonstration that, it was hoped, would help explain to the local populace why Cook was seemingly so harsh towards them when they conducted similar acts. One such time came when the ship's butcher was destined for a date with the cat-o'-nine-tails. Banks took up the story of the punishment, which was initially planned to be carried out on the beach:

> ... the crowd of people who were with us hindered it
> from being performed. In consequence of this I took
> them [the islanders] on board of the ship where Captain
> Cook immediately ordered the offender to be punished;
> they stood quietly and saw him stripped and fastened to
> the rigging but as soon as the first blow was given,
> interfered with many tears, begging the punishment
> might cease – a request which the Captain would not
> comply with ...

And the islanders appeared to have no understanding of the meaning of theft. If they wanted something and could grab it, then they would disappear into the coconut palms with it. Banks explained the issue this way: 'great and small chiefs and common men all are firmly of opinion that if they can once get possession of anything it immediately becomes their own.' However, that changed on Tuesday, 2 May, when an unknown islander overstepped the mark by taking one of the instruments that was crucial for the observation of the transit of Venus: the astronomical quadrant.

This prized item was stolen from within the fort, and the moment he became aware of the theft, Cook took the law into his own hands. After impounding all the large canoes that were in the bay, he advised the islanders that the boats would not be released until information was forthcoming as to who had stolen the quadrant and where it was located. The threat worked: word soon arrived that the thief had decamped to an eastern point of the island, so Banks and Green headed in that direction. It was a successful mission, with both the quadrant and the villain located.

On 30 May, there was another cause for concern, when the ship's carpenters hauled the longboat from the water and discovered that its bottom was little different from honeycomb. The dreaded teredo worm had taken a distinct liking to the boat's timbers and literally made a meal of it. A similar problem was discovered later, when the ship's anchors were hauled up. The toredo worms had all but eaten away their timber stocks.

As is quite often the case in these latitudes, the weather regularly turned inclement, delivering thunderstorms and heavy rain to the region. This caused Cook and Banks to decide that, as a precaution against unfavourable weather impacting on the observation of the transit of Venus, they should establish three locations for viewing the event. Cook and Green would stay at Matavai Bay, while a group led by Banks went to a distant island. A third group would be sent 30 nautical miles away to Motu Tapiri, a small islet off the east coast.

Any apprehension regarding the weather was eliminated from the moment the sun blazed its way above the horizon on the day of the transit – Saturday, 3 June. The opportunity that this presented for the mission was apparent in Cook's notes. Even so, considering that this event was the primary reason for the expedition, they were remarkably few words: 'This day proved as favourable to our purpose as we could wish. Not a Cloud was to be seen the whole day, and the Air was perfectly Clear, so that we had every advantage we could desire in observing the whole of the Passage of the planet Venus over the Sun's Disk … Dr Solander observed as well as Mr Green and myself …'

Much to Cook's delight, when the other two parties returned to Matavai Bay after the transit, they confirmed that they too had achieved satisfactory results: 'This evening the Gentlemen that were sent to observe the Transit of Venus, returned with success; those that were sent to York Island were well received by the Natives.'

Once back aboard the ship, all the relevant data gathered from the observations was collated, and with that, the first major purpose of Cook's voyage had been achieved. It was at this point therefore that the captain opened his second packet of secret instructions from the Admiralty and acquainted himself with the next challenge required of him.

Within twenty-four hours, preparations for departure were underway, but it would take more than a month for them to be completed. The equipment used in the observation was transferred back to the ship, the fort dismantled, additional ballast in the form of river stones was placed in *Endeavour*'s bilge, sails and spars repaired, and provisions and water taken aboard.

While this work was being undertaken, the lure of love and the thought of a life spent in this Eden in the South Seas proved too much for some. Two young marines, Clement Webb and Samuel Gibson, headed for the mountains determined to desert the ship and remain with the women they had come to love. Cook would not tolerate this blatant display of insubordination, knowing all too well that such an act would set a precedent for the crew over the remainder of the voyage. Armed officers, assisted by island men, were immediately despatched to search for the deserters, and the following day, they were back aboard the ship, destined to be punished.

On 13 July, after a stay of nearly three months, the time came to sail away from this paradise. Interestingly for Cook, in the preceding weeks several islanders had requested to accompany the Englishmen aboard *Endeavour*. After much deliberation, it was decided that such a person might 'be of use to us in our future discoveries', as the captain recorded:

> We resolved to bring away one whose name is Tupia, a
> Chief and a Priest. This man had been with us most part

> of the time we had been upon the Island. We found him
> to be a very intelligent person ... and was the likeliest
> person to answer our Purpose. For these reasons, and at
> the request of Mr Banks, I received him on board,
> together with a young Boy, his Servant [Tiata] ...

The weight of emotion, both on board the ship and onshore, had become heavier by the hour as the time neared to hove the anchor and hoist sail. It had been only two years since Wallis was there with *Dolphin*, which was when the islanders first became aware of the alien world from which their visitors had come, an event that initiated a huge change to their way of life.

As the longboat and pinnace were hoisted aboard and secured on the waist of the ship, the wails of sadness coming from the canoes surrounding *Endeavour* became increasingly loud and vigorous. It was an equally dramatic moment for Tupia, who was departing paradise for experiences that were beyond his imagination. Seeking to make his farewell that bit more conspicuous, he climbed to the masthead with Banks so he could wave to his people in the canoes and onshore. With that done, he returned to the deck and from then on showed no further emotion.

Everyone else on board, especially Cook, had to determinedly disconnect themselves from the extraordinary experiences of the previous months. As commander of the mission, he needed to shift his attention, and that of his men, towards the distant horizon, and the important discoveries he hoped to make there.

Captain Wallace had made his discovery of Otaheite – or King George the Third's Island, as he named it – simply because he happened to be sailing *Dolphin* some distance to the south of what, by mid 1767, was the proven safe track for square-rigged ships traversing the South Pacific. Until then, vessels making an east–west crossing in this part of the world, after having either rounded Cape Horn or sailed through the Straits of Magellan, took up a course south of the Equator in order to exploit the warm downwind sailing that came with the prevailing south-east trade winds. This was considered to be a safe route because there were established stopover points at which to replenish vital stocks of water and food. To sail in higher latitudes further south, and therefore into unknown territory, was to court fatal consequences, so, through circumstance rather than desire, a large part of the South Pacific remained beyond any explorer's reach. Now though, following the discovery of Otaheite, there was a point from which an expedition aimed at exploring the waters to the south and west could be launched. Consequently, it was Cook's commission to do just that: to see if there was anything of significance to be found, and in particular, to search for *Terra Australis Incognita*.

With his ship well prepared, and laden with as much food and water as she could carry, Cook knew he had the capacity to meet the challenge that had been presented to him in the second set of instructions from the Admiralty. These secret orders said, in part:

> Whereas there is reason to imagine that a Continent or
> Land of great extent, may be found to the Southward of
> the Tract lately made by Captn Wallis in His Majesty's
> Ship the Dolphin ... or of the Tract of any former
> Navigators in Pursuit of the like kind, You are therefore
> in Pursuance of His Majesty's Pleasure hereby required
> and directed to put to Sea ... You are to proceed to the
> Southward [of Otaheite] in order to make discovery of
> the Continent abovementioned until you arrive in the
> Latitude of 40°, unless you sooner fall in with it. But not
> having discovered it or any Evident sign of it in that
> Run you are to proceed in search of it to the Westward
> between the Latitude beforementioned and the Latitude
> of 35° until you discover it, or fall in with the Eastern
> side of the Land discovered by [Abel] Tasman and now
> called New Zealand ... if you shall fail of discovering the

> Continent beforementioned, you will with upon falling
> in with New Zealand carefully observe the Latitude and
> Longitude in which that Land is situated and explore as
> much of the Coast as the Condition of the Bark, the
> health of her Crew, and the State of your Provisions will
> admit ...

Cook subsequently plotted a course, initially to the north-west, then south and finally to the west – a plan that would fulfil the requirements of these instructions.

Abel Janszoon Tasman had become the first European to discover New Zealand when he sighted its Southern Alps on 13 December 1642. Although Dutch cartographers soon registered it by its modern title, the name Tasman gave his discovery was Staten Land, which he hypothesised was probably part of a huge continent that stretched across the Pacific to South America. Just a few weeks before this sighting, he had registered another important addition to the world map: the southern tip of Van Diemen's Land (Tasmania). As with the New Zealand coast, should Cook be successful in discovering unknown lands, it was his responsibility to prepare charts of the newly found shorelines for the Admiralty, not dissimilar to those he had produced when surveying the shores of Newfoundland.

Additionally, their Lordships had ordered him to pursue friendship and potential trade opportunities with the local people, and 'with the Consent of the Natives ... take possession of Convenient Situations in the Country in the Name of the King of Great Britain: Or: if you find the Country uninhabited, take Possession for His Majesty by setting up Proper Marks and Inscriptions, as first discoverers and possessors.' Equally, Banks and his party were obliged to collect as many samples of the local flora and fauna as possible.

There was one other proviso. The captain was reminded that this was a secret mission, and because of this, his entire crew, should they enter any foreign port, were 'not to divulge where they have been until they have permission to do so'.

Cook's reason for initially sailing to the north-west from Matavai Bay was so he could visit and explore islands that the natives of Otaheite had told him existed in that region. With Tupia helping to pilot the vessel, it took *Endeavour* two days to cover the 120 nautical miles to the first of those islands, Huaheine – one of the group that is today known as the Society Islands.

Fortunately for those on board, who were keen to regain their sea legs and thus avoid mal de mer, the weather was relatively benign. In fact, the winds were so light that Tupia felt obliged to do everything within his power to muster up a breeze and make the ship gain speed. In this regard, Banks appeared dubious of their guest's capabilities, writing: 'Our Indian often prayed ... for a wind and as often boasted to me of the success of his prayers, which I plainly saw he never began til he saw a breeze so near the ship that it generally reached her before his prayer was finished ...'

Over the ensuing weeks, Cook's expedition discovered an impressive scattering of tropical islands and peoples who, in general, were as welcoming as those they had encountered in Otaheite. However, there were still times when the Englishmen were seen as invaders, even though Tupia did his best to assure the natives that they came in friendship and peace. One such incident saw islanders in a canoe try to capture one of the small boats that was carrying Banks and others towards the shore. It was not until the marines fired their muskets into the air that this attack came to a sudden end, with the aggressors leaping into the water and swimming towards land.

Wherever possible, Cook did as directed under his secret instructions, raising the Union flag and taking possession, in the King's name, of any islands he discovered. He even left the chief of Huaheine a small plate stamped with an inscription that read: 'His Britannick Majesty's Ship, Endeavour, Lieutenant Cook, Commander, 16th July, 1769 Huaheine'. He also found previously unknown Raiatea and other islands in this group, which he claimed for Great Britain, before deciding that the time had come to turn south.

One of the reasons for the Admiralty's instruction to sail south in this region was because, while *Dolphin* had been sailing in the waters around Otaheite, crew-members firmly believed that they could see the faint outline of a coast in that direction. Cook, however, would soon confirm that this so-called sighting was, in fact, 'Cape Flyaway', a seafarer's reference to something that always confused lookouts – a bank of dark cloud sitting low on the horizon.

The extent of Banks' observations while in the South Seas was nothing short of vast, and led to him writing a 21,000-word appreciation of the findings he and his 'gentlemen' had made. It detailed the people, their habitats and their customs. Banks noted with interest the large outrigger canoes and catamarans, termed 'pahees' by the islanders, some of which were more than 50 feet in overall length. 'With these boats they venture themselves out of sight of land,' he wrote in wonder. 'They [apparently] go on voyages of twenty days.' His surprise was no doubt caused by the fact that he had no comprehension of the remarkable navigational skills of the Polynesian people. Had Banks made enquiries he would have learned little, if anything, from the natives. Their form of navigation was a natural skill handed down through the generations. It involved the observation of the position of stars at night, the flight paths of birds by day, and the angles of waves. Occasionally a crude map made from twigs or palm fronds was used.

On 15 August 1769, *Endeavour* crossed the Tropic of Capricorn (approximately 350 nautical miles to the south of Tahiti) on her passage south, heading for 40 degrees latitude, as directed. Men were aloft around the clock, to ensure that there was every possible chance of sighting land. From near the masthead the observed horizon was 20 miles or more, while at deck level it was less than half that. Even so, Cook and Banks were confident that no major landmass was in close proximity to *Endeavour*'s position – simply because a large south-westerly swell, which had obviously been generated deep in the

Southern Ocean, was making its presence felt on the vessel, and among some of the crew. Seasickness was, by then, prevalent among the men.

The incessant rolling motion of the ship, combined with the creep of cold weather that was felt more with each day as *Endeavour* pushed towards the higher latitudes, took an unfortunate toll. Banks noted: 'Our hogs and fowls begin to die apace, of the latter a great many, want of proper food and cold which now begins to pinch even us is I suppose the cause …' However, the well-insulated sheep were managing to survive.

For the crew, life on board was miserable, as a series of gales swept in from the west, bringing with them bold and bulging rain-bearing clouds that, all too often, deluged the ship. Each one of these fronts was accompanied by a considerable increase in wind strength, and that demanded a rapid response from the crew on watch: the configuration of sails had to be changed as quickly as possible – either hauled up, reefed, lowered, reset or re-trimmed.

For those on deck who were executing these manoeuvres, there was no escape from the pelting rain and biting cold, while below, where headroom was virtually nonexistent for the fifty or so men off-watch, it was dark, damp and full of fetid air. For some men, the only escape came via the bottle, and on 28 August, Cook recorded that booze beat the man:

> Fresh Gales and Cloudy, with rain on the Latter part. At 10 departed this Life Jno. Rearden [John Reading], Boatswain's Mate; his Death was occasioned by the Boatswain out of mere good Nature giving him part of a Bottle of Rum last night, which it is supposed he drank all at once. He was found to be very much in Liquor last night, but as this was no more than what was common with him when he could get any, no farther notice was taken of him than to put him to Bed, where this morning about 8 o'clock he was found Speechless and past recovery. Wind Northerly; course South …

By 2 September, Cook had fulfilled another one of his orders from the Admiralty. His journal entry that day confirmed for the Lords that he had, by sailing to 40 degrees south, achieved all that was asked of him in the waters to the south of Tahiti, with no tangible result: 'Very strong Gales, with heavy squalls of Wind, hail, and rain. At 4 p.m., being in the Latitude of 40 degrees 22 minutes South, and having not the least Visible signs of land, we wore, and brought too under the Foresail, and reefed the Mainsail ...' In reaching this point and not making any discoveries, Cook had made another mark on history, by disproving the long-held belief that this unexplored part of the world was, most definitely, where the Great South Land would be found.

Savage storms that had mustered in the Southern Ocean were soon pushing *Endeavour* to the edge in survival conditions. Apart from the threat of serious damage to the sails and rig, the ship was being brutally punished by huge breaking seas. The largest of the waves saw the decks buried under tons of white foaming water: each time this occurred, she would rise like a wounded beast, bucking and tossing to rid herself of the bone-chilling water that was cascading across her decks in great torrents. The men on deck, soaked to the skin, could only hang on and hope they weren't swept over the side.

   If there was any solace for the crew, it came with the knowledge that they had a remarkable seafarer for a captain: a man whose experience over tens of thousands of ocean miles gave him the ability to preserve his ship and his crew in threatening predicaments such as this. 'I did intend to have stood to the Southward if the winds had been Moderate,' Cook wrote of his deliberation in these conditions, 'but as the weather was so very Tempestuous I laid aside this design, and thought it more advisable to stand to the Northward into better weather, least we should receive such Damage in our Sails and Rigging as might hinder the further Prosecutions of the Voyage ...'

   Endeavour was held on this course until the weather improved to the degree whereby the helm could be put down and the ship steered to the west, towards the point where Tasman had first sighted New Zealand. By doing that, Cook knew it was inevitable that he would sight land.

While working at his charts and plotting this course, no doubt Cook would have been aware also of the circumstances of Tasman's time in New Zealand, which, in one particular instance, was most disturbing. After first sighting the alps and logging his position off the western coast, Tasman sailed his ship, *Heemskerck*, north in company with the armed support vessel *Zeehaen*, then rounded a promontory (which Cook would later name Cape Farewell) and entered a large bay, where both ships anchored. The small boats were hoisted out and rowed towards shore – an act that the Maoris there saw as an invasion by aliens transported into their world by the most unusual object they had ever seen. A group of Maoris aboard a large canoe was seen to intercept one of *Heemskerck*'s boats, first ramming it before attacking the occupants. Four of Tasman's crew were killed in the fight that followed, hence the name Murderers Bay. It was renamed Golden Bay in 1857 after gold was discovered nearby.

Endeavour sailed a looping course to a point some 600 nautical miles to the north of her turning point at 40 degrees south. It was then that the wind gods finally loosened the grip that had impeded her progress west, delivering conditions that would allow the captain to put his ship on a course that aimed directly at the position given by Tasman for where he saw the alps. Cook was now certain that they would soon see New Zealand, so he made a promise to his crew that he would name a feature on the coast after the person who was first to see it. To encourage alertness, he offered an additional incentive: a gallon of rum.

Understandably, the thought of reaching land brought an increasing level of excitement to the men. On 1 October, Sydney Parkinson, now the sole artist in Banks' research group, noted that it was decided the entire crew should share in a special treat: there were still seventeen sheep remaining in their meat supply, so 'though we had been so long out at sea, in a distant part of the world, we had a roasted leg of mutton, and French beans for dinner, and the fare of Old England afforded a grateful repast'.

Whenever it was calm enough to launch one of the ship's boats, Banks and his team continued to collect whatever samples they could to assist in their research. As a consequence, the great cabin was filled with examples of their finds and abuzz with speculation about what lay ahead, as Banks explained on 3 October:

> Now do I wish that our friends in England could by the assistance of some magical spying glass take a peep at our situation: Dr Solander sits at the Cabin table describing, myself at my Bureau Journalising, between us hangs a large bunch of sea weed, upon the table lays the wood and barnacles; they would see that notwithstanding our different occupations our lips move very often, and without being conjurors might guess that we were talking about what we should see upon the land which there is now no doubt we shall see very soon ...

Indeed, on the morning of 6 October, it became apparent that the ship was nearing the coast. Seals, which, it was known, never venture far from shore, were sighted, as were barnacle-encrusted tree branches; in addition, the colour of the ocean was becoming paler. Suddenly, at 2 pm (now 7 October ship time), a shrill cry came from high in the rig: '*Land ho! Land ho!*' It was Nicholas Young, the surgeon's servant boy, who was at the masthead. For some time, his sharp young eyes had been focused on a faint outline on the distant horizon, off the bow. After a while he convinced himself that what he was seeing was definitely not another 'Cape Flyaway'. This object had not moved nor changed shape ... it was definitely land!

Men on deck shouted below to those off-watch that land had been spotted. In an instant, the sleepy-heads had rolled out of their hammocks and scampered up the companionway ladders leading to the deck – every one of them hoping to see for himself what 'young Nick' had just sighted. They weren't to be rewarded, however, since deck level was far too low to allow visual contact with the horizon at that distance. In fact, with *Endeavour* making less than 3 knots in a very light east-north-easterly breeze, those on deck would have to wait some hours yet. Not until just before sunset could they experience the satisfaction of seeing for the first time what was believed to be New Zealand. According to his journal entry, Banks was not alone in believing that it was so: 'all hands seem to agree that this is certainly the Continent we are in search of.'

Cook, too, had no doubt that this was New Zealand, simply because of *Endeavour*'s relatively close proximity in latitude and longitude to that given by Tasman, even though they were approaching from the east. He could only wonder how great this landmass might be … and was it *Terra Australis Incognita*? That would be known once they had followed the Admiralty's instructions and explored this little-known coast to the best of their ability.

'*View of the Peak, & the adjacent Country, on the West Coast of New Zealand*'. (Sydney Parkinson). State Library of NSW, Mitchell Library Q78/10, a039026.

CHAPTER NINE

A Tale of Two Islands

A light breeze continued to hobble *Endeavour*'s passage towards the eagerly anticipated landfall, where the men would finally get to go ashore and forget the rugged times they had experienced since departing Otaheite almost three months before. Now, as frustratingly slow as their progress was at the time, the onset of darkness caused Cook to call for the sail area to be reduced, and the ship slowed even more.

A safe approach would therefore be made in daylight, before which Cook recorded his first impressions of the immediate area: 'We saw in the Bay several Canoes, People upon the Shore, and some houses in the Country. The land on the Sea Coast is high, with Steep Cliffs; and back inland are very high Mountains. The face of the Country is of a hilly surface, and appears to be clothed with wood and Verdure.'

As it would be revealed, they were approaching New Zealand's North Island, and destined to land at a location about halfway along its eastern coast. Cook noted that it was the afternoon of 9 October 1769 (8 October on today's calendar) when they sailed into the bay he had observed. Once inside, and with *Endeavour* in safe water about 2 miles from shore, he called for the best bower to be released from the cathead and let run to the bottom.

Not surprisingly, the entire crew were overcome with the excitement that came with being confronted by a barely known, unmapped part of the world. Yet this would prove to be an inauspicious start to their exploration of the coastal boundaries of this land.

The Maoris onshore could only have watched in awe as an alien object of proportions and form they had never previously witnessed, yet manned by oddly dressed humans, entered their home waters and anchored in the north-east corner of the bay. The site was just off the entrance to a small river, the Turanganui, which, at 300 yards in length, is claimed by many to be the shortest river in the southern hemisphere. Today the town of Gisborne stands on its eastern bank.

Eager to acquaint himself with the local people, Cook boarded the pinnace with Banks and Solander, and headed for shore, accompanied by a party of armed men aboard the yawl. As they reached the beach, the Maoris retreated hurriedly towards their huts, about 300 yards inland, so Cook had some men remain to protect the boats while he and others set off in pursuit, in the hope that they could establish some form of dialogue. But while this was happening, other Maoris emerged from hiding 'in the woods' and made a move to attack the four men manning the yawl, as Cook later reported:

> The coxswain of the Pinnace, who had the charge of the Boats, seeing this, fired 2 Muskets over their Heads; the first made them stop and Look round them, but the 2nd they took no notice of; upon which a third was fired and killed one of them upon the Spot just as he was going to dart his spear at the Boat. At this the other three stood motionless for a Minute or two, seemingly quite surprised; wondering, no doubt, what it was that had thus killed their Comrade; but as soon as they recovered themselves they made off, dragging the Dead body a little way and then left it.

On hearing the shots coming from the beach, Cook immediately returned to the boats and ordered all his men back to the ship. The following morning, after seeing Maoris gathered onshore once more, he decided to try again to make peaceful contact:

> Mr Banks, Dr Solander, and myself at first only landed, and went to the side of the river, the natives being got together on the opposite side. We called to them in the George Island Language, but they answered us by flourishing their weapons over their heads and dancing, as we supposed, the War Dance; upon this we retired until the marines [who were carrying the Union Jack] were landed which I ordered to be drawn up about 200 yards behind us. We then went again to the river side, [where] Tupia spoke to them in his own Language, and it was an agreeable surprise to us to find that they perfectly understood him. After some little conversation had passed one of them swam over to us, and after him 20 or 30 more; these last brought their Arms with them, which the first man did not. We made them every one presents, but this did not satisfy them; they wanted but everything we had about us, particularly our Arms, and made several attempts to snatch them out of our hands. Tupia told us several times, as soon as they came over, to take care of ourselves for they were not our friends; and this we very soon found, for one of them snatched Mr. Green's hanger [short sword] from him and would not give it up; this encouraged the rest to be more insolent, and seeing others coming over to join them, I ordered the man who had taken the Hanger to be fired at, which was accordingly done, and wounded in such a manner that he died soon after.

Another three Maoris were wounded before this confrontation ended. Cook then ordered his men back to the ship.

The words of the president of the Royal Society, the Earl of Morton, which were imparted to Cook prior to his departure from England, must have been ringing in the captain's ears. His Lordship had suggested most strongly that Cook and his men do everything within their power to be tolerant of, and kind to, the indigenous people they met during their journey. Unfortunately, this first encounter with the Maoris of New Zealand was in direct contrast to what they had experienced with the islanders of Otaheite. Even so, the captain would before long reveal an inherent wisdom that would, throughout his life as a seafarer and explorer, put him in a position where he could measure a moment and, more often than not, transform a dangerous confrontation with the indigenous people into one of cautious understanding and respect between two distinctly different cultures.

Cook remained determined to try to make peace with these people, but what would follow was almost beyond belief. The following day, when aboard one of *Endeavour*'s small tenders, he attempted to intercept two canoes carrying a small group of Maoris that were out on the bay, but they would have no part of the visitors, and paddled as hard as they could to get away. Shots were then fired over their heads in a bid to stop them, but that, too, failed. Instead, it had the opposite effect: they turned and prepared to attack the visitors. 'This obliged us to fire upon them,' a regretful Cook later explained, 'and unfortunately either two or three were killed and one wounded.'

However, three young men, who had jumped overboard from a canoe, were retrieved and taken back to *Endeavour*, 'where they was Clothed and Treated with all imaginable kindness ... and to the Surprise of everybody became at once as cheerful and as merry as if they had been with their own Friends'. Cook reflected on the incident in his journal:

> I am aware that most Humane men who have not
> experienced things of this nature will Censure my
> Conduct in firing upon the People in their Boat, nor do

> I myself think that the reason I had for seizing upon her
> will at all justify me; and had I thought that they would
> have made the Least Resistance I would not have come
> near them; but as they did, I was not to stand still and
> suffer either myself or those that were with me to be
> knocked on the head …

This life-threatening confrontation placed an equally
burdensome load of emotion on Banks, who was in the thick of
the action alongside Cook. He had been the first to fire at, and
strike down, the 'indian' who was making off with Green's
short sword the previous day. He was also there for the skirmish
with the men in the canoes. This was the closing entry in his
journal for the day: 'Thus ended the most disagreeable day My
life has yet seen, black be the mark for it and heaven send that
such may never return to embitter future reflection.'

The three men were returned to the beach the following
morning, but they refused to part company with Cook and his
group, 'pretending that they should fall into the hands of their
enemies who would kill and eat them'. So they were taken back
to the ship. Soon afterwards, however, when Cook and his men
were challenged by three large groups of Maoris on the beach –
almost 200 in all – Tupia was able 'to Parley with them' to the
point where the friendly intentions of the visitors were
eventually recognised.

It was Cook's plan to commence his coastal exploration of
this land on the morning of 11 October, so the evening before,
he again put the three local men ashore. Much to his relief, this
time they appeared to be welcomed by their own people. Also,
before weighing anchor, the captain did as he had promised and
named a prominent coastal feature in this region, the headland at
the south-western end of the bay, 'Young Nick's Head', in
honour of the boy who first sighted the coast. (Although there
was no record of him receiving the promised gallon of rum, it is
assumed that it was handed over.) Cook chose to name the
expanse of water where they were anchored 'Poverty Bay'

because, he explained, 'it afforded us no one thing we wanted' in the form of foodstuff, except for a few herbs that could be used for the prevention of scurvy.

The shrill of the bosun's whistle, then the corresponding call that the bower was aweigh, came at 6 am. While the monotonous sound of the wooden pawls on the windlass encouraged the men who were working hard to haul in the heavily tarred bower cable, other men were busy on deck at the three masts, hauling down sails so they could be set and trimmed to best suit the gentle northerly breeze that was fanning across the bay. At the same time the captain stood on the quarterdeck, watching every manoeuvre that came as a response to orders from Lieutenants Hickes and Gore. He had already advised the sailing master, Molyneux, what the desired course to the south would be – one that would, in general, follow the flow of the coastline.

Endeavour's offing from the shore would depend on the depth of water and the all-important surveillance from lookouts stationed near the masthead. It was certainly hoped that the course would be close enough for observations to be made that would lead to the creation of relatively accurate preliminary charts and notes relating to the coastline. The key part of this initial exploration was to sail no more than 150 nautical miles to the south, to around 41 degrees latitude, a position that would roughly correspond with the latitude that Tasman was on when he made his first sighting of land when approaching from the west. Then, depending on what had been found and what could be seen to the south, Cook would decide to either continue sailing south or return to the north and explore the coast in that direction.

While the Yorkshireman probably gave it little thought, this was a momentous period in his life as a mariner and explorer: he was about to embark on his first true voyage of discovery on which he would explore a foreign landmass, the extent of which was hitherto unknown to Europeans. It meant he was also highly likely to make a considerable contribution to the map of the world.

After two days, though, Cook had come to the disappointing realisation that one of his biggest challenges during this time would be dealing with the New Zealand Maoris, who continually demonstrated high levels of aggression. *Endeavour* was then less than 100 nautical miles south of Poverty Bay, and in a position similar to that experienced on his day of arrival. Some of the Maoris they were encountering were peaceably inclined and accommodating, but at this time the majority alongside the ship were chanting war songs while they shook their 'pikes' (spears) in defiance, and threatened to kill every man aboard *Endeavour*.

On approach to Hawke's Bay – which Cook named after the First Lord of the Admiralty, Sir Edward Hawke – the wind went from fair to nothing, and this encouraged a group of Maoris to come offshore in their canoes. Much to the pleasure of Cook and Banks, these people were friendly; they accepted an invitation to board the ship, then when it came time to leave, they departed without rancour. However, they unknowingly left three of their group behind and, quite amazingly, did not return to collect them. Of more surprise perhaps, the guests showed no alarm, and were quite happy to stay aboard until the next morning. It was soon after sunrise when men on deck noticed another canoe in close proximity, so they hailed it to come alongside in order that the guests could be taken back to the coast. Yet the Maoris would not approach until their three compatriots assured them, as Cook noted, 'we did not Eat men'.

In a foretaste of many more incidents over the ensuing weeks, the first attempts to attack the ship came on 13 and 14 October, one involving some 150 Maoris aboard nine very large canoes. A prompt display of British firepower – first musket shots in their general direction, then a booming shot from a 4-pounder carriage gun mounted on deck – resulted in the attackers paddling away in great haste.

A far more dramatic situation developed on the 15th, when *Endeavour* was next to a prominent headland at the southern end of Hawke's Bay. The episode took place when some of those on board began bartering with a group of Maoris, as Cook recalled:

> ... one of the Boats came alongside and offered us some more fish. The Indian Boy Tiata, Tupia's Servant, being over the side, they seized hold of him, pulled him into the Boat and endeavoured to carry him off; this obliged us to fire upon them, which gave the Boy an opportunity to jump overboard. We brought the Ship too, lowered a Boat into the Water, and took him up unhurt. Two or three paid for this daring attempt with the loss of their lives, and many more would have suffered had it not been for fear of killing the Boy. This affair occasioned my giving this point of land the name of Cape Kidnappers ...

After two more days of slow progress, *Endeavour* was at 40 degrees 34 minutes south, and here Cook deliberated with others about their observations so far and what they might expect to find ahead. As a result, he made a decision on the next stage of their exploration that would prove to be very astute:

> Seeing no likelihood of meeting with a Harbour, and the face of the Country Visibly altering for the worse, I thought that the standing farther to the South would not be attended with any Valuable discovery, but would be losing of Time, which might be better employed and with a greater Probability of success in examining the Coast to the Northward. The Bluff head or high point of land we were abreast off at Noon I have called Cape Turnagain because here we returned ...

During their passage to the south, both Cook and Banks were impressed by the snow-capped mountain ranges they were seeing to the west, many with their peaks protruding above elongated banks of white cloud. Later, once *Endeavour* had turned around and was to the north of Poverty Bay, they also became increasingly enthused by the number of bays and inlets they were then observing.

A potential tragedy was averted at Anaura Bay, north of Gisborne, when Banks, Solander and Tupia went ashore in the ship's boats, which had been sent to find water. Late in the day, some of the Maoris offered to transfer the trio back to the ship in one of their canoes, but it was swamped while trying to make its way out through the surf. The visitors were then forced to stay ashore for the night. In the morning they 'embarked again and came without incident to the ship'.

It was too rough for *Endeavour* to anchor there, so Cook backtracked to Tolaga Bay, 25 nautical miles north of Poverty Bay, where they were also exceedingly well received by the indigenous people. Once ashore, Banks and his men went 'botanizing' – collecting samples of the flora as well as some artefacts – while Cook did his own exploring. Of note, he wrote, 'We saw no four-footed Animals, either Tame or Wild, or signs of any, except Dogs and Rats' (which history would later confirm were the only quadrupeds in New Zealand). He also had some hands collect the wild celery that they found in what is now known as Cook's Cove, a wedge-shaped inlet at the southern end of this bay: 'This [celery] is found here in great plenty, and I have caused it to be boiled with Portable Soup and Oatmeal every morning for the people's breakfast … I look upon it to be very wholesome and a great Antiscorbutic.' The same cove proved to hold a treasure trove of natural wonderments for Banks et al., as well as a good source for water and wood. Twelve tons of water was put aboard the ship along with close to three boat-loads of firewood.

On 31 October, Cook made numerous observations regarding a 500-foot-high bluff that his ship was rounding at the time while riding a fresh south–easterly gale: 'This point of Land I have called East Cape, because I have great reason to think that it is the Eastern-most land on this whole Coast.' His supposition would subsequently prove correct. Then, after clearing that cape, *Endeavour* sailed through the night on a gentle, arcing course to the west over a distance of 33 nautical miles until, at 9 am, another impressive 500-foot cape was abeam. This one had a profile that sloped down to the coast. It so happened that while Cook and others were detailing the primary features of this very conspicuous landform, another small armada of canoes carrying hostile Maoris made an approach from the shore, obviously with the intention of attacking this strange vessel. One canoe was so large that it carried sixty warmongering warriors. Their display of aggression increased as the canoe closed on the ship – the men were chanting songs of defiance while making powerful and threatening gestures with their spears. Cook had tired of this all-too-regular sabre-rattling, so he responded in what would be seen in this era as an appropriate, but not provocative, manner:

> ... it fully appeared that they came with no friendly intentions; and I at this Time being very busy, and had no inclination to stay upon deck to watch their Motions, I ordered a Grape shot to be fired a little wide of them. This made them pull off a little, and then they got together either to consult what to do or to look about them. Upon this I ordered a round shott to be fired over their heads, which frightened them to that degree that I believe they did not think themselves safe until they got ashore. This occasioned our calling the Point of land off which this happened, Cape Runaway ...

This was the day when the men aboard *Endeavour* saw their first 'double canoe' in New Zealand waters: a large catamaran measuring about 70 feet overall. It was crowded with Maoris, and stayed in company with the ship until dark, then turned back towards shore – 'but not before they had thrown a few stones', Cook noted. This last episode occurred while *Endeavour* was crossing what Cook would name Bay of Plenty, because of the fertile appearance of the coastal strip and hills beyond.

Much to everyone's surprise, the same canoe returned the next morning, now under sail. Its occupants approached as close as they dared to *Endeavour*, and immediately commenced a bombardment of rocks onto her deck. A warning shot from a musket-bearing marine brought the assault to a rapid conclusion, but these friend-or-foe confrontations involving up to forty-five canoes at one time would continue to occur on a daily basis.

After crossing Bay of Plenty, *Endeavour* followed the eastern coastline of what fifty years later would become known as the Coromandel Peninsula (named after the RN ship), and rounded another rugged headland midway along its length. She then entered a 6-mile-wide bay where Banks described the shoreline as 'barren and rocky but many Islands were in sight'. Cook began easing his ship around the rim of this bay under reduced sail while searching for an inlet that would provide a well-protected anchorage.

Again, the visitors were being shadowed by several canoes, all the way to where Cook elected to anchor, and always remaining a safe distance away. The locals held that position throughout the afternoon, watching things happen on this strange vessel that were way beyond their comprehension. They saw the anchor being lowered, figures scampering through the rig and others working on deck, all making sure that everything was shipshape. It was not until nightfall that these Maoris moved within hailing distance to deliver a message. As the captain noted with interest, they were 'so generous as to tell us that they would come and attack us in the morning'.

They lied. Instead, the warriors returned in the depth of night with the intention of raiding what they expected to be a ship full of sleeping sailors. But the men standing watch on deck saw them approaching and raised the alarm. The would-be attackers could only abandon their plan and hurriedly paddle off into the darkness.

Cook's reason to name this expanse of water Mercury Bay was simple: it was here that they would go ashore and set up a base to observe the transit of Mercury, on Thursday, 9 November. If successful, this would allow the captain to establish a very accurate longitude for their location at the time – a valuable reference point for ongoing navigation. These transits occur at a rate of thirteen or fourteen each century, either in May or November. They are more frequent than the transit of Venus because Mercury, being closer to the sun, completes more orbits.

Good fortune played into Cook's hands when an old man, 'Torava', who was obviously a Maori chief, came aboard not long after *Endeavour* had anchored. He was feted with presents, including cloth and iron, after which, with Tupia acting as an interpreter, he explained that his people were 'very much afraid' of the visitors. Not surprised to hear this, Cook then made an assurance: 'we promised friendship if they would supply us with provisions at their own price.' It was a promise that brought the desired result because, when the Englishmen went ashore after breakfast that morning, 'The Indians who were on one side [of the river] made all the signs of friendship imaginable, beckoning to us to land among them.'

On the day of the transit, Cook, Second Lieutenant Hickes and others took their instruments ashore and set up a position where they could best observe the event. They landed along the south of the bay at what is now Cooks Beach, near the Purangi Estuary. The weather could not have been more favourable – clear skies – but regrettably, while preparations were underway, the attention of all those onshore was drawn to the sound of gunfire emanating from the ship. It came after a large number of native canoes went alongside *Endeavour* to engage in bartering, and a subsequent incident had fatal consequences. One of the Maoris, who had been given a piece of cloth by Third Lieutenant Gore, then refused to hand over the cloak he had agreed to trade. Instead, the canoe moved away from the ship, and according to Banks, 'they immediately began to sing their war song as if to defy any revenge those on board might choose to take; this enraged the … lieutenant so much that he levelled a musket at the man who had still got the cloth in his hand and shot him dead.'

Having received a report on the incident, the captain later expressed his disappointment: 'Mr Gore fired a Musket at them, and, from what I can learn, killed the Man who took the Cloth; it did not meet with my approbation, because I thought the Punishment a little too severe for the Crime, and we had now been long Enough acquainted with these People to know how to Chastise Trifling faults like this without taking away their Lives …' Despite the incident, Cook and his men were able to maintain what he described as 'a great deal of good nature and friendship' with the Maoris, who, as Banks noted, 'acknowledged that the dead man deserved his punishment'.

This would prove to be another location where there was a proliferation of food, including cockles, clams, oysters, fish and lobsters. Banks proclaimed the oysters as being 'as good oysters as ever came from Colchester and about the same size', and, when it came to the lobsters: 'We have had them in tolerable plenty in almost every place we have been in and [these] are certainly the largest and best I have ever eat.' There was also ample wild fowl to be had, including shags – or cormorants – of which Banks and his party managed to shoot twenty. This quarry was then broiled for a meal where everyone declared 'they were excellent food'.

Endeavour remained at Mercury Bay for eleven days, during which time Banks' team explored, sketched and detailed the people and their surroundings extensively. Meanwhile, Cook conducted surveys on behalf of the Admiralty, for incorporation into charts of the region that would later be recognised as exemplary. He also visited a small fort that the local people had built to defend themselves in the event of an attack from other tribes. This particular contact with the Maoris finally reinforced what for Cook had been a growing belief for some weeks now, about which he wrote: 'they confirm the Custom of Eating their Enemies, so that this is a thing no longer to be doubted.'

In his role as ship's captain, Cook put his men on parade,

had them clean the vessel from stem to stern, and ordered that the rig, sails and equipment be checked thoroughly. On board *Endeavour*, he continued to enforce strict discipline among the crew, his log recording one instance that necessitated the lash: 'Samuel Jones, Seaman, having been confined since Saturday last for refusing to come upon deck when all hands were called, and afterwards refused to Comply with the orders of the officers on deck, he was this morning punished with 12 lashes and remitted back to confinement.'

As stipulated in his orders from the Admiralty, Cook laid claim to the previously uncharted territory on behalf of his sovereign. 'Before we left this bay,' he reported, 'we cut out upon one of the Trees near the Watering Place the Ship's Name, date, etc., and, after displaying the English Colours, I took formal possession of the place in the Name of His Majesty ...'

In 1879, 110 years after Cook's time in Mercury Bay, New Zealand author John White published *The Ancient History of the Maori*, a remarkable six volumes covering the lives and traditions of New Zealand's first settlers. Their heritage dates back to more than 500 years before the European visitors' arrival there, when Polynesians crossed the ocean in their large canoes and settled in the new land. In his fifth volume, White printed an historic account of Cook's stay, as recalled by an old chief, Te Horeta te Taniwha, who was a young boy living in the main settlement of Whitianga when *Endeavour* was in the bay. It provides a valuable insight into the impressions that the Englishmen made on the local people. It was as if they were space invaders.

> In the days long past, when I was a very little boy, a
> vessel came to Whitianga ... and when our old men saw
> the ship they said it was a tupua [a supernatural object
> carrying goblins], and the people on board were strange
> beings. The ship came to anchor, and the boats pulled
> onshore. As our old men looked at the manner in which
> they came onshore, the rowers pulling with their backs
> to the bows of the boat, the old people said, 'Yes, it is

so: these people are goblins; their eyes are at the back of their heads; they pull onshore with their backs to the land to which they are going'. When these goblins came onshore we [the children and women] took notice of them, but we ran away from them into the forest, and the warriors alone stayed in the presence of those goblins; but, as the goblins stayed some time, and did not do any evil to our braves, we came back one by one, and gazed at them, and we stroked their garments with our hands, and we were pleased with the whiteness of their skins and the blue eyes of some of them.

The goblins had walking-sticks which they carried about with them, and when we arrived at the bare dead trees where the shags roost at night and have their nests, the goblins lifted the walking-sticks up and pointed them at the birds, and in a short time thunder was heard to crash and a flash of lightning was seen, and a shag fell from the trees; and we children were terrified, and fled, and rushed into the forest, and left the goblins all alone. They laughed, and waved their hands to us, and in a short time the bravest of us went back to where the goblins were, and handled the bird, and saw that it was dead. But what had killed it?

After the ship had been lying at anchor … [they] made many of us desirous to go and see the home of the goblins [on board *Endeavour*].

There was one supreme man in that ship. We knew that he was the lord of the whole by his perfect gentlemanly and noble demeanour. He seldom spoke, but some of the goblins spoke much. But this man did not utter many words. His language was a hissing sound, and the words he spoke were not understood by us in the least.

At 7 am on 15 November, *Endeavour* weighed anchor and made sail in a light westerly breeze, heading out of Mercury Bay and resuming a course to the north. After sailing for three full days, the ship rounded yet another promontory, this one being named by the captain after one of his former commodores, Lord Colville. It was at the head of a large expanse of water (now known as Hauraki Gulf), which, as Cook and his men would soon discover, extended 50 nautical miles to the south.

After shoal water caused *Endeavour* to be anchored at a point around 30 nautical miles in, Cook and Banks, hoping to explore some of the interior of the country, took to the boats and rowed another 20 nautical miles to the gulf's south-eastern corner. There they discovered a river, which they investigated by boat for more than 10 miles inland. The river, and the heavily wooded forests that often lined its shores, reminded the pair of London's River Thames, so they gave it that name.

Endeavour was forced to remain at anchor in the Firth of Thames for some days due to foul weather, then, once conditions improved, she made haste to the north. All on board were captivated by the spectacular scenery they were observing off the ship's port side, particularly around Bream Bay, with its backdrop of bold, high peaks. But the peace was broken when local Maoris once again harassed the ship.

The most menacing situation came after *Endeavour* rounded a headland that Cook recorded as Cape Brett – so named, in an apparent exercise in wordplay, after Rear Admiral Sir Piercy Brett, because one of the rocks there had a large hole 'pierced' through it. Having cleared this cape by a safe margin, *Endeavour* entered another area of great natural beauty, which Cook christened with the logical title 'Bay of Islands'. No sooner had she anchored off the island of Motuarohia, however, than she was surrounded by an exceptionally large fleet of canoes.

In his usual manner, the captain made every effort to confirm his peaceful intentions. After inviting some of the Maoris to join him aboard the ship so they could be presented with gifts, he was alerted to the fact that others, still in their canoes, were trying to steal the anchor buoy. Their efforts were soon curtailed after muskets and cannons were fired their way.

Following this incident, Cook decided that it would be prudent to move the ship farther offshore. Cook, Banks and Solander were then rowed ashore 'in the Pinnace and Yawl, manned and Armed', still hoping to engage the local people in friendly discussion – yet their reception was far from that.

From the moment they stepped onto the sand, the visitors were surrounded by hundreds of agitated Maoris. Some immediately took up their glazed-eye war dance, while others tried to seize the boats that had brought these foreigners ashore. Realising that an extremely dangerous confrontation could develop at any moment, Cook had Hickes fire his musket over their heads, but it had little effect. By now, the threat had escalated into a situation in which the shore party fully expected to be attacked; worse than that, along with the few hundred Maoris on the beach, hundreds more were seen lining the hills around the cove. As before, musket-fire into the air proved no deterrent, and it wasn't until *Endeavour* – from about three-quarters of a mile away – blasted cannonballs over the heads of the aggressors that they scattered in every direction.

'In this Skirmish only one or two of them was Hurt with small Shot,' Cook recalled in his journal, 'for I avoided killing any one of them as much as Possible, and for that reason withheld our people from firing.' The tactic worked, because later that day, when he met with a group of the Maoris, he found them to be 'meek as lambs'.

After departing from this large, picturesque bay on 5 December, *Endeavour* sailed slowly into the night on a gentle breeze – but the casual nature of the scene soon turned to one of concern when the wind went calm. It became apparent that *Endeavour* was entering a danger zone: she was being carried by a fast-running current towards a nearby rocky island. The captain ordered that the boats be put over the side and launched as quickly as possible, so they could try to tow the ship away from threat. This effort, coupled with the benefit of a soft southerly breeze, which appeared unannounced, combined to save the day.

About an hour later, though, when the man in the chains swinging the lead was reporting the water depth to be 17 fathoms, a sudden, unexpected thump reverberated through the ship. There was a look of shock on everyone's face: *Endeavour* had struck an isolated submerged rock less than 5 fathoms below the surface! Good fortune was with them again, as the contact proved to be a glancing blow: the ship slid back into deep water. Men had already darted down the companionway ladders and into the bilge to see if the hull had been breached. They returned to the quarterdeck with the news that all was well. The hull remained sound.

Rather than there being a let-up from such anxious moments, the crew then experienced a tormenting two weeks of sailing as *Endeavour* battled adverse headwinds and fierce gales. It was enough to test the mettle of any seafarer, but Cook, as frustrated as he was, pressed on. It took ten days to slog just 100 nautical miles upwind to the north-west – but there was worse to come. On 18 December the ship had 'not gained one Inch to windward in this last 24 hours', the captain reported. The only cause for encouragement came via the few canoes that ventured offshore, despite the conditions, to observe this incomprehensible vessel. When they came within hailing distance, their Maori crews provided some welcome news: only a few miles further to the north-west, the coast turned westwards, and once there the pain that came with this upwind sailing should come to an end.

A day later, *Endeavour* was rounding that much-desired corner of land, and accordingly Cook declared: 'The Point of Land … I have called North Cape, judging it to be the Northernmost Extremity of this Country …'

Unfortunately, though, there was no reprieve from the weather. Conditions remained nothing short of atrocious, and as a result, the busiest men on the ship were the sail-makers, plying needle and thread to patch and repair torn and tattered wet sails that had proved to be no match for the howling winds. But, as demanding as that task might have been, it was the men aloft near the masthead, the lookouts, who suffered most. Biting wind and rain speared through their clothing while they clung desperately to the rigging each time the mast lurched into a wild gyration, arcing through the air in response to the impact that a gigantic wave, or a savage gust of wind, delivered to the ship. These crewmen were forever peering through the wind-driven rain, hoping beyond hope that any threatening outline of land, or breaking surf indicating the presence of a reef, would emerge through the dim and murky curtain that was the limit of their vision, and allow them to take evasive action.

Before long, Cook had had enough: he decided it best to abandon their westerly course and head north-west, away from land. The move eased the pressure on the crew for just twenty-four hours, until the lookouts hailed that they could see Three Kings Islands, located 30 nautical miles to the north-west of Cape Maria Van Diemen. Tasman had discovered and named these features when cruising north along the west coast of New Zealand 126 years earlier, before he'd headed off into the Pacific.

It was not until Christmas Eve that the storms finally parted company with *Endeavour* and her weather-weary crew. Banks subsequently reported on the various stages of that year's Christmas celebrations, from preparation through consumption to aftermath:

> Land in sight, an Island or rather several small ones most probably 3 Kings. Calm most of the Day: myself in a boat shooting in which I had good success, killing chiefly several Gannets or Solan Geese. As it was the humour of the ship to keep Christmas in the old fashioned way it was resolved of them to make a Goose pie for tomorrow's dinner.
>
> Christmas day: Our Goose pie was eat with great approbation and in the Evening all hands were as Drunk as our forefathers used to be upon the like occasion.
>
> December 26: This morn all heads ached with yesterday's debauch.

The last thing that everyone aboard *Endeavour* would have expected to see at this time was another ship – but it almost happened.

While the Englishmen were enjoying their Christmas Day festivities, just 100 nautical miles south-east of their position, a 650-ton French 36-gunner, *St Jean Baptiste*, was at anchor. Her presence resulted from the ship's captain, Jean-François-Marie de Surville, a merchant seafarer, wanting to find a 'rich land' that the British had reportedly discovered in the South Pacific – undoubtedly Otaheite. After de Surville had departed from India and sailed to the east, scurvy became rampant among his crew, so, using Tasman's charts, he opted to head towards New Zealand, where his men might be able to recuperate. In December 1769, *St Jean Baptiste* made landfall on the northern part of New Zealand's west coast; by Christmas, after sailing west to east around North Cape, the French ship had anchored at Doubtless Bay, 30 miles north of the Bay of Islands. In doing so, the Frenchmen traversed the same waters that *Endeavour* was sailing at the time. Despite de Surville's efforts, his men continued to die, so he decided to sail directly to Peru in the hope that medical assistance could be found there.

For Cook and his crew, the break from the fiendish weather was all too brief, at just forty-eight hours.

> … we made Sail … under the Foresail and Mainsail, but was soon obliged to take in the latter as it began to blow very hard and increased in such a manner that by 8 o'Clock it was a mere Hurricane attended with rain and the Sea run prodigious high. At this time we wore the Ship … under a Reefed Mainsail, but this was scarcely done before the Main Tack [a corner of the mainsail] gave way and we were glad to take in the Mainsail and lay-to under the Mizzen staysail.

Even so, Cook was able to sail a course to the south – something he desperately wanted to achieve after the navigation plots he'd placed on his charts had convinced him 'that the Northern part of this land must be very narrow'. Referring to the 50-mile-long narrow neck of land known today as Aupouri Peninsula, his theory would soon prove to be correct.

His first challenge was to fix the position of Cape Maria van Diemen, and this he did with incredible precision. Modern technology reveals that his latitude was exact and his longitude only 3 miles out. It was a similar case when he plotted North Cape. These achievements stand to this day as part of the enduring testimony to Cook's outstanding ability as a navigator.

The wind turned light to such a degree that Cape Maria van Diemen remained in sight for three days, which gave Cook ample time to reflect on the horribly wild weather that he, his men and the ship had endured since rounding Cape Brett. It had been thirty-four days since they were at that cape, which was only 100 nautical miles away via the most direct course. In his journal, Cook bemoaned the adverse conditions over that period, while noting how much worse it could have been for *Endeavour*: 'it will hardly be credited that in the midst of summer ... such a gale of wind as we have had could have happened, which for its strength and continuance was such as I hardly was ever in before. Fortunately at this time we were at a good distance from land otherwise it might have proved fatal to us ...'

Incredibly, having departed from Massacre Bay in December 1642 and headed north up the western coast of the North Island, Abel Tasman had not landed anywhere else. So, early in January 1770, it was Cook's opportunity to gather some of the finer details, although the weather would make it a hostile lee shore for much of the 350-plus nautical miles that lay ahead. He explained the limitations this imposed for the second day of the new year, 'having no land in sight, not daring to go near it as the wind blew fresh right onshore and a high rolling Sea from the Same Quarter, and knowing that there was no

Harbour that we could put into in case we were Caught upon a lee shore'.

Two days later, a similar circumstance saw the great seafarer apply some self-admonishment:

> Nothing is to be seen but long sand Hills, with hardly
> any Green thing upon them, and the great Sea which
> the prevailing Westerly winds impel upon the Shore
> must render this a very Dangerous Coast. This I am so
> fully sensible of, that … once clear of it I am determined
> not to come so near Again, if I can possibly avoid it,
> unless we have a very favourable wind indeed …

The fact that at no time while sailing along this coast did they encounter any native canoes also confirmed the inhospitable nature that the region presented for seafarers.

It was not until 8 January that wind conditions – a light north-easterly – gave Cook the necessary confidence to take up a course relatively close to the coast. From a few leagues offshore, Banks saw the land as being fertile, yet the savage nature of the westerly and south-westerly gales precluded any thought of making landfall. Nevertheless, Cook was able to map the coast in a general sense by calculating the angles of the shoreline.

These coastal highlights continued to be noted; then, on 13 January, there came the most remarkable feature of all, according to Banks: 'This morn soon after day break we had a momentary view of our great hill the top of which was thick covered with snow … How high it may be I do not take upon me to judge, but it is certainly the noblest hill I have ever seen …' An equally impressed Cook recorded in his journal: 'at 5 a.m. saw for a few Minutes the Top of the Peaked Mountain above the Clouds … I have named it Mount Egmont in honour of the Earl of Egmont. The shore under the foot of this Mountain forms a large Cape which I have named Cape Egmont …'

Banks had an additional observation, concerning the 'very pleasant and fertile' countryside inland from the mountain, noting that 'with our glasses we could distinguish many white lumps in companies of 50 or 60 together which probably were either stones or tufts of grass but bore much the resemblance of flocks of sheep'. In fact, these were unusual white plants that are now referred to as 'vegetable sheep'.

On 15 January, it was apparent to Cook that the coastline was disappearing into the distance in a south-easterly direction, and not realising at this stage that New Zealand comprised two main islands, he understandably assumed he was entering a 'very broad and deep bay'. His immediate objective, though, was to find a suitable anchorage where many pressing tasks could be undertaken. For one, with it being six months since sailing away from Matavai Bay, *Endeavour*'s speed was now being impeded by the considerable amount of weed and crustacean that had taken up residence on the hull below the waterline: she needed to be careened so that the bottom could be scrubbed. There were also some defects to be repaired, and there was a need for wood and water to be collected. Finally, the captain was all too aware that a period of respite onshore would be much appreciated by the men as an escape from their claustrophobic life below deck.

The wind strength and direction overnight propelled *Endeavour* more to the east than hoped, but at daylight on 16 January, the eyes of those on deck were greeted by the sight of spectacular, almost fjord-like inlets; some of them 'miserably barren' and other parts heavily wooded and backed by imposing hills. The wind had died by then, and there was a considerable tidal current running, so, to avoid rocks that were all-too apparent, the captain ordered that the boats be launched to tow the ship towards shore and a suitable anchorage. At two o'clock, *Endeavour* was securely moored in a 'very snug cove' on the north-western side of the inlet. It featured a beautiful, 200-yard-long sandy beach, and the hills surrounding it were 'an entire forest'. History records that the Englishmen had entered the

Marlborough Sounds region, at the top of New Zealand's South Island.

No sooner had the anchor cable been made fast than several canoes filled with Maoris paddled up to the ship and made their presence felt by heaving some stones onto *Endeavour*'s side. That done, there was an immediate about-face when Tupia engaged the men in a form of dialogue and invited them aboard the ship – an invitation some accepted, but only briefly. 'After this they retired to their town,' Banks recalled, before detailing his own activities: 'we went ashore abreast of the ship where we found good wood and water and caught more fish in the seine than all our people could possibly destroy, besides shooting a multitude of Shags ...'

The following morning, Cook ordered that the ship be eased onto the beach and careened. While this was being done, about 100 Maoris arrived in canoes and gave every sign that they would become troublesome. The captain's response was swift: he called for some small shot to be fired at one of the ringleaders, and from that moment on, they stayed a good distance away.

On 17 January, after the ship had been careened again so that the opposite side of the hull could be scrubbed, Cook, Banks and others left in one of the boats to do some exploring. They spotted a few Maoris onshore in a small bay and went to join them, only to be confronted with more chilling evidence of cannibalism, as Cook recorded in his journal:

> Soon after we landed we meet with two or three of the
> Natives who not long before must have been regaling
> themselves upon human flesh, for I got from one of
> them the bone of the Fore arm of a Man or Woman
> which was quite fresh, and the flesh had been but lately
> picked off, which they told us they had eat; they gave us
> to understand that but a few days before they had taken,
> Killed, and Eat a Boat's Crew of their Enemies or
> strangers, for I believe they look upon all strangers as

> Enemies … There was not one of us that had the least
> doubt but what these people were cannibals …

The careening work was completed by the 18th, and over the
next few days *Endeavour*'s crew were set new tasks. These
included repairing and filling water casks, caulking the topsides,
cutting firewood, harvesting grass for feed for the sheep they
were carrying for a meat supply, and firing up the forge so that
broken ironwork could be repaired, especially the all-important
braces for the tiller: without them the ship could not be steered
properly.

At one stage, while the men were busy going about their
duties, Maoris came alongside the ship offering to sell the heads
of men 'they had lately killed; both the Hairy Scalps and Skin of
the faces were on'. There was no suggestion of cannibalism in
this instance, and Banks bought one of the heads to add to his
wide-ranging and extensive collection of items pertaining to
this voyage, a collection he would present to the Royal Society
once back in London. Whenever possible, he and Solander
were onshore collecting plants, mosses and other samples of
flora that took their interest, while Parkinson busied himself
with sketching anything that appealed to his artistic eye.

On 23 January, Cook's exploration of this region took on a
level of intrigue. In the company of one of the sailors, he
climbed to the top of a high hill on Arapawa Island, 6 nautical
miles by boat to the south-east of where *Endeavour* lay at
anchor. He later wrote that he was soon 'abundantly
recompensed for the trouble I had in ascending the Hill, for
from it I saw what I took to be the Eastern Sea, and a Strait or
passage from it into the Western Sea'.

This assumption led to Cook, Banks and Solander going
ashore as often as possible to climb other hills in the hope of
gaining different perspectives on what they were increasingly
confident was a strait; all three men were almost certain that
they were now on a separate large island from the one on which

Endeavour had landed after sailing in from Otaheite. Unfortunately, sometimes due to 'impenetrable woods', they were unable to achieve a definitive answer – although, an animated conversation with one of the Maoris they came upon strongly supported the existence of a strait. Cook decided that the only way to prove the point was to sail *Endeavour* to the east from what he would name Queen Charlotte Sound, in honour of the wife of King George III. The bay where the ship was careened was placed on the captain's chart as Ship Cove, and the strait they were about to discover would, at Banks' insistence, become Cook Strait.

Over the next few days, the wind was uncooperative – too little or too much – so *Endeavour* remained at anchor until 6 February. Then, despite there being only a faint breeze that day, Cook decided they could wait no longer: the anchor was hove up, and the ship was warped out of the bay, then put under sail.

It became obvious that this water was indeed a strait, but any pleasure that came with the discovery quickly evaporated. A strong tidal current was carrying *Endeavour* at 4–5 knots towards a cluster of rocks off Arapawa Island, and because there was little wind to fill the sails, she could not be steered clear. The only hope for avoiding shipwreck was to get the best bower released and lowered as quickly as possible – but the ship was in 75 fathoms of water, and at that depth the anchor might never hold … By the time it had hit the bottom and taken a bite, an incredible 150 fathoms' worth of cable had been released.

While this was happening, the officers on the quarterdeck could only watch anxiously as the gap between the ship and misfortune continued to close at a rapid rate. All ears were trained on the crewman assigned to taking a transit with a feature onshore, hoping for his call announcing that the ship's run had been halted … The call came when *Endeavour* was just 300 yards from the rocks.

Cook had to accept that they had 'narrowly escaped being dashed against the Rocks' because of a last-minute change in the direction of the current. Once the situation on board had stabilised, with the current continuing to hold *Endeavour* a safe distance from the threat (which he named The Brothers soon afterwards), it was time to hove the anchor back aboard: a near back-breaking task that took three hours!

While scanning the horizon, Cook observed a headland in the distance to the north-east – a craggy ridge rising from the water. Because of its prominence, he named it Cape Palliser, in honour of his great mentor, Sir Hugh. This headland would soon be recognised as the southernmost point of New Zealand's North Island, and the eastern entrance to Cook Strait.

At this point, the intention was to turn south-west, and discover where the coastline would take them, but when *Endeavour* took up this new course, considerable debate developed on the quarterdeck as to whether or not there was land beyond the horizon astern of the ship. Speculation centred on the possibility of there being an isthmus extending to the south-east from the last remaining portion of uncharted coastline on the northernmost of the two main islands, between Cape Palliser and Cape Turnagain to the north. Cook saw only one way to resolve the issue: he abandoned his plans to head to the south-west, instead opting to sail around Palliser until either Turnagain was reached or their direct course was interrupted by a dramatic, eastward change in the direction of the coast.

Having long cleared Cape Palliser, hazy conditions prevailed until 9 February, when *Endeavour* was just 20 nautical miles south of her target. Once the weather cleared and the lookout at the masthead declared that he could see Cape Turnagain, another piece of the puzzle had been solved. Cook wrote of the moment: 'I then called the officers upon the deck and asked them if they were now satisfied that this land was an Island to which they answered in the affirmative ...'

Endeavour was tacked and set on a course to the south-west, so that the exploration of the eastern coast of the separate landmass to the south could begin. Two weeks later, Cook had the ship edging back towards land while she made between 6 and 7 knots riding the front of a fresh northerly gale. The exhilaration of making such progress was quickly dampened, however, when a southerly squall proved to be too much for the main topgallant mast and the fore topmast studding-sail boom, bending both timber spars beyond their limit until the sound of splintering wood and flogging canvas filled the air. Crewmen – the majority barefoot, as was usually the case – scampered hand-over-hand up the ratlines like monkeys, in response to orders shouted from below: the spars had to first be contained to prevent any further damage aloft, then lowered to the deck. Much to Cook's delight, the ever-efficient carpenters aboard the ship set about their task and had the broken mast and spar 'soon replaced by others'.

By now, *Endeavour* had sailed 300 nautical miles down the east coast of this southern island and was off a barren and foreboding headland that Cook named Cape Saunders. Two elements were curtailing any desire the crew may have held to go ashore: the wild weather that was prevailing, and the generally inhospitable nature of the coastline they were observing. This caused Cook little concern, though, because he held a 'fear of losing time and the desire I had of pushing to the southward in order to see as much of the coast as possible, or if this land should prove to be an island to get around it'. It turned out to be a wise decision as, had he taken *Endeavour* too close to the coast over the next couple of days, she would have been trapped by a savage gale, which struck virtually unannounced.

This change in the weather forced him to sail to the south-east for almost two weeks, and by the time he managed to struggle his way back towards the shore, *Endeavour* was off the desolate and uninviting southern tip of the landmass. It was here, on 9 March, that they were again lucky to escape being wrecked.

> At 4 a.m. Sounded, and had 60 fathoms; at daylight we
> discovered under our lee bow Ledges of Rocks, on
> which the Sea broke very high … The wind being at
> North-West we could not weather [clear] the Ledge, and

as I did not care to run to leeward, we tacked and made a
Trip to the Eastward; but the wind soon after coming to
the North enabled us to go clear of all ... These rocks are
not the only dangers that lay here, for about 3 Leagues to
the Northward of them is another Ledge of Rocks ...
whereon the Sea broke very high. As we passed these
rocks in the night at no great distance, and discovered
the others close ... at daylight, it is apparent that we had
a very fortunate Escape. I have named them the Traps,
because they lay as such to catch unweary Strangers ...

These were challenging and dangerous waters on the fringe of
the Southern Ocean. It was not surprising therefore that the
captain's convincing theory that they were now at the southern
extremity of this land caused a feeling of great relief to prevail
among the crew. Cook explained in his journal entry of 10
March: 'I began now to think that this was the southernmost
land and that we should be able to get round it by the west, for
we have had a large hollow swell from the southwest ever since
we had the gale of wind from that quarter which makes me
think that there is no land in that direction ...'

That same day, the captain decided to make a dramatic turn
to the north with the intention of returning to the coast and
resuming his exploration. What he did not realise was that the
mass of land he had sighted five days earlier, whose
southernmost point he had named South Cape, was actually a
large island, now known as Stewart Island.

By 14 March, Cook had rounded and named West Cape
and had *Endeavour* heading north. He was impressed by the
fjord lands along this stretch of coastline, with their
dramatically spectacular entrances. They invited a visit, but
the pressure of time, together with a wealth of knowledge
that only a skilled seafarer such as Cook possessed, caused him
to resist the temptation and continue on his northerly course.
One inlet, which would later be named Doubtful Sound, he
found particularly appealing:

> The Land on each side of the entrance of this harbour
> riseth almost perpendicular from the sea to a very
> considerable height and this was the reason why I did not
> attempt to go in with the ship because I saw clearly that
> no winds could blow there ... it certainly would have
> been highly imprudent in me to have put into a place
> where you could not have got out but with a wind that
> we have lately found does not blow one day in a month.
> I mention this because there were some on board who
> wanted me to harbour at any rate without in the least
> considering either the present or future consequences.

Once north of this highly indented part of the coastline, the captain found that the land was 'not distinguished by anything remarkable', although he did make special mention of the rugged, and often snow-capped, mountain ranges that stood as a backdrop to the coast for much of its length, and the amount of fog that they experienced. He then added: 'No country upon earth can appear with a more rugged and barren aspect than this doth from the sea for as far inland as the eye can reach nothing is to be seen but the summits of these Rocky mountains which seem to lay so near one another as not to admit any Valleys between them ...'

On Tuesday, 27 March 1770, Captain James Cook wrote himself into the history books and made a significant change to the map of the world. He concluded of his circumnavigation of New Zealand: 'This country, which before now was thought to be a part of the imaginary Southern Continent, consists of 2 large Islands, divided from each other by a Strait or Passage ...'

He was, quite rightfully, well pleased when reflecting on his achievement. With the winter months not far away, he had just one further thought: 'As we have now circumnavigated the whole of this Country it is time for me to think of quitting of it ...'

CHAPTER TEN

Bound for
Van Diemen's Land

James Cook wasted no time in sailing from New Zealand. On 31 March 1770, when he was advised that everything on board was stowed and the ship ready to sail, he declared that they would depart as soon as the weather allowed. Prior to this, he had reviewed his orders from the Admiralty relating to the next part of the voyage. They read in part:

> ... if you shall fail of discovering the Continent
> beforementioned, you will upon falling in with New
> Zealand ... explore as much of the Coast as the Condition
> of the Bark, the health of her Crew and the State of your
> Provisions will admit of having always great Attention to
> reserve as much of the latter as will enable you to reach
> some Port where you may procure a Sufficiency to carry
> You to England either round the Cape of Good Hope, or
> Cape Horn as from circumstances you may judge the
> Most Eligible way of returning home.

He would also have consulted Banks and his fellow officers, regarding the options for returning home. Cook explained his decision in the following terms:

To return by the way of Cape Horn was what I most wished, because by this route we should have been able to prove the Existence or Non-Existence of a Southern Continent, which yet remains Doubtful; but in order to Ascertain this we must have kept in a higher Latitude in the very Depth of Winter, but the Condition of the Ship, in every respect, was not thought sufficient for such an undertaking. For the same reason the thoughts of proceeding directly to the Cape of Good Hope was laid aside, especially as no discovery of any Moment could be hoped for in that route. It was therefore resolved to return by way of the East Indies by the following route: upon Leaving this Coast to steer to the Westward until we fall in with the East Coast of New Holland, and then to follow the direction of that Coast to the Northward, or what other direction it might take us, until we arrive at its Northern extremity ...

It is interesting to note that there was no specific reference in the Admiralty's orders for Cook to continue the search for *Terra Australis Incognita* once his exploration of New Zealand was complete. However, there is no doubt that, with such a large tract of unexplored ocean lying to the west of his current position, this would have appealed to his inquisitive nature.

Cook's choosing to sail towards Van Diemen's Land meant that his desired destination was the same position that had served as Abel Tasman's point of departure from that coastline, before the Dutch navigator headed for New Zealand during his voyage of 1642–43. Cook had applied a similar strategy when using a reference point of Tasman's to find the coast of New Zealand.

It was not by choice that Tasman had departed the coast of Van Diemen's Land when he did. He had hoped to continue north, but forces of nature dashed his plans. Powerful headwinds that swept down this exposed coast forced his two ships offshore and into a wide open sea, to the point where the Dutchman had no option but to continue sailing eastwards. However, just before leaving, Tasman had a crewman swim ashore and plant the Dutch flag in the sand, thereby claiming the region in the name of his motherland. The location, on the south-east coast of Tasmania, is close to what is now known as Marion Bay.

Tasman's mission was not dissimilar to Cook's, in that he was sailing through that part of the world in the hope of discovering the Great South Land. But incredibly, apart from finding Van Diemen's Land, Tasman did not sight the coastline again. And this was despite sailing *Heemskerck* and her support vessel in a large and sweeping anticlockwise loop around the continent in search of it – a loop that took in his discovery of New Zealand.

From Cook's perspective, knowing that in 1616 another Dutchman, Dirk Hartog, had discovered a 250-nautical-mile stretch of unexplored coastline, part of what is now Western Australia, holding *Endeavour* on a course towards Van Diemen's Land would quite possibly lead to something out there being discovered. But would it be large or small?

Another precedent for Cook, although its influence on his voyage appears to have been negligible, concerns the controversial Dieppe maps, and in particular, the so-called Dauphin map. The Dieppe maps have been much debated for centuries. They are a series of maps created between 1536 and 1566 in the town of Dieppe – a major port on France's northern coast, and the centre of map production in Europe during that era – that purportedly showed the known landmasses of the world. The Dauphin, the first work in the series, was a gift for the Dauphin of France (the heir apparent to the throne, in this case the future King Henry II), and it revealed a stretch of coastline in the Far East not seen on any previous maps, and labelled 'Java la Grande'. Believers to the modern-day are convinced that this represents the first known outline of the east coast of Australia, even though it is not drawn in the position that we know today. The same advocates claim that Java la Grande came into existence as a result of a voyage led by a

Portuguese navy officer, Cristóvão de Mendonça, between 1521 and 1524. His mission was possibly launched with the aim of intercepting Ferdinand Magellan, who, it was feared, was heading towards the Spice Islands from the east, with the intention of plundering their wealth on behalf of the King of Spain. At this time, the waters that Magellan was believed to be sailing were unexplored, so when Mendonça set sail from a Portuguese base in Malacca aboard one of the three caravels prepared for the undertaking, he was heading into unknown territory. Much speculation exists as to what happened during that expedition, right down to the wreck of one of his caravels supposedly being seen by shipwrecked sailors on a beach near Warrnambool, Victoria, in 1836. The ship was almost entirely covered by sand.

It must be said that most of the evidence relating to the Portuguese, via Mendonça's voyage, being the first known discoverers of Australia's east coast is purely speculative. According to the true believers, if one takes the drawing of Java la Grande attributed to Mendonça and reconstructs it using modern-day navigation technology, there is a strong argument to suggest it is an outline of the same coast that Cook was destined to explore and chart most accurately.

Although the Lords could well have doubted their accuracy, the Admiralty was well aware of the Dieppe maps. So if Cook had sighted the Dauphin or others in the series, before departing from England, he would have had a sense of what might lie ahead. Interestingly, Banks is known to have owned one of the Dieppe maps, the Harleian, but it seems unlikely that he had it with him when aboard *Endeavour*. In 1790, Banks donated this map to the British Museum.

There were anxious moments for the captain and his crew as *Endeavour* was guided towards the west and the open sea that lay beyond Cook Strait. On the morning of 2 April, she was in very deep water and making slow speed when what gentle breeze there was suddenly disappeared. *Endeavour* was then in danger of being washed onto rocks, which were 3 miles away, until a most fortuitous puff arrived, got the ship moving and eliminated the threat. This would not be the last time that the vagaries of the weather would intervene and save the ship and its men. Later, before actually sailing away from the coast, *Endeavour* passed the northernmost tip of the South Island, which Cook named, appropriately, Cape Farewell.

For the first sixteen days of this passage, the wind and waves were most docile: it was a pleasant time for all. Banks and his gentlemen observed 'things we have seen upon the sea [that] are so extraordinary … the Tropic bird, flying fish and Medusa Porpita are animals very seldom seen out of the influence of trade winds'. The crew on watch, who had little to do when it came to tending the sails, filled much of their time creating junk, or oakum, by picking apart old ropes into small pieces so they could be used for caulking or padding. The sound of hammering and sawing came from nearby as the carpenter continued with his nine-day repair of the ship's yawl, while the sail-maker, sitting on the deck, took the opportunity to apply his craft to the heavy canvas sails, which had become increasingly worn. Such conditions belied the fact that in later years this same stretch of water, the Tasman Sea, would be recognised by mariners as being among the most volatile and storm-lashed in the world.

On 18 April, the calm was broken by a violent mood swing in the weather. In no time, the situation changed from serenity to turmoil as a horrid storm smashed into the ship from the south-west, direct from the Southern Ocean. This system was so powerful that Cook had no choice but to lower the topgallant yards, turn downwind and run with the storm under greatly reduced canvas. 'Wind southerly,' he recorded in his log, 'a hard gale with heavy squalls attended with showers of rain and a great sea from the same quarter … At six o'clock the gale increased to such a height as to Oblige us to take in the Fore topsail and Mainsail and run under the Foresail and Mizzen all night …'

Among Banks' team, artist Sydney Parkinson was in awe of the magnitude of this storm and its threatening nature to men and ship. He wrote: 'we had a broken sea that caused the ship to pitch and roll very much at the same time; we shipped a sea fore and aft, which deluged the decks, and [might possibly] have washed several of us overboard ...'

This was probably the worst weather that *Endeavour* had experienced since departing England close to twenty months earlier. It was as if this sea was determined not to give up easily on its secret: the large and unmapped landmass lying to the west. At the same time, though, the forced change of course to the north-west was actually making that discovery more likely ... that is, if *Endeavour* could survive the hammering that nature was hurling at her, where some of the waves would have been near 40 feet high – almost half the height of the mainmast. Apart from the skill being demanded of the helmsman, who was battling to guide the ship through the maelstrom, the leadsman was required to step beyond the bulwark and into the chains every two hours to sound the depth. A shoaling bottom would possibly be an indication that they were closing on land.

Through expeditious seamanship, *Endeavour* survived the storm virtually unscathed, and when Cook was able to put some relatively accurate navigation plots on the chart, there was an interesting revelation: their position was around 150 nautical miles to the north of Tasman's plot for the coast of Van Diemen's Land, yet they had sighted no land. Only a matter of hours later, however, there were some encouraging signs. Seabirds known to exist only in close proximity to a shoreline were sighted, and an obviously exhausted small land bird was seen to take refuge in the rigging for a much-needed rest.

Even so, the mystery regarding the coast of Van Diemen's Land continued to grow. A later set of plots had *Endeavour* 60 nautical miles to the west of Tasman's last known position on the coast – yet the lookouts aloft still could not sight land. Cook did not question the accuracy of Tasman's plots, so he could only assume that the coast Tasman saw took a dramatic turn to the west somewhere to the south of their current position. There was a real chance, therefore, that *Endeavour* had missed Van Diemen's Land altogether and was sailing west into a wide expanse of open ocean. Still, they pressed on.

It was at 6 am on the following day – Thursday, 19 April 1770 – when *Endeavour* was still sailing in a fresh gale, that history was made. Cook recorded in his journal, somewhat casually: 'saw land extending from NE to W at the distance of 5 or 6 Leagues.'

Over the next hour or so there was much discussion as the ship closed on the expanse of coast that was increasingly apparent off her starboard bow, particularly about what new course should be adopted so that it could best be explored. For Cook, the priority was to get *Endeavour* to Batavia (now the Indonesian capital of Jakarta): this was a key part of the plan for returning to England. So, with that destination being to the north of their current position, the captain decided on a change of course to parallel the coast in that direction, back to the north-east. That coastline would prove to be more than 2000 nautical miles in length and one that they would see and sail along for the next four months.

Before making the call to wear ship and steer north-east, Cook declared that the southernmost point of land they could see to the west, which was the first cape they had sighted, would be named Point Hicks in recognition of Lieutenant Zachary Hickes – whose surname Cook continually spelled 'Hicks' in his log and journal – he being 'the first who discovered this land'. It is here also that Cook made some remarkable observations that would be proved correct almost thirty years later. By considering their position relative to Tasman's, and the circumstance of their surroundings, Cook hypothesised that it was unlikely that the land they were now seeing and Van Diemen's Land were joined: Van Diemen's Land was quite probably an island. Sure enough, the waters they were sailing were what is now known as Bass Strait, which separates the Australian mainland from Tasmania; Point

Hicks, in the far east of Victoria, is today part of Croajingolong National Park.

The following day, the hazy weather cleared, affording all on board a better opportunity to 'View the Country which had a very agreeable and promising Aspect'. The observers noted, with considerable interest, that the land was obviously inhabited: smoke from small fires was seen drifting skywards. Just who these people were created absorbing speculation.

Having sailed along the coast for 40 nautical miles towards the north-east, and with darkness approaching, Cook had the majority of sails taken in and the ship brought-to for the night so she could drift slowly offshore. This was the most appropriate safety measure they could take in these foreign waters, while also ensuring that the exploration of the coast could continue the next day from virtually the same point. Before changing course, though, they came upon another cape, one where the land was seen to take a definite turn to the north. Cook subsequently named this place Cape Howe in recognition of Richard, Earl Howe, one of the Lords of the Admiralty when *Endeavour* sailed from England. The same headland would later be identified as the most south-eastern point of the unexplored landmass that lay beyond it.

Next morning, when eight bells sounded, signalling 4 am for the middle watch, it was considered safe for *Endeavour* to sail back to the coast and resume the exploration. This was the start of a very exciting time for everyone on board, simply because they knew that they were observing a coastline that no European before them had seen. For an explorer like Cook, it was akin to striking gold. By midday, with Cape Howe well in her wake, *Endeavour* was on a course just east of north. For some hours 'flying squalls of rain' had been experienced, but with those having cleared, all on deck were getting their first real appreciation of the form of the land, which was about 3 leagues away to the west. Cook described it as being 'diversified with hills, ridges, plains, and Valleys, with some few small lawns; but for the most part the whole was covered with wood, the hills and ridges rise with a gentle slope; they are not high, neither are there many of them'. Banks' description was typically imaginative and detailed:

> Large fires were lighted this morn about 10 O'Clock, we supposed that the gentlemen ashore had a plentiful breakfast to prepare. The country tho in general well enough clothed appeared in some places bare; it resembled in my imagination the back of a lean Cow, covered in general with long hair, but nevertheless where her scraggy hip bones have stuck out farther than they ought [whereby] accidental rubs and knocks have entirely bared them of their share of covering.

That same day, there was a sudden scramble to get on deck from below. The reason: to see three waterspouts that had spiralled down from lead-coloured clouds to the surface of the sea, and were now performing cobra-like twists and turns over the ocean. When Cook returned to business, he expressed his surprise at the apparent lack of harbours of any size along the coast so far. Part of the reason for this perception might have been because, for much of this time, *Endeavour* was up to 6 leagues offshore. Their distance from the coast also contributed to there being few references to specific features – that is, until 75 nautical miles north of Cape Howe, when a 2650-foot peak pierced the distant horizon. Master's Mate Richard Pickersgill, who had been with Wallis on *Dolphin*'s previous voyage into the Pacific, recalled of the sighting: 'Saw a high land [the captain] called the Dromedary from its resemblance to that animal ...' This pinnacle, subsequently renamed Mount Gulaga, would prove to be one of the highest on the east coast.

Later, through patient observation using his telescope, and the eagle eye of the lookout, Cook was finally able to mark the existence of a bay. He wrote the name 'Bateman Bay' alongside it on his chart as a tribute to Nathaniel Bateman, captain of *Northumberland* when he served as master.

On 22 April, *Endeavour* was still tracing the shoreline but making very little headway in a near calm. The coast was now enveloped by heavy rain-bearing clouds of dreary grey, and the ship was being rolled in a gentle manner by the motion of the large ocean swell. Each sway from side to side was accompanied by a loud, thumping sound as the sails were turned inside out. It was a frustrating time for all. At noon, having tired of this uncomfortable experience, the captain called for the crew to wear ship and sail offshore. That brought a much-preferred change of wind angle: the sails filled, in what little breeze there was, and the ship was moving. *Endeavour* sailed on into the night, covering almost 30 miles before wearing again and taking up a near reciprocal course towards land.

A full day had passed by the time the coast finally hove into view, and with the weather having cleared, there was much to see. Pickersgill wrote of one standout feature, about 10 miles inland to the north-west, which he described as 'a remarkable peaked hill with a tuft of trees on this resembling the top of a Pidgeon house'. To no-one's surprise, it was entered on Cook's chart as Pidgeon House Hill.

When *Endeavour* had reached the coast after that night offshore, Cook was given something else to contemplate: the ship had been carried some 9 nautical miles to the south of where they expected to be. Soon afterwards, he had an explanation for this loss of ground. He and his fellow officers had just become the first known navigators to experience the powerful flow of the East Australian Current – a south-flowing stream of warm water that has its origins in the Coral Sea to the north, and has been known to run at up to 7 knots. During the weeks ahead, this same current would further frustrate *Endeavour*'s advance north. Another observation they made at this point was that the air continued to be much clearer here than what they were used to in the northern hemisphere.

Once back on course and heading north, the Europeans finally had their first visual contact with those responsible for the smoking campfires onshore. '[We] steered along shore North-

North-East, having a Gentle breeze at South-West,' Cook wrote of this momentous occasion, 'and were so near the Shore as to distinguish several people upon the Sea beach. They appeared to be of a very dark or black Colour; but whether this was the real Colour of their skins or the Clothes they might have on I know not ...' Banks noted an apparent difference between the practices of these people and those of the Polynesians encountered earlier in the expedition: 'Since we have been on the coast we have not observed those large fires which we so frequently saw in the Islands and New Zealand made by the Natives in order to clear the ground for cultivation; we thence concluded not much in favour of our future friends ...'

The crew were being tested on many fronts as they did their best to keep the ship moving in very light airs, trying to counter the negative influence of the southerly current they were now conscious of. These exasperating conditions continued throughout 24 April, at which point they were approaching what would later become known as Jervis Bay, and for days to follow.

At one stage, when their progress was again thwarted by a lack of wind and too much adverse current, they were forced 20 nautical miles back to the south-west, and while the sailors accepted the loss in 'northing' as inevitable, it was a negative that soon became a positive – of sorts. *Endeavour* was then just south of where the city of Wollongong is sited today, on the New South Wales South Coast, and it was time to do something different, as recounted by Cook:

> Saturday, 28th. In the P.M. hoisted out the Pinnace and
> Yawl in order to attempt a landing, but the Pinnace took
> in the Water so fast that she was obliged to be hoisted in
> again to stop her leaks. At this time we saw several
> people a shore, 4 of whom were carrying a small Boat or
> Canoe, which we imagined they were going to put in to
> the Water in order to Come off to us; but in this we
> were mistaken. Being now not above 2 Miles from the

Shore Mr. Banks, Dr. Solander, Tupia, and myself put
off in the Yawl, and pulled in for the land to a place
where we saw 4 or 5 of the Natives, who took to the
Woods as we approached the Shore; which disappointed
us in the expectation we had of getting a near View of
them, if not to speak to them. But our disappointment
was heightened when we found that we nowhere could
effect a landing by reason of the great Surf which beat
everywhere upon the shore.

The following morning (28 April, ship time), the chance to sail
into a safe anchorage further to the north presented itself. 'At
daylight in the morning we discovered a Bay,' Cook wrote,
'which appeared to be tolerably well sheltered from all winds,
into which I resolved to go with the Ship, and with this View
sent the Master in the Pinnace to sound the Entrance, while we
kept turning up with the Ship, having the wind right out. At
noon the Entrance bore North-North-West, distance 1 Mile.'

After the signal came from Molyneux, aboard the pinnace,
that it was safe to proceed into the bay, *Endeavour*'s sails were
trimmed to best utilise the south-easterly breeze on a course
that was to the west. What followed in the captain's description
held echoes of their arrival in Poverty Bay in New Zealand, but
not with the same level of aggression from either side.

... we stood into the bay and Anchored under the South
shore about 2 miles within the Entrance in 5 fathoms,
the South point bearing South-East and the North point
East. Saw, as we came in, on both points of the bay,
several of the Natives and a few hutts; Men, Women,
and Children on the South Shore abreast of the Ship, to
which place I went in the Boats in hopes of speaking
with them, accompanied by Mr. Banks, Dr. Solander,
and Tupia. As we approached the Shore they all made
off, except 2 Men, who seemed resolved to oppose our
landing.

Cook ignored the threat, as the Englishmen held the upper hand in any potential showdown. Instead, he had the men who were rowing them ashore increase their rate, in the hope that the natives would remain and he would be able to communicate with them. As the stroke rate went up, oars thumped in unison in their slots along the gunwale, and when close enough to the water's edge, he made an effort to establish some form of dialogue.

> … this was to little purpose, for neither us nor Tupia could understand one word they said. We then threw them some nails, beads, etc., ashore, which they took up, and seemed not ill pleased with, in so much that I thought that they beckoned to us to come ashore; but in this we were mistaken, for as soon as we put the boat in they again came to oppose us, upon which I fired a musket between the 2, which had no other Effect than to make them retire back, where bundles of their darts lay, and one of them took up a stone and threw at us, which caused my firing a Second Musket, loaded with small Shot; and although some of the shot struck the man, yet it had no other effect than to make him lay hold of a shield or target to defend himself.

There was nothing more they could then do but go ashore. The six men on the oars dug deep with their blades once again and began propelling the 18-foot-long pinnace towards the beach, until the stem and keelson cut a fine furrow in the sandy shallows, and they came to a gentle stop. At this moment, Cook handed a historic act to his wife's cousin, seventeen-year-old Isaac Smith.

'Jump out, Isaac!' the captain called to the young lad, who was squatting in the bow of the pinnace.

With that, Smith stood up, put his foot on the gunwale, then leapt out and firmly planted his feet in the sand. In doing so, he became the first European to set foot on the east coast of the continent.

Unfortunately, as Cook noted, the welcome that followed from the indigenous people was not what had been hoped for: 'we had no sooner [landed] than they throwed 2 darts at us; this obliged me to fire a third shot, soon after which they both made off, but not in such haste but we might have taken [captured] one; but Mr Banks being of Opinion that the darts were poisoned, made me cautious how I advanced into the Woods ...'

The captain and his men began moving among the trees fringing the beach, all the time looking to make contact with the people and gain their confidence – but it was as if they had vanished. Incredibly, though, they left some small children behind in one of a few crude bark huts set among the trees, not far from the beach. Equally basic in form were the three canoes that were lying on the sand. Cook described these craft as 'the worst I think I ever saw; they were about 12 or 14 feet long, made of one piece of the Bark of a Tree, drawn or tied up at each end, and the middle kept open by means of pieces of Sticks by way of Thwarts.'

When Banks returned to the ship that evening, the entry he made in his journal included the comment: 'The people were blacker than any we have seen in the Voyage tho by no means negroes.' He also left no doubt that he had seen what would become known as a boomerang, although not in use. This made him probably the first European to register the existence of the amazing aerodynamic implement.

Each of these [men] held in his hand a wooden weapon about 2½ feet long, in shape much resembling a scymeter [scimitar]; the blades of these looked whitish and some though shining so much that they [might have been] made of some kind of metal, but myself thought they were no more than wood smeared over with the same white pigment with which they paint their bodies.

Early the following morning, after he had donned his uniform, Cook stepped out of his small cabin, moved a few paces forward and climbed the steep ladder leading to the quarterdeck. Once there, he met with his senior officers and announced his plan for the day: some of the crew were to go ashore and collect wood and water, and grass for the sheep, while the pinnace would be hoisted out and manned so that he could explore, survey and chart part of the expansive bay that encircled them.

By the end of the day, the captain and his men were pleased with their achievements – except that they had again failed to get anywhere near the local people. But while that was a source of disappointment to Cook, the fishing was not:

> After I had returned from sounding the Bay I went over
> to a Cove on the North side of the Bay, where, in 3 or 4
> Hauls with the [net], we caught about 300 pounds weight
> of Fish, which I caused to be equally divided among the
> Ship's Company. In the A.M. I went in the Pinnace to
> sound and explore the North side of the bay, where I
> neither met with inhabitants or anything remarkable …

Banks continued to create a highly detailed journal on his experiences in this bay. He was thoroughly pleased by the number of new plant species that he and Solander were taking from the shore, while at the same time being intrigued by the seemingly contradictory actions of the natives. Sometimes they were seen to be making threatening gestures with their spears, as if determined to rid their home waters of the visitors; at other times, they appeared receptive to their presence. Even so, each time the Europeans approached them, they 'ran away into the woods before the boat was within half a mile of them, although [we] did not even go towards them'. This was completely contrary to what had been experienced in New Zealand.

Banks' notes described flora and fauna of Australia's natural landscape that are now iconic, including a tree that yielded 'gum' – the eucalypt. When it came to the fauna, the likes of which had never previously been seen, there was a need for comparisons:

[We saw] one quadruped about the size of a Rabbit. My Greyhound just got sight of him and instantly lamed himself against a stump which lay concealed in the long grass; we saw also the dung of a large animal [a kangaroo] that had fed on grass which much resembled that of a Stag; also the footsteps of an animal clawed like a dog or wolf [dingo] and as large as the latter; and of a small animal whose feet were like those of a polecat or weasel [bandicoot]. The trees over our heads abounded very much with Loryquets [lorikeets] and Cockatoos of which we shot several; both these sorts flew in flocks of several scores together ...

Endeavour lay at anchor for a week in this bay, until 6 May. This was longer than Cook had planned, but with northerly winds prevailing, and his course being in that direction, he could only wait for a breeze that was more suitable for progress. At this stage, the captain and his entire crew could also reflect on the benefit of the strict dietary regimen that Cook had introduced at the time of departure from England: in the twenty months that they had been at sea, the ship had remained free of scurvy. It was a remarkable achievement in this era, one for which Cook was well worthy of high praise. Even so, there were moments of sadness, as was the case when the ship's thirty-year-old poulterer succumbed to tuberculosis on 1 May. 'Last night Forby Sutherland, Seaman, departed this Life,' wrote Cook, 'and in the A.M. his body was buried ashore at the watering place, which occasioned my calling the south point of this bay after his name.'

The delayed departure gave Cook additional time to further explore and map the bay, particularly to the south-west, and after having done so he wrote of the waterway: 'It is capacious, safe, and Commodious.' It would appear that he and Banks agreed that this would be a suitable location for the establishment of a settlement, should that ever be required by the government. As it turned out, Banks recommended the area to the House of Commons Committee in 1779 when they were considering suitable sites for a penal colony. This need was brought about because the prisons and the prison hulks on the Thames were full to overflowing. No doubt Cook would have supported Banks' suggestion, if there had been opportunity to get his opinion.

Eighteen years later, when the governor-designate of the proposed penal colony of New South Wales, Captain Arthur Phillip, led the First Fleet into the same anchorage, the bay was not what he expected to find: it was nowhere near as impressive as he had been led to believe. His concerns were that the waters were too shallow, and more importantly, that there was not a supply of fresh water capable of supporting a settlement.

It was because of the abundance of stingrays in this bay and their size – the day before *Endeavour* set sail, Gore caught two stingrays, each one weighing near 300 pounds – that Cook chose to name the location Stingray Harbour. It would stay that way until the ship was well to the north, when, having been impressed by the 'great quantity of New Plants' that Banks and Solander had collected there, Cook decided to refer to it on his charts and in his records as Botany Bay. The delay regarding its eventual official name is confirmed in Banks' journal entry for 3 June, four weeks after departure, when he wrote that he had seen 'a small canoe fitted with an outrigger, which made us hope that the people were something improved as their boat was far preferable to the bark Canoes of Stingrays bay'.

CHAPTER ELEVEN

Unknown Land, Unknown Reefs

Before sunrise on 6 May, Cook climbed the companionway ladder leading to the quarterdeck, and once there, immediately sensed a gentle offshore breeze that was wafting across the bay: perfect for getting underway. 'Having seen everything this place afforded,' he wrote that day, 'we, at daylight in the morning, weighed with a light breeze at North-West, and put to Sea ...'

His overview of what was the first contact by Europeans with aborigines in this part of the unknown continent, albeit contact from afar, revealed a level of disappointment:

> ... we could know but very little of their Customs, as we
> never were able to form any Connections with them;
> they had not so much as touched the things we had left
> in their Huts on purpose for them to take away. [They]
> do not appear to be numerous, neither do they seem to
> live in large bodies, but dispersed in small parties along by
> the Water side. Those I saw were about as tall as
> Europeans, of a very dark brown Colour, but not black,
> nor had they woolly, frizzled hair, but black and lank like
> ours. No sort of Cloathing or Ornaments were ever seen

by any of us upon any one of them, or in or about any of
their Huts; from which I conclude that they never wear
any. Some that we saw had their faces and bodies painted
with a sort of White Paint or Pigment ...

With the best bower raised to the cathead and stowed, then the
stream anchor, which had been used for added security, hauled
aboard, *Endeavour*'s bow headed eastwards and, as sail after sail
was hauled down and trimmed, so the ship gained speed. Before
long the crew felt the first motions that came with being at sea:
the high-volume apple-cheek-shaped forward sections of the
vessel's bow causing her to rise gently in response to the
oncoming swell, before pressing into the shallow trough that
followed.

Once well clear of the entrance, and with the leadsman
confirming that there was plenty of water under the keel, the
captain called for the helm to be put down and the ship turned
to larboard (port). The course was then to the north, and as the
turn was made, the crew responded by going to their assigned
tasks, re-trimming the sails to suit the south-easterly breeze, then
making fast the sheets and braces on hardwood belaying pins. In
Endeavour's wake lay tribute to the two men who had worked so
diligently at their task while in the bay. The southern headland
of Stingray Harbour was named Point Solander, and the
northern, Cape Banks.

While all this activity was happening on deck, the three
cooks had been busy below deck preparing a special meal, about
which Banks reported:

The land we sailed past during the whole forenoon
appeared broken and likely for harbours ... We dined to
day upon the stingray and his tripe: the fish itself was not
quite so good as a skate nor was it much inferior, the
tripe everybody thought excellent. We had with it a dish
of the leaves of [wild spinach] boiled, which eat as well
as spinach or very near it.

As was always the case, Banks had been dining with the captain in the great cabin. His footman, James Roberts, who was eating the exotic stingray with the crew in their crowded quarters forward, saw things differently: 'served it to the ship's company instead of salt provisions. It was very strong and made a great many of the Ship's Company sick which eat of it.'

Meanwhile, the voyage continued. '[We] steered along shore North-North-East,' Cook wrote in his journal, 'and at Noon we were by observation in the Latitude of 33 degrees 50 minutes South, about 2 or 3 Miles from the Land, and abreast of a Bay, wherein there appeared to be safe Anchorage, which I called Port Jackson.' Once more, his inspiration for the name came from among his superiors at the Admiralty, in this case George Jackson, later Sir George Duckett, First Baronet.

One can only ponder on the thought that, if Cook had not been delayed in Botany Bay, might he have taken the time to hoist out the pinnace and sail it into this other bay to find out what was there, or at least alter *Endeavour*'s course to the west for a much closer look from on deck. Had he done either, he would have been in awe of what lay beyond the commanding sandstone cliffs that stood at its entrance: one of the most magnificent deep-water safe havens imaginable – Sydney Harbour. However, on this day, with a highly favourable wind coming over the aft starboard quarter, and time being of the essence, Cook decided that he must push on.

That afternoon, after sailing just 17 nautical miles further north, he recorded another find of note: 'Monday, 7th. Little wind, Southerly, and Serene pleasant Weather. At sunset ... some broken land that appeared to form a bay bore North 40 degrees West, distant 4 Leagues. This Bay I named Broken bay ...'

There are suggestions by some historians that it was actually Broken Bay, not Port Jackson, that Captain Arthur Phillip set out to investigate in January 1788, after Botany Bay had proved to be unsuitable for the proposed penal colony. Their belief is that while he was sailing north in search of this bay, Phillip took the opportunity to enter Port Jackson in order to see if it might offer safe anchorage and a much-needed water supply for the near 1400 people in his charge, approximately half of whom were convicts (543 men and 189 women, including some wives of male convicts). He went no further. On 26 January, while the eleven ships in the First Fleet began arriving in Port Jackson from Botany Bay, Phillip stepped ashore up-harbour in 'Sydney Cove' and raised the British flag.

Endeavour was barely past the northern entrance to Broken Bay when the wind went foul from the north, before evaporating altogether. The greatest influence on their passage then was the southerly current: it caused the ship to be swept back to the south more than 15 nautical miles over a 48-hour period. Finally, by 11 May, the wind pattern was back in the ship's favour and she was again on course, paralleling the coast.

Whenever appropriate, Cook applied names to prominent coastal features – among them, Port Stephens, Smoky Cape and the Solitary Isles. However, *Endeavour*'s offing from the coast, the time of day, or poor weather, resulted in him not registering many landmarks that are well known today, such as the entrance to Newcastle's Hunter River, or the Clarence or Richmond rivers to the north.

Ever since they had rounded Cape Howe on 20 April, the coast had tended east of north, but on 15 May, that changed. The captain would later realise that the proud promontory he saw ahead that day was the easternmost point of the coast. He named it after John Byron, a pioneer of British exploration in the Pacific and captain of *Dolphin* during her first circumnavigation, in 1764–66.

> Tuesday, 15th. Fresh Gales at South-West, West-South-West, and South-South-West. In the P.M. had some heavy Squalls, attended with rain and hail, which obliged us to close reef our Topsails. At 8[pm] we brought too until 10, at which time we made sail under our Topsails. Having the Advantage of the Moon we steered [north]

keeping at the distance of about 3 Leagues from the land.
As soon as it was daylight we made all the sail we could,
having the Advantage of a fresh Gale and fair weather …
A Tolerable high point of land bore North-West by
West, distant 3 Miles; this point I named Cape Byron. It
may be known by a remarkable sharp peaked Mountain
lying in land North-West by West from it.

The crewman running the log line out over the taffrail on the
poop deck confirmed that the speed was between 5 and 6 knots
as *Endeavour* rounded Cape Byron, and it was here that Cook
observed the change: as far as he could see, the coast tended west
of north. They had covered another 25 nautical miles when, just
before sunset, powerful white breakers were seen pounding onto
an offshore reef, fine on the larboard bow. Cook responded
immediately, calling for the ship to be hauled up to an offshore
easterly course. It would be maintained all night, until first light
confirmed that it was safe to resume the desired northerly course
under full sail. All too aware of the hazards presented by those
reefs, Cook named a nearby elevated coastal feature Mount
Warning and noted in his journal that the reefs 'may always be
found by the peaked mountain before mentioned, which bears
South-West by West from them'. His name for the point off
which the shoals lay was the similarly themed Point Danger;
today, the same headland marks the border between New South
Wales and Queensland, at Tweed Heads.

Since sailing from Botany Bay, there had been regular sightings
of campfires along the coast but no real sign of people. The
crew noted that occasionally these local inhabitants were seen
on the headlands, but they showed no interest in this modern
sailing ship, which, because they had not harnessed wind energy
for their own canoes, most likely appeared to be propelled by
magical forces. Banks recorded something of one such group:
'Some people were seen, about 20 … we observed them with
glasses for near an hour … Not one was once observed to stop

and look towards the ship; they pursued their way in all appearance entirely unmoved by the [nearness] of so remarkable an object as a ship ...'

While Banks and Solander continued their observations from the deck, Parkinson was ensconced in the great cabin, creating, with painstaking precision, drawings of all the plants that had been collected in Botany Bay. At one stage he completed ninety-four sketches in a two-week period. Banks explained that these plants had been kept fresh through being wrapped in wet cloths and stored in tin chests.

Yet another headland soon held Cook's interest, one that he would name Point Lookout. It is found at the northern tip of what is now identified as North Stradbroke Island – due east of where Brisbane stands today. The waters here were also named by Cook, in this case with a title that was destined to remain misspelled: 'On the North side of this point the shore forms a wide open bay, which I have named Morton's Bay, in the Bottom of which the land is so low that I could but just see it from the Topmast head ...'

The name came in recognition of James Douglas, 14th Earl of Morton, a Scottish astronomer who became president of the Royal Society in 1764. Unfortunately, and unbeknown to Cook, Banks and Solander, the Earl of Morton had died less than eight weeks after *Endeavour*'s departure from England, in August 1768. It was due to a spelling error in the published account of Cook's voyage that the name became Moreton Bay. The mistake also applied to the next promontory he passed, which he named Cape Morton.

Once the ship had cleared this cape, Cook's attention was caught by three conspicuous features on the otherwise low coastline: 'Three Hills lay to the Northward ... they are very remarkable on account of their Singular form of Elevation, which very much resembles Glass Houses, which occasioned my giving them that Name ...'

By midday on 19 May, *Endeavour* was sailing along a 65-mile beach and approaching the northern end of what would later become known as Fraser Island. Today it is recognised as the world's largest sand island, covered in lush subtropical vegetation and many lakes. Its highest ridge is more than 750 feet above sea level.

This day was plagued by light winds. While the ship made headway at just 1 knot, Banks hoisted out aboard one of the small boats to see what he could find drifting by in the form of sea life or flotsam, and to observe birds. Twenty-four hours later, Cook had named Indian Head (because natives were seen to be assembled on it) and Sandy Cape, the northernmost point on Fraser Island. Once again, though, danger loomed.

At 7 am on 21 May, with *Endeavour* in deep water a few nautical miles off Sandy Cape, and with the masthead lookout unable to see land anywhere to the west – the water would prove to be a 50-mile-wide bay there – Cook called for the ship to be hauled up and trimmed for a course in that direction. That is, until 'we discovered a Reef stretching out to the Northward as far as we could see'. With breakers seen to stretch back towards the cape, so blocking their course to the west, there was an immediate call to change course to the north. From then on, it was down to the leadsman: from his precarious position, leaning out over the side from the chains at the bottom of the foremast rigging, he continually threw the lead and called out the depth to the officers on the quarterdeck.

This reef, which forms an impassable barrier for more than 20 miles north of Sandy Cape, was made conspicuous by the chain of surf that was breaking onto it, and Cook accordingly gave it the name Break Sea Spit. It was yet another maritime death trap lying in wait to claim the unwary, but fortunately for this crew, fair winds and clear weather enabled them to steer *Endeavour* wide of the threat.

In his journal entry for the day, Cook described how they found their way around the reef:

> Monday, 21st. In the P.M ... when judging there was
> water for us [to sail] over [the shoal], I sent a Boat ahead

to sound, and upon her making the Signal for more than
5 fathoms we hauled our wind and stood over the Tail
of it in 6 fathoms. From 6 fathoms we had the next Cast,
13, and then 20 immediately, as fast as the Man could
heave the Lead ...

Such a close call was not lost on a non-mariner like Banks:

... our usual good fortune again assisted us, for we
discovered breakers which we had certainly ran upon
had the ship in the night sailed 2 or 3 leagues farther
than she did. This shoal extended a long way out from
the land for we ran along it till 2 O'Clock and then
passed over the tail of it in seven fathoms water. While
we were upon the shoal innumerable large fish, Sharks,
Dolphins etc. and one large Turtle were seen ...

As *Endeavour* then glided to the west in a light and favourable
breeze, the lookout at the masthead was focused on the horizon
off the bow, looking for the coastline the captain was confident
they would soon find. This was a belief founded on the
Yorkshireman's nous and instinct as a seafarer: his ability to
analyse the depth of the sea, its tides, currents and the features
of its surface were all part of his exemplary skill. The same talent
led to him believing that the expanse of sea to the south of their
position was a large and open bay (he was correct on both
counts). Cook would later name it Hervey's Bay, in honour of
naval officer Augustus John Hervey, who became the Third
Earl of Bristol and a Lord of the Admiralty the year *Endeavour*
returned to England.

Twenty-four hours later, as darkness settled on what had
been a day of serene sailing in a soft south-easterly breeze, Cook
opted for a slowly-slowly approach. *Endeavour* was then in only
6 fathoms of water, and with land then barely visible ahead, he
decided it best to anchor for the night and make a cautious
approach the following morning. On today's chart, their

anchorage was about 5 nautical miles offshore and 15 nautical miles north-north-west of the Burnett River, which runs through Bundaberg.

The next day, they were 30 nautical miles further north, anchored in a 'large open bay' and destined to go ashore for exploration activities. The captain's mind was firmly focused on another disturbing issue, however – a serious breach of discipline.

> Last night, sometime in the Middle watch, a very extraordinary affair happened to Mr Orton, my Clerk. He having been drinking in the evening, some Malicious person or persons in the Ship took Advantage of his being Drunk, and cut off all the Cloaths from off his back; not being satisfied with this, they sometime after went into his Cabin and cut off a part of both his Ears as he lay a Sleep in his Bed. The person whom he suspected to have done this was Mr Magra, one of the Midshipmen; but this did not appear to me. Upon enquiry, however, as I had been told that Magra had once or twice before this in their drunken Frolics cut off his cloaths, and had been heard to say (as I was told) that if it was not for the Law he would Murder him, these things considered, induced me to think that Magra was not Altogether innocent … I shall say nothing [more] about it, unless I shall hereafter discover the Offenders, which I shall take every method in my power to do, for I look upon such proceedings as highly dangerous in such Voyages as this, and the greatest insult that could be offered to my Authority in this Ship …

Cook knew all too well the strain that came with so many men being confined on a small ship for so long, and that as a result, they took to the bottle for relief. But discipline had to be maintained, and to do that he needed to exhibit authority. His actions were swift: he dismissed Magra from the quarterdeck and suspended him from all duty aboard the ship, even though he was not found guilty of any offence. At the same time, the captain recognised that Orton 'is a man not without faults; yet from all the inquiry I could make, it evidently appeared to me that [he was] so far from deserving such Treatment'. It was not until a note appeared in Cook's journal on 14 June that there appeared to be any form of resolution: 'This day I restored Mr Magra to his duty as I did not find him guilty of the crimes laid to his charge.' The only reference to the incident that possibly shed light on who the perpetrator was came in Parkinson's journal, when *Endeavour* was in Batavia some months later. Parkinson wrote of a recent deserter, Patrick Saunders: 'One of our midshipmen ran away from us here, and it was suspected that he was the person who cut off Orton's ears …'

This could well have been the case. Saunders was known to have been dis-rated from midshipman to able seaman on the day that Magra was dismissed from the quarterdeck.

Try as they did while at Hervey Bay, those who went ashore saw no natives. Just some smouldering fires and abandoned bark huts, which indicated that the local people had left quite recently, possibly to escape the aliens on their shores. Now, though, at this anchorage 50 nautical miles to the north, about twenty of them were seen by men remaining on board the ship. This group walked down to the water's edge, looked at the ship for a few minutes, then casually returned to the woods as if nothing was out of the ordinary. Those sailors on land saw a wide variety of birdlife, and shot a bustard – which led to the area being named Bustard Bay. The town of 1770 is now on the shore of that bay.

This newly discovered land was again proving to be awe-inspiring for Banks and Solander. It was a naturalist's heaven. Banks wrote that some of the plants they had seen were known to be native to the East Indies.

The research team came across many nests of ants, which, when disturbed, 'came out in large numbers and revenged themselves very sufficiently upon their disturbers, biting sharper than any I have felt in Europe'. Then, among the mangrove swamps, there were the green caterpillars that 'ranged by the side of each other like soldiers'; and if 'these wrathful militia were touched but ever so gently,' Banks observed, 'they did not fail to make the person offending them sensible of their anger, every hair in them stinging much as nettles do'.

Sails were set and the anchor weighed at 5 am on 24 May. After cruising north in light airs at no more than 3 knots, they came across a headland that, as Cook calculated, lay almost directly on the Tropic of Capricorn. As a result, he named the headland, 20 nautical miles north of where the city of Gladstone is now found, Cape Capricorn. The presence of an increasing number of small islands and associated reefs then caused him to see the ship brought-to for the night, essentially holding station until daylight, so that unseen dangers were avoided. A harrowing forty-eight hours was to follow, and that was merely a precursor to what lay ahead.

On 27 May, while sailing through the Cook-named Keppel Group of islands, *Endeavour* went within 2 feet of running aground. It was an urgent holler from the leadsman of '*Three fathoms!*' that saw Cook instantaneously shout for the best bower to be released, in the desperate hope that the ship's progress could be brought to a halt. Prudent seamanship had seen him earlier order for both bowers to be hauled to their respective catheads and be ready for release at a moment's notice; and this was the moment. By the time the ship settled back on the anchor cable, Cook recorded: 'we had only 16 feet, which was not 2 feet more than the Ship drew …'

There was then a great sense of urgency because if the tide dropped that much, or more, *Endeavour* would be on the bottom. The captain directed Molyneux to take out two boats and search for a channel that was deep enough to get the ship back into safe water. But the master returned with the news that in some areas there was only 2½ fathoms. By day's end, it was as if divine providence had intervened – or maybe the 'usual good fortune' that Banks referred to had played a hand in their favour. 'In the Evening the wind veered to East-North-East,' Cook recorded, 'which gave us an opportunity to stretch 3 or 4 miles back the way we Came before the Wind Shifted to South …'

Circumstances could not have been better, as winds from the east–north–east are extremely rare at that time of the year. Cook was able to backtrack his ship to a point where she was anchored in deep water, while the search for a passage north was carried out. The eventual track that Cook adopted was first towards the east, until *Endeavour* was well clear of the islands and reefs, and then to the north.

Unknown to the captain, there was now an outside barrier existing some 60 miles to the east of the ship, one that would offer few opportunities to sail a course to the open ocean, should that become necessary. The Great Barrier Reef is one of the world's seven natural wonders: the largest feature on earth established by living creatures. It is made up of myriad islands, lagoons, atolls, coral outcrops and sand cays – a work of nature that stretches over more than 2300 kilometres (1800 nautical miles) along the coast. In total, it covers an area almost identical in size to Germany. Cook had no reason at this stage to consider changing course and sailing to the outside of the reef, but the rapidly growing labyrinth of navigational challenges was beginning to frustrate this usually well-composed master mariner. He was virtually sailing blind, by day and night. His only charts were the ones he was creating as he went, so every ounce of navigational talent he possessed was being drawn on.

Cook was now forced to probe his way north. He had Molyneux out in the boat ahead, sounding and signalling if it was not safe to proceed in that direction. On 28 May, the captain named Cape Townshend, 60 nautical miles north of the Keppel Group and surrounded by what would become known as the Northumberland Islands. *Endeavour* came to anchor not far from there, Cook's plan being to take the opportunity to 'examine the country' and generally survey it while waiting for the waxing moon to bring valuable assistance to night-time navigation, should they be forced to sail through the darkness. He named one inlet Thirsty Sound because 'we could find no fresh water'. This respite was brief, although it allowed Banks and his people the opportunity to go ashore and 'botanize'. The number and variety of butterflies, in particular, took their attention.

It was 6 am on the last day of May when they weighed anchor and continued on. Cook was obviously not aware that from here, the Great Barrier Reef began to converge on the coast to a point to the north where it was just 10 miles off the mainland: *Endeavour* was about to sail into a 400-nautical-mile potentially lethal maze of islands and reefs. From here on, until safe sea-room was achieved, Cook would have his ship sailing hundreds of yards astern of one of the boats, which was also under sail. Molyneux and his men aboard the boat were continually sounding the depths, making sure that *Endeavour*'s course was confronted with no threat in the form of a shoal. The moment there was any doubt, a signal would be made aboard the boat, so that Cook could either call for the bower to be dropped or the course changed. There were also signals flown from the ship when necessary. An ensign flying from the peak of the mainmast meant that the boat showing the way should either keep pace with or go further ahead of the ship. When a flag was hoisted on the boat, it signalled to the ship that she was entering dangerous waters and that the course should be changed accordingly. This flag remained aloft until the ship changed course or anchored.

The lookouts near the masthead were equally busy, scanning the waters ahead for any sign of danger, and those on deck and on watch found the going no easier. The captain had them on a 'split yarn' (high alert) in case an emergency should suddenly confront the ship. All things aboard *Endeavour* that were vital for her manoeuvrability and preservation were either stowed or secured in a way that they could be accessed instantly and released, especially the sheets, braces and buntlines controlling the sails.

The next stage, over a course curving to the north-west and covering 100 miles, was not without some close calls, but they continued on at between 1 and 3 knots. Eventually, at 8 pm, Cook was forced to anchor because he 'was not sure that there was a passage this way'.

At 5 am on 1 June, he had the ship underway once more, on the same course to the north-west. Three hours later, however, it became apparent that they were entering a large bay. He named it Repulse Bay before backtracking and sailing to the east, in search of the coast running north.

During the middle of the day on Sunday, 3 June, the lookouts reported from the masthead that there was a passage to the north. Cook then called for the ship to be turned to larboard and the braces hauled aft, for what would be an ambling downwind run at about 3 knots through some of the most beautiful island scenery in Australia. 'This passage I have named Whitsunday's Passage,' Cook later wrote, 'as it was discovered on the Day the Church commemorates that festival, and the isles which form it Cumberland Isles, in honour of His Royal Highness the Duke of Cumberland'. Despite there being seventy-four islands in this group, Cook identified only one of them with a name: Pentecost Island – a spectacular pinnacle of rust-red rock, capped by dense green foliage. The island is situated 4 miles south-east of the now well-known holiday destination of Hamilton Island.

The ongoing passage to the north was undertaken with great caution, while Cook did everything he could to map the remarkable coastline he and all on board had been observing off their larboard side for the 1200 nautical miles since first sighting Point Hicks. For some incomprehensible reason, though, Cook did not consider this immense seaboard to be part of a huge continent. He remained convinced that *Terra Australis Incognita*, if it existed, would be found elsewhere. However, his challenge right then was to safely navigate his ship through the increasingly dangerous, reef-riddled coast and back to England with news of his discoveries.

Although the lack of communication continued, the Europeans finally saw some aborigines who reacted to their presence with something other than indifference. Parkinson wrote: 'On one of [these islands], which is not more than two miles in circumference, we saw a company of the natives, entirely naked and of a dark complexion, standing quite still and beholding the ship with astonishment. At night we saw a fire which yielded a very grateful odour, not unlike that of burning the wood of gum.'

At 2 pm on 10 June, *Endeavour* was anchored off what is now Mission Beach, and Cook and others went ashore looking for a water supply.

> My intention was to have stayed here at least one day, to have looked into the Country had we met with fresh water convenient, or any other Refreshment; but as we did not, I thought it would be only spending of time, and losing as much of a light Moon to little purpose, and therefore at 12 o'Clock at night we weighed and stood away to the North-West, having at this time but little wind, attended with Showers of rain. The Shore between Cape Grafton and the ... Northern point [which we could see] forms a large but not very deep Bay, which I named Trinity Bay, after the day on which it was discovered; the North point [I named] Cape Tribulation, because here began all our Troubles.

It was the evening of Monday, 11 June. *Endeavour* was 17 nautical miles north-north-east of Cape Tribulation and 10 nautical miles away from the nearest part of the coast, due west. She was barely heeled in the light breeze while sailing under double-reefed topsails, and the captain was confident that, by applying considerable caution and great diligence, it would be safe to sail into the night. What he didn't realise was that the majority of the reefs his ship was skirting were concealed just below the sea surface, even at low tide. This was a game of roll the dice to learn your fate.

> Wind at East-South-East ... At 6 [pm] we shortened Sail, and hauled off shore East-North-East and North-East by East, close upon a Wind. My intention was to stretch off all Night as well to avoid the danger we saw ... Having the advantage of a fine breeze of wind, and a clear Moon light Night in standing off from 6 until near 9 o Clock, we deepened our Water from 14 to 21 fathoms, when all at once we fell into 12, 10 and 8 fathoms. At this time I had everybody at their Stations to put about and come to an Anchor ...

While *Endeavour* was being prepared for anchoring, the man calling the depth confirmed the ship was already back in deep water. 'I [then] thought there could be no danger in standing on,' Cook recorded later in his journal. 'Before 10 o'Clock we had 20 and 21 fathoms, and continued in that depth until a few minutes before 11, when we had 17, and before the Man at the Lead could heave another cast, the Ship Struck and stuck fast ...'

'Two of the natives of New Holland 'advancing to combat'. (Sydney Parkinson). State Library, Mitchell Library Q78/10 / a039031

CHAPTER TWELVE

The Race to Save *Endeavour*

*E*ndeavour blundered onto the reef doing only 2 knots, but even so, with 368 tons of momentum behind her in the form of her displacement, she gouged her way across the coral to a point where she was well aground.

The crunch came like an explosion for the crew on deck, who, until that moment had been lounging around, chatting and enjoying light-weather sailing on a balmy, moonlit night. The impact was so abrupt that those who were standing were suddenly hurled forward, staggering like drunkards while they tried to regain their balance. Others grabbed what they could to avoid being thrown around. For a split second, there was a look of disbelief among all hands, then the flooding realisation of what had happened. With that, the adrenaline kicked in.

Those below who had been sleeping in their hammocks were jolted out of their comatose state by the impact, and in an instant they were rushing up the companionway ladders to be topside. They knew immediately what had happened, yet the urgency of the moment hit like a shockwave as panicked orders flew from the quarterdeck.

Some hands took to hauling up or lowering sails to take the pressure off the ship, while others hastily hoisted out the boats in readiness for whatever task was necessary. Simultaneously, barefoot crew scampered up the ratlines towards the starlit heavens – 80 feet up to the topmasts – all responding to orders calling for the topgallants, yards and topmasts to be lowered all the way down to the deck. This alone was a monumental task, but it had to be done, and done quickly, to stop the ship from being blown further onto the reef.

The captain knew immediately that their predicament had the potential for calamity: it was now almost high tide, so the opportunity to re-float his ship on the next rising tide was diminishing rapidly. If there was a godsend, it was that the wind was light and the seas were near calm. But how long would that last? The prevailing wind in the region was the south-easterly trade wind that usually blew at between 20 and 30 knots, and when it was at its worst, it created a powerful and nasty sea – conditions that could only have driven the ship further onto the reef and possibly caused her to break up. There was no indication at that time that the relatively benign conditions were turning for the worse, but still there was no time to waste.

Endeavour's bow was pointing to the north-east, yet, as the men in the boats would soon reveal, only about 100 feet out to starboard (one ship-length) the water depth was between 8 and 12 fathoms – plenty in which to float the ship. There was also deep water a short distance off her stern. The only good news to be had was that, hard aground as the vessel was, she was taking on only a small amount of water. As yet, there was no major breach of the hull. That being the case, the first task was for the longboat to take an anchor out to the deep water off her starboard bow, the plan being to then drag the ship in that direction and re-float her. But despite every effort of the men who were on the anchor cable manning the capstan amidships, *Endeavour* refused to budge. A new plan had to be implemented. In anticipation of the next high tide in the morning, as Cook later recorded, 'we went to work to lighten her as fast as possible, which seemed to be the only means we had left to get her off.'

Toiling overnight, crewmen heaved more than 10 tons of iron ballast out of the bilge and onto the lower deck, from where it was tossed out through the two small ports in the ship's stern.

Yet, the captain reported, 'as this was not found sufficient we continued to Lighten her by every method we could think of ...'

Six carriage guns were next to go over the side, while the majority of the water casks were emptied. Finally, almost every other heavy item not deemed essential – 'Stone Ballast ... Hoop Staves, Oil Jars, decayed Stores, etc.' – was also jettisoned.

As frightening as this situation was for Banks and his accompanying landsmen, he revealed great admiration for the efforts of captain and crew:

> The officers behaved with inimitable coolness void of all
> hurry and confusion ... All this time the Seamen worked
> with surprising cheerfulness and alacrity; no grumbling
> or growling was to be heard throughout the ship, no not
> even an oath ... About 1am the water was fallen so low
> that the Pinnace touched ground ... after this the tide
> began to rise and as it rose the ship worked violently
> upon the rocks so that by 2 she began to [take on] water
> and [this] increased very fast.

By the time of that high tide, at around 10 am on 12 June, the crew had jettisoned some 40 or 50 tons in excess weight. Fortunately, the weather remained favourable, but the attempt to re-float her failed, since the tide peaked lower than the previous evening's high. This meant that the crew then had about twelve hours to prepare for the next high tide, while hoping that the ship did not sustain any further damage.

The new plan involved an attempt to drag *Endeavour* back over the coral the way she had come. Two bower anchors were set, one off the starboard quarter and the other directly astern, after which their respective cables were 'hove taut' using blocks and tackles. But while this was happening, the situation with the ship only deteriorated:

> As the Tide fell the ship began to make Water as much
> as two pumps could free: at Noon she lay with 3 or 4

Strakes heel to Starboard ... [at] 5 o'Clock p.m. the tide
we observed now begun to rise, and the leak increased
upon us, which obliged us to set the 3rd Pump to
work ... we should have done the 4th also, but could
not make it work.

At 9 pm, *Endeavour* had been aground for twenty-three hours.
By that stage, the tide had lifted the ship into an upright
position, but even so, for the first time, the captain was
beginning to think that all might be lost. 'The Leak gained
upon the Pumps considerably,' he wrote. 'This was an alarming
and, I may say, terrible circumstance, and threatened immediate
destruction to us. However, I resolved to risk all, and heave her
off in case it was practical, and accordingly turned as many
hands to the Capstan and Windlass as could be spared from the
Pumps ...'

Banks' journal entry echoed the desperate situation they
faced: 'The dreadful time now approached and the anxiety in
everybody's countenance was visible enough ... fear of Death
now stared us in the face ...'

The strongest men applied every ounce of strength they had
to the bars of the capstan and windlass, cranking them inch by
inch to the point where the load on the bower cables must have
had them close to their breaking strain of 55 tons – but they
held. Suddenly, the ship lifted slightly with the run of a wave
along her length. With that, she moved a little aft, only for her
hundreds of tons to then be jolted back down onto the reef.
Another wave similarly lifted the ship, and again she moved
backwards before another shuddering jolt, and another, and
with each movement astern the men hurriedly took up the
slack. This gain increased progressively until finally the moment
came: 'about 20 Minutes past 10 o'Clock the Ship floated, and
we hove her into Deep Water ...'

There's no doubt that the captain would have heaved a sigh
of relief. His belief that the collier design was the best for an
expedition such as this had just been borne out. *Endeavour*'s full

and flat sections amidships provided exceptional buoyancy, and it was that buoyancy that had contributed so much to her being re-floated. A design featuring slacker bilges would more than likely have capsized on the reef and never been saved from such a predicament.

But the battle was only half won. There was already almost 4 feet of water in the bilge from stem to stern, and with 'the Leak increasing upon us', the ship remained in danger of sinking. The captain ordered all available hands to the pumps while others worked on getting some sails set.

By 11 am, *Endeavour* was limping towards the coast under greatly reduced sail. The leadsman worked nonstop and the lookouts aloft scanned the sea ahead to ensure the ship was on a safe course. The best bower had been recovered, but the small bower was snagged and had to be cut away, cable and all. Meanwhile, the exhausted men at the pumps were relieved to learn that they were finally pumping more water out of the bilge than was coming in. Yet there was to be no rest. While they continued to work at the pumps, others were busy converting an old lower steering sail into a large patch so that they could 'fother' the forward section of the ship from the outside in the area where the leak appeared to be. In his journal, Cook explained the procedure:

> We Mix Oakum and Wool together and chop it up Small, and then stick it loosely by handfuls all over the Sail, and throw over it Sheep dung or other filth. Horse Dung for this purpose is the best. The Sail thus prepared is hauled under the Ship's bottom by ropes, and [moved around] until one finds where it takes effect [on the leak]. While the Sail is under the Ship the Oakum is washed off, and part of it carried along with the water into the Leak, and in part stops up the hole ...

The following day, 13 June, a south-easterly breeze remained soft, so conditions were ideal for attempting the fothering exercise. And it worked: 'the Leak decreased, so as to be kept clear with one Pump with ease; this fortunate circumstance gave new life to everyone on board …'

The captain realised that if the leak could not be slowed, and the weather turned against them, there was little hope of *Endeavour* remaining afloat. If that became the case, he intended to run the ship ashore on an island or the coast, 'where out of her Materials we might build a Vessel to carry us to the East Indies'. But now, with the leak under control, a new plan was being hatched: they would sail north along the shore, in search of a suitable harbour where the damage could be repaired.

For safety, the wounded ship was anchored during the hours of darkness. When Cook awoke next morning, he received the highly satisfying news that the light south-easterly continued to prevail. He therefore wasted no time in ordering for the anchor to be weighed at 6 am so that they could continue on their downwind run along the coast. While the crew readied the ship for sailing, he also ordered that two boats be hoisted out and sailed ahead of *Endeavour*, sounding the depth as they went.

They found no port that day, so at sunset the bower was let go once again and *Endeavour* was set up for another night at anchor. That same evening, though, the search came to an end: 'At 8 o'clock the Pinnace, in which was one of the Mates, returned on board, and reported that they had found a good Harbour about 2 Leagues to leeward. In consequence of this information we, at 6 a.m., weighed and run down to it, first sending 2 Boats ahead to lay upon the Shoals that lay in our way …' Once off the port, *Endeavour* was anchored so that Cook could board the pinnace and be taken into what proved to be a river entrance. 'I went myself and Buoyed the Channel,' he wrote, 'which I found very narrow, and the Harbour much smaller than I had been told, but very convenient for our Purpose …'

It was Friday, 17 June, when *Endeavour* sailed into this river, which would soon bear her name. Just over a century later,

Cooktown would be founded on its southern bank close to the entrance where *Endeavour* was beached.

On approach, Cook had his men lighten the ship forward so that she could be grounded as far up the river bank as possible, bow first. Not only would this ensure that the carpenters had good access to the damaged section, once the ship was finally secured onshore, but it offered the crew the best chance of coping with the tidal rise and fall, which averaged around 8 feet. By the 17th, the weather had turned for the worse, with lashing rain and a strong wind. As a result, the ship's entry into the river, which presented a wide, sweeping bend to port near its mouth, was far from straightforward, as reported by Cook:

> Most part strong Gales at South-East, with some heavy showers of rain in the P.M. At 6 a.m., being pretty moderate, we weighed and run into the Harbour, in doing of which we run the Ship ashore Twice. The first time she went off without much Trouble, but the Second time she Stuck fast; but this was of no consequence any farther than giving us a little trouble, and was no more than what I expected as we had the wind. While the Ship lay fast we got down the Foreyard, Foretopmast, booms, etc., overboard, and made a raft of them alongside …

Twenty-four hours later, the remaining four cannons had been lifted out of the hold and moved aft to the quarterdeck, while the spare anchor and any stores and ballast still in the hold were taken ashore by boat. When the next high tide arrived, *Endeavour* was positioned half-a-mile inside the entrance 'on a Steep beach on the south side'. The crew then set up a camp on the beach, which included a tent for the few men who were sick – those '8 or 9, afflicted with different disorders, but none very dangerously ill'. At this time, Banks noted that Tupia was showing the symptoms of scurvy, and that the astronomer, Charles Green, 'was also in a poor way'.

Five days after *Endeavour* had entered the river, she was finally secured in a satisfactory manner on the sand and, at low tide, ready for an assessment of the damage her hull had sustained. During Cook's inspection, at 2 am that day, he realised that a piece of coral rock had played a role in the ship remaining afloat after she had been winched off the reef.

> ... the Rocks had made their way through 4 planks ...
> and wounded 3 more ... Fortunately for us the Timbers
> in this place were very close; otherwise it would have
> been impossible to have saved the Ship, and even as it
> was it appeared very extraordinary that she made no
> more water than what she did. A large piece of Coral
> rock was sticking in one Hole, and several pieces of the
> Fothering, small stones, etc., had made its way in, and
> lodged between the Timbers, which had stopped the
> Water from forcing its way in in great Quantities.

The carpenters began their task at 9 am while the armourers, with their equipment set up on the beach, busied themselves making bolts and nails. Other crewmen were assigned to maintenance jobs on board. Meanwhile, with the ship safely harboured and the repair work underway, the captain's primary concern was to reduce the threat that would continue to come from shoals and reefs once they put to sea from this location. For this reason, he committed Molyneux to go offshore and sound the depths, in the hope that the sailing master could find a safe passage back to deep water.

It would be seven weeks before *Endeavour* was re-floated and set to sail again – seven weeks that gave Banks and his colleagues the best possible chance to appreciate the flora and fauna of this remarkable new land. On 23 June, the day after the repairs commenced, Cook sent some men into the countryside for a pigeon-shooting excursion, during which 'One of the Men saw an Animal something less than a greyhound; it was of a Mouse Colour, very slender made, and swift of Foot …' Banks recorded a far more colourful description: 'A seaman who had been out in the woods brought home the description of an animal he had seen composed in so Seamanlike a style that I cannot help mentioning it: it was (says he) about as large and much like a one gallon keg, as black as the Devil and had 2 horns on its head.' This was, no doubt, the first reported sighting of a kangaroo – rather than its droppings.

The following day, it was Cook's turn:

> I saw myself this morning, a little way from the Ship,
> one of the Animals before spoke of; it was of a light
> mouse Colour and the full size of a Grey Hound, and
> shaped in every respect like one, with a long tail, which
> it carried like a Greyhound; in short, I should have taken
> it for a wild dog but for its walking or running, in which
> it jumped like a Hare or Deer …

In additions to these sightings, there was evidence that, as at Botany Bay, the indigenous people in the area were doing everything possible to avoid being seen by the foreigners.

Monday, 9 July, was especially memorable for every man. It had been twelve months since they were in Otaheite, and that was the last time they had enjoyed fresh meat in any form. Now though, Molyneux returned from an excursion with a prize catch of three large turtles, weighing a total of 791 pounds. 'This day all hands feasted upon Turtle for the First time,' Cook diarised. As memorable as this occasion was, for the ship's commander, Banks and others the following day was one of considerable historic significance. It marked the first direct contact made with the Australian aboriginal on this coast, as Cook recalled:

> In the A.M. 4 of the Natives came down to the Sandy
> point on the North side of the Harbour, having along
> with them a small wooden Canoe with Outriggers, in

which they seemed to be employed striking fish, etc.
Some were for going over in a Boat to them; but this I
would not suffer, but let them alone without seeming
to take any Notice of them. At length 2 of them came
in the Canoe so near the Ship as to take some things we
throwed them. After this they went away, and brought
over the other 2, and came again alongside, nearer than
they had done before, and took such Trifles as we gave
them; after this they landed close to the Ship, and all 4
went ashore, carrying their Arms with them. But Tupia
soon prevailed upon them to lay down their Arms, and
come and set down by him, after which more of us
went to them, made them again some presents, and
stayed by them until dinner time, when we made them
understand that we were going to eat, and asked them
by signs to go with us; but this they declined, and as
soon as we left them they went away in their Canoe ...
They were wholly naked, their Skins the Colour of
Wood soot or a dark chocolate, and this seemed to be
their Natural Colour ... Some part of their Bodies had
been painted with red, and one of them had his upper
lip and breast painted with Streaks of white, which he
called Carbanda. Their features were far from being
disagreeable; the Voices were soft and Tuneable, and
they could easily repeat many word after us, but neither
us nor Tupia could understand one word they said ...

Banks believed, following his encounter with the natives, that
the name of the odd-looking animal that so held the
Englishmen's interest was 'Kangooroo' or 'Kanguru'. However,
over the years a suggestion has emerged that the aborigines
were actually confused by his gestures and verbal enquiry, and
that the word 'kangooroo' actually meant 'I don't know' or 'I
don't understand'.

It was not until the middle of July, four weeks after
Endeavour had entered the river, that Lieutenant Gore shot one

of these animals so that Banks and his people would have a specimen to study. Banks noted that his greyhound, Lady, had claimed a small kangaroo, but was unable to catch the larger, more mature ones because they were far too nimble for the dog. On inspecting Gore's prize, the captain commented, 'It bears no sort of resemblance to any European animal I ever saw.' Then the following day: 'Today we dined of the animal shot yesterday and thought it excellent food.' Of greater interest to the rest of the crew, the men sent out to haul the seine net in the river were having considerable success, meaning that fresh fish was a regular part of their diet.

On 18 July, while the men were in the early stages of preparing the ship for sea and the carpenters entered the final stages of their difficult repair to her hull, Cook, Banks and Solander crossed the river for an expedition that saw them walk 8 miles to the north, along the shore of the coast. During the trek, they were pleased to encounter natives who showed no sign of fear whatsoever. However, this trip up the coast also brought the captain further cause for concern regarding the success of his mission. '[We] ascended a high hill, from whence I had an extensive view of the Sea Coast,' he wrote, 'it afforded us a melancholy prospect of the difficulties we are to encounter, for in whatever direction we looked it was covered with Shoals as far as the Eye could see ...'

Cook was pleased with the relationship that had formed recently between his party and the natives, but this all changed with a confrontation that came about the following day. The Englishmen had continued to catch turtles, an act that the indigenous people appeared to view as theft: the turtles were native property, dead or alive. This incident started when some of the natives accepted an invitation to go aboard *Endeavour*.

> Those that came on board were very desirous of having
> some of our Turtle, and took the liberty to haul two to
> the Gangway to put over the side; being disappointed in
> this, they grew a little Troublesome, and were for

throwing everything overboard they could lay their hands
upon ... I offered them some bread to Eat, which they
rejected with Scorn, as I believe they would have done
anything else excepting Turtle. Soon after this they all
went ashore, Mr Banks, myself, and 5 or 6 of our people
being there at the same time. Immediately upon their
Landing one of them took a Handful of dry grass and
lighted it at a fire we had ashore, and before we well
knowed what he was going about he made a large Circuit
round about us, and set fire to the grass in his way, and in
an instant the whole place was in flames. Luckily at this
time we had hardly anything ashore, besides the Forge
and a Sow with a litter of young Pigs, one of which was
scorched to Death in the fire. As soon as they had done
this they all went to a place where some of our people
were washing, and where all our nets and a good deal of
linen were laid out to dry; here with the greatest
obstinacy they again set fire to the grass, which I and
some others who were present could not prevent, until I
was obliged to fire a Musket loaded with small Shott at
one of the Ring leaders, which sent them off ...

By 20 July, *Endeavour* was deemed to be ready to put to sea. But
on that same day, the captain's deep concern about the
navigational hazards ahead was further roused. He had sent
Molyneux out in the pinnace yet again, looking for an escape
route through the coral maze, but on returning, the master's
news was everything Cook did not need to hear: there was no
safe passage for the ship to the northward at low water.
Dwindling food supplies put additional pressure on this stage of
the voyage, one that would be of undetermined duration and
distance to the East Indies, 'through an unknown and perhaps
dangerous Sea'.

Contrary winds and unsuitable tides kept *Endeavour* in port
for another frustrating twelve days, until the morning of 4
August. 'The wind continued moderate all night,' Cook

recorded of that day, 'and at 5 a.m. it fell calm; this gave us an opportunity to warp out. About 7 we got under sail, having a light Air from the Land, which soon died away, and was Succeeded by the Sea breezes from South-East by South, with which we stood off to Sea East by North, having the Pinnace ahead sounding ...'

At midday, when *Endeavour* was in a comfortable depth of water, Cook called for the best bower to be dropped. They were less than 10 nautical miles east-north-east of the Endeavour River, alongside what Molyneux had named Turtle Reef. When the anchor was set, the captain climbed up the ratlines to the masthead to get a view of the reefs that surrounded them. It was a vista that left him in no doubt that their situation was dire – so serious, in fact, that at one stage he even considered sailing back to the south. That would have been upwind, however, and ships like this were incapable of sailing upwind effectively, especially when in restricted water. After assessing the situation, he decided to hove the anchor and proceed north, but now with even greater caution.

The gain was only 8 miles, to a position a similar distance to the east of Cape Bedford, before it became too dangerous to proceed any further, so Cook called for the ship to come to anchor once more. Minutes later, another challenge appeared: the south-east wind had quickly increased in strength to gale force, and soon after, *Endeavour* 'drove' – began to drag her anchor. All 1¼ tons of it was being dragged through the muddy bottom like a giant plough. Now there was real danger. The captain called for additional cable to be released – close to 200 fathoms' worth – in the expectation that this would be sufficient for the anchor to take a bite. But still it didn't. His next call was to release the small bower as well, in the forlorn hope that two anchors would arrest their drift. That too failed, and *Endeavour* continued on her path towards the submerged coral and apparent destruction, still at the mercy of the relentless gale.

Cook, the master mariner, knew there was only one option remaining, one that would reduce the load on the anchor cables, and therefore give the bowers a greater chance to halt the ship's alarming charge towards the reefs downwind. They had to reduce windage aloft. The best men were ordered to climb the rig and strike – that is, lower almost to the deck, 80 feet below – the topgallant yards, the topgallant mast, other yards and the remaining topmasts, some of which weighed close to a ton. The tactic worked, although *Endeavour* dragged for 3 nautical miles through the reefs before the anchors finally held.

Before bringing down the topmasts, Cook had scaled the mainmast so he could get an overview of their surroundings. What he observed confirmed his worst fears: 'I saw that we were surrounded on every side with Shoals and no such thing as a passage to Sea but through the winding channels between them dangerous to the highest degree in so much that I was quite at a loss which way to steer when the weather will permit us to get under sail …' One sight brought some semblance of optimism, however. 'On the Easternmost [reef] that we could see the Sea broke very high, which made me judge it to be the outermost; for on many of those within the Sea did not break high at all …'

Cook's conclusion would prove correct. It was the outer edge of the reef, which was just 15 nautical miles away. He now knew that if he could thread *Endeavour* through the incalculable number of coral barriers that stood between the ship's present position and that 'outermost' reef, it would take them to the much-needed sanctuary of the open sea. To achieve that, he would have to call on every seafaring and navigational skill he possessed. In recognising the challenge, Cook was also convinced that it was highly probable no explorer before him had ever had his ship imprisoned by such a threatening circumstance. This was one challenge from which it could be said that there was little chance of escape, but if anyone had the ability to do so, it was Cook.

In the time since Cook discovered this remarkable barrier of reefs, a plethora of ships have been claimed by it. Ironically, one of the most noteworthy of these came almost exactly twenty-one years after *Endeavour*'s entanglement, and it came as a direct result of the mutiny involving a young seafarer who would be sailing master for Cook on his fateful final voyage: William Bligh. HMS *Pandora* was returning to England in 1791 with some of the arrested *Bounty* mutineers on board when she slammed onto the Great Barrier Reef some 200 nautical miles north of where *Endeavour* was sailing at this time. Thirty-five lives were lost.

Endeavour lay in wait for the gale to subside, and all that time a careful watch was kept on the highly strained anchor cables, and the chafe points that existed where these heavy ropes exited through the hawseholes. Every time the ship pitched in response to a wave, or lay back due to yet another savage gust, an enormous shock-load was exerted on the cables at those points.

After lying at anchor for over two days, *Endeavour* was finally under sail again at 3 am on 10 August, heading northwards along the coast, hoping to find a safe channel between the coral reefs that would take them east to the outer reef, then the open sea. The ship's master was again in the pinnace out ahead, taking soundings and showing the way. Simultaneously, the crew set about re-hoisting into place the topmasts and yards and re-rigging the halyards and lines. As Cook recalled, everyone was beginning to believe they might be safe: 'We now judged ourselves to be clear of all Danger, having, as we thought, a Clear, open Sea before us; but this we soon found otherwise ...'

The captain's 'found otherwise' moment came when he, Molyneux and others had been to the masthead yet again to observe their surroundings. It took very little time for them to agree that, once more, *Endeavour* appeared to have nowhere to go, so she was brought to anchor close to shore, 9 nautical miles north-west of a headland he called Cape Flattery – so named because of the false sense of security they had just experienced.

Endeavour was then 40 nautical miles north of present-day Cooktown. When the ship was settled on the anchor, Cook went to the shore in the hope that, by climbing a high hill, he might be able to see a path through the hazard-strewn waters and out to the far edge of the reef. This effort was to no avail, however. As an alternative strategy, he, Banks and a select crew boarded the pinnace, carrying a twin-mast settee rig, and sailed to the highest of three islands visible about 20 nautical miles to the north-east. They took sufficient provisions to last three days, during which time Cook recorded in his journal:

> Sunday, 12th … I immediately went upon the highest hill on the Island, where, to my Mortification, I discovered a Reef of Rocks lying about 2 or 3 Leagues [to the east] extending in a line North-West and South-East, farther than I could see, on which the sea broke very high. This, however, gave me great hopes that they were the outermost shoals, as … there appeared to be several breaks or Partitions in the Reef, and Deep Water between it and the Islands …

Cook and his party stayed at the top of the hill until near sunset, hoping the hazy weather would clear and consequently give them a better view of the outer reefs. When that didn't eventuate, they returned to the beach and camped for the night. At 3 am next day, the captain sent out the pinnace with one of the mates in charge, to take soundings and survey one of the channels they had observed running through the reef, approximately 10 nautical miles away. Although the weather on the island that day didn't favour Cook's observations, the pinnace returned with encouraging news: there was deep water all the way to the outer reef. Before quitting this island, Cook named it Lizard Island, because 'The only land Animals we saw here were Lizards'.

On returning to the ship and consulting with Molyneux – who had carried out his own, unsuccessful search for a safe passage, to the north of their anchorage – the captain confirmed that they would be sailing east and escaping to deep water through the outer reef. Cook later wrote of their escape on 14

August and the pressure that all aboard had been under for close to three months:

> Winds at South-East, a steady gale. By 2 o'Clock we just fetched to windward of one of the Channels in the outer Reef I had seen from the Island, we now tacked and Made a short trip to the South-West while the Master in the Pinnace examined the Channel, he soon made the Signal for the Ship to follow, which we accordingly did, and in a short time got safe out. The moment we were without the breakers we had no ground with 150 fathom of Line, and found a well grown Sea rolling in from the South-East, certain signs that neither land nor shoals were in our neighbourhood in that direction, which made us quite easy at being freed from fears of shoals etc – after having been entangled among them more or less ever since the 26th of May, in which we have sailed 360 Leagues without ever having a Man out of the Chains heaving the Lead when the Ship was under way, a circumstance that I dared say never happened to any ship before …

Freedom at last – or was it?

Cook camped for seven weeks at the mouth of the now-named Endeavour River to make repairs after hitting the reef; from the Hawkesworth edition of the account of the voyage. State Library of NSW, Mitchell Library X980/26 / a6430022.

CHAPTER THIRTEEN

The Width of One Wave

As fate would have it, within a couple of days of *Endeavour* having threaded her way to apparent safety, the captain was facing the most dire situation he would ever experience under sail.

After the three months Cook and his crew had been sounding and weaving their way through the maze of coral death traps that made up the Great Barrier Reef, the men on board were relieved to reach deep water. But the safety it brought was paid for with the lost opportunity of mapping this newly apprehended coast, and the risk of missing any passage that might exist between New Holland and New Guinea.

After two days of sailing well wide of the reef, Cook ordered for the ship to change course to the west-north-west, so that contact could be re-established with either the outer reef or the mainland. With that objective achieved they could once again continue with their exploration towards the north. This would, however, be the moment that led to *Endeavour* returning to the life-threatening clutches of what loomed as an unconquerable force – the thundering surf pounding onto the reef. With the wind having faded to nothing, and the sails responding only to the continuous roll of the powerful ocean swells with a mighty thumping sound as they turned inside out, the ship was being dragged uncontrollably in the pre-dawn darkness by a tidal current towards a point of no return.

Despite every effort by the crew, this drift towards destruction continued unabated. No setting of sails, weighing of anchors or launching of small boats to tow the ship was having any effect. Before long, on Thursday, 16 August, *Endeavour* was on the cusp of being picked up by a huge wave, where – as if taking one last breath – she would heave, then be rolled and slammed onto the reef with such violent force that her thick white oak hull planks and frames would be splinters in no time.

'The Large Waves of the Vast Ocean meeting with so sudden a resistance [from the reef] makes a most Terrible Surf, breaking Mountains high' was the image indelibly printed on the captain's mind. Such that: 'between us and destruction was only a dismal valley the breadth of one wave … we had hardly any hopes of saving the ship,' he wrote.

Incredibly, when only a boat-length away from the reef – just the width of one of these giant waves – there was deliverance. Had it not arrived, then the life of every man on board, and the mission, would have been terminated. Salvation came in the form of a puff of wind: barely definable, but enough to bring desperately needed pressure to the sails.

As Cook explained, it was only because their senses were on such high alert that they were able to sense this waft at all. 'At any other time in a calm we should not have observed it,' he remarked. Still, it was only strong enough to propel *Endeavour* a mere 200 yards from the brink before the calm returned. Anxiety and adrenaline continued to pump at an unprecedented rate through the veins of every man aboard as their situation again deteriorated. Having thrown pieces of paper into the water to measure the ship's rate of drift, those on the quarterdeck looked on in dread at the progress of these floating items. There was no doubting it: they were heading back towards the surf, back towards the relentless explosion of foam on the still frighteningly close coral reef.

Once again, it seemed that their end was nigh.

Further agonising torment followed until Aeolus, the God of Wind, dealt them another card, and what Banks would describe as 'our friendly little breeze' returned once more. It lasted about as long as the first puff: enough to take them back to a position 200 yards from the breakers, where, as Banks professed: 'We were still, however, very in the jaws of destruction.'

Fate's pendulum then tipped further towards good fortune. By now, the sun was well above the horizon, and in the improving visibility, the lookout bellowed to Cook and others on the quarterdeck that he could see a narrow channel leading to the inside of the reef, about a quarter of a mile ahead. Cook immediately sent the mate out in a boat to examine it. He returned to say the channel was not much wider than the length of the ship, but that *Endeavour* would be able to pass through it and into smooth water. Added to this encouraging development, it became apparent during the few minutes of ensuing discussion that the tide, too, was finally turning in their favour. It was on the ebb, and before long, water was gushing 'like a millstream' out of the channel they could see. While this pushed them away from their newfound opportunity, it was actually good news, since the ever-increasing distance between *Endeavour* and the channel – and with it, the dangers posed by the reef – afforded Cook and his fellow officers more breathing space in which to plan their next move.

Eventually, the ship was carried 2 miles from the threat, to a location where the man aloft was able to sight an even more favourable gap in the coral. The captain then sent Lieutenant Hickes to explore.

At two o'clock Mr Hicks returned with a favourable account of the opening, it was immediately resolved to try to secure the Ship in it, narrow and dangerous as it was it seemed to be the only means we had of saving her as well as ourselves. A light breeze soon after sprung up at ENE which with the help of our boats and a flood tide we soon entered the opening and was hurried through in a short time by a rapid tide like a Mill race

which kept us from driving against either side though
the channel was not more than a quarter of a Mile
broad ...

Once inside the reef via the pass – which he not surprisingly
named Providential Channel – Cook called for the bower to be
let go in 19 fathoms of smooth water. As the cable slithered
rapidly along the foredeck and out through the hawsehole, the
crew were still in a state of disbelief. It was the master's mate,
Pickersgill, who best put their emotions in perspective. He
wrote of the recent near miss as being 'the narrowest escape we
ever had, and had it not been for the immediate help of
providence we must inevitably have perished'.

Additionally, there had been another challenging situation
to contend with during their time outside the reef, yet its
importance was by this time seen as being relatively trivial. It
was discovered that when *Endeavour* was surging down large
seas, water continually flooded into the ship's bilge as a result of
the earlier repair work on her bow not having extended high
enough above the waterline. As a result, several crewmen were
tasked with the constant and frenetic pumping out of the bilge.
The mentally drained commander of this expedition, the person
responsible for the lives of all ninety men on board, went to
considerable lengths to register the drama that came so close to
bringing their world to an end – possibly for his own benefit as
much as anyone else's. Two days earlier, he had been rejoicing
in the belief that they had escaped the perils of the inner reef.
That joy compared little with the overwhelming relief he felt
now that *Endeavour* was riding safely at anchor, within that same
reef.

... such are the Vicissitudes attending this kind of
Service and must always attend an unknown Navigation:
Was it not for the Pleasure which Naturally results to a
man from being the first discoverer, even was it nothing
more than Sands and Shoals, this Service would be

insupportable especially in far distant parts like this, short
of Provisions and almost every other necessary …

He then defended his decision to explore the reef-strewn
coastline as far as he did:

The world will hardly admit of an excuse for a man
leaving a Coast unexplored he has once discovered, if
dangers are his excuse he is then charged with
Timorousness and want of Perseverance and at once
pronounced the unfittest man in the world to be
employed as a discoverer; if on the other hand he boldly
encounters all the dangers and obstacles he meets and is
unfortunate enough not to succeed, he is then charged
with Temerity and want of conduct …

This thought caused Cook to state his belief that in no way
could he be declared guilty of 'Timorousness and want of
Perseverance', since he had never previously been confronted
by more danger than at this time. He conceded that 'perhaps in
prudence' he should never have exposed his 'single ship'
expedition to such danger – but that was in hindsight.

With those thoughts now spelt out via the tip of his quill, he
had to contemplate where to go from here. Should they once
more try to navigate their way north through a labyrinth of coral
traps perfectly disguised by the sea surface, or return to the more
recent plan of sailing towards New Guinea on a course outside
the main reef? While the first option was like trying to dodge
cannonballs in battle, the latter meant that Cook would run the
risk of not satisfying his desire to confirm the existence, or not,
of a strait separating New Guinea from the northern extremity of
this coast of New Holland.

He chose the former.

The distance north from Cook's Passage, near Lizard Island,
where *Endeavour* had made good her escape to freedom from

the confinement of the inner reef, to Providential Channel, where she now lay at anchor back inside the reef, was 150 nautical miles, and with the remainder of this coast to the north yet to be revealed, Cook could only speculate how many more miles of navigational torture lay ahead. It would prove to be 130 nautical miles to that point – York Cape – which he named in honour of Prince Edward, Duke of York and Albany, the younger brother of King George III. Originally the name applied only to the particular headland he observed, but now Cape York is the name applied to the entire peninsula, covering 53,000 square miles.

It was now critical they get to Batavia and replenish the ship's rapidly dwindling stores. So, at 6 am on 18 August, less than twenty-four hours after setting the best bower, the men were at the windlass for the back-breaking task of hauling it on board. Before setting sail, the captain ordered men to take the boats to an area of reef nearby, to see what they might be able to realise in the way of food. They returned with 270 pounds of meat from shellfish, 'mostly cockles [giant clams] as large as two men can move, and contain about 20lbs of good meat'.

The helmsman then put the wheel down and *Endeavour* bore away, ever so slowly, in response to the moderate south-east breeze, and set on a course to the north-west-by-west. The procedure that followed was the eighteenth-century equivalent of traversing a minefield in modern-day battle. Every one of the thousands of coral outcrops lurking just below the surface was like an explosive device capable of destroying the ship. This was to be the ultimate team effort for everyone aboard *Endeavour*, one in which both wind and tide – which Banks noted 'ran immensely strong' – also came into play.

Only the most trusted lookouts were aloft, while the crew on deck maintained split-yarn vigilance. The bowers had been suspended at their respective catheads, and those hands nominated to be on the foredeck and tend them were ready to release one or both at a moment's notice. The wind strength was being monitored constantly so that sails could be adjusted, in order to maintain a cautious speed of between 2 and 3 knots. Out on the water, there was almost always a couple of boats ahead of the ship: their crews sounding the depths, ever watchful for signs of danger. Finally, for added security, two men were often employed in the chains – one either side of the ship – heaving the lead and calling the depths. Then there was the helmsman: his high level of concentration could not wane for a second, nor could his hearing, as he stayed alert to any call requiring a sudden change of course. At night they would come to anchor, as it was far too dangerous to proceed in the dark.

On 21 August, *Endeavour* was at what would soon prove to be the northern tip of this mighty peninsula. 'We observed that the main[land] looked very narrow,' Banks wrote, 'so we began to look out for the Passage we expected to find between New Holland and New Guinea.'

The ship was guided through this narrow, mile-long passage then anchored, with the plan being for a small party to go ashore, climb a nearby hill and survey their surroundings. This was a wise move, according to Banks, since: 'It gave us the satisfaction of seeing a strait, at least as far as we could see, without any obstruction. In the Evening a strong tide made us almost certain [of this].'

Banks again made note of how the natives had, all the way along the New Holland coast, held a nonchalant attitude towards the presence of the ship and its men. During this excursion ashore, three 'Indians' on a beach close by took only a casual interest in their arrival, then 'walked leisurely away'. It was no different the following morning, when 'three or four women appeared upon the beach gathering shellfish: we looked with our glasses and to us they appeared as they always did, more naked than our mother Eve'. But, as for interest in the European visitors, there was none.

It was on Wednesday, 22 August 1770, that Lieutenant James Cook went ashore on another island, less than 10 miles from where he rounded York Cape, and made history in the name of England.

Having satisfied myself of the great Probability of a passage, thro' which I intend going with the Ship, and therefore may land no more upon this Eastern coast of New Holland, and on the Western side I can make no new discovery ... the Eastern Coast from the Latitude of 38 degrees South down to this place, I am confident, was never seen or Visited by any European before us; and notwithstanding I had in the Name of his Majesty taken possession of several places upon this Coast, I now once More hoisted English Colours, and in the Name of His Majesty King George the Third took possession of the whole Eastern coast from the above Latitude down to this place by the Name of New Wales, together with all the Bays, Harbours, Rivers, and Islands, situate upon the said Coast; after which we fired 3 Volleys of small Arms, which were answered by the like number from the Ship ...

Gunner Stephen Forwood said of the ceremony: 'At 6pm possession was taken of this country in His Majesty's name, and this announcement from the shore by volleys and answered from on board with colours flying and concluding with three cheers.'

Cook named this island Possession Island, and the passage through which *Endeavour* passed, after rounding York Cape, Endeavour Strait. Historians continue to debate the reasons for his naming the entire coastline New Wales and later New South Wales.

Endeavour was soon set on a course to the north-west, but the waters she was sailing were still full of surprises, in the form of sandbanks and reefs. A most cautious approach to navigation remained paramount, therefore. By now, the last visible remnants of New Holland had faded into the hazy horizon directly astern: the ship was bound for Batavia, having covered more than 2000 life-threatening nautical miles since sighting Point Hicks 126 days earlier. Along that coastline – one of the few that had remained unknown to Europeans – Cook, the explorer, had attached 112 names to outstanding topographical features, bays and capes.

Nevertheless, the same explorer took no respite from his research into this part of the world. Right then, as *Endeavour* began breasting a rising swell, there was yet another satisfying conclusion to be savoured:

> ... the wind had got to South-West, and although it blowed but very faint, yet it was accompanied with a Swell from the same quarter. This, together with other concurring Circumstances, left me no room to doubt that we were got to the Westward of Carpentaria or the Northern extremity of New Holland, and had now an open Sea to the Westward; which gave me no small satisfaction, not only because the danger and fatigues of the Voyage was drawing near to an end, but by being able to prove that New Holland and New Guinea are two separate Lands or Islands, which until this day hath been a doubtful point with Geographers ...

The separation between these two lands would become known as Torres Strait.

By now, everyone aboard the ship was craving Batavia and the fresh food it would provide, but more importantly, to soon be home in England with their loved ones. They had been beyond the horizon for more than two years and had had no communication with the outside world via any other vessel; understandably, they were eager to see home waters and thereby erase the fear for their safety that families had harboured since *Endeavour* set sail from Plymouth. So far, every aspect of this circumnavigation had been a remarkable success – even down to the ship still being free from scurvy. Accordingly, considering all that had been achieved to date, there was no doubt that this could already be declared the most successful voyage of discovery ever undertaken.

As *Endeavour* made her way to the west–north–west, the captain was still not certain they were free of the threats of shoals and reefs, so an attitude of prudent seamanship remained. The master was still out in a boat sounding the depths; the lookout remained highly vigilant, and the ship lay at anchor during the hours of darkness.

At night, Cook often sat at his desk and worked under the flickering light of a lantern, updating his notes relating to the voyage. At this juncture, with his exploration of the east coast of New Holland completed, he penned a report titled *Account of the New Wales Coast*. It included a most remarkable and absorbing judgement of the indigenous people:

> From what I have said of the Natives of New Holland they may appear to some to be the most wretched People upon Earth; but in reality they are far more happier than we Europeans, being wholly unacquainted not only with the Superfluous, but the necessary Conveniences so much sought after in Europe; they are happy in not knowing the use of them. They live in a Tranquillity which is not disturbed by the Inequality of Condition. The earth and Sea of their own accord furnishes them with all things necessary for Life. They covet not Magnificent Houses, Household-stuff, etc.; they live in a Warm and fine Climate, and enjoy a very wholesome Air, so that they have very little need of Clothing; and this they seem to be fully sensible of, for many to whom we gave Cloth, etc to, left it carelessly upon the Sea beach and in the Woods, as a thing they had no manner of use for; in short, they seemed to set no Value upon anything we gave them, nor would they ever part with anything of their own for any one Article we could offer them. This, in my opinion, Argues that they think themselves provided with all the necessarys of Life, and that they have no Superfluities …

It was hoped that the remainder of the passage to Batavia would be free of drama, but that was not to be the case. On the morning of 24 August, while the best bower was being raised, the large swell that was running put such a shock-load on the bower cable that the rope parted, dropping its heavy load. The anchor was the most vital piece of equipment with regard to the safety of the vessel; it was something that the ship simply could not be without. And bowers were impossible to replace on a voyage such as this, or manufacture on board.

The second bower was released as soon as the crew became aware of problem. The lost anchor now lay in 8 fathoms of water, and Cook had no option but to do everything in his power to recover it. Once the situation on board was stabilised, he had two boats go out and sweep the bottom with a hawser suspended between them. This attempt was unsuccessful, so the ship remained at anchor there for another night. The following morning, the first sweep with the hawser snagged on the bower and it was then hauled to the surface.

Endeavour then continued sailing to the north-west, towards the coast of New Guinea. This was a time when every man could have been forgiven for thinking that they were about to experience deep water, and freedom from the danger-laden days they had endured in recent months. But again it was not to be the case. As recorded by Cook, one last, menacing threat to their security lay in wait: 'Sunday, 26th … the boat which was ahead made the signal for Shoal Water, immediately upon which we let go an Anchor, and brought the Ship up with the sails standing … and at the same time we saw from the Ship Shoal Water in a manner all round us … [and] there was no way to get clear but the way we came.'

His journal confirmed that he saw this as yet another amazing escape from shipwreck, one in which only alertness and a prompt reaction had saved the day. He noted that, had it not been high tide, *Endeavour* would have struck the rocky bottom. If that had happened, the pounding of her hull on the seabed, caused by the surge of the sea that was running at the time, would have 'bulged' her – that is, caused planks to be sprung and the ship to take on water at a rapid rate.

Because of this situation, Cook abandoned his plans to land on the mainland coast of New Guinea. Instead, he called for *Endeavour* to sail on a course to the west, so that the strong easterly wind that was blowing would propel her away from the shoals they continued to encounter. This would prove to be a day of perfect downwind sailing, when the driver – a square sail set on a yard that is hoisted to the peak of the gaff on the mizzen mast – could be hoisted and trimmed to suit the breeze.

Banks at this time was busy writing a report in his journal – filling page after page with a 10,700-word commentary relating to his experiences and observations while sailing the coast of New Holland. When his daily journal resumed on 1 September, the ship was heading towards Frederick Hendrik Island, on the south-western coast of New Guinea, where they stopped two days later. An excursion ashore, led by Cook, Banks and Solander, proved little different from what they had experienced so often in New Zealand and at times along the coast of New Holland: when they landed, natives appeared and made threats; the Englishmen fired their muskets and the natives retreated. On this landing, they were met by three natives, who took umbrage at the presence of the foreigners, but after the New Guineans retreated into the woods, they returned to the beach with around 100 armed warriors. As Banks later explained, that was enough: he and his compatriots were now tired of dealing with such confrontations. '[We] immediately concluded that nothing was to be got here but by force,' the naturalist wrote, 'which would of course be attended with destruction of many of these poor people, whose territories we had certainly no right to invade either as discoverers or people in real want of provisions; we therefore resolved to go into our boat and leave entirely this coast …'

Following the abortive excursion, Banks described a new condition that had only recently struck the crew:

As soon as ever the boat was hoisted in we made sail and
steered away from this land to the No small satisfaction
of I believe three fourths of our company: the sick
became well and the melancholy looked gay. The
greatest part of them were now pretty far gone with the
longing for home which the Physicians have gone so far
as to esteem a disease under the name of Nostalgia;
indeed I can find hardly anybody in the ship clear of its
effects but the Captain, Dr Solander and myself. Indeed,
we three have pretty constant employment for our
minds which I believe to be the best if not the only
remedy for it ...

As difficult to comprehend as it might have been for most of the
men aboard the ship, at this stage of their circumnavigation,
they were only just beyond half-distance on the long journey
home. In reality, the latter half of the voyage would be
considerably quicker, as no more exploration was required
under the Admiralty's orders.

While the stopover in Batavia was essential for the
replenishment of supplies, there was also a growing need for the
ship to be overhauled. Not surprisingly, after such an arduous
voyage of, to date, some 25,000 nautical miles – more than the
circumference of the Earth – *Endeavour*'s bones were getting
tired. She was leaky, metal fittings were failing, rigging was
worn, and she would probably need to be careened for cleaning
below the waterline. Additionally, the crew were getting restless:
they wanted to be on land, and as a result there was pressure on
the captain to change his plans and stop at Fort Concordia (in
present-day Kupang, on the island of Timor), which was
considerably closer.

'I was strongly importuned by some of my Officers to go to
the Dutch settlement at Concordia for refreshments,' Cook
wrote in his journal, 'but this I refused to comply with,
knowing that the Dutch look upon all Europeans with a Jealous
Eye that come among these Islands, and our necessities were

not so great as to oblige me to put into a place where I might expect to be but indifferently treated.'

His theory was put to the test when he did decide to stop, at the island of Savu, 100 nautical miles to the west of Timor. Cook had the ship anchored and sent Lieutenant Gore and others ashore to ask if they could procure provisions there. After two days of effort, Gore was finally advised by the 'king' for that part of the island that he could supply nothing unless it was authorised by the Dutch governor. That same day, at 2 pm, the governor and this self-styled monarch went aboard *Endeavour* with Gore, who was ordered to leave two crewmen ashore as hostages. Cook later described the visit:

> We entertained them at Dinner in the best Manner we could, gave them plenty of good Liquor, made them some considerable presents, and at their going away Saluted them with 9 Guns. In return for these favours they made many fair Promises that we should be immediately supplied with everything we wanted at the same price the Dutch East India Company had it; and that in the morning Buffaloes, Hogs, Sheep, etc., should be down on the beach for us to look at, and agree upon a price.

However, possibly due to an overindulgence of alcohol by the guests, none of these promises were honoured the following morning. There was no livestock or produce to be seen.

Relations between the two sides then became increasingly strained, but persistence paid off. And this was despite the visitors receiving formal advice that they would be allowed to remain on the island for only one more day, and in that time they had to complete all their purchases. This they did, as Banks recounted:

> The refreshments we got consisted of 8 Buffaloes, 30 Dozen fowls, 6 sheep, 3 hogs, some few but very few limes and cocoa nuts, a little garlic, a good many eggs,

above half of which were rotten, an immense quantity of Syrup [marmalade] which was bought for trifles, several hundred gallons at least – upon the whole, enough stock to carry us to Batavia, and syrup for futurity …

Endeavour set sail for Batavia soon afterwards, with a captain whose attitude towards dealing with the Dutch remained unchanged.

It was then a frustrating five-week passage to Batavia, due to headwinds, calms and navigation charts for the region that the forever-meticulous ship's captain found to be horribly inaccurate. On 21 September, from a position well offshore, the ship rounded Java Head – now known as Tanjung Layar, the westernmost promontory on the island where Jakarta is located. There was then only 130 nautical miles to cover before they reached their destination on the north-western coast of Java, and Cook knew it could not come soon enough. One of his main concerns was the rapidly deteriorating condition of the sails, something that was confirmed for him yet again when he tacked the ship onto a course that would clear the cape by a comfortable margin: 'very unsettled squally weather which split the Main Topsail very much, and obliged us to bend the other; many of our Sails are now so bad that they will hardly stand the least puff of Wind …'

Nine exasperating days passed before *Endeavour* finally reached Batavia, because of strong adverse currents and fickle winds – conditions that caused the anchor to be hove fifteen times to prevent the loss of hard-gained ground. Once in port, the priority became the condition of the ship, and the carpenter, Satterley, promptly presented a report on the defects he had found. He described the overall condition of the hull as 'very leaky', and she was taking on a considerable amount of water throughout the bilge: up to 1 foot every hour. On considering Satterley's report, Cook and his officers concurred that there was a need for a complete overhaul of much of the vessel before she could be sailed to Europe.

Two days after arriving, and while plans were being put in place for repairs, it became clear to the captain and his entire crew that, had the lightning chain not been fitted to the ship prior to their leaving home two-and-a-half years earlier, they might have been spending much more time in Batavia than planned.

> About 9 o'clock in the Evening we had much rain, with
> some very heavy Claps of Thunder, one of which
> carried away a Dutch Indiaman's Main Mast by the
> Deck, and split it, the Main topmast and Topgallant mast
> all to shivers. The ship lay about 2 Cables lengths from
> us, and we were struck with the Thunder [lightning] at
> the same time, and in all probability we should have
> shared the same fate as the Dutchman, had it not been
> for the Electrical Chain which we had but just before
> [hoisted to the masthead]. This carried the Lightning or
> Electrical matter over the side clear of the Ship. The
> Shock was so great as to shake the whole ship
> very sensibly …

Batavia presented Cook with the first opportunity to comply with another of his orders – to forward a copy of his journal to the Admiralty at the first practicable opportunity. He put it aboard a Dutch ship that was heading for Europe, and sent with it a covering letter outlining his achievements to date, which the Admiralty would no doubt have found to be richly rewarding. It read in part:

> … we discovered the East Coast of New Zealand, which
> I found to consist of 2 large Islands … both of which I
> circumnavigated. On the 1st of April, 1770, I quitted
> New Zealand, and steered to the Westward, until I fell in
> with the East Coast of New Holland, in the Latitude of
> 38 degrees South. I coasted the shore of this Country to
> the North, putting in at such places as I saw Convenient,

until we arrived in the Latitude of 15 degrees 45 minutes South, where, on the night of the 10th of June, we struck upon a Reef of Rocks, where we lay 23 Hours, and received some very considerable damage. We were detained repairing the damage we had sustained until the 4th of August, and after all [that] put to Sea with a leaky Ship, and afterwards coasted the Shore to the Northward through the most dangerous Navigation that perhaps ever a ship was in, until the 22nd of the same month, when, being in the Latitude of 10 degrees 30 minutes South, we found a Passage into the Indian Sea between the Northern extremity of New Holland and New Guinea ...

Unassuming individual that he was, Cook could look back on this voyage with great pride. He had exceeded the demands of his orders, placed a spectacular new coastline on the map of the world, and managed to keep the incidence of scurvy among his crew down to a level that was unprecedented. But fate was about to take an undesired twist, bringing a sad series of events to the final stage of his circumnavigation. The first hint of what was to follow came on Friday, 26 October, when his journal read: 'Set up the Ship's Tent for the reception of the Ship's Company, several of them begin to be taken ill, owing, as I suppose, to the extreme hot weather.'

Banks provided more details: 'We now began to feel the ill Effects of the unwholesome climate we were in: our appetites and spirits were gone but none were yet really sick, except poor Tupia and Tiata, both of which grew worse and worse daily so that I began once more to despair of poor Tupia's life ...'

Work had already started on repairing *Endeavour*, but as each day passed, more men were falling ill. The cause was a curse that came with this steamy, rain-sodden environment: dysentery. With the ship destined to be in port for another ten weeks, the disease would prove to be a death sentence for many of *Endeavour*'s crew, all of whom had survived after being taken to the threshold of tragedy so many times during this voyage.

The first death came on 7 November, and ironically it was the surgeon who was the first to succumb, as Cook recorded: 'We had the misfortune to lose Mr Monkhouse, the Surgeon, who died of a Fever after a short illness, of which disease and others several of our people are daily taken ill, which will make his loss be the more severely felt ...'

On 27 December, close to three months after docking at Batavia, *Endeavour*'s repairs were finished and she was ready to put to sea. By then this destination, which had been so ardently desired prior to arrival, had become a curse. Apart from the surgeon, both Tupia and Tiata had died from the disease, as had one of the servants, John Reynolds, and three seamen. Dysentery was carving its way through those on board like a scythe: at times barely a dozen men were well enough to work at their assigned tasks. Banks and Solander were among those struck down by the disease. At no stage, however, is there any reference to the captain falling seriously ill.

Not even Christmas Day could raise any sense of enthusiasm from the men. But the following day, when the time arrived for the anchor to be weighed so that *Endeavour* could move away from the port, Banks wrote of a new-found energy among the crew: 'There was not, I believe, a man in the ship but gave his utmost aid to getting up the Anchor, so completely tired was every one of the unwholesome air of this place. We had buried here 8 people ... in general, however, the Crew was in rather better health than they had been a fortnight before ...'

Unfortunately, though, when *Endeavour* did finally depart, she took the disease with her, and this circumstance, coupled with the sweltering and steamy heat of the monsoon season, kept the ship's sick list at a disconcertingly long length. There was little that could be done to assist those most afflicted, so much so that by halfway through the voyage to Cape Town, twenty-two men were dead, their bodies having been buried at sea. This included Banks' assistant naturalist, Herman Spöring, astronomer Charles Green, two of the three midshipmen, the bosun and one of the carpenters.

Cook's journal entry for 31 January 1771, painted a dire picture:

> In the course of this 24 Hours we have had 4 men died of the Flux [dysentery], viz., John Thompson, Ship's Cook; Benjamin Jordan, Carpenter's Mate; James Nicholson and Archibald Wolf, Seamen; a melancholy proof of the calamitous situation we are at present in, having hardly well men enough to tend the Sails and look after the Sick, many of whom are so ill that we have not the least hopes of their recovery …

The captain lamented: 'a Man was no sooner taken with [the disease] than he looked upon himself as Dead. Such was the Despondency that reigned among the Sick at this time, nor could it be by any Means prevented.'

When *Endeavour* arrived off Cape Town on 15 March, Cook arranged for twenty-eight of the sick to be transferred ashore for treatment. The ship remained in port a month while everything was done to save the men, but still they continued to die.

Just prior to leaving the Cape, Cook learned that he might be confronted by another challenge on the 6000-plus nautical-mile homeward run: a Dutch ship brought news 'that a War is daily expected between England and Spain'. It might also involve France. They would have to be on their guard.

By 15 April, *Endeavour* was ready to put to sea. Three men had died during this stay, and eleven others arrived back aboard that day, the last of the patients receiving treatment onshore. The anchor was weighed and sails set at 3 pm on 16 April, but within an hour there was more distressing news. This time, according to Cook, dysentery was not the cause: 'At 4 departed this Life Mr Robert Molyneux, Master, a young man of good parts, but had unfortunately given himself up to Extravagancy and intemperance, which brought on disorders that put a Period to his Life …'

The threat of war caused Cook to sail 1700 nautical miles north-west to St Helena Island where, for the purposes of protection in the North Atlantic, she joined up with a convoy of East India ships, which was under the escort of the 50-gun HMS *Portland*. The fleet made sail on 4 May, with all captains doing everything possible to ensure that the ships remained in tight formation as they sailed north towards the Equator. As an added precaution, Cook had his men practise cannon and light arms fire on a regular basis. After six days of sailing, however, he was becoming increasingly concerned: his cumbersome and slow converted collier would almost certainly lose visual contact at some stage and become vulnerable to attack. Sure enough, once the fleet had crossed the Equator and headwinds began to prevail, *Endeavour* fell out of the pack and was soon going it alone.

On Sunday, 26 May, the ship was again shrouded in sadness:

> About 1 o'Clock P.M. departed this Life Lieutenant
> Hicks, and in the Evening his body was committed to
> the Sea with the usual ceremonies. He died of a
> Consumption [tuberculosis] which he was not free from
> when we sailed from England, so that it may be truly
> said that he hath been dying ever since, tho' he held out
> tolerable well until we got to Batavia ...

By now, the crew were beginning to wonder if they would ever reach home. *Endeavour*, having sailed near 50,000 nautical miles, was literally falling apart at the seams. The hull was again leaking badly, but of more concern was the condition of the masts and sails. Near the end of June, the carpenter reported to Cook that the main topmast was sprung (split) as a result of the two windward-side backstays having broken. Sails were also blowing apart every time the ship encountered squalls. Two weeks later, the captain was to learn that they had already been given up for lost:

> At 9 a.m. spoke to a Brig from Liverpool ... bound for
> Grenada. We learnt from this Vessel that no account had
> been received in England from us, and that Wagers were
> held that we were lost. It seems highly improbable that
> the Letters sent [via] the Dutch ships from Batavia
> should not come to hand, as it is now 5 months since
> these ships sailed ...

For Banks, who had already lost his spaniel earlier in the trip, there was a level of grief when he went to his cabin one day and found that his greyhound had died suddenly from an unknown cause. However, while the two canines had departed the world, the nanny goat was as healthy as the day she went aboard the ship and was now about to complete her second circumnavigation.

There was elation across the ship on Wednesday, 10 July 1771, and Cook's journal revealed the reason: 'At Noon we saw land from the Mast Head, bearing North, which we judged to be about the Land's End.'

After being away on a voyage of discovery that would prove to be the most remarkable in the annals of maritime history, *Endeavour* was back in home waters. It was also the voyage that proved to the world that through cleanliness and the utmost attention to good diet, the scourge of scurvy could be minimised. Even so, the ship returned with its journal revealing a terrible loss of life. Of the ninety-four men who were aboard *Endeavour* when she sailed away from Plymouth on 26 August 1768, only fifty-four returned. In another sobering statistic, thirty-one of the thirty-eight deaths occurred after the ship reached Batavia, the majority as a consequence of dysentery.

On Saturday, 13 July, the captain made his final entry in *Endeavour*'s log: 'At 3 o'clock in the PM anchored in the Downs, and soon after I landed in order to repair to London.'

CHAPTER FOURTEEN

A Battle of Wills

Lieutenant Cook's desire to return home to his family in London without delay was as compelling as his willingness to comply with the last of his orders from the Admiralty. The Lords' final directive specified: 'upon your Arrival in England, you are immediately to repair to this office in order to lay before us a full account of your proceedings in the whole Course of your Voyage.'

This he did, more than likely while heading to the family home at Mile End. No doubt, he was anxious to not only see his wife, Elizabeth, but also to learn how their offspring were faring, in an era when childhood deaths were not uncommon. The reunion must have been a time of great joy and relief for the captain's wife, due in no small part to the speculation that had grown regarding *Endeavour*'s possible fate. With the ship feared missing, Elizabeth could well have been preparing her two young sons for the possibility that their father would not be returning home.

For Cook, now aged forty-two, the homecoming was coloured by both happiness and despair. His wife remained the proud and caring mother he knew so well, but she greeted him with the tragic news that their only daughter, four-year-old Elizabeth, had died just three months before his return, and baby Joseph had lived for only a month after being born on the day that *Endeavour* set sail from Plymouth. Yet there was the satisfaction of seeing that the two eldest boys, James, aged seven, and Nathaniel, six, were thriving. Added to this mix was an emotional burden for all: with the man of the house having been away for three years, there was the difficult period of becoming reacquainted as a family, and of him needing to adjust to life ashore. Throughout his absence, Cook had lived in the confines of a very small cabin aboard an overcrowded ship, which was forever moving, sometimes violently, at the whim of wind and waves. Now, he had to adapt himself to a stable, comfortable and considerably larger home environment.

While relishing being back in the family fold, Cook's dedication to duty would have remained at the forefront of his daily activities, with one of his priorities being to write letters to the parents of those who had died during the expedition. One such parent was George Monkhouse, who lost two sons – William, the ship's surgeon, and Jonathan, a midshipman. Cook also spent much of his shore-time over the coming months rewriting his journals and checking the charts and sketches that documented the *Endeavour* voyage.

During these first few weeks at home, he no doubt keenly awaited a response from the Lords of the Admiralty regarding his reports of the voyage. He could only hope that the navy chiefs would be highly satisfied with his discoveries. The wait lasted almost three weeks. On 1 August, the Lords met to consider the captain's documents, and the following day, the Secretary of the Admiralty, Philip Stephens, penned the eagerly awaited letter and had it delivered to Cook's home. It was everything that this explorer could have hoped for. It read in part: 'having laid [your documents] before my Lords Commissioners of the Admiralty I have the pleasure to acquaint you that their Lordships extremely well approve of the whole of your proceedings and they have great satisfaction in the account you have given them ...'

A Yorkshireman to the heart, the unassuming Cook remained reserved in his demeanour, despite the significance of his achievement. He had just commanded the most successful voyage of discovery the world had known, thus elevating England to a new level of eminence throughout Europe. Meanwhile, the aristocratic, socially prominent and always-eloquent Banks, and his associate Daniel Solander, were being celebrated across London society. The press referred to this as 'Mr Banks' Voyage', and the finds were deemed to be more than impressive: he and Solander had returned with news of almost forty previously undiscovered islands, as well as evidence of the most remarkable species of plants and animals, the likes of which had never been seen in Europe. There was little or no mention of Cook in these reports. It was as if he had sailed the ship at Banks' behest – a sailing master doing as ordered by his gentleman commander.

In no time, Banks and Solander were being presented to King George III by the president of the Royal Society, Sir John Pringle, and soon afterwards it was suggested that Banks should lead another expedition into the South Pacific. Such was the euphoria around the man that, according to later claims, some in the upper echelon of society urged that New South Wales be renamed Banksia. On a personal front, somewhat unchivalrously, Banks ended his relationship with Miss Harriet Blosset. He had established this relationship just before setting sail on *Endeavour* and many expected their liaison to lead to a betrothal, as marriage was discussed on his return. Miss Blosset reportedly suggested that they wait at least two weeks to discuss the matter further, and if, at that time, his desire for marriage remained genuine, 'she would gladly attend him to church'. It appears he virtually ignored her during that period – behaviour that did not impress many of those who knew him well. Eventually, he advised her in a letter that marriage was not for him, and eased his conscience by pompously making an arrangement for her: 'The marriage is not to take place and she is to have £5000,' he told a friend.

The pinnacle of recognition came Cook's way on 14 August 1771. This was the day when the First Lord of the

Admiralty, Lord Sandwich, proudly introduced him to the King at St James' Palace in London, so that all aspects of the incredible voyage could be explained in detail to the much-impressed monarch. No doubt there would also have been discussion about a new voyage of discovery for Cook, something that had already been mooted by Lord Sandwich. Making this day even more meritorious for the highly acclaimed sailor, confirmation came through that he had been promoted to the rank of commander within the Royal Navy. He received his commission from the King at this meeting.

By now, Cook had bidden farewell to his wonderful ship, and to his men, some of whom would sail with him again. The now-famous nanny goat was retired from active duty and took up residence in the lush gardens at Cook's home. It would appear that the shock of shore life after two circumnavigations was too much for her, though, as she died just a month later.

Endeavour was moved to Woolwich soon after their return, and there she was refitted and sheathed once again. For three years, she transported stores to the Falkland Islands, before becoming a troop transport during the American War of Independence. The former collier suffered a most inglorious fate, however, when the British scuttled her near the harbour entrance at Newport, Rhode Island, in August 1778, to form part of a blockade against a French attack. In recent years, considerable effort has gone into trying to locate the wreck of the famous ship.

Cook's affection for *Endeavour* was evident in a letter he wrote to his former employer and mentor John Walker, soon after arriving back in London. 'I sailed from England as well provided for such a voyage as possible,' he said, 'and a better ship for such a Service I never would wish for.' A few weeks later, in another letter to Walker, Cook alluded to the possibility of a second expedition into the Pacific: 'Another Voyage is thought of [by the Admiralty], with two Ships, which if it takes place I believe the command will be conferred upon me ...'

His theory at this stage was that any search for a southern continent would have to be well to the south, in the higher latitudes, a theory with which Banks concurred. Using the extensive knowledge he now held of the region where he thought this landmass might be, Cook had already mapped out a plan that would allow him to cover the greatest expanse of ocean in the time available. He proposed to enter the region via a stopover in New Zealand, after rounding the Cape of Good Hope, and sail across the Southern Ocean on the prevailing westerly winds. By arriving there in September, he could carry out his search throughout the entire summer, before returning to England via Cape Horn in fair weather. Cook's plan would come unstuck, but through no fault of his own.

Cook proposed that the new project should be a two-ship expedition because of the near-cataclysmic experiences he and his crew had endured in the reef-strewn northern waters of New Holland. The second vessel would provide added security. The Admiralty agreed, and on 25 September – little more than two months after *Endeavour* reached England – the Lords directed the Navy Board to pursue the purchase of two ships most suited for the proposed mission.

With *Endeavour* having proved to be the perfect vessel for the first voyage, there was little wonder that, on Cook's suggestion, the Navy Board purchased the colliers *Marquis of Granby* and *Marquis of Rockingham*. The former was larger than *Endeavour* by about 100 tons and offered a bigger cargo hold, as well as more space between decks for crew comfort. *Marquis of Rockingham* was 28 tons lighter in burthen, at 340 tons, which was an ideal size for a support vessel. Most satisfying for Cook was that their pedigrees were the same as *Endeavour*'s, having both been built at the Fishburn yard in Whitby. They were renamed HMS *Drake* and HMS *Raleigh*, respectively. Cook was assigned to command *Drake*, and 36-year-old Tobias Furneaux – who had circumnavigated the globe as second lieutenant aboard Captain Wallis' *Dolphin* in 1766–68 – was made commander of the support vessel. When speaking of his new command, Cook wrote, 'She was the ship of my choice and as I thought the fittest for the Service she was going upon of any I had ever seen.'

The fit-out of both ships, which started at Deptford almost immediately, was scheduled to take four months to complete. The Admiralty advised Cook that it would like the voyage to begin in March the following year, which was distinctly possible. Now the Admiralty's favourite son, he was given carte blanche when it came to procuring whatever was needed, including the best equipment, provisions and the latest navigational aids.

Fortunately for the Cook family, not all of his time was spent working. In December, he went to Great Ayton, Yorkshire, to see his 77-year-old father, a widower since Grace had passed away in February 1765. Elizabeth, now pregnant for the fifth time, travelled with him for what would be her first-ever meeting with her father-in-law, who was living with one of Cook's sisters, Margaret Fleck, the wife of a local fisherman. The family reunion would have been euphoric, especially for a very proud James Cook senior, whose son had gone from being a farm boy in Yorkshire to one of the great master mariners and explorers of all time.

It had been a demanding three-day journey to get there – more than 250 miles by carriage. The latter stages, over particularly rough roads, combined with the bitter cold of mid-winter to take quite a toll on Elizabeth. Because of this, she remained in Great Ayton while her husband travelled on horseback to Whitby for a few days to visit John Walker. While there, he also visited the Fishburn shipyard to report on how suitable and seaworthy *Endeavour* had proved to be on the circumnavigation, and to inform the owners that *Marquis of Granby* and *Marquis of Rockingham* had been purchased for the next voyage of discovery. His fame had preceded him to Whitby, as was apparent when he visited his old lodgings at the Walker household. Cook walked through the door to an unrestrained and highly emotional welcome from Mary Prowd, the elderly housekeeper who, ignoring her employer's instructions to recognise the captain with all due formality, threw her arms around her hero, hugged him and cried: 'Oh honey James! How glad I is to see thee …'

New Year's Eve was celebrated at his father's residence. Then, on 4 January, the captain and his wife were on their way back to London, a city that was invariably smog-ridden throughout the winter months due to the burning of coal in homes, as well as the many factories operating in these early days of the Industrial Revolution.

After returning to town, the commander was soon informed that there was a move afoot by Secretary of State Lord Rochford to change the names of the two recently converted colliers. Rochford was convinced that because of Britain's strained relationship with Spain, which had been inflamed by the recent explorations in the Pacific, the Spanish would find the names *Drake* and *Raleigh* offensive – the two eponymous Englishmen having been among their country's greatest adversaries historically. Rochford therefore proposed that the vessels be renamed *Aurora* and *Hispenis*, two choices that Lord Sandwich disliked, although he recognised the sensitivity surrounding the issue. Instead, the First Lord of the Admiralty declared, 'The names pitched upon for the two Discovery ships are Resolution & Adventure,' and that they became.

Meanwhile, in further planning his second voyage of discovery, Cook extensively researched the tracks of all previously known forays into the Pacific, with particular regard to the circle of latitude 40 degrees south of the Equator – which in today's nomenclature passes through Bass Strait and New Zealand's Cook Strait. This led to him writing to Sandwich in February 1772 with a more specific outline for the course of the voyage:

> Upon due consideration of the discoveries that have been made in the Southern Ocean, and the tracks of the Ships which have made these discoveries; it appears that no Southern lands of great extent can extend to the Northward of 40° of Latitude, except about the

> Meridian of 140° West [about 600 nautical miles east of
> Tahiti], every other part of the Southern Ocean have at
> different times been explored to the northward of the
> above parallel. Therefore to make new discoveries the
> Navigator must Traverse or Circumnavigate the Globe
> in a higher parallel than has hitherto been done, and this
> will be best accomplished by an Easterly Course on
> account of the prevailing westerly winds in all high
> Latitudes.

In simple terms, *Resolution* and *Adventure* were destined to sail into some of the bleakest and most hostile southern waters ever traversed, all in search of a continent that might not exist. Cook added that 'the general route must be pursued otherwise some part of the Southern Ocean will remain unexplored', a theory with which Sandwich agreed.

It must be asked why neither Cook nor his superiors proposed that he further trace the coastline of New South Wales to prove if it might form part of the Great South Land, especially considering the remarkable length of coastline that he had charted with *Endeavour*. One can only interpret this as reflecting their continued belief that the continent so eagerly sought was independent of the region formerly known as New Holland.

Work on the refit of the two ships was proceeding according to plan, and a March departure date remained likely – until Joseph Banks stepped in. It appears that the wave of euphoria that had elevated the 29-year-old to the highest levels of public recognition had also led to a proportionate swelling of his ego. This spelled trouble for Cook, and for the mission. Continued references in the press to 'Mr Banks' Voyage' aboard *Endeavour* saw Banks become the unofficial legend of British maritime exploration with the announcement of a second Pacific voyage. Illustrative of the plaudits being heaped on this young man, the eminent Swedish scientist Carl Linnaeus signed off his letter to

Banks with the Latin line '*Vale vir sine pare*' – 'Farewell oh unequalled man'.

Banks' involvement in the second voyage came about through an invitation from Lord Sandwich. The immediate response was that he would be glad to participate in the forthcoming expedition, and that Dr Solander would join him. Due to Banks' high profile in the press, and in the absence of any mention of Cook's appointment as commander, it was immediately assumed by the British public that Banks was going to lead the second voyage of discovery, and he did nothing to dispel this. Such an assumption allowed Banks' self-aggrandisement to escalate unabated: Lord Sandwich's enquiry, and the publicity that followed, led the non-seafaring Lincolnshire estate owner to convince himself that it was 'his' expedition.

Sure enough, Banks was soon receiving applications from people across Britain and Europe, and even from sailors within the Royal Navy, either requesting to be part of the venture or making suggestions for particular areas of research during the expedition. Banks duly vetted all these applications while seeking appropriately qualified (and not so qualified) members of his entourage. In no time, the proposed team had grown to fifteen in number, including scientists, draughtsmen, secretaries, servants and – incredibly – two horn players to entertain them along the way.

The most qualified and desirable member of this group was James Lind, from Edinburgh, whose written invitation from Solander had urged: 'Will You my Dear Doctor give us leave to propose You, to the Board of Longitude, as willing to go out as an Astronomer. Your well known character makes us all beg, pray & long for your affirmative answer … Good God, we shall do wonders if you only will come and assist us.' On learning of Lind's appointment, and parliament's subsequent commitment of a special grant of £4000 to support the Scotsman in his quest to make discoveries, Cook wrote somewhat sarcastically: 'but what the discoveries were, the Parliament meant he was to make, and for which they made so liberal a Vote, I know not.' Another notable inclusion in Banks' team was Johann Zoffany, a German-born artist who had been appointed as a founding member to the Royal Academy of Arts in 1769.

Banks was becoming increasingly excited by the opportunities he saw coming his way on this voyage, which he knew would delve deep into the Southern Ocean. He wrote to his friend Comte de Lauraguais in France: 'Oh how Glorious would it be to set my heel upon the [south] pole! And turn myself round 360° in a second.' It was equally important to him to be on the expedition that would, more than likely in his mind, finally identify the location of the fabled great southern continent.

When Banks first saw 'his' ship, *Resolution*, at the navy dockyard at Deptford, he was far from impressed. Not because of any (nonexistent) expert opinion he might have had of her lines and nautical attributes, but because he did not see her as being big enough to accommodate his ever-expanding team, which now looked likely to exceed the sixteen originally planned, including Solander and himself. This disappointment led to him going immediately to his friend, Lord Sandwich, with the demand that the vessel be modified extensively to house his party and the exorbitant amount of equipment they intended to take with them – or he would cancel the voyage. Banks' direct approach to Sandwich was symptomatic of his belief that he was in command while Cook would be nothing more than the ship's master, answerable to him.

The fact that both Palliser, as Comptroller of the Navy, and Cook had agreed that no significant modifications should be made to what was a proven design, meant nothing to Banks. He simply by-passed the experts and won the day with Lord Sandwich, who ordered that the Navy Board proceed with Banks' desired changes. *Resolution* was to be altered considerably through the addition of a heavily built upper deck, a heightened waist amidships, and a poop deck with a cabin to accommodate Cook, who was thereby evicted from the captain's cabin, and again denied exclusive use of the great cabin. Banks had decided that only he and his chosen people would utilise these areas.

Such was the publicity surrounding the voyage that innumerable people visited *Resolution* while she was in dock, in order to gain a better appreciation of the undertaking. Their presence impeded the shipwrights, carpenters and riggers working on the changes, which led Cook to remark, with a degree of cynicism: 'many of all ranks ... Ladies as well as gentlemen, for scarce a day past on which she was not crowded with Strangers who came on board for no other purpose but to see the Ship in which Mr Banks was to sail round the world.'

Cook, the seafarer, was becoming increasingly concerned about the time that was being taken to make the alterations instigated by Banks. A March departure was now completely out of the question. There were continual delays and inevitably, as each problem unfolded, Banks would vent false frustration and threaten not to go on the voyage.

Regardless of these antics, not to mention his belief that the original configuration was the best choice for the upcoming expedition, Cook got on with the job of co-ordinating the refit. Instead of commenting on the changes, he accepted the direction that came from the Navy Board, with his characteristic stoicism. He knew that the sea trials before departure would reveal that *Resolution* had been made so top-heavy that she would be unseaworthy. However, he would later regret not expressing his objections to the design changes. It had been an expensive mistake in more ways than one: most critically, *Resolution*'s departure would be delayed by more than two months.

On 12 May 1772, *Resolution* was deemed ready for her trials. After weighing anchor she moved down the Thames to The Nore, a sandbank marking the point where the river meets the North Sea. There, as soon as the bower was released, the pilot who had guided her to the anchorage demanded to be taken ashore, refusing to sail the ship any further. He considered her crank – so top heavy that she was in danger of capsizing even with a minimal amount of sail set. One experienced crew-member described the vessel as 'an exceeding dangerous and unsafe ship', while Charles Clerke, a veteran of the *Endeavour* voyage and Cook's second lieutenant for the forthcoming expedition, wrote to Banks and left him in no doubt as to his opinion: 'By God, I'll go to Sea in a Grog Tub, if desired, or in the Resolution as soon as you please; but must say I think her by the far most unsafe Ship I ever saw or heard of.'

For Cook also, the passage to The Nore was enough. It was time for him to stand his ground. He immediately advised the Admiralty and the Navy Board that he would not put to sea in this ship as it was. This was a declaration that any professional seafarer, especially in the naval hierarchy, would understand, and it had the desired impact. Within days, his superiors ordered that *Resolution* be taken south to the dock at Sheerness so that almost every one of the modifications demanded by Banks could be removed. Most importantly, the new top hamper had to be demolished.

With *Resolution* returned to her original proportions, Banks travelled to Sheerness for a first-hand look at what had happened to 'his' ship, and when he saw her he threw what can only be described as an almighty tantrum. A midshipman, John Elliott, who was there at the time, would later write:

> Mr Banks was requested to go to Sheerness and take a view of the accommodations, as they now stood, to try if he could go out in her, for in no other state could she go to sea, and go she must … When he saw the ship, and the Alterations that were made, He swore and stamped upon the Wharf like a Mad Man; and instantly ordered his servants, and all his things out of the ship.

Banks then made a disastrous mistake: he wrote a 2000-word rant to Lord Sandwich in which he vented his anger and frustration, and did everything possible to justify the importance of his role in the expedition. He even went to the extent of suggesting that HMS *Launceston*, a 44-gun ship, be put at his disposal for the mission. As much as Banks tried to create a case in defence of the now-rejected ship configuration, the letter simply revealed his ignorance of all things maritime. Cook biographer John Cawte Beaglehole summed it up perfectly: Banks failed to understand that 'accommodation was to be made for the passengers such as would fit the ship, not such as would fit the ship to the passengers'.

It would later be revealed that Banks had an ulterior motive when it came to passenger accommodation and his own private quarters. But that would not become apparent until after *Resolution* arrived in Madeira.

He also launched an ill-judged broadside at Cook. There were other captains of equal, if not superior, ability, Banks opined; these seafarers would be more suited to the task than one who obviously believed that the success of the expedition relied so much on the design and build of the ship.

Lord Sandwich immediately fired back a powerful response, which no doubt scored a direct hit on Banks. It had been drafted for two reasons: firstly, to put Banks in his place, and secondly, to head off any intentions he may have held of starting a confrontation with the navy via the press. But while Banks did not pursue support through print, it came anyway via letters to editors. A typical example appeared in the June issue of *The Gentleman's Magazine*, in which the writer was convinced that everything relating to this voyage revolved around Banks, and that the navy had scorned the wishes of the King:

> As the expedition with a view to new discoveries, which Mr Banks, Dr Solander and Mr Zoffany were to embark in, is now, after raising the expectations of the literati throughout Europe to the highest pitch, abruptly laid aside … [it] is a memorable instance how little it is in the power of Majesty to perform, when the servants of the Crown are determined to oppose the Sovereign's will.

The consequences of Banks' petulant behaviour were simple and definite: he and his party would not be undertaking this second voyage of discovery with Commander Cook. This was good news for all concerned – except for Banks. Midshipman Elliott again provided an overview of the situation: 'upon the whole it has always been thought that it was a most fortunate circumstance for the purpose of the voyage that Mr Banks did not go … for a more proud, haughty man could not well be, and all his plans seemed directed to show his own greatness, which would have accorded ill with the discipline of a man of war …'

In contrast with the near-farcical situation surrounding *Resolution*, *Adventure*'s refit had been completed without drama and on schedule. Since then, her captain, Tobias Furneaux, had sailed her to Plymouth, where she was lying idly at anchor, awaiting the arrival of the expedition's lead ship.

Despite the many distractions, Cook had to maintain composure and keep his concentration on the task ahead. Most importantly, he needed to select a highly talented crew for *Resolution*, to ensure that the mission was given every chance of success. The man chosen as master, Joseph Gilbert, was of a similar age to Cook, and as the voyage progressed, he became a strong supporter of the captain.

Cook was most pleased to welcome aboard twelve men who had served with him aboard *Endeavour*, including Charles Clerke and Robert Cooper, the last of whom had been promoted to the rank of lieutenant. For Elizabeth Cook's cousin, nineteen-year-old Isaac Smith, the taste of adventure experienced on the previous voyage was such that he too had signed on for another circuit around the world. Representing the Royal Society this time were astronomers William Wales aboard *Resolution*, and William Bayley aboard *Adventure*, while William Hodges would serve as artist on the lead ship.

With Banks having met his match in the showdown with Sandwich, he decided the best way to assuage his anger was to charter a fully crewed ship and have his already assembled entourage join him on a voyage to Iceland to study that region. His replacement aboard *Resolution* was a man well known to both Banks and Solander within the Royal Society, Johann Reinhold Förster, a German-born man of religion who was also a botanist and philosopher. In addition, it would soon be realised, he was a man devoid of any attractive character traits. One Cook biographer, Richard Hough, wrote of Förster: 'Johann either made enemies or aroused exasperation by his pedantry, self-righteousness, vanity, habitual acrimony and downright rudeness.' His offensive demeanour led to many confrontations with the crew during the voyage, to the extent that he was floored in one round of fisticuffs, and on a number of occasions was threatened with being thrown overboard – but he lasted the distance. Förster was accompanied by his seventeen-year-old son, Georg, who fortunately did not inherit any of his father's irksome traits and was seen to be highly intelligent.

Of all the equipment put aboard *Resolution*, the most notable and exciting was the Larcum Kendall K1 chronometer, which was a replica of the acclaimed Harrison H4 – the most advanced timepiece in the world for the calculation of longitude. The H3, the predecessor of the H4, had taken its creator, John Harrison, seventeen years to make. The H4 was noted for its accuracy and the fact that, because it was virtually frictionless, the system required no oiling. Also, with pendulums having proved to be unreliable aboard a ship, Harrison's chronometers had opposing balances in their mechanisms, a feature that eliminated the effect of the ship's pitching and rolling motion on the clocks. The K1, like the H4, had the appearance of a large pocket watch of almost 5 inches diameter. The H4 was noted for having a jewelled mechanism and was said to be 'a thing of beauty'. In describing his timepiece, Harrison said: 'Fifty years of self-denial, unremitting toil, and ceaseless concentration. I think I may make bold to say, that there is neither any other Mechanism or Mathematical thing in the World that is more beautiful or curious in texture than this my watch or timekeeper for the Longitude.' It must have come as a great relief for Cook to realise early in the voyage that the K1 performed as well as Harrison's H4. Because of this, his navigational plots would be considerably more precise than those he was able to make on *Endeavour*. In an earlier trial of the H4 on a 1300-nautical-mile passage from England to Madeira, the Harrison clock proved to be absolutely accurate when applied to the ship's navigation, while the common dead-reckoning method, which was used for a comparison, proved to be out by 86 nautical miles.

As the work on *Resolution* neared completion, Cook applied himself to victualling the ship, personally ordering the majority of the supplies and supervising their stowage. This was a considerable task, as the expedition was likely to take two years to complete and the ship had a crew of 118. The provisions included 60,000 pounds of biscuits, 7637 pieces of salted beef, each weighing 4 pounds, twice that amount of salted pork, 1900 pounds of suet, 3100 pounds of raisins, 642 gallons of wine, 19 tons of beer and 1400 gallons of spirits. In general, the average daily allocation per man while at sea included a pound of biscuits and either as much beer as he could drink or a pint of wine, or half a pint of brandy, rum or arrack.

With the health of his crew being uppermost in his mind, the captain again put aboard foods that he saw as being essential for their wellbeing. This included 20,000 pounds of sauerkraut, salted cabbage and cakes of meat essence, which, through the addition of wheat and water, became a broth; and 210 gallons of olive oil. There were also 30 gallons of carrot marmalade in the larder. Livestock, including bullocks, sheep, pigs and goats (the latter simply to supply milk), was corralled on the main deck, while chickens and geese were housed in pens.

As always, the crew list changed right up until the last minute. When it came to a voyage of this duration, it was very common for there to be a considerable number of desertions prior to the ship departing home waters. In this case, a total of fifty-eight sailors decamped from *Resolution* before she set sail, but they were replaced without too much difficulty.

The expedition was three months behind schedule as a result of Banks' interference. It was not until 21 June – the longest day of the year – that *Resolution* was finally deemed ready to sail from Sheerness, bound for Plymouth. On the same day, back in London, it was time for the commander to endure yet another farewell from his family, and for his wife, still just thirty years of age, to realise that her seafaring husband was about to leave her once again for an indeterminable amount of time. Such was the lot of a mariner's wife. At this point, Elizabeth was only three weeks away from giving birth to their third son, George – a child that Cook would never see. The infant lived for less than three months.

Resolution and *Adventure* in the Long Reach on the Thames 1772, as painted by Francis Holman. State Library of NSW, Dixson Galleries DG 22 / a2827001.

CHAPTER FIFTEEN

Second Time Around

The day after farewelling his family, Cook was aboard *Resolution* and calling for the anchor to be weighed and sails set. Ahead lay an eleven-day passage to Plymouth, where *Adventure* had been awaiting the arrival of her lead ship since the middle of May. Slow as it was, this voyage provided a valuable sea trial for *Resolution* and gave the crew ample time to familiarise themselves with every aspect of operation, from the rig and sails to the balance of the helm, and how she responded to the wheel when the course was changed.

A pleasant surprise came on approach to Plymouth when the Admiralty yacht *Augusta* hove into view, with Lord Sandwich and the Comptroller of the Navy, Commodore Hugh Palliser, on board. The vessel was returning the two men to London after they had been inspecting dockyards along the coast. With the weather being fair, they took the opportunity now to go aboard *Resolution* for final discussions with Cook, and, in particular, to get his appraisal on how the ship was handling.

> I was now well able to give them and so much in her
> favour that I had not one fault to allege against her … It
> is owing to the perseverance of these two persons that
> the expedition is in so much forwardness, had they given

way to the general Clamour and not steadily adhered to
their own better judgement, the Voyage in all
probability would have been laid aside ...

The captain's satisfaction with his newly refitted ship also led to
him writing to Stephens immediately after arriving in Plymouth
to confirm that his vessel offered everything he expected of her.

While *Resolution* and *Adventure* lay at anchor in close
proximity in Plymouth Sound, and final preparations for the
voyage were made, Cook received a package from the
Admiralty in London containing his instructions for the
expedition. Dated 25 June 1772, they held no surprises for the
captain, primarily because he had been party to the initial draft.
He also knew that should he execute these directions to the full,
he would become the first maritime explorer to circumnavigate
the world twice, and in opposing directions.

In short, the first part of his orders stated that after reaching
the Cape of Good Hope, he was to fall as far south as possible in
search of Cape Circumcision, the position of which had been
approximated when sighted by French explorer Jean-Baptiste
Bouvet on 1 January 1739 – the day of the Feast of the
Circumcision. The odds were stacked against Cook in this
endeavour: the actual existence of the cape remained
questionable, and the latitude and longitude that Bouvet
recorded were, more than likely, quite inaccurate. Should Cook
locate the cape, he was then to explore what he could of that
coastline, 'Prosecuting your discoveries as near to the South
Pole as possible' and 'keeping in as high a latitude as you can'.
However, if Cape Circumcision proved to be little more than a
feature on a small island, he should move on and continue
sailing on an east-about circumnavigation in search of the still-
mythical Great South Land.

Bouvet's writings regarding what he had seen gave rise to a
general belief that it could be part of a significant find. He
described the area around the cape as being desolate and
covered by glaciers, and suggested that all the signs of a

considerable landmass were evident – ice, seaweed, seals and penguins included. On the other hand, his pilot believed that what they had seen was nothing more than a small island. There was only one certainty for Cook and his expedition: it was going to be a bitterly cold, storm- and blizzard-ravaged mission to a region where few men had dared to venture.

Of all the tasks to be completed before departure, Cook's most important one was to set the highly valued timepieces – the chronometers – to the most accurate time possible, thereby ensuring there was every chance that their calculation of longitude during this passage around the world was as near to correct as possible. This undertaking proved to be a delicate but successful operation.

It was a cloud-shrouded sunrise on the morning of 13 July, but the wind was most favourable. At 6 am, the captain called for all required hands to be on deck aboard *Resolution*, and signalled for the same action aboard *Adventure*. From that moment, the shrill of the bosuns' whistles could be heard while commands were shouted from the quarterdeck for all to hear, each one aimed at getting the ships underway.

Only Cook knew the contents of his orders from the Admiralty, so everyone else on board could only speculate about where exactly they were heading. Nor could they say how long they would be absent from home waters. This was reflected to some degree in a simple note that Richard Pickersgill, now Lieutenant Pickersgill following a recommendation from Cook, wrote in his journal that day: 'Farewell old England'. There is little doubt that, at some stage during the departure, every man would have looked aft over the taffrail with a degree of emotion, watching the coastline become increasingly faint. Not even the stoic captain was spared this experience, as he would later reveal in a letter to John Walker in Whitby:

> I should hardly have troubled you with a letter was it
> not customary for men to take leave of their friends
> before they go out of the world, for I can hardly think

myself in it so long as I am deprived from having any connections with the civilised part of it, and this will soon be my case for two years at least. When I think of the inhospitable parts I am going to, I think the voyage dangerous. I however enter upon it with great cheerfulness, providence has been very kind to me on many occasions, and I trust in the continuation of the divine protection; I have two good ships well provided and well manned.

It was an easy passage over more than 1000 nautical miles to Madeira, during which the men had every opportunity to adjust to life at sea. Once anchored at their destination, the desired provisions were taken aboard: wine, in particular. The captain was determined to implement the same pioneering dietary and hygiene regimen for his crew as he had applied so successfully aboard *Endeavour*. This was evident to the men of *Resolution* and *Adventure* when he bought hundreds of bunches of onions for the crew, explaining that it was 'a Custom I observed last Voyage and had reason to think that they received great benefit therefrom'.

The stopover in Madeira was also the last opportunity Cook would have for some time to write to the Admiralty on various matters including his assessment of the performance of the ship at sea:

… Resolution answers in every respect as well, nay even better than we could expect. She steers, works, sails well, and is remarkably stiff and seems to promise to be a dry and very easy ship in the sea. In our passage from Plymouth we were once under our courses but it was not wind that obliged the Resolution to take in her topsails, though it blowed hard, but because the Adventure could not carry hers. In point of sailing the two sloops are well matched; what difference there is is in favour of the Resolution.

While in Madeira, there came an unexpected moment of mirth for Cook and his crew – many of whom still had Banks' buffoonery during the preparations for this voyage fresh in their minds. While ashore in the town of Funchal, they learned that three months earlier – which was when *Resolution* had originally been due to depart from Plymouth – a 'gentleman' named Burnett had arrived from England, saying that he was there to join Banks' ship when she reached port. It is believed that Banks, having abandoned this mission, wrote to Burnett in Funchal, advising him that he would not be arriving on *Resolution*. With that, this so-called gentleman took the next available ship back to Europe, although not before the locals had realised that Burnett was not a man, but a woman dressed in men's garb. In fact, 'Mr Burnett' was Banks' mistress, whom he was planning to smuggle aboard for the voyage. Cook found it amusing to think that Banks obviously believed that he could deceive the captain and all on board. He would later remark: 'every part of Mr Burnett's behaviour and every action tended to prove that he was a woman. I have not met with a person that entertains a doubt of a contrary nature.'

From Madeira, the next stage of the voyage – to the Cape Verde Islands, then on to Cape Town – was relatively uneventful. More stock and poultry went aboard at the islands, and a number of crew bought monkeys to keep as pets. However, after heading back to sea, Cook realised that these primates were the source of offensive excrement on the deck, so he ordered that the animals be thrown overboard: he would have nothing on his ship that might threaten the health of his men. 'The captain paid more attention to the health of his people than to the lives of a few monkeys,' wrote *Resolution*'s astronomer, William Wales. This was also evident in Cook's demands that the men should bathe themselves and wash all linen regularly, and that the ship be 'cleaned and smoked betwixt decks in order to clear and air the sloop'. Bedding was also aired, and the bilges sluiced with salt water on a regular basis.

With the two ships sailing south in company, every opportunity was taken to ensure that they were of comparable speed in a wide range of conditions – something that would make it easier for them to stay in visual contact during the more difficult stages of the voyage. Initially *Resolution*, due to her greater size and spread of sail, was the faster vessel, but before long, *Adventure* could match her. On 20 August, a carpenter's mate, Henry Smock, who had been working over the side of *Resolution* replacing a scuttle (a hatch), slipped and fell into the ocean and was not recovered. The Equator was crossed on 9 September, and that occasioned the usual induction ceremony for any first-timers: a complete dunking in the sea, or fines in the form of alcohol for those who chose to avoid the experience. The celebration continued well into the night.

By the end of October, *Resolution* and *Adventure* were riding snugly at anchor in the shadow of Cape Town's imposing Table Mountain. Cook noted with pride that 'at this time we have not one man on the Sick list, the People in general have enjoyed a good state of health ever since we left England'. Captain Furneaux had lost two midshipmen to a mystery illness, apparently contracted while they were in the Cape Verde Islands, but otherwise his men, too, were in good health. Cook's strict dietary regimen was vindicated further when two Dutch ships arrived in Cape Town while outward bound from Europe to the East Indies. Their officers reported that they had lost almost 200 men to scurvy since departing from their home port.

While in Cape Town, the two astronomers on the mission, Wales and William Bayley, spent considerable time checking the accuracy of the chronometers against celestial observations. Subsequently they reported that the Kendall timepiece was exceeding expectations, but the same could not be said of *Adventure*'s Arnold versions of the same watch, which had proved unreliable for accurate navigation.

The stopover in Cape Town also provided Cook with a final opportunity to send numerous letters back to England – to the Admiralty, family and friends. The most noteworthy was to Joseph Banks. It was the first step in a reconciliation that would come about after his return from this voyage:

> Dear Sir,
> Some Cross circumstances which happened at the latter part of the equipment of the Resolution created, I have reason to think, a coolness betwixt you and I, but I can by no means think it was sufficient to me to break off all correspondence with a Man I am under many obligations to …

On the afternoon of 23 November, little more than three weeks after arriving at Cape Town, *Resolution* and *Adventure* were again sailing in company and heading for the open sea. As they left Table Bay, the captain called for a fifteen-gun salute to recognise the local garrison. Then, having cleared the land, he entered a simple note in his journal: 'I directed my course for Cape Circumcision.'

Just one day later, the near 200 men making up the complement of the two ships were getting a not-so-subtle taste of what lay ahead. Barely south of the Cape of Good Hope, *Resolution* and *Adventure* were riding 'strong gales with hard Squalls, rain & hail' and rolling heavily in a building Southern Ocean swell. Biting cold, snow and ice would soon be bringing another testing dimension to this voyage, so in preparation, the commander called for each man to be issued with 'a Fearnought Jacket and a pair of Trowsers, which were allowed by the Admiralty'. Both items were made from a heavy woollen fabric, but the jackets did not have long sleeves.

Beyond that issue, it was up to the crewmen to do what they could to counter the cold, but their protection was minimal: vests, woollen sweaters, lightweight caps or hats, thin leather shoes and stockings. Some compensation would come three weeks later when Cook, feeling considerable compassion for his men in the freezing conditions, 'Set all the Tailors to work to lengthen the sleeves of the Seamen's jackets and to make Caps to shelter them from the severity of the Weather, having ordered a quality of Red Baize to be converted to that purpose.' Besides the clothing, Cook had another measure to help his men cope with the cold: 'an additional glass of Brandy every morning enables them to bear the Cold without Flinching.'

A week after departing from Cape Town, *Resolution* spent twenty-four hours lying-to at the mercy of 'very hard gales with rain and hail ... the sea running very high'. Regardless of the ferocious nature of the conditions and the biting cold, men were required to go aloft, while 'waisters' – the crewmen working the waist deck area – acted in support of them, the task being to lower to the deck the topgallant yards. This action was undertaken during gales to reduce windage aloft, thus making the ship more stable.

Around this time, the first moment of drama occurred. Approaching midnight, a scuttle in the topsides that gave access to the bosun's storeroom burst open through the force of a wave and water began flooding into the hull. By the time the crew discovered the problem, 2½ feet of water was cascading through the bilge. Men rushed to secure the hatch while others manned the pumps and cleared the ship of the water.

Despite the conditions throughout that night, the two ships remained in contact, aided by position indicators known as 'false fires' – combustible material set alight in containers placed high in the rig. Unfortunately, though, the cold and the lumbering motion of the ship saw the livestock and poultry aboard *Resolution* suffer, her captain recording: 'the Weather ... makes great destruction among our Hogs, Sheep and Poultry, not a night passes without some dying, with us, however they are not wholly lost for we eat them notwithstanding.'

On 11 December, *Resolution* and *Adventure* had plunged to a point 1100 nautical miles south of the Cape of Good Hope, and there a fearsome initiation into sailing in high latitudes really began for every member of the mission. On what started out as a foggy day, a gale howled in from the north-west bringing with it snow and sleet. At 1 pm, the men on watch, who were huddled behind whatever protection they could find, heard a call from the lookout at the masthead. A dreaded new danger was in their midst: the first iceberg to be sighted was off the bow, and it was twice as high as the mainmast. The next day the captain's note in his journal read: 'Sleet and snow ... Thermometer was one degree below the Freezing point. Passed six Islands of Ice this 24 hours, some of which were near two miles in circuit and about 200ft high.'

There was plenty more to come in this icy wilderness – a daunting frontier for everyone on board. They found themselves surrounded by mountains of ice 'farther than the eye could reach'. Cook wrote: 'the day being so foggy at times that we could not see a Ship's length. Betwixt 12 at night and 7 in the Morn, 4 Inches thick of Snow fell on the Decks ... the Thermometer most of the time five degrees below the Freezing point so that our Rigging and sails were all decorated with Icicles.'

Every man on deck faced an extreme test of endurance in such horrendous weather, a challenge that is barely imaginable. They were constantly caked in snow, fighting the relentlessly savage bite of a howling wind and, while tending the sails, having to get their hands around sheets, halyards and lines that were virtually frozen stiff. Added hell came in the form of large rolling seas, and foaming white water cascading across the decks.

The icebergs were so large that they created a lee of sheltered water on their downwind side, so Cook took the first available opportunity to guide *Resolution* into one of those lees and have *Adventure* follow. He then signalled for Furneaux to join him aboard *Resolution*, and there advised him of the destination the two ships would head for in the event of them becoming separated, and what date they should rendezvous there. It was to be Queen Charlotte Sound in New Zealand. Both captains were pleased with the stoicism of their crew and the performance of their ships. In comparing the two vessels, Third Lieutenant Clerke wrote: 'Adventure we find to be the most weatherly Ship in a Gale tho' this [*Resolution*] is as good a Sea Boat as can possibly swim.'

Having traversed the latitudes of the Roaring Forties, the ships were now in what would become known as the Furious Fifties, and destined for the Screaming Sixties – all in a quest to fill in the features of the Earth's surface that remained a mystery. At this stage, the only certainty for the mission was that *Resolution* and *Adventure* were once more destined to be exposed to heinous, ice-laden storms over the ensuing weeks while the search for Cape Circumcision – or any part of what might be an undiscovered continent – continued. One mighty storm, one gargantuan breaking wave of 50 feet or more in height, or a collision with an unseen iceberg in the middle of the night – any of these and other terrifying possibilities could send the ships into oblivion. Still they pressed on.

Every man, from the commander to the lowliest cabin boy, was new to sailing in this situation. So it was a case of 'learn as you proceed', as Cook was quick to observe: 'Dangerous as it is sailing amongst the floating Rocks in a thick Fog and unknown Sea, yet it is preferable to being entangled with Field Ice under the same circumstances. The danger to be apprehended from this Ice is the getting fast in it where, beside the damage a ship might receive, might be detained some time ...'

One week later it was 25 December, and every man had earned the right to some good cheer. 'At Noon seeing that the People were inclinable to celebrate Christmas Day in their own way,' their commander wrote, 'I brought the Sloops under a very snug sail [in case I] should be surprised with a gale [of] wind with a drunken crew, this action was however unnecessary for the wind continued to blow in a gentle gale ...'

The men had been hoarding their liquor in anticipation of the day, so there was little wonder that mirth and good humour reigned throughout the ship. A similar celebration took place aboard *Adventure*, which came alongside *Resolution* in the early evening so that the crews could salute each other with three rousing cheers.

If the men wanted a snowman as part of the festivities, they needed only to look aloft, towards where the ever-alert lookout was perched on the highest trestletrees on the mainmast. With every snowfall, the poor soul assigned to this task would soon be covered in white.

The following day, the lead ship and her consort were back under sail, on course for the coordinates that Bouvet had provided for his sighting of land. As they went, Pickersgill wrote of the eager anticipation confronting the men: 'We being Now across M. Bouvet's track to ye Eastward of Cape Circumcision, expect to find land hourly, though sailing here is rendered very Dangerous.' He told how the threats from ice and storms had every man on deck on high alert, and how orders and responses had to be shouted at the highest volume, just to be heard over the howl of the wind and the roar of the bursting seas. These were 'rigorous circumstances'.

By the end of December, Cook was becoming frustrated in his search for Bouvet's supposed discovery. He had guided his two ships to the approximate position that the Frenchman plotted for the landmass, but there was nothing to be seen. After yet another day of searching, he wrote of his conclusion:

> The Weather was so clear, that land even of a moderate
> height might have been seen 15 Leagues, so that there
> could be no land betwixt us and the Latitude of 58
> degrees. In short, I am of opinion that what M. Bouvet
> took for land and named Cape Circumcision was nothing
> but Mountains of Ice surrounded by field Ice. We
> ourselves were undoubtedly deceived by the Ice Hills the
> Day we first fell in with the field Ice.

He then aired his frustration, saying he was 'only sorry that in searching after those imaginary Lands, I have spent so much time, which will become the more valuable as the season advanceth'.

Even so, a sixth sense had Cook believing that there was a major landmass to be found somewhere in the southern half of the world. What he would never know was that the cape he was searching for was a tiny island, just 5 miles long and measuring a total of 19 square miles, almost all of which was covered by a glacier. Bouvet's coordinates for its position were inaccurate by a considerable margin, and it would not be for another thirty-five years that Bouvet Island was sighted. When it was, it became recognised as the most remote speck of land on earth – more than 1000 miles from anywhere else.

Cook's supposition regarding the existence of Cape Circumcision led to him writing on the same day: 'it is plain that if there is land [in this region] it can have no great extent North and South, but I am so fully of opinion that there is none that I shall not go in search of it, being now determined to make the best of my way to the East in the Latitude of 60 degrees or upwards.' He added that he would then continue his exploration, as *Resolution* took up a course to the east and south in search of whatever else might be out there.

By 9 January 1773, both ships were running low on water and here the captain implemented what he would realise to be 'the most expeditious of watering I have ever met'. The two ships sailed into a field of 'growlers', to use the modern term – large chunks of ice – where he called for the vessels to be stopped and the boats hoisted out, so that as much ice as possible could be collected and lifted onto each of the ships using a block and tackle. The initial procedure took close to six hours to complete; in that time, the ice was further broken up using ice axes, and then melted, thus contributing 15 tons of fresh water for *Resolution* and 9 for *Adventure*. The entire operation lasted three days and, by then, *Resolution* had an additional 40 tons of water on board.

Cook the explorer soon became Cook the scientist, a man fascinated by icy-cold seawater. He had a thermometer attached to a line and sent it down to the 100-fathom mark, and on its recovery, learned that the water temperature was 32 degrees at that depth. This brought him to a question: 'Some curious and interesting experiments are wanting to know what effect cold has on Sea Water in some of the following instances: does it freeze or does it not? If it does, what degree of cold is necessary and what becomes of the Salt brine? for all the Ice we meet with yields Water perfectly sweet and fresh ...'

The search for land of any form then continued, initially to the east. As soon as the weather conditions were in his favour, however, Cook had the ships make a major course change towards the south and hold it until, during the middle of the day on 17 January, he became the first explorer to venture beyond 66 degrees south – the latitude of the Antarctic Circle. This is the northernmost latitude of the southern hemisphere, where in high summer the sun remains above the horizon around the clock.

Twenty-four hours after this historic event, *Resolution* and *Adventure* were at a remarkable 67 degrees 15 minutes south, and it was here, having himself climbed the icy rigging to the position of the lookout, that Cook realised he had reached the limit of his exploration in the high latitudes. '[The] ice was so thick and close that we could proceed no further,' he wrote. 'From the masthead I could see nothing to the Southward but Ice ... I did not think it was consistent with the safety of the Sloops or any ways prudent for me to persevere in going farther to the South as the Summer was already half spent ...'

Cook was then a mere 75 miles to the north of the Antarctic continent, the existence of which was not even apparent until its discovery in 1840 by a United States navy expedition commanded by Charles Wilkes. Cook might well have got there first had it not been for the impenetrable barrier of ice that confronted his ship.

He then chose the option of going in search of the Kerguelen Islands – an archipelago of more than 300 mainly barren and rocky outcrops, the largest of which has an area of 2577 square miles. They had been discovered the previous year by a Frenchman, Yves-Joseph de Kerguelen-Trémarec, who, like Cook, had been searching for the Great South Land. Cook and his officers learned of Kerguelen-Trémarec's discovery while in Cape Town.

This new search had the two ships sailing to the north-east. When the weather allowed it, during the day they would sail abeam of each other, 4 or more miles apart, in order to scan the widest possible area of ocean, while at night the vessels would close in and thus minimise the risk of losing visual contact. This was again another fruitless search, due in part to the conditions, but more importantly because, once again, the coordinates given for the islands were not as accurate as Cook's navigation. Time would reveal that *Resolution* and *Adventure* did not come within 300 miles of their target. Clerke summed up the situation: 'We've been for these 6 or 7 days past cruising for the Land the Frenchman gave intelligence of at the Cape of Good Hope – if my friend Monsieur found any Land, he's been confoundedly out in the Latitude & Longitude of it, for we've searched the spot he represented … and the devil an Inch of Land is there.'

Having exhausted every possibility available to him to locate the Kerguelen Islands, Cook abandoned the effort on 6 February, and with *Adventure* in company, 'bore away East a little all sails set'. It was time to move on while the summer season remained in their favour and see what land, if any, might be lying ahead, awaiting discovery.

Within two days, though, there was a significant setback to the mission, when the ships became separated in a thick fog and both visual and sound-signal contact was lost. Prior to the arrival of the fog, *Adventure* was seen sailing on a parallel course to *Resolution*'s, about a mile off her larboard quarter. There was no cause for immediate concern aboard *Resolution*, when Cook implemented the standard procedure for retaining contact via the sound of cannon-fire:

> At 9 o'Clock we fired a gun and repeated it at 10 and
> at 11 and at Noon made the Signal to Tack and Tacked
> accordingly, but neither this last Signal or any of the

> former were answered by the Adventure which gave us
> too much reason to apprehend that a separation would
> take place ... In short we were entirely at a loss, even to
> guess by what means she got out of the hearing of the
> first gun we fired ...

By mid-afternoon, with still no indication of *Adventure* being in proximity, either visually or via return cannon fire, Cook accepted that he had no option but to move to the next stage of the search and return to the position where the support vessel was last seen. Captain Furneaux was expected to have followed the same instructions at about the same time. A cannon aboard *Resolution* was then fired every thirty minutes while, during the hours of darkness, they lit more false fires at the masthead in the hope that those aboard *Adventure* might see the glow.

Despite their best efforts, for over forty-eight hours there was no sign of the missing ship. It was decision time for the commander, who was confident that nothing untoward had happened to their consort: 'Having now spent two Days out of the three assigned to look for each other, I thought it would be to little purpose to wait any longer ... I therefore made sail to the SE with a very fresh gale at WBN accompanied with a high Sea.' *Resolution*'s ultimate destination was then, as prearranged with Furneaux, Queen Charlotte Sound.

From the moment that the course to the east was resumed, so too was the alertness of all those aboard when it came to searching for land. It was only three days later, on 13 February, that they observed possible signs of terra firma being nearby, in particular the presence of an increasing number of penguins about the ship. There was then considerable debate among the officers as to the direction in which land might lie. Here, again, logic and natural instinct informed Cook's opinion:

> Some said we should find it to East others to the North,
> but it was remarkable that not one gave it as his opinion

that any was to be found to the South which served to
convince me that they had no inclination to proceed any
farther that way. I however was resolved to get as far to
the South as I conveniently could without losing too
much easting although I must confess I had little hopes of
meeting with land, for the high swell or Sea which we
have had for some time from the West came now
gradually round to SSE so that it was not probable any
land was near between these two points and it is less
probable that land of any extent can lie to the North …

His reasoning was based on the fact that Tasman had tracked
through the Southern Ocean to the north of *Resolution*'s
position, so, had any large landmass been there, it would almost
certainly have been discovered. Additionally, he expected that
Furneaux would probably sail a similar course to Tasman's
while heading for New Zealand. History later confirmed that
Resolution was in relatively close proximity to land when the
penguins were sighted, but it was a very small island – Heard
Island – a rugged, snow-capped peak that was given a place on
the world map after being sighted in 1853 by Captain John
Heard. At this stage in Cook's voyage, with there being no
definitive evidence of land, he drew a new conclusion: 'it is
now impossible for us to look upon Penguins to be certain signs
of the vicinity of land or, in short, any other Aquatic birds
which frequent high latitudes.'

During the next week, the crew of *Resolution* were
fortunate to observe two remarkable natural phenomena. On 17
February, they were possibly the first Europeans to witness the
spectacular Aurora Australis in the southern skies. Cook wrote
of this: 'Last night Lights were seen in the Heavens similar to
those seen in the Northern Hemisphere commonly called the
Northern lights, I do not remember of any Voyagers making
mention of them being seen in the Southern before.' Then, on
22 February, they watched in awe as a gigantic iceberg capsized:
'After Dinner hoisted out two Boats and set them to take up Ice

while we stood to and from under the island [iceberg] which was about half a mile in circuit and three or four hundred feet high, yet this huge body turned nearly bottom-up while we were near it.'

Cook continued to maintain an easterly course virtually along the latitude of 60 degrees south, and in doing so courted danger around the clock because of the hundreds of icebergs and large pieces of ice that stood in their way. Until this point, he had been harbouring a desire to venture once more into the Antarctic Circle, but not any longer. '[The] pieces which break from the large Islands are more dangerous than the Islands themselves,' he reasoned, 'the latter are generally seen at a sufficient distance to give time to steer clear of them, whereas the others cannot be seen in the night or thick weather till they are under the Bows.' Interestingly, when the position of *Resolution* at this time is considered, had Cook turned due south as planned, he could well have sighted land – Antarctica.

Despite the bleak and harsh environment that the crew had to endure, Cook continued to insist that personal hygiene and a tidy general appearance be maintained. He punished men who had dirty hands by withholding their daily grog allowance. When it came to the state of a crewman's clothing, Clerke noted: 'Captain Cook having Observed many of the People in rather a ragged condition, this forenoon he gave them some Needles thread and Buttons, that they may have no excuse for their tattered [appearance] … they also have every Saturday to themselves to wash etc – that they may likewise have no excuse for a dirty, or improper appearance.'

By 8 March, *Resolution* was beginning to clear herself from the fields of ice and icebergs, but even so, six days later, the ship was covered in a blanket of snow from stem to stern. On 17 March, when Cook's latest plot gave a position of some 900 nautical miles south of Van Diemen's Land, it was time to escape the misery of the region. 'We then bore away NE', he reported, 'and at Noon steered North inclining to the East with a Resolution of making the best of my way to New Holland or

New Zealand, my sole motive for wishing to make the former is to inform myself whether or no Van Diemen's Land makes a part of that continent ...'

Unfortunately for Cook, incessant gales and storms from the western sector soon had him giving up any hope of visiting Van Diemen's Land: he could no longer achieve the northing required to reach that destination. But as bad as the weather was, *Resolution* was handling the conditions superbly, one day averaging almost 7 knots for an entire twenty-four hours under greatly reduce sail. It led Cook to write of his ship: 'Upon the whole she goes as dry over the Sea as any ship I ever met with.'

The new course had *Resolution* sailing towards New Zealand's South Island, and this was first sighted on 25 March. Two days later, she was anchored in the rugged and boldly beautiful Dusky Sound, on the south-west corner of the island, a place of breathtaking scenery – steep and lofty escarpments shrouded in dense, unbroken dark-green expanses of foliage, with pure white waterfalls cascading into the sea like long bridal veils. While exploring the region by boat, botanist Johann Förster found a waterfall of 'more beauty and grandeur than anything, I had hitherto seen'. A torrent of water near 8 yards in circumference fell for more than 100 yards from high above, before exploding onto the rocks below and creating a very fine vapour-like mist.

Cook again took up his quill, making notes in his journal that reflected the magnitude of the undertaking they had just completed. They had reached safe sanctuary after more than '117 Days at sea in which time we have Sailed 3660 Leagues [11,000 nautical miles] without once having sight of land'.

Of major importance to the commander was that, after such a severe test of human endurance in one of the world's harshest environments, only one crew-member was showing any sign of scurvy. Clerke recognised this all too well:

> We've now arrived at a Port with a Ship's Crew in the
> best Order that I believe ever was heard of after such a

long Passage at Sea – particularly if we come to consult
Climates; this happy state of Health was certainly owing to
the Extraordinary indulgencies of [wort], Wheat, Malt etc
etc together with the strict attention paid by Capt. Cook
to the People's Cleanliness.

Within hours of arriving in Dusky Sound, the captain elected to move his ship to an anchorage that Pickersgill had found while exploring the southern shoreline. It was heaven-sent. The water was so deep that *Resolution* was moored bow and stern to trees in a tight and well-protected cove; and, much to the delight of the men, the ship sat so close to the shore that trees growing horizontally out from the rocks formed a natural gangway which they could use to go ashore. The crew took every advantage of this bonus: with maintenance work needing to be done, tents and equipment were carried to the shore and set up near a stream that provided a crystal-clear water supply. *Resolution* had come through her arduous Southern Ocean test remarkably well, with only a few signs of leaks. Some of her ironwork needed attention, so by 1 April, the forge was fired up and the sound of hammer on metal was echoing around the hills. The sail-makers and riggers were similarly busy carrying out minor repairs.

The ultimate reward came when the captain ordered that 'spruce beer' be brewed. Aside from the enjoyment provided by this new liquid refreshment, there was an abundance of fresh food from land and sea for everyone to share. Fish and crawfish were easy game, while seals provided food and lamp oil, Clerke noting that some of the men were adamant that seal steaks were superior to beef. Ducks and other wild fowl also made for wonderful meals.

Nature's role as a generous provedore was reflected in the names that Cook gave to features in the region, such as Supper Cove, Duck Cove and Luncheon Cove. In the case of Goose Cove, however, it earned its title on his chart for another reason. He decided that this inlet, situated on a large island he had explored and would subsequently name Resolution Island, was the ideal place to set free the remaining geese he had brought from Cape Town, hoping they would 'breed and may in time spread over the whole Country'. When the founders of European settlement in New Zealand arrived here in around 1840, though, there was not a goose to be seen.

Cook made contact with the Maoris on many occasions while in this region, and much to his relief, there were no aggressive confrontations like those he had too often experienced during his first visit to New Zealand. All exchanges passed amicably enough. His patience and diplomacy during these interactions left a lasting impression on Midshipman Elliott, whose published memoir would offer an insightful assessment of his captain:

> ... certainly no man could be better calculated to gain the confidence of Savages than Captain Cook. He was Brave, uncommonly Cool, Humane and Patient. He would land alone unarmed – or lay aside his Arms, and sit down, when they threatened with theirs, throwing them Beads, Knives, and other little presents, then by degrees advancing nearer, till by Patience, and forbearance, he gained their friendship, and an intercourse with them; which to people in our situation, was of the utmost consequence.

Although it rained frequently, the crew enjoyed a month of respite and recovery in this pristine environment. Then it came time to head to Ship Cove in Queen Charlotte Sound and, hopefully, a rendezvous with *Adventure*.

Spectacular snow-capped peaks were a blunt reminder that winter was approaching, yet there was no sign of strong winter winds pushing in from the south-west. There were many calms, and this frequently resulted in *Resolution* being towed towards the open sea by the boats, or lying at anchor close to the coast. Such idle time was not wasted, of course: men went ashore either on hunting expeditions or to explore. One of these exploratory missions could have had calamitous consequences.

It came when the captain directed Lieutenant Pickersgill to take Förster and his son in the pinnace to see what they could find in a large inlet that appeared to carve its way inland. They were away for thirty-six hours, and during that time a brutal thunderstorm, packing howling winds, snow and hail, descended from the heavens. In Förster's description, it was 'as if all nature was hastening to a general catastrophe … our hearts sunk with apprehension lest the ship might be destroyed by the tempest or its concomitant ethereal fires [lightning], and ourselves left to perish in an unfrequented part of the world.' Fortunately, men and ship survived.

When a highly preferred south-easterly breeze wafted its way off the land on the morning of 11 May, Cook needed no encouragement to weigh anchor. Every man was ready to sail, and before long *Resolution* was surging north, aided by a powerful swell from the south-west. From there it was a relatively casual few days of sailing towards Cape Farewell and then into Cook Strait.

On 18 May, *Resolution* was 'welcomed' into Queen Charlotte Sound by a series of spiralling waterspouts, one of which caused some anxiety when it passed within 50 yards of the stern. The spouts soon dissipated, and not long afterwards came the sight and sound everyone had hoped for. As Cook recorded: 'At Daylight in the Morn we were … at the entrance of Queen Charlotte Sound and soon after we discovered the Adventure in Ship Cove by the Signals she made …'

Those signals came in the form of cannon-fire, and almost immediately the booming sound of *Resolution*'s cannons were also echoing through the hills surrounding the cove. Simultaneously, great joy surged through the crew of *Adventure*. Having had no sign of their lead ship for fourteen weeks, they had become convinced that *Resolution* was lost, probably to the force of an immense Southern Ocean storm.

By six o'clock that evening, *Resolution* was riding safely at anchor in close proximity to *Adventure*, which had been in the cove for eleven days. Not long after all was made secure, Captain Furneaux climbed up the side of *Resolution* and stepped onto the deck, eager for discussions with his expedition commander.

Furneaux explained to Cook that, having given up all hope of re-establishing contact with *Resolution*, he had set a course for Van Diemen's Land, and once there anchored in a well-sheltered bay, which he named Adventure Bay in honour of his ship. (Furneaux mistook the land surrounding this bay as being part of the Tasman Peninsula, when in fact he was on the eastern side of Bruny Island.) *Adventure* stayed there for five days, while his men gathered wood and collected water. With that done, he used the remaining time before they were due in Queen Charlotte Sound to explore the coast to the north. This led to him now being able to advise today that he was uncertain whether Van Diemen's Land was an island or part of the east coast of New Holland. He explained that when *Adventure* reached what is today known as Banks Strait, off the north-east corner of Van Diemen's Land, the water showed signs of shoaling, suggesting to him and his crew that they were entering a large bay. Their desire to continue with this exploration was curbed by the arrival of a strong wind from the south-east, a circumstance that threatened to make the coast a dangerous lee shore for *Adventure*. The captain therefore opted for the security of sea-room, considering it 'more prudent to leave the Coast and steer for New Zealand'. He made what was a bold, but unsubstantiated, proclamation at this point: 'it is my opinion that there are no Straits between New Holland and Van Diemen's Land, but a very deep bay.'

Cook listened intently, in particular to Furneaux's descriptions of the aboriginals he had seen around Adventure Bay and their lifestyle. The commander judged that they were little different from the indigenous people he had encountered while sailing north along the coast of New Holland in 1770. He could then reach only one conclusion, and thus abandoned his earlier thought about Van Diemen's Land being an island. Later that day, when he retired to the great cabin to update his journal, he wrote that it was 'highly probable that the whole is one continued land and that Van Diemen's Land is a part of New Holland'.

Two days after rendezvousing with *Adventure*, Cook decided to give the remaining sheep – a ram and a ewe – a new lease of life, onshore. In doing so, he employed the same hope he had embraced when releasing the geese in Dusky Sound. However, it was short-lived: 'Last night the Ewe and Ram I had with so much care and trouble brought to this place, died, we did suppose that they were poisoned by eating of some poisonous plant, thus all my fine hopes of stocking this country with a breed of sheep were blasted in a moment …'

In the northern hemisphere, the winter months usually meant that Royal Navy sailors were granted shore leave while their ships were docked for repairs and maintenance, and Furneaux obviously believed this would apply for the men of *Resolution* and *Adventure*, who had been sailing in the most trying conditions since leaving home ten months earlier. Accordingly, while waiting in Queen Charlotte Sound for the anticipated arrival of *Resolution*, he had erected tents on the shore – some to accommodate the ailing members of his crew, many of whom were suffering the effects of scurvy. He also established vegetable gardens, with a view to harvesting crops during the coming months. Cook's plan was vastly different, however. There was no time to waste. He wanted both ships back at sea as soon as possible.

The commander's aim for the next stage of this voyage of discovery was built around his new belief that New Holland and Van Diemen's Land were one. This meant that they no longer needed to sail to Van Diemen's Land, as Cook had originally intended to do, to solve that particular geographical mystery. Instead, they would concentrate their search for the Great South Land – *Terra Australis Incognita* – in the South Pacific, to the east of New Zealand. He was convinced that there was no possibility of a continent existing in the region he had just navigated, between Cape Town and New Zealand, so the new challenge was to determine if such a landmass occupied a significant part of the South Pacific.

His intention, as he advised Furneaux, was to sail through the areas that he had not crossed during *Endeavour*'s circumnavigation. Despite it being winter, he would head south into the Roaring Forties once more, sailing between the latitudes of 41 degrees and 46 degrees south (the latitude of the southern tip of New Zealand) until reaching a point close to the longitude of Otaheite, but 1700 nautical miles south of it. If no land was sighted, then the course would change dramatically to the north – destination: Matavai Bay. There the ships could be reprovisioned and the men catch up on some eagerly anticipated shore leave among the ravishing coffee-skinned island beauties they had heard so much about. Cook could see no reason to continue on an easterly track towards Cape Horn while sailing in the Roaring Forties, because the direction and size of the Southern Ocean swells he'd experienced when rounding Cape Horn from east to west, with *Endeavour*, left him in no doubt that there was no continent to the west of the Horn.

> It may be thought by some an extraordinary step in me to proceed on discoveries as far south as 46° in the very depth of Winter for it must be owned that this is a Season by no means favourable for discoveries. It nevertheless appeared to me necessary that something must be done in it, in order to lessen the work I am upon, lest I should not be able to finish the discovery of the Southern part of the South Pacific Ocean the ensuing Summer, besides if I should discover any land in my route to the East I shall be ready to begin with the Summer to explore it; setting aside all these considerations I have little to fear, having two good Ships well provided and healthy crews ...

There was a rider attached to Cook's plan: should no continent be found while en route to Tahiti, the two ships would return to New Zealand 'by the shortest route', and once there, he would extend his search by sailing directly south, as deep as possible into the Southern Ocean. This would be the final part of the search in that particular region, and represent the completion of his orders relating to the search for the mythical continent in that part of the South Pacific and Southern Ocean.

Activities for each new day on board ship started at 4 am with the bosun rousing the required crewmen from their hammocks with a shout and the shrill tone of his whistle. On the morning of 7 June 1773, the call was for 'All hands'. The crisp morning breeze was ideal for the departure of the two ships from the cove, so it was time for the crew to prepare for putting to sea.

At 7 am, when everything was in readiness, the captain called for the anchor to be weighed. The sound of the ratchets clacking away on the windlass, and the call for men to heave simultaneously on cables, halyards and lines, filled the morning air.

Within a few hours, *Resolution* and *Adventure* were sailing east out of Cook Strait, on their way to unravelling another mystery relating to the geography of planet Earth.

On his second voyage Cook ventured south of the Antarctic Circle three times; Williams Hidges, artist on *Resolution*, captured the event of harvesting water for the ships from an iceberg. State Library of NSW, Mitchell Library SAFE / PXD 11 Volume 5, 26 / a156043.

CHAPTER SIXTEEN

Return to Otaheite

To venture into the Southern Ocean in the depths of winter is something that even today's mariners tend to avoid. So, to be there in a wooden sailing ship, at the mercy of full-blown storms and mountainous seas, icebergs and snow, was tempting fate in the extreme. But Cook had a job to do, and he was obviously confident that his men and ships had the ability to cope with the worst that nature could muster. Into the Southern Ocean they plunged, and within a matter of days the crews of both vessels were being put to the test, continually countering the widely varying extremes of wind and wave. They would set every conceivable sail when the wind was light, then reef and double-reef the sails, and finally strike the yards in the most punishing and life-threatening conditions.

On two occasions aboard *Resolution*, the force of waves on the near 60-square-foot rudder proved too much for the timoneer manning the wheel, who was desperately gripping its spokes while fighting the enormous pressure on the helm. His efforts were no match for the impact that came when a huge wave slammed into the rudder and took control of the steering mechanism, forcing the wheel into a rapid, uncontrolled gyration. As a consequence, the man steering was literally hurled over the top of the wheel and onto the deck on the opposite side, as if he were a rag doll.

Conditions remained challenging for much of the time while the ships sailed an easterly course along the latitudes of the Roaring Forties, yet the only drama of note involved one of the goats, which, like many other animals, were left to roam around the waist of the ship. Förster wrote on 9 July:

> A very great & mountainous Swell from the South,
> which makes the Ship roll very much. In one of these
> deep rolls, a young goat born on board this Ship about
> the Tropics, had the misfortune to fall overboard from
> the booms where he went in order to come at the Hay
> in the Longboat. He swam at first hard, we brought to &
> hoisted a boat out; but he was drowned before they
> could take him up.

Four days later, the always expressive but often ostracised Förster recorded that it was one year since *Resolution* and *Adventure* had set sail from England. With a flourish of his quill, the naturalist wrote in his journal: 'May providence continue to guard us against Misfortunes & Accidents, & procure me opportunities to describe & discover many useful things in these Seas & the Lands therein, for the benefit of mankind … and to the Satisfaction of the great & benevolent monarch, who ordered this expedition …'

For almost a month, the horizon ahead and abeam of the two ships had remained devoid of any sign of land, so on reaching his designated point to the south of Otaheite on 14 July, the captain directed for their course to be steered to the north-east as planned. This change meant that they would traverse the last remaining sector of the South Pacific that had not been the subject of exploration, and therefore either discover the mythical continent or eliminate this part of the world from the list of possible regions where the Great South Land might be found.

The decision to climb north towards the tropics came as a source of great relief to the crew of *Adventure*, in particular, as scurvy was beginning to take hold among the men. Yet any hope that the weather would become more benign was little other than fantasy. Both ships remained under considerable pressure from the elements, and as a result the men on watch were kept extremely busy. Cook's journal offered further description of the efforts being undertaken to master the conditions:

> First part fresh gales and gloomy weather. At 2pm single reefed the Top-sails and presently after the Clew of the fore top-sail gave way which obliged us to unbend the sail and bring another to the yard ... At 8 double reefed the Top sails and handed [lowered] the Mizzen Top-sail, The gale kept increasing in such a manner as to bring us at 2 am to hand the Fore Top-sail and sometime after the Main Topsail and to strike Top gallant yards, the Fore Top-mast staysail being split we unbent it and bent another ...

On 23 July, *Adventure*'s cook, Murduck Mahony, became the first man to lose his fight against scurvy. Furneaux recorded that Mahony had 'been a long time bad', and he was one of twenty-two on the ship's sick list at this time, with most suffering from either scurvy or rheumatic complaints. 'Capt Cook appointed Wm Chapman one of our Seamen, who is Aged & having lost the use of 2 of his fingers to be Cook of the Adventure', added Furneaux.

During the first week of August, the expedition was somewhere in the region of the uninhabited Pitcairn Island, about 1200 miles south-east of Otaheite. This island was discovered in July 1767 by British sailor Captain Philip Carteret, who named it after fifteen-year-old midshipman Robert Pitcairn, the first of his crewmen to sight its coastline. Pitcairn became famous in 1789 after being chosen as a hideaway by the mutineers from HMS *Bounty*. Cook called for every effort from his lookouts to sight this small, remote and rugged outcrop.

'[We] looked out for it but could see nothing excepting two Tropic birds,' the captain noted, and with that he declared that there was no undiscovered continent in this part of the world: 'No discovery of importance can be made, some few Islands is all that can be expected while I remain within the Tropical Seas.'

Adventure's sick list had now grown to number thirty, all incapacitated by scurvy and deteriorating rapidly. With Furneaux struggling to find sufficient fit men to sail the ship, he turned to his commander for assistance. Both vessels were then brought to a near halt so that *Adventure*'s boats could be sent to *Resolution* to collect the thirteen men Cook offered to fill the void. The condition of the crew aboard the support ship caused Cook to decide that, instead of going directly to Matavai Bay, in the north of Otaheite, he should change course and head for a sheltered bay in the Tautira region, on the island's south-east coast. This would allow the men to rest and get fresh food sooner, and hopefully recover. However, it turned out to be a decision that came close to bringing an end to the entire mission.

At sundown on 16 August, the jagged profile of Otaheite's imposing mountains was there for all to see, about 8 leagues away. It was vital that a safe and steady approach be made to land there in daylight, in order to locate a passage through the fringing reef towards a safe anchorage. Around midnight, just before retiring for a few hours' sleep, Cook issued specific instructions to the lieutenant on watch regarding the course and speed he wanted the ship to maintain overnight. Something went wrong, however – possibly because some of the men on watch nodded off. The captain recorded the sight that greeted him after he'd climbed the companionway ladder to the deck: 'when I got up at break of day I found we were steering a wrong course and were not more than half a league from the reef which guards the South end of the Island ...'

The circumstances could hardly have been more alarming. Cook shouted a terse order for an immediate change of course – to haul off to the north – but the cumbersome *Resolution* was slow to respond in what was only a very light breeze. In no time at all, the draught of air evaporated, and the ship was left floating on a glassy sea just a short distance away from the reef.

Here was another classic example of the perilous life that early mariners faced on expeditions such as this. For better or worse, they were always in the hands of the elements, and through either human error (as was the case in this instance) or the vagaries of the weather, a ship could suddenly be finely balanced between annihilation and salvation.

Cook drew on every ounce of expertise he had amassed over his three decades at sea to devise a plan to save the ship. The immediate action was to hoist out the boats and have those aboard them attempt to tow *Resolution* away from the pending calamity. *Adventure* was caught in the same predicament, and likewise had little, if any, opportunity to escape. Most disturbingly, there was no sign of a breeze anywhere on the horizon which might help eliminate the threat, so it was only the efforts of the men towing that saw both vessels barely holding their ground – and that soon changed.

As an additional distraction, albeit one that came with all the right intentions, a small armada of canoes had arrived from the shore to welcome the visitors, and many of the natives insisted on clambering aboard *Resolution*. Cook later recalled the situation at this point:

> … we came before an opening in the reef by which I hoped to enter with the Sloops as our situation became more and more dangerous, but when I examined the natives about it they told me that the Water was not deep … it however caused such an indraught of the Tide as was very near proving fatal to both the Sloops, the Resolution especially, for … they were carried by it towards the reef at a great rate; the moment I perceived this I ordered one of the Warping Machines [anchoring devices] which we had in readiness to be carried out with about 3 or 4 hundred fathoms of rope to it, this proved

> of no service to us ... The horrors of ship-wreck now
> stared us in the face, we were not more than two Cables
> length from the breakers and yet could find no bottom to
> anchor, the only means we had left us to save the Ships;
> we however dropped an anchor but before it took hold
> and brought us up, the Ship was in less than 3 fathom
> water ... the Adventure anchored close to us on our
> starboard bow and happily did not touch ...

This rather underplayed the proximity of the vessels to one another, as *Resolution*'s resident astronomer, William Wales, noted: 'the two Ships riding alongside of each other so near that a tolerable Plank would have reached from her Gunnel to ours.'

Now there was a danger that the surge of a wave could well thump *Resolution*, in particular, onto the coral reef and cause her hull planks to open up. Cook's crew worked relentlessly towards trying to save their ship, a task made even more demanding by the temperature having already hit a stifling and sticky 95 degrees Fahrenheit. Cook wrote of the strategy that he and his senior officers implemented: '[We] carried out a Kedge Anchor and a hawser and the Coasting Anchor ... by heaving upon these and cutting away the Bower Anchor we saved the Ship.' As was so often the case in such situations, the greatest boon came with a change in the strength and direction of the tidal current. Soon it was strong enough to give *Resolution* an offing of some 2 miles from the reef.

Cook then had the boats go to the assistance of *Adventure*, but as they did, a light offshore breeze developed, sufficient to fill her sails and get her moving away from the reef. Reflecting the desperate nature of their escape, Furneaux had had no option but to cut away the bowers that had been holding the ship while on the edge of the reef. His journal read: 'got under sail with the land wind, leaving behind her three anchors, her coasting Cable and two Hawsers ...'

Anders Sparrman, a botanist aboard *Resolution*, was greatly impressed by how Cook and his crew dealt with their desperate moment, particularly 'the celerity [speed] and the lack of confusion with which each command was executed to save the ship ... I should have preferred, however, to hear fewer "Goddamns" from the officers and particularly the Captain, who, while the danger lasted, stamped about the deck and grew hoarse with shouting.' That shouting led to Cook's voice beginning to fail, so Sparrman suggested that the captain might use a 'speaking-trumpet', which the captain did, and that he should also distribute them to 'those officers who appeared to me most efficient in handling the vessel'. The botanist's account continued:

> They thanked me for my idea which ... was the only active part I played on the operations ... As soon as the ship was once more afloat, I went down to the Ward Room with Captain Cook who, although he had from beginning to end of the incident appeared perfectly alert and able, was suffering so greatly from his stomach that he was in a great sweat and could scarcely stand.

Cook was no doubt exhausted, both mentally and physically, and it was Sparrman who came to his assistance again, with 'an old Swedish remedy' – a solid swig of brandy. And it worked: 'His aches vanished immediately, his fatigue a few minutes later and, after a good meal, we soon regained our accustomed energy.'

Both ships were then forced to spend another night at sea, one that saw everyone on high alert as it was laced with heavy tropical rain and squalls. They sailed short tacks in deep water until first light, when they were able to negotiate a safe passage through a gap in the reef. They then anchored in a lee that provided good protection from the constant pulse of the south-easterly trade wind.

On two occasions, when the ships were riding securely at anchor inside the reef, Cook ordered a couple of launches and *Resolution*'s cutter, commanded by the master, Joseph Gilbert, to put to sea and try to recover the abandoned anchors. The salvage teams were able to retrieve *Resolution*'s bower but could not locate any of *Adventure*'s. They would remain lost to the depths until 1978, when an American expedition found and salvaged two of her anchors.

While at this anchorage, there was also the need for a burial at sea. Isaac Taylor, a marine, died from a 'consumptive disorder', which had plagued him since departing England. As was always the case when a man died, his body was sewn into a canvas hammock or old sail, which was then weighted with cannonballs or other heavy objects. One of the ship's boats then carried Taylor's body out beyond the reef, where, in keeping with Royal Navy tradition, it was consigned to the deep, feet first.

Their stay in the south of Otaheite lasted just a week – sufficient time for the sick men aboard *Adventure* to be heading back to good health through rest and a diet of fresh local foods, especially fruits and meat. They were then strong enough to cope with the remaining 30-nautical-mile coastal passage to Matavai Bay. The stopover was also long enough for the captain to reacquaint himself with the customs and lifestyle of the islanders, as well as recognising the changes that had come as a consequence of their contact with Europeans, particularly their use of tools made from iron to shape their canoes. One thing that had not altered was the penchant of the Tahitian men, in particular, to be light-fingered. It was a timely reminder of what the sailors should be prepared for when they reached Matavai Bay.

On 24 August, the two ships were readied to put to sea and sail north. Although light airs made it a slow 48-hour passage, the reception that the Englishmen received after rounding Point Venus and sailing into the anchorage made everything worthwhile. The islanders were overjoyed to know that the great man, Cook, had returned after an absence of four years.

The day after arriving, the commander and Furneaux sailed a short distance along the coast in the pinnace to meet with the king, named Otoo, or Tu for short. The latter, a strapping young man, some 6 feet 3 inches in height, was initially 'mataou'd' (frightened) of the ships' guns and therefore somewhat apprehensive of their arrival, but he soon made the visitors most welcome. Cook was to learn that the structure of the island's social hierarchy had changed significantly since he was last there: many chiefs had died in battles between opposing tribal groups. One of Tu's first questions for the newcomers concerned the whereabouts of Tupia, and here Cook had the unfortunate task of informing him that the former chief and priest had died, along with many of his own men, before reaching England.

Cook found this young king to be more difficult than the chiefs he had encountered during his 1769 visit to the island. But Tu liked gifts, and the sound of bagpipes, so Cook obliged. On 28 August, as the captain explained, he 'entertained him [Tu] with the Bag-pipes of which musick he was very fond, and dancing by the Seamen'.

There was no reason to stay in Tahiti any longer than necessary on this visit, so, as the captain reported: 'The sick being all pretty well recovered, our water casks repaired and filled and the necessary repairs of the Sloops completed [I] determined to put to sea without Loss of time.' On Wednesday, 1 September, just six days after their arrival, his men pulled down the tents that had been set up on the beach to accommodate the sick, and the fabric observatory that Wales had erected on nearby Point Venus. At 3 pm that day, the wind, most fortuitously, swung to the easterly sector, making the situation ideal for weighing anchor and setting sail.

The eventual destination on this stage of the voyage was again Queen Charlotte Sound, but there was some island-hopping to be done beforehand: starting with Huaheine, just 100 nautical miles to the north-east. Once there, *Resolution* was successfully navigated through a narrow channel and into a lagoon, but *Adventure* was not so fortunate. She was caught in stays (that is, the ship failed to complete a tack), and then, having lost all speed, she drifted sideways onto the reef.

Showing considerable foresight, Cook had taken a precautionary measure. On realising how difficult the entry had been for *Resolution*, he already had his ship's launch hoisted out and manned in case *Adventure* should need assistance. Fortunately for the mission's support vessel, there was not a large swell running, and once the men aboard the launch had positioned her anchors adequately, Furneaux was able to orchestrate a manoeuvre that hauled her back into deep water without any damage to the hull.

Huaheine supplied the provisions of food that could not be procured in Matavai Bay and it also brought a level of embarrassment for a particular member of the expedition team – all because the islanders took a liking to the visitors' clothing. 'Mr Sparrman, being out alone botanizing,' Cook penned in his journal, 'was set upon by two men who stripped him of everything he had but his Trowsers, they struck him several times with his own hanger [sword] but happily did him no harm … a man … gave him a piece of cloth to cover himself and conducted him to me.'

In the meantime, Pickersgill, whom the captain had commissioned to purchase the required provisions, had secured some 400 hogs and all the fruit and vegetables they required. Just before the Englishmen left Huaheine, some of the more prominent members of the local community put a proposition to Cook: that he take his ships and attack their principal enemies, the men of nearby Bora Bora, on their behalf. These islanders were described by Midshipman John Elliott as 'the finest race of Men, and the greatest warriors'. This fact did not concern Cook, who simply declined the request.

The two ships then sailed a mere 26 nautical miles to the west, to the island now known as Raiatea. Once there, Pickersgill was assigned another task: to find enough food for the 400 hogs. This he did by taking two of the ship's small boats and a party of marines to a nearby island, where they spent the night. Securing the food was easy compared with trying to reassemble the soldiers, however. 'When the morning came,' wrote Pickersgill, 'I got up by times for to get away as early as possible, but enquiring for the people, I found most of them absent and on further examination, found them one in one house and one in another all straggled about the Woods, each man with his Mistress.'

By 18 September 1773, Cook had completed his sweep through this small and supremely beautiful group of islands and was heading west once more, with a change of plan. He had abandoned his desire to sail directly to New Zealand from this region. Instead, as he explained, the quest would continue: 'I directed my Course to the West inclining to the South as well to avoid the tracks of former Navigators as to get into the Latitude of Amsterdam Island discovered by Tasman in 1643, my intention being to run as far west as that Island ...'

Three days later, he discovered a trio of small islands, which he initially named the Sandwich Islands in honour of Lord Sandwich. Subsequently, though, he retitled them Herveys Islands, 'in honour of Captain Hervey of the Navy and one of the Lords of the Admiralty'.

Cook now had his men sailing in full exploration mode – on high alert. The majority of this territory was uncharted so there was every chance that they could stumble across an unknown reef or atoll at any time. This continued for the remainder of September until the ships reached the Tongan group of islands, before anchoring at Middleburg Island, a short distance to the south-east of Amsterdam Island. The sailors were stunned by the beauty of this South Pacific paradise, which the second lieutenant aboard *Adventure*, James Burney, described as being as 'beautiful as can be imagined – equal to any landscape I ever saw'. As a downside, though, the islanders here were 'people friendly & well disposed but great Thieves on which account we had some quarrels with them'.

Nevertheless, the visitors were welcomed wholeheartedly on Middleburg Island. Within a matter of hours, there was a large reception for them, during which the sailors entertained their hosts by playing the bagpipes – a source of immense intrigue to the locals. Cook sampled the local liquor, kava, which was made by a crude and most unhygienic method: men would chew the root of the kava plant, spit the pulp into a wooden bowl, add cold water, then drink the concoction as quickly as possible. It is a debilitating fluid when consumed in its rawest state, making most of the body's appendages go numb.

The overall beauty of this region had the naturalists and artists marvelling at an environment they could never have imagined. Less welcome, the thieving here was also unlike anything previously experienced. When William Wales went ashore, he was welcomed by a crowd of between 400 and 500 exuberant natives. The longboat could not be beached because the water was too shallow, so Wales removed his leather shoes and waded to the beach. Once there, he placed the shoes between his feet to protect them, but that was not good enough. In a flash, they were gone: 'they were instantly snatched away by a Person behind me. I turned round & just saw him mixing with the Crowd but it was in vain for me to attempt following him bare-footed over such sharp coral rocks, as the shores are composed of.' The captain later negotiated for the recovery of the astronomer's footwear.

One theft could have had a significant impact on the recording of the voyage to date, and again, Wales was involved. It happened after he decided to stay on the ship while the officers and his colleagues in the research group went ashore. During the afternoon, one of the natives who was on board was 'discovered coming out at the scuttle of the Master's Cabin, out of which he had taken [the master's] and the Ship's Log books, his Daily assistant, Nautical Almanack & some other Books', according to Wales' report. Crewmen on deck immediately took up their muskets and fired at the man and his accomplices, who then 'threw the books overboard & all jumped after them. The Books were all picked up & the canoe [in which the men had arrived at the ship] filled & sunk alongside ...'

*

On Friday, 8 October, the perfect circumstances existed in the form of a pleasant easterly breeze, so Cook signalled that it was time to depart. His intention was to sail directly to New Zealand, a passage of around 1200 nautical miles that would take about twelve days to complete.

Soon after sunrise on 21 October, the east coast of New Zealand's North Island was sighted, and before long the captain had it plotted as being Table Cape, around 200 nautical miles to the north of Cape Palliser at the eastern entrance to Cook Strait. The following day, the ships were beginning to feel the full force of a westerly gale, the persistence of which had dramatic consequences. The first drama came aboard *Resolution* when a savage squall sent the fore topgallant mast spearing towards the deck, and soon after this, sails began to blow apart. It was a nightmarish time for all on deck, but particularly for those who were then sent aloft to man the yards and retrieve the broken mast.

The ships plugged on to the south under greatly reduced sail. On the 25th, Cook made a journal entry that put the conditions into perspective. He wrote that the storm 'came on in such fury as to oblige us to take in all our sails with the utmost expedition and to lay-to under our bare poles ... The sea rose in proportion with the Wind so that we not only had a furious gale but a mountainous Sea also to encounter.'

On 26 October – the day before his forty-fifth birthday – when sailing near Cook Strait, the men aboard *Resolution* lost visual contact with the support vessel, which was being blown away to leeward from the coast. *Adventure* was sighted again the next day as a speck on the horizon to the south. By now, Cook Strait was living up to the reputation it holds today as being a cauldron for gales, and because of this, as Burney would note aboard *Adventure*, 'The 29th at Night we lost Sight of her [*Resolution*] the third Time. After this we never had the good fortune to meet her again.'

On 2 November, *Resolution* was battling a fresh southerly gale in Cook Strait, but still the captain was confident that they would reach Queen Charlotte Sound on the next flood tide. 'Vain were our expectations,' he wrote, adding that the next day, 'we discovered a new inlet which had all the appearance of a good harbour ...' His hope now was to reach this inlet – Wellington Harbour, as it would be named, after the hero of Waterloo – and anchor in its confines. But the turn of the tide brought a reversion to the original plan. Ship Cove was again their destination, and they reached there on 3 November.

Cook fully expected *Adventure* to be waiting in the cove for them, but she wasn't. It was a situation that would lead to one of the worst imaginable outcomes.

Cook's reception in Hawaii on his return from the Arctic was exceptional. The locals came out in force to inspect the ships, and trade and offer gifts. This illustration by John Webber shows King Terre'oboo being rowed to *Resolution* to offer Cook gifts. State Library of NSW, Dixson Library DL PXX 2, 35 / a1673038.

CHAPTER SEVENTEEN

Close Calls and an Atrocity

After a few days had passed, Cook and his men were becoming increasingly anxious regarding the whereabouts of *Adventure*. The captain knew that his support ship did not possess the same capabilities as *Resolution* when sailing upwind in extreme conditions, as had prevailed for much of the time prior to reaching Queen Charlotte Sound, but even allowing for that, *Adventure* was well overdue. On 10 November, Clerke wrote: 'We're all much surprised that our Consort, the Adventure, does not make her appearance nor are we able to form any idea what can have detained Her so long.'

In the meantime, *Resolution*'s crew carried out extensive maintenance on all parts of the ship, including overhauling the rig, caulking hull and deck planks, and 'boot topping' – scrubbing marine growth from around the ship's waterline over her entire length. There was considerable disappointment for all when more than 4000 pounds of bread was found to be mouldy and rotten, as a result of the storage casks having been made from green (not dried) timber, and the high humidity that had been experienced in the tropics. Also, with galley duties having used up much of the coal placed as ballast in the ship's bilge, Cook ordered that two launch-loads of ballast, in the form of rocks and shingle, be taken aboard and stored in the main hold. It was vitally important that the ship have maximum stability for the coming voyage, which would see her returning to Antarctic waters.

With each new day, concern for the safety of *Adventure* and her crew grew, as reflected in an entry in Cook's journal:

> I went in the Pinnace over to the East Bay, accompanied by some of the officers and gentlemen; as soon as we landed we went upon one of the hills in order to take a view of the Straits to see if we could discover anything of the Adventure, we had a fatiguing walk to little purpose for when we got to the top of the hill we found the Eastern horizon so foggy that we could not see above two or three miles.
>
> … as to the Adventure I despair of seeing her any more but am totally at a loss to conceive what is become of her till now. I thought that she might have put into some port in the Strait … and there stayed to complete her Wood and Water; this conjecture was reasonable enough at first, but the elapsation of twelve days has now made it scarce probable …

All that Cook could do was mount a search for *Adventure* in the region of Cook Strait once *Resolution* sailed from Queen Charlotte Sound. This departure was accelerated when, on 23 November, Cook, Pickersgill and a few of the crew went to the beach in the cove for some relaxation, only to discover that the Maoris there had recently killed a young man, and having apparently feasted on some body parts, were treating his remains with what the Englishmen considered to be utter disrespect. Later, when the captain returned to the ship, he was confronted by an abhorrent scene. The young man's head had been brought aboard and placed atop the capstan on the quarterdeck. Cook would later write that, to the disgust of all his men, 'a piece of the flesh had been broiled and eat by one of the Natives in the presence of most of the officers.'

This scene led to him making his most profound statement regarding cannibalism in New Zealand:

> That the New Zealanders are Cannibals can now no longer be doubted, the account I gave of it in my former Voyage was partly founded on circumstances and was, as I afterwards found, discredited by many people … This custom of eating their enemies slain in battle (for I firmly believe they eat the flesh of no others) has undoubtedly been handed down to them from the earliest times.

By 24 November, everything was in readiness for *Resolution* to put to sea. At four o'clock the following morning, the anchor was weighed and the ship glided out of the cove on a light northerly breeze. Before leaving, Cook ensured that should Furneaux arrive at Ship Cove, there would be a message waiting for him.

> This morning before we sailed I wrote a memorandum setting forth the time we arrived last here, the day we sailed, the route I intended to take and such other information as I thought necessary for Captain Furneaux to know and buried it in a bottle under the root of a tree in the garden in the bottom of the Cove in such a manner that it must be found by any European who may put into the Cove. I however have not the least reason to think that it will ever fall into the hands of the person I intended it for, for it is hardly possible that Captain Furneaux can be in any part of New Zealand and I not have heard of him in all this time.

It was Cook's intention to search as much of the sound and the coastline of the strait as possible, and this he did, 'firing guns every half hour without seeing or hearing the least signs of what we were in search after'. At six o'clock on 25 November, the captain reluctantly gave up any hope of finding *Adventure*.

> All the officers being unanimous of opinion that the
> Adventure could neither be stranded on the Coast or be
> in any of the Ports in this Country determined me to
> spend no more time in search of her, but to proceed
> directly to the Southward ... I can only suppose that
> Captain Furneaux was tired with beating against the
> north-west winds and had taken a resolution to make
> the best of his way to the Cape of good hope, be this as
> it may I have no expectation of joining him any more ...

In reality, Furneaux was still endeavouring to reach Queen Charlotte Sound, his ship having been defeated continually by gale-force winds from the western sector. Lieutenant James Burney wrote in his journal during this episode: 'Our ship in her best trim is not able to keep up, or carry Sail with the Resolution – at this time we fall bodily to Leeward being quite Light & so crank that we are obliged to Strike to every Squall – and so unmanageable that there is no getting her round either one way or another [tacking or wearing ship].'

Because of this, *Adventure* had been blown offshore time after time, but the captain persevered and finally reached Ship Cove five days after *Resolution* departed. Burney would then note:

> On coming in we were greatly disappointed at not
> finding the Resolution here. As soon as the Ship was
> Secured a Boat was sent to the Watering place ... in our
> garden Stood a Large Tank of Wood on the Top of
> which was carved LOOK UNDERNEATH – we were
> not long in obeying the directions & found buried in a
> Bottle under the Log a Letter [from Cook].

Adventure was in no fit state to return to sea immediately. Considerable repairs needed to be made, and it wasn't until 17 December that she was ready to sail again. That same day, tragedy struck.

Furneaux had ordered ten armed sailors to take the cutter to Wharehunga Bay, 6 nautical miles to the east of Ship Cove, to collect what wild greens they could for the ship's larder. They were directed to return by mid-afternoon, but there was no sign of the party as night descended on the sound.

At first light the next morning, Burney and ten fully armed marines were sent in search of the men. On arrival at a cove in Wharehunga Bay, they saw a large double-hulled Maori canoe on the beach, and upon investigation, discovered in one of the hulls a rowlock from the cutter, a shoe belonging to a crew-member, and what they hoped was dog flesh. They then walked up the beach to where some food baskets were found, and when these were cut open, Burney made a ghastly discovery: the hacked-up and freshly cooked remains of human bodies. There was no question that these belonged to the missing men, because among the flesh was a hand with a distinctive tattoo – containing the letters 'TH' – which was that of Thomas Hill, one of the men aboard the cutter.

The search party then rowed into another cove, where they were confronted by about 400 Maoris, some of whom taunted them. There they came across what Burney described as 'such a shocking scene of Carnage & Barbarity as can never be mentioned or thought of, but with horror'. More body parts from the lost crewmen were scattered around, while others were being cooked on a fire. The Maoris were treating the Englishmen as invaders, an enemy, and the accepted custom of cannibalism prevailed.

Burney had his men gather up some of the strewn body parts, to serve as evidence for Furneaux, before leaving the ghastly scene. The moment they arrived back at the ship and informed the captain of the massacre, he accelerated his plans for departure. The anchor was weighed at daylight the following morning, and four days later, Cape Palliser was in *Adventure*'s wake as she headed away from New Zealand on an easterly course.

By now, Furneaux knew that to pursue *Resolution* would be futile, so he set course for Cape Horn. They were homeward bound. However, by the time *Adventure* reached the Horn, the captain had to consider two emerging problems: his ship was becoming unseaworthy as a result of the battering she had absorbed during more than eighteen months at sea, and they were running low on provisions. He therefore continued towards the east, bound for Cape Town, where both predicaments could be remedied. *Adventure* reached England on 14 July 1774, two years and one day after sailing away from Plymouth.

Cook had abandoned his search for *Adventure* once *Resolution* cleared Cape Palliser. Initially, she was trimmed for an easterly course, but soon he called for the timoneer to put the helm down and turn towards the south. This was the first stage of a plan he had developed in recent weeks and shared with only his senior officers: to continue the search for the Great South Land as far south as possible. It was not his practice to keep the men of the lower deck similarly informed, because such knowledge might create discord among them. When it became apparent to all where they were heading, Cook was pleased to note that his men were happy to continue without a consort, 'to the South or wherever I thought properly [to] lead them'.

Within a matter of days, Cook had made his first declaration relating to this exploration. With there being a considerable swell running from the south-west, he was convinced that there was no continent in the near vicinity, and that any land that might exist could only be to the south of 60 degrees latitude.

By mid December, *Resolution* was back among the ice, sailing under greatly reduced canvas in a gale, but still managing to cover between 130 and 150 nautical miles most days. Being summertime in the southern hemisphere, darkness lasted for only a few hours in such high latitudes, so Cook was able to press his ship onwards in relative safety because of the extended daylight. Even so, nothing could be done to prevent the dramas brought on by the occasional rogue sea. 'The Storm & Sea much increased,' Förster wrote at one point. 'At 9 o'clock, there came a huge mountainous Sea & took the Ship in her middle, & overwhelmed all her parts with a Deluge. The table in the Steerage, at which we were sitting, was covered with water, & it put our candle out; the great Cabin was quite washed over & over by the Sea coming through the Sides of the Ship.' He added: 'A cruise among the inhospitable Ice Islands is a dismal prospect & shocking to humanity.'

On 15 December, *Resolution* was inside the Antarctic Circle for the second time on this voyage, and the fields of ice were beginning to pose a serious threat to the ship. Fog was closing in; then, more alarmingly, they were embayed by a rapidly expanding field of ice and icebergs – there was nowhere for the ship to go but back the way she came. As the vital change of course was being implemented, the already dangerous situation turned into one of emergency, duly announced by a bellowed 'All hands on deck!' With the expected sense of urgency, men rushed up the companionway ladders and leapt onto the deck, the look on every face reflecting shock – the captain's included.

They were confronted by a huge iceberg, and there was every good chance that the ship might strike it with a glancing blow. The first order was for as many men as possible to grab what light spars they could and be ready to fend off this monstrous island of ice. The helmsman was able to turn the ship, however, and she was then set up on a reciprocal course, much to everyone's great relief. Elliott wrote in his journal that it was 'the most Miraculous escape from being every soul lost, that ever men had'.

The danger they faced was not lost on anyone, especially the ever-restrained captain.

One of these masses [of ice] was very near proving fatal to us, we had not weather [cleared] it more than once or twice our length, had we not succeeded this circumstance could never have been related. According to the old proverb a miss is as good as a mile, but our situation requires more misses than we can expect, this together with the improbability of meeting with land to

> the South and the impossibility of exploring it for the ice
> if we did find any, determine me to haul to the north.

From that moment, every man on deck, but more so the lookouts aloft, had their eyes peering anxiously forward and off the bows, looking for any additional threat to the vessel that might emerge through the murk. Cook planned to continue sailing south the moment they were clear of this danger and the weather had turned in their favour. And there was no holding him back once these requirements were met. On 24 December, *Resolution* was beyond 67 degrees south in conditions that beggar belief:

> ... wind northerly a strong gale attended with a thick
> fog Sleet and Snow which froze to the Rigging as it fell
> and decorated the whole with icicles. Our ropes were
> like wires, Sails like board or plates of Metal and the
> Shivers [sheeves] froze fast in the blocks so that it
> required our utmost effort to get a Top-sail down and
> up; the cold so intense as hardly to be endured, the
> whole Sea in a manner covered with ice ...

It was in conditions like this that Cook had to apply a technique needed to make the ship safer. The sails were virtually frozen stiff, so *Resolution* had to shake herself free of this burden, as well as the snow and ice accumulated in the rig. The helmsman would be ordered to put down the helm, turning the bow towards the direction of the wind. Then, with a thunderous sound, the sails would flog wildly, causing the ice that was sheathing them to fall to the deck like glass from a broken window. At the same time, the entire rig would shudder so violently that the mass of snow on the masts and yards would be shaken free and disappear downwind in an enormous white cloud.

Resolution was now at the limit of navigation: Cook told his officers on the quarterdeck that it was time to sail to the north, away from this icy wilderness. His decision was equally influenced by a growing belief that there was no land to be found in this region.

The following day was Christmas Day, and the extreme weather conditions, clear skies notwithstanding, made for a modest celebration. As expected, the grog bottles came out, and before long most of the men were melancholy, if not very drunk.

Cook had applied strict discipline among the crew from the start of this voyage, and the cat-o'-nine-tails had seen not-infrequent action since then. Two days after the new year of 1774, there came a breach that the captain deemed to be extreme. Midshipman Charles Loggie, who was well under the influence of alcohol, drew a knife and slashed two of the young seamen. The assailant was subsequently 'sent before the mast', where he was punished in no uncertain fashion with the lash.

Another two days later, *Resolution* was at the latitude of 55 degrees south and holding a north-westerly course. Despite his conviction that they were not in the proximity of any large landmass, Cook was considering making one more probe as far south as possible, just to make sure. It was still too early to do so, as was apparent twenty-four hours later, when the ship was confronted by some of the worst weather that the Southern Ocean could muster at that time of year: very strong gales with excessively heavy squalls, accompanied by ugly, grey, voluminous breaking seas, some around 50 feet high, their crests a couple of hundred yards apart. Each time one of these ocean monsters hammered the ship, she would shudder and roll violently in response. Worse still, whenever a wave broke over the deck and cascaded from one bulwark to the other, it became apparent that the caulking work done in Queen Charlotte Sound was ineffective. Bitterly cold water gushed through the gaps in the deck planks and poured below, drenching the men's hammocks and bedding, and generally making life almost unbearable. It was like water torture.

By 11 January, the conditions had driven *Resolution* another 400 nautical miles north, and now, with the weather turning in his favour, it was decision time for the captain. At noon he wrote, 'being little more than two hundred Leagues from my track to Otaheite in 1769 in which space it was not probable anything was to be found, we therefore hauled up SE with a fresh gale.' They were heading to the Antarctic Circle for the third time!

Making Cook's life easier as a navigator was the continuing accuracy of the Kendall timepiece, particularly with regard to the calculation of longitude. He was full of praise for this chronometer, as it held its time in all conditions: '[I] determined our Longitude beyond a doubt. Indeed our error can never be great so long as we have so good a guide as Mr Kendall's watch.'

Resolution pressed on south in sometimes horrid conditions, yet the men rarely grumbled, even when the need arose for some to climb up the ratlines and tend the sails. By Sunday, 30 January, Cook and his crew were creating maritime history in a previously unseen, incomprehensible environment.

> A little after 4 AM we perceived the Clouds to the South
> near the horizon to be of an unusual Snow white
> brightness which denounced our approach to field ice,
> soon after it was seen from the Mast-head and at 8
> o'Clock we were close to the edge of it which extended
> East and West in a straight line far beyond our sight ...
> The Clouds near the horizon were of a perfect Snow
> whiteness and were difficult to be distinguished from the
> Ice hills whose lofty summits reached the Clouds. The
> outer or Northern edge of this immense Ice field was
> composed of loose or broken ice so close packed
> together that nothing could enter it; about a Mile in
> began the firm ice, in one compact solid body and
> seemed to increase in height as you traced it to the
> South; In this field we counted Ninety Seven Ice Hills or
> Mountains, many of them vastly large ... I will not say it
> was impossible anywhere to get in among this Ice, but I
> will assert that the bare attempting of it would be a very

> dangerous enterprise and what I believe no man in my situation would have thought of. I whose ambition leads me not only farther than any other man has been before me, but as far as I think it possible for man to go, was not sorry at meeting with this interruption, as it in some measure relieved us from the dangers and hardships, inseparable with the Navigation of the Southern Polar regions. Since therefore we could not proceed one Inch farther South, no other reason need be assigned for our Tacking and stretching back to the North, being at that time in the Latitude of 71°10' South, Longitude 106°54'W ...

Cook's coordinates for *Resolution* placed her about 130 nautical miles north of what is today Antarctica's Walgreen coast.

He now made the decision to sail to the north, and towards warmer weather, comfortable in the knowledge that while no land had been discovered, he had done everything possible to find it. And besides, there was already ample success in the ship's wake.

As the men on watch started to tend the sheets, braces and lines in preparation for the call to tack, there was some friendly rivalry between two of the crew. First a young midshipman, George Vancouver – who years later would be honoured for his achievements in life by having a city in British Columbia named after him – scurried out to near the tip of the bowsprit and shouted back to his crewmates that he was further south than any man had ever been ... Not to be outdone, Anders Sparrman, who was sitting well aft in the great cabin at the ship's stern, then laid claim to the honour because, as the ship glided through her turn, that was the most southerly point that any part of *Resolution* had achieved.

The crew could have been forgiven for thinking that their exploration efforts were coming to a close and that they would soon be heading home. But nothing was further from the mind of the expedition commander. The voyage was far from complete; the exploration had to continue, but in what direction he wasn't sure. Cook would no doubt have spread out his charts on the table in the great cabin once again, in order to compare the tracks of *Endeavour* and *Resolution* with the course taken by others who had sailed across the Pacific and through the Southern Ocean. This research would reveal what regions remained to be explored – uncharted areas that were large enough to conceal a yet-to-be-discovered continent.

After poring over the charts, he realised that there were two options open to him: he could return to the waters south of Cape Town, in the vicinity of Bouvet's 1739 find, or track through the wide expanse of the Pacific that remained generally untouched by European explorers. He firmly believed that there was nothing to be found to the east, between *Resolution*'s current position and Cape Horn. So, considering that, and the fact that winter was approaching, the answer was to search the tropical regions of the Pacific. This was obviously a scenario that Cook had considered when leaving his message for Furneaux at Ship Cove. Part of that note read: 'if I do not find a Continent or isle between this and Cape Horn in which we can Winter perhaps I may spend the winter within the Tropics ...' Such a plan would ensure that he could complete this voyage of discovery to the fullest since, after exploring the Pacific, he could again turn his attention to the Southern Ocean waters around the region of Bouvet's supposed cape while sailing for home the following summer.

Cook now plotted a course towards Easter Island, located 2000 nautical miles to the west of the Chilean coast, before advising his senior officers where they were heading. He was prepared for this decision to meet with a level of negativity, but instead he 'had the satisfaction to find they all heartily concurred in it'. Again, the tars were not made aware of this latest plan.

On 23 February, as *Resolution* continued on her way towards the warmer climes, there was concern for the captain, who had fallen ill with stomach cramps – 'to the grief of all the ship's company', wrote John Marra, a gunner's mate. Cook tried to brush it off, noting in his journal: 'I was now taken ill of the Bilious colic and so Violent as to confine me to my bed, so that the Management of the Ship was left to Mr Cooper my first Officer who conducted her very much to my satisfaction.' The ship's surgeon, James Patten, did everything he could for the captain, and Cook recognised his efforts in the journal. He also recorded that 'a favourite [pet] dog belonging to Mr Forster fell a Sacrifice to my tender Stomack; we had no other fresh meat whatever on board and I could eat of this flesh as well as broth made of it, when I could taste nothing else, thus I received nourishment and strength from food which would have made most people in Europe sick'. Two days later, Förster was no doubt pleased to observe how his 'sacrifice' had aided the patient's recovery: 'the Capt is much better, sits up, & eats something, but is very weak, & quite emaciated, & will continue so for a good while, unless we meet with Land, & get some refreshments.'

Many of the men were becoming ill, in fact, and Wales had a theory on the cause of this – namely, the rapid transition from a world of freezing rain, sleet, snow and icebergs to warmer weather. 'It's scarcely 3 weeks ago we were miserable on account of ye cold,' the Royal Society's astronomer wrote, 'we are now wretched with ye heat.'

On 11 March, land was sighted from the masthead, but it wasn't until two days later that, with the use of telescopes, it could be confirmed as Easter Island. Cook then wrote: 'In stretching in for the land we discovered people and those Monuments or Idols mentioned by the Authors of Roggeveen's Voyage which left us no room to doubt but it was Easter Island.' It was Jacob Roggeveen, a Dutchman, who had discovered this island for Europe, on Easter Day, 5 April 1722.

Cook could not find a suitable sheltered harbour in which to anchor, so he chose an exposed bay near the southern extremity of the western coastline. However, almost as soon as the best bower was released from the cathead and had plunged to the seabed, it became apparent that this bay was a poor holding ground; more than likely, *Resolution* would drag anchor in strong winds and a surging sea. He therefore informed the officers that the stay here would be as brief as possible. But they would not sail before Förster and twenty-six of the ship's complement had gone ashore to investigate the incredible features of the island and collect plant specimens.

Cook himself went onto the island, but he was not strong enough to undertake the proposed trek to the far side. For those who went, it was a strenuous day's work, but a valuable and interesting exercise all the same. When Förster returned to *Resolution*, he wrote about his impression of the huge stone statues of Easter Island:

> We stood directly across the country … till we came to the other side of the island & there we found 7 stone pillars, 4 of which were still standing … One of the standing ones had lost its hat … In what manner they contrived these structures is incomprehensible to me, for we saw no tools with them … The Images represent Men to their waist, the Ears are large and they are about 15 foot high & above 5 foot wide; they are ill shaped & have a large solid bonnet on their head like some of the old Egyptian divinities … These pillars intimate that the Natives were formerly a more powerful people, more numerous & better civilised.

Both he and Pickersgill reported to Cook that the island offered little in the way of water and provisions, so after taking aboard what they could, the captain called for a departure on 17 March. He would later write his own appraisal of this island, which he found to be like no other in the Pacific. He made particular note of the 700 or so people who lived there: 'They are certainly of the same race of People as the New Zealanders and the other islanders, the affinity of the Language, Colour and some of their customs all tend to prove it.' This similarity between the peoples, of two opposite sides of the Pacific no doubt confounded Cook, as it raised questions regarding their migration patterns, long-distance seafaring skills and ability to navigate. Time would reveal that the Polynesians were among the world's greatest navigators.

The need for food and water, combined with the desire to explore, led to Cook deciding to make for the spectacular and tropical Marquesas Islands – some 770 nautical miles to the north-east of Otaheite on 10 degrees south latitude, and over 2000 miles north-west of *Resolution*'s present position. The first European to sight and visit the Marquesas was Spanish navigator Álvaro de Mendaña y Neira, in 1595, during the second of his two voyages aimed at solving the mystery of *Terra Australis Incognita*.

By now, the tars of the lower deck had realised that they would not be heading home any time soon, yet their complaints were few. As Marra would point out, the captain's quest for the best possible food for his men was much appreciated: 'It preserved the crew in health, and encouraged them to undergo cheerfully the hardships that must unavoidably happen in the course of so long a voyage.' But Cook's own health failed again, partly due to sunstroke; according to Marra's account, 'eating lard and salt pork plenteously' had also contributed to the captain having 'fallen again into his constipation and bilious complaint'. It took him five days to recover.

With the Marquesas Islands lying to the north-west, *Resolution* was booming along on the face of a strengthening south-east trade wind, surging down blue Pacific rollers and churning out a bold, white bow wave that would have done any ship proud. Every conceivable sail was set to suit the conditions – spritsails, studding sails, the spanker and driver included – all billowing forth and contributing to a scene that sailors' dreams are made of.

Still, as delightful as this was, some sailors continued to go beyond the boundaries of the Articles of War and were duly disciplined. Bowles Mitchell, at the time a midshipman, told of one such incident: 'Wm Wedgerborough marine confined, there being strong presumptive proof, of uncleanliness ... and proof positive in point of Drunkeness ... Read the articles of war & Punished Wm Wedgerborough marine with a dozen lashes.'

Cook was concerned about the accuracy of the longitude given for the Marquesas, because it was recorded using far more basic navigational equipment, almost two centuries earlier. He therefore sailed to approximately 9 degrees south latitude, before turning his ship west in search of the mainly volcanic islands making up the group. The task for the lookouts was somewhat easier than normal, because the highest peak in the group, Mount Oave, stood 4000 feet above sea level, meaning that it could be seen on a clear day from more than 50 nautical miles away. The first island to emerge above the horizon was not on Cook's chart, so he named it Hood Island as a tribute to sixteen-year-old Alexander Hood. The latter, a cousin of Admiral Lord Hood, was the first person to sight it, on 7 April 1774, while on lookout duty at the masthead.

Having spent three weeks sailing from Easter Island to the Marquesas, the crew were captivated by the natural beauty of this new destination. When Mendaña had come across them all those years before, he sighted and named only four islands out of the fifteen that are now known to be in the group. The Spaniard made special reference on his chart to a bay at Vaitahu, on the western side of Tahuata Island, so Cook decided to search for it and anchor *Resolution* within its confines. Unfortunately, though, as *Resolution* was being prepared for anchoring there, a violent, bullet-like blast of wind descended from the hills, causing the sails to flog, the masts to shake and the ship to heel dramatically. Worse still, in being caught unawares, the crew could do little to prevent her from being blown to within a boat-length of a jagged reef that was to leeward. The savage squall disappeared as quickly as it had arrived, thankfully, and with it gone, and composure having returned on board, the captain opted to anchor further offshore.

While sailing towards this anchorage, *Resolution* was welcomed on a number of occasions by men aboard large canoes, which had a lateen rig and sails made from woven matting, probably palm fronds. The usual form of trading started almost immediately – iron nails and cloth for fruit and hogs – but it seemed that some of the islanders had a different attitude to business. 'In this Traffic they would frequently keep our goods and make no return,' Cook reported, 'till at last I was obliged to fire a Musket ball Close past one man who had served us in this manner after which they observed a little more honesty …'

And that was only the start. It became apparent that these people were as adept at pilfering as the natives that the crew had encountered in Otaheite and elsewhere. Cook was boarding the pinnace with a view to going ashore when he learned that some of the islanders had just stolen an iron gangway stanchion from the opposite side of the ship. 'I told the officers to fire over the Canoe till I could get round [there] in the Boat,' the captain later recalled, 'unluckily for the thief they took better aim than I ever intended and killed him the third Shot, two others that were in the same Canoe jumped overboard …'

While the scenically beautiful Marquesas provided ample drinking water to refill *Resolution*'s barrels, Cook was not able to secure the provisions required to restock the ship. So it was time to move on again, now towards a place where he fully expected to find everything he needed: Otaheite. It would also enable Wales to use his navigation instruments at a known point on the island and, accordingly, check the accuracy of the Kendall.

When the ship's anchor was weighed on 12 April, after just five days in the Marquesas, Cook was comfortable in the knowledge that it had been a successful fact-finding mission. He had been able to far more accurately position these islands on the map of the Pacific, and by the time *Resolution* was clear of the group, he had also added three previously undiscovered islands to the same map.

*

After sailing 500 nautical miles to the south-south-west, Cook opted to land in the Tuamotu Archipelago, since it provided both Förster and himself with their first opportunity to go ashore at an atoll and take a close look at how it was formed. Their chosen destination was Takaroa, a loop-like atoll of 15 nautical miles in length, where the distance between ocean and lagoon was on average little more than a few hundred yards. The reception from the people there was not overly friendly, however, so Cook returned to *Resolution*, weighed anchor and 'ordered two of three Guns to be fired over the little isle the Natives were upon in order to show them that it was not their own Superior strength and Numbers which obliged us to leave their isle'.

It was now the captain's intention to keep moving along his desired route through the unmapped parts of the Pacific, via Otaheite, with some level of haste. Then, if nothing of major importance was discovered, they would head to Ship Cove in Queen Charlotte Sound for a winter break.

Having sailed on port tack for the majority of the course from the Marquesas Islands, *Resolution* anchored in Matavai Bay early on the morning of 22 April. Within twenty-four hours, the islanders – who were again delighted to see their favourite visitor from alien shores – were bringing all the desired produce to the ship for trade. Even the king, Tu, arrived with a gift of twelve hogs. While this was happening, Wales had set up his observatory on the beach to take his sights and check the Kendall chronometer. At the same time, the crew set about undertaking extensive maintenance aboard the ship. After going ashore himself, the captain was pleased to note that the islands had enjoyed a good wet season and fresh food was plentiful.

Of particular interest to all of the visitors was the large number of new canoes that had been built, which was as a direct result of the iron tools that Cook had traded or given to the islanders during previous visits. Then, on 26 April, the Englishmen were stunned by the arrival in Matavai Bay of an enormous fleet of double-hulled canoes that were being prepared for a battle with the natives of the island of Moorea, 15 nautical miles across the channel to the north-west. It was a battle that could start at any time. 'In these 330 Canoes,' wrote Cook, 'I judged there were no less than 7760 Men, a number which appears incredible.' Equally impressive was another double-hulled craft that was nearing completion – one that could lay claim to being the largest vessel of its type in the South Pacific. It was 108 feet in length (almost as long as *Resolution*) and destined to be propelled by more than 100 paddlers. With the battle pending, there were apparently suggestions from Tu that Cook might like to stay longer and provide the full firepower of *Resolution* to support the proposed raid.

The captain was pleased to note that there was no reason to delay his ship's departure from the island due to illness among his crew, since: 'As to Sick we had none.' His initial plan was to stay on Otaheite for less than a week, but by the time the required amount of food and water had been collected and the considerable level of hospitality reciprocated, it would be three weeks before they departed.

One thing that hadn't changed was the natives' habit of pilfering, and here Cook took it upon himself to deal out twelve lashes to an islander who had stolen a water cask. The hope was that this would deter others from being light-fingered, but it had little impact. Less than a week later, a sentry who had been posted onshore fell asleep one night, midway through his watch, and when he woke up, his musket had been stolen. The weapon was recovered, but not without considerable effort on the captain's part. Cook's proactive role in searching for the stolen item offended the king, however, to the point where the relationship between the two men broke down. They only reconciled after the musket was recovered.

On Saturday, 14 May, by which time *Resolution* had a 'vast supply of provisions' on board, she set sail from Matavai Bay. First though, Cook ordered that a salvo from her 'great guns' be fired in Tu's honour.

But suddenly, as all sails were being hauled down from the yards and trimmed for *Resolution*'s course out of the bay, towards Huaheine, there was a commotion on deck. John Marra, the gunner's mate, had decided that the hospitality in Otaheite had been so much to his satisfaction that he had no desire to leave. Being a good swimmer, he made a sudden dash for the side of the ship and leapt over the bulwark and into the water, with the intention of returning to shore. But luck was not on his side. The captain promptly brought the ship to, hoisted out a boat and retrieved his errant crewman. The moment he was back on deck, Marra was put 'in confinement till we were clear of the isles'. He was not punished at the time because Cook deemed him to be a valuable member of the crew, and also because the young sailor had been encouraged to desert with the full knowledge of the king. Remarkably, this was not the first time that Marra had decided to literally jump ship. He had done the same thing as *Resolution* departed from Deptford, even before the expedition was underway.

Resolution was at anchor at Huaheine the following day. Then, after an eight-day stay on the island – where the welcome and the supply of provisions was as bountiful as during the previous visit – it was time to visit Raiatea, a similar-sized island just west of Huaheine. Again, *Resolution* went remarkably close to being driven onto a reef as she entered the harbour. It was a situation in which only Cook's careful planning and skills as a seafarer kept her in deep water. He later reported on this close shave: 'The two points of the reef which form the entrance on which the Sea broke with Such height and Violence as was frightful to look at; having all our Boats and Warps in readiness we presently carried them out and Warped the Ship into safety.'

As he was preparing to depart Raiatea on 4 June, Cook was shocked to hear from an islander that two English ships, one under the command of Joseph Banks, the other under Tobias Furneaux, had arrived in Huaheine. The captain immediately made plans to send one of the ship's boats to Huaheine with orders for Furneaux, but within a matter of hours the man making the claim (who had promptly disappeared into the hills) was deemed to be lying. It was all part of a practical joke, a habit for which the islanders were well known.

The crew returned to preparing their ship for departure, and as they set sail, they demonstrated their appreciation of the hospitality they had received on Raiatea by setting off fireworks and firing cannons in salute of 'his Majesty's Birth Day'. Cook's final note was that he set his course to the west, 'and took our final leave of these happy isles and the good People in them'.

Resolution's new track was to the west, and on 17 June, while en route to Tonga, she passed a previously undiscovered island, which Cook named Palmerston Island. For much of this passage he brought the ship to at night, to lessen the chance of their coming to grief on any uncharted reef or atoll.

On 27 June, *Resolution* was anchored off Nomuka, in the Tongan group of islands, and once again, every man was welcomed in typical island fashion. Offsetting what was perhaps an even greater display of friendliness compared with the previous stopovers, petty (and not so petty) thieving was an art form with these people also. The first such incident came when the surgeon, James Patten, had his musket stolen while he was away hunting wild fowl. Soon afterwards, some of the cooper's tools, as well as a second musket, disappeared from where they'd been left on a beach. Cook called in the marines to pursue the perpetrators, which they did and the muskets were duly recovered.

Later, the captain discovered one of the adzes that had been stolen, and through actions and words he left the culprit in no doubt that he wanted the item returned. She would have no part of it, until remorse set in. The woman not only returned the adze to Cook, but offered him a form of apology he wasn't prepared for:

> ... this woman and a man presented to me a young
> woman and gave me to understand she was at my service.
> Miss, who probably had received her instructions, I found

wanted by way of Handsel [an advance payment], a Shirt
or a Nail, neither the one nor the other I had to give
without giving her the Shirt on my back which I was not
in a humour to do. I soon made them sensible of my
Poverty and thought by that means to have come off
with flying Colours but I was mistaken, for I was made to
understand I might retire with her on credit, this not
suiting me neither the old Lady began first to argue with
me and when that failed she abused me … Sneering in
my face and saying, what sort of a man are you thus to
refuse the embraces of so fine a young Woman, for the
girl certainly did not [want] beauty which I could
however withstand, but the abuse of the old Woman I
could not and therefore hastened into the Boat, they then
would needs have me take the girl on board with me, but
this could not be done as I had come to a Resolution not
to suffer a Woman to come on board the Ship on any
pretence whatever and had given strict orders to the
officers to that purpose …

Despite the thefts, Cook and his men had nothing but the highest
admiration for the islanders they met while cruising through this
archipelago. On departing the region, he would write: 'this
group [of islands] I have named the Friendly Archipelago as a
lasting friendship seems to subsist among the Inhabitants and their
Courtesy to Strangers entitles them to that name.'

Cook's plan for exploring this part of the Pacific included an
attempt to find 'Quirós's Isles', which he believed were about
1000 nautical miles north-west of the Friendly group. His
interest was stimulated by the knowledge that when Spain's
Pedro Fernandez de Quirós found these islands in 1606, he was
so certain that he had discovered part of the perimeter of the
mythical *Terra Australis Incognita* that he named it 'Terra
Austrialia del Espíritu Santo' (Southern Land of the Holy Spirit).
Resolution was soon underway once more, and on 3 July, having
sailed north-west, arrived at a small and previously uncharted

island, Vatoa. This stay was brief, and with nothing to be seen on the immediate horizon, Cook continued in his efforts to locate the 'Isles', which he was convinced lay to the north-west. Had he headed more to the north from Vatoa, he would have made yet another great discovery: Fiji, an archipelago comprising more than 332 islands. Tasman recorded some of the most northerly islands in this group when he sailed through the region in 1643, but the major part of Fiji would be recorded by Captain William Bligh in 1789, following the *Bounty* mutiny.

Cook's determination to unravel the entire riddle of this part of the Pacific saw him adopt a zigzag course to the north-west, so that the greatest possible area of ocean could be scoured. The ship proceeded at maximum speed through the daylight hours, then, for safety reasons, was brought back to a near-drift at night.

It was 3 pm on Sunday, 17 July, when land was next sighted, but a howling gale out of the south-east – which saw many sails 'split and torn to pieces' – made for a difficult approach. Even so, he soon entered an important note in his journal: 'I made no doubt but this was the Australia Del Espiritu Santo of Quiros.' Over the next six weeks, *Resolution* circumnavigated almost all of the eighty-three islands in the group, which stretched for more than 300 nautical miles in a line to the south-south-east. Cook subsequently applied his own name to them – the New Hebrides (today Vanuatu). Initially he tracked south, then back to the north, charting the majority of islands along the way.

The first anchorage there that Cook chose was off Malekula Island, and inevitably natives were clambering aboard in no time, initially full of curiosity and friendship. Soon though, fear was the prevailing emotion: this came about after one of the islanders, armed with a bow and what the visitors thought was a poison arrow, threatened to shoot a member of the crew. The aggressor was immediately peppered with small shot, but it was the noise of the musket discharging that caused most alarm among the natives. They immediately began leaping overboard – some through the stern windows of the great cabin, others from up the rigging – and began swimming ashore. Simultaneously, many of the islanders who had remained in the canoes took up their weapons and started firing a fusillade of arrows towards the ship. But, as the commander explained, 'a Musket discharged in the air and a four pounder over their heads sent them all off in the utmost confusion.'

A week later, some of *Resolution*'s men were in fact poisoned. The cause was from an altogether more natural source. Cook explained:

> The Night before we came out of Port two Red fish about the size of large Bream and not unlike them were caught with hook and line of which Most of the officers and Some of the Petty officers dined the next day. In the Evening every one who had eat of these fish were seized with Violent pains in the head and limbs, so as to be unable to stand, together with a kind of Scorching heat all over the Skin, there remained no doubt but that it was occasioned by the fish being of a Poisonous nature and communicated its bad effects to every one who had the ill luck to eat of it even to the Dogs and Hogs, one of the latter died ... We had reason to be thankful in not having caught more of them for if we had we should have been in the Same Situation ...

The visitors also became aware of what, due to the dense amount of smoke, appeared to be a large forest fire high on a nearby island. Darkness revealed that it was actually an erupting volcano, throwing up large volumes of smoke and fire, and making 'the same noise like thunder'.

The reception from the natives in the New Hebrides had generally been affable so far, but that changed when the ship landed at Eromanga Island. Hundreds of fully armed warriors formed a semicircle on a beach, where their chief had encouraged Cook to come ashore, and the moment he stepped off the pinnace and onto the sand – as usual, in uniform – he sensed a trap, simply because of the way the chief was talking to his men and gesticulating. Cook did an immediate about-turn, hurrying back up the boarding plank of the pinnace while ordering his own men to retreat as quickly as possible. With that, the natives tried to restrain the boat, grabbing the oars, so that Cook knew there was only one effective form of defence: to shoot the chief for his treachery, the hope being that this would bring the shock needed to quell the threat. The musket misfired, however, and suddenly a hail of arrows, spears and rocks targeted the boat, slightly wounding two of the crew. Cook called on his marines to take up their arms and return fire, which they did. As this was happening, other crewmen rowed the pinnace and cutter back to the ship, achieving a lucky escape for all. Once there, the men clambered up over the side and onto the deck, where they began helping others who were already initiating plans to weigh anchor and get the ship under sail as soon as possible.

Later, Cook would ponder the reason for this attack. A significant point for consideration was that these people were Melanesian, very different from the Polynesians who had mostly shown great warmth towards the visitors. One theory that subsequently emerged was that the Englishmen, being white, might have been seen by the Melanesians as ghosts – the spirits of the islanders' ancestors. But there is no known reason why these people would want to kill their ancestors.

By the middle of August, when the ship was at anchor at Tanna Island, Cook decided to continue his cruise around the New Hebrides by exploring the islands all the way to the north of the group. Once there, *Resolution* rounded the island that Quirós had named Austrialia del Espíritu Santo (today known just as Espiritu Santo).

It appears that, for much of the time during this particular part of his circumnavigation, Cook held no great desire to revisit Queen Charlotte Sound, his primary goal being to reach

Cape Horn by November that year and enter the South Atlantic. But once again, the temptation to explore and discover new lands was becoming all too powerful. So he put New Zealand back on the agenda, noting that he must do this 'while I had yet some time left to explore any lands I might meet with between this and New Zealand, where I intended to touch to refresh my people and recruit our stock of wood and Water, for another Southern Cruise'. By 1 September, *Resolution* was sailing away from modern-day Vanuatu. She was being steered into the open ocean towards the south on a course that would take her to New Zealand's west coast.

On departing from the New Hebrides, Cook could satisfy himself with the knowledge that he had confirmed the existence and location of Quirós's Isles, and at the same time was able to highlight the navigational inaccuracy that emerged from the 1768 visit by Frenchman Louis-Antoine, Comte de Bougainville.

While en route to New Zealand, Cook made two other important discoveries that were inscribed onto the map of the South Pacific. Three days after leaving the New Hebrides, yet another large island was located. As *Resolution* closed on this coast from a north-easterly direction, Cook and his men realised that they were observing a very large tract of mountainous terrain – land that stretched from horizon to horizon, one that would eventually be revealed to be more than 200 miles long and around 30 miles wide. A suitable anchorage was located on the eastern shore, and *Resolution* sheltered there for a week. While at anchor, Wales and Clerke went ashore and set up the observatory, so that they could monitor an eclipse of the sun – much to the intrigue of the friendly natives – while the always energetic, but still generally unpopular, Förster botanised extensively. There was again a lesson for Cook and some of the officers relating to poisonous fish, in this case toadfish:

> A Fish was procured from the Natives by my Clerk …
> only the Liver and roe was dressed of which the two Mr

> Forsters and myself did but just taste. About 3 or 4
> o'Clock in the Morning we were seized with an
> extraordinary weakness in all our limbs attended with a
> numbness ... I had almost lost the sense of feeling ... We
> each of us took a Vomit and after that a sweat which gave
> great relief ... When the Natives came on board and saw
> the fish hanging up, they immediately gave us to
> understand it was by no means to be eat ...

An air of sadness enveloped the entire ship while anchored here when the ship's butcher, Simon Monk, fell down the forward hatch and died soon afterwards as a result of his injuries. It was the third loss of life among the crew since leaving England.

For an expedition commander, and as required by the Admiralty, a very important undertaking was to take possession of each new land for King and Country. Cook did so and recorded the find as follows:

> [This main island] will prove at least 40 or 50 leagues
> long, & is therefore the greatest new Tropical Island we
> have hitherto seen ... It lies NWbW & SEbE, but seems
> to be but narrow across ... It deserves to be called New-
> Caledonia, as we do not know its true Name, for what
> we got from the Natives were only Names of Districts
> on the Isle ...

Resolution sailed the 300 nautical miles of the eastern side of this archipelago, much of the time paralleling the extensive coral reef along the coast. Then, when the ship was close to its southern extremity, the men sighted a beautiful small island surrounded by long strands of golden sand beaches and azure waters, and cloaked in palms and pine trees. Cook appropriately named it the Isle of Pines. But as beautiful as this island was, there was nothing attractive about the shallows the ship encountered south of New Caledonia. At one stage, *Resolution* appeared to be in an inescapable trap: she was surrounded by reefs, where large waves were breaking into wild furrows of white water. Once again, it was only through the great skill of the captain, the dedication of the crew, and possibly an additional influence from above, that the threat was overcome.

From there, it was a 1200-nautical-mile passage south-east to Queen Charlotte Sound. When *Resolution* was near halfway, a call laden with considerable excitement came from the lookout stationed high in the rig. He had spotted a previously undiscovered island – small, with a rocky shoreline, and crowned in vivid green. As Cook's journal confirmed, a stopover was essential:

> Hoisted out two boats in which myself, some of the
> officers and gentlemen went to take a view of the Island
> and its produce ... We found the Island uninhabited ...
> the chief produce of the isle is Spruce Pines which grow
> here in abundance and to a vast size, from two to three
> feet diameter and upwards, it is of a different sort to
> those in New Caledonia and also to those in New
> Zealand and for Masts, Yards [etcetera] superior to both.
> We cut down one of the Smallest trees we could find
> and Cut a length of the upper end to make a Topgallant
> Mast or Yard ... Here then is another Isle where Masts
> for the largest Ships may be had ...

Cook claimed the island in the name of King George and identified it as Norfolk Isle, 'in honour of that noble family', in particular, as Wales would note, the Duchess of Norfolk. The anchor was then weighed and the south-easterly course resumed, this time with a highly favourable northerly wind blowing.

The perfect setting came to an abrupt end, however, when a spring storm hurtled out of the heavens, bringing with it thunder, lightning and a strong wind that 'split the jib to pieces'. The moment the lightning appeared, the men on watch hurriedly hauled the lightning chain to the masthead to provide the maximum possible protection for their ship.

It was 19 October 1774 when Cook recorded: 'being little wind, weighed and Warped into the Cove [in Queen Charlotte Sound] and there moored a cable each way, Intending to wait here to refresh the Crew, refit the ship in the best manner we could and complete her with Wood and Water.'

The captain went ashore personally and searched for evidence of *Adventure* having been there. 'As soon as I landed I looked for the bottle I had left behind in which was the Memorandum it was gone, but by whom it did not appear.' It certainly looked as if foreigners had been there, though, as trees had been felled using saws and axes. There were also signs that an astronomer had had his equipment set up on the shore: it could be no other person than William Bayley, from *Adventure*.

The captain and crew were no doubt pleased to know that their fellow expedition members had reached safe sanctuary in Ship Cove. But for now, they remained unaware of the atrocity that had befallen the ten men from *Adventure* at the hands of the Maoris.

In New Zealand waters, *Endeavour* was frequently confronted by war canoes manned by aggressive Maoris. State Library, Mitchell Library Q78/10 / a039022.

CHAPTER EIGHTEEN

One Last Look

The commander sensed an air of apprehension among the Maoris as his men set about the repair work on *Resolution* in Ship Cove, readying her for the arduous homeward voyage. While the locals had been generous in supplying the visitors with considerable quantities of fish previously, they were now noticeably reserved in their contact with the Englishmen. Cook was eager to know if they were aware of *Adventure*'s recent stay at the cove and whether they had any specific details. Eventually, some information was forthcoming.

Through a very limited form of dialogue with the Maoris, some of Cook's men learned that a ship not dissimilar to *Resolution* had apparently been wrecked in the nearby strait, and the natives there had killed and consumed anyone from her crew who had made it to shore. Cook found that the claim did not stand up to scrutiny, however, since: 'when I examined them on this ... they not only denied it but seemed wholly ignorant of the matter.' He suspected that miscommunication was to blame: 'our people had Misunderstood them ... the story referred to some of their own people and boats.'

The major requirements for the overhaul of the ship were for extensive caulking of the topsides and deck – a makeshift job, as all the proper caulking fibre had already been used; considerable maintenance of the fore and main topmasts, which had to be lowered to the deck; and the replacement of many sails. With there being no need for cannons during the planned trip across the Southern Ocean, six of them were lowered from the deck and into the hold, so that their weight would contribute to the stability of the ship.

Wales had been busy taking no end of observations from a small base set up onshore, and he soon established that the captain's positioning of Ship Cove on the chart created in 1770 was out by as much as 40 nautical miles. Ever methodical, Cook then set about taking additional sights along with Wales. When these were completed, the captain had to agree that he was 20 miles in error. As he had done elsewhere throughout the voyage, Cook spent considerable time studying the magnetic variation of the compass and the dip in the compass needle, the results from which he recorded in his journal.

The crew enjoyed whatever free time they could by going ashore and relaxing, but, as always, there were breaches of discipline. John Marra, the young man who had tried to desert as they were sailing away from Matavai Bay, had his name entered in the ship's log once more for the wrong reasons: 'Punished Jno Marra with a Dozen Lashes for Drunkenness and going off the Ship without leave.' While the log suggested that he had again been planning to desert, that was certainly the intention of another crewman less than a week later. 'Punished Jno Keplin with a dozen lashes for leaving the Boat when on duty and declaring he would go with the Indians,' wrote Joseph Gilbert, *Resolution*'s sailing master. 'He thought proper to come back of himself.'

On 10 November, when the ship was ready to put to sea, Cook called to hove up the anchor and 'drop out of the cove' to a location on the sound. From there, she awaited the arrival of a favourable wind, one that would allow her to sail to the east and back into the Southern Ocean. The wait was brief – just until daylight the following morning. A few hours later, when Cape Palliser was abeam to the north, Cook wrote: 'From this cape I shall for the third time, take my departure … we steered SBE [south by east] all sails Set, with a view of getting into the Latitude of 54 degrees or 55 degrees. My intention was to cross this vast Ocean nearly in these Parallels, and so as to pass over those parts which were left unexplored last summer.'

Soon after clearing the coast of New Zealand, the mechanically minded Wales devised and made an instrument to accurately measure the number of degrees the ship would roll in large seas, and the angle of heel when sailing 'upon a wind'. This device intrigued Cook, who noted a few days later: 'The greatest Angle he [Wales] observed her to Roll was 38 degrees ... when the Sea was not unusually high so that it cannot be reckoned to be the greatest Roll she made.'

A little more than two weeks after setting sail, on 27 November 1774, when *Resolution* was at latitude 55 degrees south, the captain made a declaration that had an air of finality to it:

> I now gave up all hopes of finding any more land in this
> Ocean and came to a Resolution to steer directly for the
> West entrance of the Straits of Magellan, with a view of
> coasting the ... South side of Terra del Fuego round
> Cape Horn to Strait La Maire. As the world has but a
> very imperfect knowledge of this Coast, I thought the
> Coasting it would be of more advantage to both
> Navigation and Geography than anything I could expect
> to find in a higher latitude ...

Over the following day, *Resolution*, as if given a free rein, recorded an impressive 184 nautical miles, an average of 7.6 knots. Second Lieutenant Clerke wrote of this achievement: 'We have had a fine steady Gale and following Sea these 24 Hours, and run the greatest distance we have ever reached in this ship [over a single day].'

It was Saturday, 17 December, when Cook announced in his journal: 'The land now before us can be no other than the west Coast of Terra del Fuego and near the West entrance of the

Straits of Magellan.' He noted with pride that, to the best of his knowledge, *Resolution* had just completed the first-ever run across the Southern Ocean from west to east in a 'high Southern Latitude'. The comment that followed this reflected his typical restraint: 'I have now done with the SOUTHERN PACIFIC OCEAN, and flatter myself that no one will think that I have left it unexplored, or that more could have been done in one voyage towards obtaining that end than has been done in this …'

After cruising along what her captain would describe as 'the most desolate and barren country I ever saw', *Resolution* sailed into a deep and sheltered sound, about 120 nautical miles west-north-west of Cape Horn, and anchored on 21 December. Here, for the first time, since leaving New Zealand, the crew were able to wood and water the ship.

Tragedy revisited the expedition the following evening, however, as noted by Lieutenant Robert Cooper: 'Found William Wedgeborough Marine missing who we imagine fell overboard last night as he was seen very much in Liquor at 12 o'clock & was drowned.' According to the captain, 'It was supposed that he had fallen overboard out of the head [the toilet at the bow] where he was last seen …' This was the second time that Wedgeborough, who was considered a troublemaker among the men, had fallen overboard.

On Christmas Eve, Cook and Pickersgill each led a shooting party to the shore, hoping to claim some fresh food for the celebratory lunch planned for the following day. It proved to be a highly successful exercise, with Cook's party bagging sixty-two geese and Pickersgill's another fourteen – thus allowing for one bird to be shared between three men – while the shags they shot were given as a bonus to the crew of the captain's pinnace. '[We] had not experienced such fare for some time,' Cook wrote of the ensuing feast. 'Roast and boiled Geese, Goose pies etc was victuals little known to us, and we had yet some Madeira Wine left, which was the only Article of our provisions that was mended by keeping; so that our friends in England did not perhaps, celebrate Christmas more cheerfully than we did ...'

Förster provided a more colourful report on proceedings:

> All went on with a great deal of mirth & Glee & we
> went to bed at 3 o'Clock in the morning at broad
> daylight. We found that we could hardly shut our Eyes
> or have the least comfortable nap, for the noise of the
> drunken Ships-Crew who were continually fighting ...
> the Captain sent all drunken noisy fellows ashore, to take
> there an airing & get sober again.

The following day, while *Resolution* remained at anchor, Cook put quill to paper to explain the obvious: 'The Festival which we celebrated at this place occasioned my giving it the name of Christmas Sound.'

The captain's journal recorded that 29 December was a significant day for the expedition: 'at half past 7 we passed this famous Cape [Horn] and entered the Southern Atlantic Ocean. It is the very same point of land which I took for the cape when I passed it in 1769 which at that time I was doubtful of.'

The next stop for *Resolution* was Staten Island, where many sea lions and fur seals were killed 'for the sake of their blubber or fat to make oil'. Their flesh was described as being 'too rank' to be eaten, but the following day Cooper wrote of 'boiled Shags and Penguins in the Coppers for the Ships Company's Dinner'.

As *Resolution* cruised along the south-west coast of Tierra del Fuego, a coast that Cook compared with that of Norway, all on deck kept their eyes peeled towards the shore, in the hope of seeing *Adventure* anchored somewhere there. Unfortunately, their alertness did not extend to anticipating the approach of a sudden and powerful squall. Before they could react, a topgallant mast, studding sail boom and studding sail had all surrendered to the force of nature. An extremely heavy burst of rain accompanied the squall, but the captain and his men were unable to benefit from the serendipity that such a development usually offered. Because of the mayhem on deck, there was no time to set the canvas canopies that were used to catch rainwater and so top up the ship's water casks.

Once clear of land and into the South Atlantic, Cook committed to continuing on with the voyage of exploration rather than sail a direct course to Cape Town. He explained his decision with reference to the theories of Alexander Dalrymple, the Scottish geographer whose place Cook had taken on the *Endeavour* expedition: '… our Course was SE with a view to discovering that extensive coast which Mr Dalrymple lies down in his Chart in which is the Gulf of St Sebastian … I had some doubts about the existence of such a coast and this appeared to me to be the best route to clear it up and to explore the Southern part of this ocean.'

They again ventured beyond 58 degrees south, and for much of the time endured very strong gales that called for the majority of sails to be either furled or heavily reefed. The Southern Ocean remained as tempestuous as ever when it came to welcoming *Resolution* back into its domain. By now, the vast majority of the crew had had enough of this level of cruelty and were anxious for Cape Town. Not the captain, though, nor Förster, judging by his own account: 'many dread to fall in with Land, for fear that this might retard our early arrival at the Cape [of Good Hope]: but as Land might have new plants, birds & fish, & the little store of brandy will of course necessitate the Captain to return in time to the Cape, I am quite impartial.'

By 14 January 1775, *Resolution* was heading towards the location 'in which Mr Dalrymple places the NE point of the Gulph of St Sebastian'. Encouraging signs came during that day when Welshman Thomas Willis, acting as lookout, called to those on deck below that what they had believed to be an ice island was actually terra firma. As the ship approached Willis Island, which it was duly named, Cook and his officers realised there was a far greater landmass beyond, lying to the east-south-east. After they had sailed along its northern coast, in fact, the new island was found to measure some 100 nautical miles in length.

This was yet another impressive addition to the world map for Cook, but not one that excited him. He had allowed himself to think that the landmass might be the southern continent he had been seeking for more than two-and-a-half years. So desolate and uninviting was this find, he immediately dismissed any thoughts of venturing ashore 'where it did not seem probable that any one would ever be benefitted by the discovery'. Elsewhere he wrote: 'I must Confess the disappointment I now met with did not affect me much, for to judge of the bulk by the sample it would not be worth the discovery. This land I called the Isle of Georgia in honour of H. Majesty.'

Clerke held a similar hope to his captain: 'I did flatter myself ... we had got hold of the Southern Continent, but alas these pleasing dreams are reduced to a small Isle.' In laying claim to the island at a location Cook called Possession Bay, the Jack was hoisted on a staff and three volleys were fired from the cannons. The island would later become known as South Georgia.

The commander's dismay was further evidenced in his admission: 'I was now tired of these high Southern Latitudes, where nothing was to be found but ice and thick fogs ...' But still he would not surrender. Soon afterwards, *Resolution* was heading south-east in search of more land, possibly even Bouvet's supposed cape, about which Cook held a new theory. Because of the recent mistake regarding the composition of Willis Island, he now thought it possible that Bouvet's discovery might similarly be disguised by a mass of snow and ice.

This continuing quest saw *Resolution* back among icebergs and growlers on 27 January. Four days later, the course that Cook was holding again brought success. This time, he discovered eight of what would later prove to be a chain of eleven primarily volcanic islands – once more barren and uninviting – stretching in a north–south arc. Cook named them Sandwich Land (later, the South Sandwich Islands). They are located more than 1300 nautical miles east-south-east of Cape Horn. Clerke said of the group: 'this Land is I believe as wretched a Country as Nature can possibly form …'

As *Resolution* sailed away, Cook penned a series of conclusions regarding this icy southern wilderness, observations that yet again reflected his remarkable instinct for maritime exploration:

> We continued to steer to the South and SE till noon at which time we were in the Latitude of 58 degrees 15' South, Longitude 21 degrees 34' West and seeing neither land nor signs of any, I concluded that what we had seen, which I named Sandwich Land was either a group of Islands or else a point of the Continent, for I firmly believe that there is a tract of land near the Pole, which is the Source of most of the ice which is spread over this vast Southern Ocean: and I think it also probable that it extends farthest to the North opposite the Southern Atlantic and Indian Oceans, because ice has always been found [by me] farther to the north in these Oceans than anywhere else which, I think, could not be if there was no land to the South … it is however true that the greatest part of this Southern Continent (supposing there is one) must lay within the Polar Circle where the Sea is so pestered with ice that the land is thereby inaccessible. The risk one runs of exploring a coast in these unknown and Icy Seas, is so very great, that I can be bold to say, that no man will ever venture farther than I have done and that the lands which may lie to the South will never be explored. Thick fogs, Snow storms, Intense Cold and every other thing that can render Navigation dangerous one has to encounter and these difficulties are greatly heightened by the inexpressible horrid aspect of the Country, a Country doomed by Nature never once to

feel the warmth of the Sun's rays, but to lie for ever
buried under everlasting snow and ice ... After such an
explanation as this the reader must not expect to find me
much farther to the South. It is however not for want of
inclination but other reasons. It would have been rashness
in me to have risked all which had been done in the
Voyage, in finding out and exploring a Coast which
when done would have answered no end whatever, or
been of the least use either to Navigation or Geography
or indeed any other Science ...

With this in mind, the captain continued sailing east for another
fourteen days in the hope that his new theories might lead him
to Jean-Baptiste Bouvet's find. But it was a mission without
success.

I had now made the circuit of the Southern Ocean in a
high Latitude and traversed it in such a manner as to
leave not the least room for the possibility of there being
a continent, unless near the Pole and out of the reach of
navigation ... Thus I flatter myself that the intention of
the Voyage has in every respect been fully Answered,
the Southern Hemisphere sufficiently explored and a
final end put to the searching after a Southern
Continent, which has at times engrossed the attention of
some of the Maritime Powers for near two Centuries
past and the Geographers of all ages ...

It was time to steer for the Cape of Good Hope, Cook adding:

My people were yet healthy and would cheerfully have
gone where ever I had thought proper to lead them, but
I dreaded the Scurvy laying hold of them at a time when
we had nothing left to remove it. Besides, it would have
been cruel in me to have continued the Fatigues and
hardships they were continually exposed to longer than

absolutely necessary, their behaviour throughout the
whole voyage merited every indulgence which was in
my power to give them.

On 18 March, *Resolution* crossed paths with a number of ships,
one of which came close enough for both she and *Resolution* to
heave to in order that communications might be exchanged. As
soon as circumstances permitted, Cook had a boat hoisted out
so that it could go to the ship.

At 1pm the boat returned from on board the Bownkerke
Polder, Captain Cornelis Bosch, a Dutch Indiaman from
Bengal; Captain Bosch very obligingly offered us sugar,
Arrack and whatever he had to spare. Our people were
told by some English Seamen on board this ship that the
Adventure arrived at the Cape of Good Hope Twelve
Months ago and that one of her boats crew had been
Murdered and eat by the People of New Zealand, so
that the story which we heard in Queen Charlottes
Sound was now no longer to be doubted, it was to this
effect: that a ship or boat had been dashed to pieces on
the Coast, but that the crew got safe onshore; on the
Natives who were present stealing some of the strangers
clothes, they were fired upon till all their ammunition
was spent, or as the Natives expressed, till they could fire
no longer, after which the Natives fell upon them,
knocked them all on the head and treated them as above
mentioned …

The 'story' Cook was referring to was the one that had come
to him from Maoris the previous October. At the time, he
wrote in his journal: 'a report has arisen … that a ship has
lately been lost, somewhere in the Strait, and all the crew
Killed by them [Maoris].'

When *Resolution* arrived in Cape Town on 21 March,
Cook received a letter written by Furneaux that acquainted him

with the loss of ten 'of his best men'. Furneaux also confirmed that he had again sailed in search of Cape Circumcision without success.

Resolution went through extensive maintenance during the five weeks she spent in Cape Town. While there, Cook received a copy of the published narrative of his first voyage, which the Admiralty had commissioned British author John Hawkesworth, LLD, to write based on Cook's notes. In no time, the captain was fuming: he was horrified by the high level of creative licence taken by Hawkesworth. At times Cook could not even place himself in the context of the copy that was supposedly referring to his endeavours.

Resolution set sail from Cape Town on 27 April, and following a stop in St Helena, she crossed the Equator and re-entered the northern hemisphere on 11 June, driven across the 'line' by a fresh east-south-easterly gale. However, even with the thought of home beckoning so enticingly, Cook decided that he should complete just one more undertaking in the interests of navigation. After sailing *Resolution* almost the entire width of the Atlantic, to just off the coast of Brazil, he was able to establish more positively the longitude of the island of Fernando de Noronha. The last stop was Fayal, an island in the Azores, from which they departed on 19 July.

Ten days later, Förster wrote of a most welcoming scene. *Resolution* had passed Eddystone Lighthouse, where all on board observed 'the first part of Englands happy Shores. The numberless Ships & finely cultivated country we see make our hearts Glad, being a Sight from which we were weaned 3 tedious long years.'

On the morning of 30 July 1775, *Resolution* was anchored in the Solent. The final note the captain would later write in his journal – a chronicle that told the remarkable story of a new world – was simple. It read in part: 'anchored at Spit-head. Having been absent from England Three Years and Eighteen Days, in which time I lost but four men and only one of them by sickness.'

CHAPTER NINETEEN

Land Fever

The 46-year-old Cook had packed his trunk and was ready to be rowed to shore in Portsmouth as soon as was practicable after the ship was anchored. The release of the best bower from the cathead signalled both the completion of the commander's second circumnavigation and the moment when his name again went into the annals of maritime history, this time in even bolder terms. He had navigated his ship across an enormous expanse of ocean in search of the much-hypothesised *Terra Australis Incognita*, and in doing so, had become the first explorer to circle the world in both directions. This recent voyage was remarkable. Over a period of three years, *Resolution* had sailed mostly through uncharted and challenging waters, from the tropics to inside the Antarctic Circle, recording a total distance of 70,000 nautical miles – equivalent to three times around the globe at the Equator.

By late afternoon that same day, Cook had stepped ashore from the pinnace and clambered up the rust-coloured stone steps to street level. There, he was immediately surrounded by a claustrophobic milieu of brick buildings, waterfront bars and people bustling about. It is quite possible that no-one recognised the great mariner and explorer: navy men coming and going were a common enough sight on Portsmouth's waterfront, after all. Not that this lack of public awareness perturbed the

Yorkshireman. His priority was to organise transport to London, where he would report to their Lordships of the Admiralty at Whitehall, before moving on to Mile End and a longed-for reunion with his wife and family.

His visit to the Admiralty was recorded by Dr Solander in a letter to Joseph Banks on 1 August. The Swedish naturalist wrote that Cook was 'in the board-room, giving an account of himself & Co. He looks as well as ever …'

News of his safe return to England was immediately reported in newspapers such as the *St James's Chronicle*. Two days later, a story in the *London Chronicle* read: 'On Sunday arrived at Spithead after an agreeable voyage around the world, Captain Cook in the storeship *Resolution*. It is said they have discovered many islands in the South Seas that never were heard of before; the inhabitants of which appear to have plenty of everything.'

The preoccupation of the Royal Navy and the nation as a whole with Britain's war with the American colonies – which had started in earnest three months before *Resolution*'s return – resulted in the voyage failing to achieve the same level of public acclaim as *Endeavour*'s homecoming of 1771. Nevertheless, on 9 August, Cook responded to a royal request by attending Buckingham House, where he briefed His Majesty King George III on the highlights of the expedition, presenting him with charts, maps and drawings. The King, an ardent supporter of this voyage of discovery, presented Cook with his commission as post-captain aboard the thirteen-year-old 74-gun HMS *Kent*. A post-captain was a naval officer who held a commission, but not the rank, as a captain, which still applied in the case of Lieutenant James Cook.

This posting lasted a matter of hours, however. The next day, much to Cook's surprise, the Admiralty appointed him to a position of fourth captain at the Royal Hospital at Greenwich, a facility for treating sick and injured RN personnel. In effect, it was a position recognising 'honourable service'. He was to receive £200 per annum, a residence, a daily allowance of 1 shilling and two-pence, and free 'fire and light'. But, while this was a most satisfactory arrangement financially, the thought of being retired from the sea and pensioned off, as honourable as it might appear, did not sit comfortably with the newly created captain. He could not envisage himself being deskbound for the rest of his naval career. So he wrote to his friend Stephens, the Secretary of the Admiralty, asking that their Lordships allow him to quit that post 'when either the call of my country for more active service or that my endeavours in any shape can be essential to the public'. They agreed to the request.

Cook's concerns about his unexpected retirement to shore duties were evident in a letter he wrote to John Walker a few days later:

> Dear Sir – As I have not now time to draw up an account of such occurrences of the voyage as I wish to communicate to you, I can only thank you for your obliging letter and kind enquiries after me in my absence. I must however tell you that the Resolution was found to answer, on all occasions, even beyond my expectations, and is so little injured by the voyage that she will soon be sent out again. But I shall not command her. My fate drives me from one extreme to another; a few months ago the whole southern hemisphere was hardly big enough for me, and now I am going to be confined within the limits of Greenwich Hospital, which are far too small for an active mind like mine. I must, however, confess it is a fine retreat and a pretty income, but whether I can bring myself to like ease and retirement, time will show. Mrs Cook joins with me in best respects to you and all your family; and believe me to be, with great esteem, Dear Sir, your most affectionate friend and humble servant – James Cook

While Cook was adjusting to an apparent life of semi-retirement, hoping he might be called on for active service in

North America, he could only have looked on with increasing frustration at what was planned for others who had been part of his recent expedition. Causing him considerable angst, no doubt, was the news that his former lieutenant, Charles Clerke, was to be appointed master and commander of *Resolution* for her return voyage to the Pacific. Tobias Furneaux was to command another ship, for the purpose of transporting home an Otaheite islander named Omai, who had become a figure of fascination within London society since arriving in England aboard *Adventure* in July 1774. Following the repatriation mission, Furneaux was then to further explore the South Seas. This plan did not eventuate, however, as Furneaux was instead assigned to captain HMS *Syren* and sent to join the war in the colonies. He died four years later, aged forty-six.

In addition, there was a disagreement brewing between Cook and Johann Förster, who was hoping to publish the official journal relating to the voyage. Eventually, Lord Sandwich intervened: Cook would write his version based on 'nautical observations', and Förster from the perspective of a naturalist, with associated 'philosophical remarks'. This decision resulted in Förster writing a snide response to Sandwich, who in turn blasted him for his attitude:

> You mention a satisfaction that you have in being eased
> from the trouble of methodizing & clearing Captain
> Cook's journal from its inaccuracies & vulgar
> expressions. I do not pretend to be a Critic; but I must
> say that I have met with very few vulgarisms or
> inaccuracies in that journal; but I have seen his journal
> misquoted, & vulgarisms introduced that were not in the
> Original.

Cook continued to see his world sail by – literally. Each day, as he looked through the window of his office at the hospital, he watched the passage of Royal Navy ships along the Thames, all the while wishing that he was captain of one of them. There was no denying it: he could not remove the need to be at sea from his heart now, any more than he'd been able to resist its calling as a teenager, when working in Mr Sanderson's establishment in Staithes. At a time when he considered himself to be in his prime, Cook had become a casual observer of all things Royal Navy. Deptford dockyard, where *Endeavour* and *Resolution* had been prepared for their voyages, was only half a mile upstream, yet it was no longer part of his world.

At least he had the satisfaction of being consulted by the Navy Board regarding the choice of a suitable support vessel for *Resolution*'s next voyage into the South Seas. Cook suggested, once again, that they look no further than a Whitby collier. In early January 1776, the Navy Board duly purchased the eighteen-month-old 298-ton *Diligence*, for £1865. She was soon being refitted as a consort and re-rigged as a brig – with three masts instead of two. She was named HMS *Discovery* and destined to have a complement of seventy men, compared with *Resolution*'s 112.

Cook was never a man to propel himself into prominence: he let his achievements speak for themselves. At the same time, he was rarely one who let an opportunity pass him by. One such circumstance came early in the new year when he was invited to a lunch hosted by Lord Sandwich and attended by Sir Hugh Palliser and Philip Stephens. The captain was very much among friends, and it was equally agreeable to him that the purpose of this gathering was to discuss his thoughts on the leadership of the upcoming expedition.

Charles Clerke was now out of the running, having been arrested and imprisoned as a result of severe debts accrued by his seafaring brother, Sir John Clerke. The latter had sailed to the East Indies in 1772 owing the huge amount of £4000 – a figure that Charles, as his brother's guarantor, could not come close to repaying.

What Sandwich, Palliser and Stephens did not realise was just how much Cook wanted to escape the drudgery of his administrative duties at the Royal Hospital – which amounted to very little – and return to the adventure and challenges of the high seas. Similarly, Cook would come to understand why he had been retired: it was thought that he had done enough, the assumption being that he would no longer want to undertake such dangerous enterprise. There is no date given for this lunch, but it quite possibly took place in late January 1776. Cook's first biographer, Andrew Kippis, described the gathering in his book *The Life of Captain James Cook*, which was first published in 1788. He wrote:

> That Captain Cook was of all men the best qualified for carrying it into execution was a matter that could not be called in question. But however ardently it might be wished that he would take upon himself the command of the service, no one (not even his friend and patron, Lord Sandwich himself) presumed to solicit him upon the subject. The benefits he had already conferred on science and navigation, and the labours and dangers he had gone through, were so many and great, that it was not deemed reasonable to ask him to engage in fresh perils.

It was soon understood that Cook would have no part of such a hypothesis. Here, suddenly, was his opportunity to escape his recent bout of 'land fever'.

The expedition was outlined to him in considerable detail: following a return to the South Seas, it involved a search for the Northwest Passage, the much-speculated-upon waters across the top of North America that might connect the Atlantic with the Pacific. As the information flowed forth, so Cook became increasingly convinced that he was the man for the task. Kippis continued: 'Captain Cook was so fired with the contemplation and representation of the object that he started up, and declared that he himself would undertake the direction of the enterprise. It is easy to suppose with what pleasure the noble lord and the other gentlemen received a proposal which was so agreeable to their secret wishes …' They had found their man.

Lord Sandwich informed the King almost immediately of Cook's decision, and within days it was common knowledge. At the end of January, the *General Evening Post* reported:

> Captain Cook in the new voyage which he is going to make is to take Omai to Otaheite, and from thence to proceed upon the Discovery of the North-West Passage to the northward of California. Parliament has just offered a reward, £20,000 to those who approach within one degree of the Pole; but there are to be no Botanists, Designers etc to accompany them.

Having negotiated with the Admiralty the parameters of his appointment, Cook then had his goose-feather quill in hand on 14 February to pen a note to John Walker in Whitby. The letter read in part:

> I should have Answered your last favour sooner, but waited to know whether I should go to Greenwich Hospital, or the South Sea. The latter is now fixed upon; I expect to be ready to sail about the latter end of April with my old ship the Resolution and the Discovery, the ship lately purchased of Mr Herbert. I know not what your opinion may be on this step I have taken. It is certain I have quitted an easy retirement, for an Active, and perhaps Dangerous Voyage. My present disposition is more favourable to the latter than the former, and I embark on as fair a prospect as I can wish. If I am fortunate enough to get safe home, there is no doubt but it will be greatly to my advantage.

The question begged to be asked: what was it that caused Cook – the man who was undeniably the world's greatest maritime explorer – to again leave his family and challenge the unknown, for a similarly unknown amount of time?

This mission, as directed by the Admiralty, was designed to solve the mystery surrounding the existence of the Northwest Passage. Others had gone before him looking for it, the most recent being John Byron in 1764. On arriving in the Pacific via the Straits of Magellan, however, the former *Dolphin* commander had decided to ignore his orders from the Admiralty and searched instead for undiscovered islands in the tropical regions of the South Pacific, rather than turning directly north. Now it was Cook's chance to add fine detail to the current knowledge of the world's oceans. Should he be successful in discovering the passage, he would reveal a new trading route between the two great oceans; one that provided a far more direct passage to the wealth of the East Indies for much of the year, by eliminating the need to sail via the wretched waters of Cape Horn, or the long route around the Cape of Good Hope. Success would also see the captain and crew of *Resolution* and *Discovery* share in the £20,000 reward promised by the government – a princely sum, although a pittance compared to the financial benefit that such a route offered to British trade.

Around this time, Clerke was one of many Royal Navy officers released from prison through an Act of Parliament, since there was now an urgent need for these experienced sailors in North America. The Admiralty had no hesitation in confirming him as captain of *Discovery*. Even so, Clerke's unbridled freedom was still to be confirmed: he would need to be back in London prior to the two ships making their final departure from Plymouth before he could be sure of sailing as scheduled.

On 16 May, while the refitting of both vessels continued at Deptford, Cook was elected a Fellow of the Royal Society. Such was the support for his admission that twenty-five members proposed him (instead of the usual three or so), the first two on the nomination document being Joseph Banks and Daniel Solander. Obviously, Cook and Banks had put their earlier differences behind them. London's famed botanist was not only highly supportive of Cook's latest expedition, but also actively involved in preparations for what was expected to be a three-year undertaking. Cook was absent for this portion of the ships' refits, however, and Banks lacked the requisite knowledge when it came to checking on the standard of workmanship at the navy dock. This had always been Cook's domain but now, with virtually no direct management, the workers took shortcuts, especially when it came to caulking the topsides and decks. It would not be until *Resolution* was under a heavy press of sail and rolling down large Atlantic swells that the problems became apparent: she was a horribly leaky ship. Water poured below, through the topsides and decks, as she lumbered from gunwale to gunwale. It was guaranteed to be a miserable existence for everyone.

The main reasons for the commander's absence from the dock was that he was busy rewriting and editing his journal from the earlier voyage, and sitting for a portrait by noted artist Nathaniel Dance. The painting, which depicts a pensive Cook in full uniform, has become the most reproduced of all that were done of the great mariner. It is interesting to note that this portrait does not show Cook with a gloved right hand, as is the case with the similarly famous John Webber portrait on display at the National Portrait Gallery in Canberra. The captain often wore a glove on that hand to conceal the wounds he had suffered in Newfoundland in August 1764, when the powder horn he was holding exploded. The Admiralty appointed Webber 'Draughtsman and Landskip Painter' for *Resolution*'s second voyage.

The captain was also enjoying his home life, with his and Elizabeth's brood having increased by one when a son, Hugh, was born nine months after his return to England. The two eldest boys, James and Nathaniel, were then aged twelve and eleven respectively. James had already entered the Royal Navy Academy at Portsmouth, and Nathaniel was about to join the navy as well. However, the family still had to cope with the sad fact that three siblings – Elizabeth, Joseph and George – had all died in infancy. In a letter that Cook sent to Lord

Sandwich at this time, he wrote: '[I] thank your Lordship for the ... Very liberal allowance made to Mrs Cook during my absence. This, by enabling my family to live at ease and removing from them every fear of indigence, has set my heart at rest and filled it with gratitude to my Noble benefactor.'

There was a plethora of features to this new expedition that Cook had to take into consideration, none more critical than the fact that it would again see them experience two climatic extremes – the steamy heat of the tropics through to the biting cold of the polar zone, with its ice, snow and howling winds. In normal circumstances, the men of the lower deck were expected to supply most, if not all, of their clothing, but this time the captain knew he had to help out. The voyage would take *Resolution* and *Discovery* inside the Arctic Circle, little different from going within the Antarctic Circle between three and five years earlier. Cook realised he had to 'weather-proof' his men as much as possible, so he placed a special clothing order with the Navy Board. This included 100 kersey (coarse wool) jackets, 60 kersey waistcoats, 40 pairs of kersey breeches, 120 linsey (woven coarse twill) waistcoats, 140 linsey drawers, 440 checked shirts, 100 pairs of checked drawers, 400 frockcoats, 700 pairs of trousers, 500 pairs of stockings, 80 worsted caps, 340 Dutch caps and 800 pairs of shoes.

The original plan was for *Resolution* to have departed from England and be heading towards the Cape of Good Hope by early April, but tardiness on the part of the dockyard workers at Deptford had seen that month come and go, with the ship still being far from ready. The crew for the mission was close to being finalised. It had been structured around Cook's affirmation that having a solid depth of seafaring experience among his senior men was crucial to the expedition's success. Here, he was pleased to be able to draw on a number of sailors who had been with him on either the previous circumnavigation or both – all of whom had no hesitation in going with the explorer again. Six men on this new voyage had been with him for both circumnavigations, and of the latest complement, twelve were returning from *Resolution*'s first voyage. The crew was a cosmopolitan combination of seafarers and supernumeraries: the vast majority were English, but the mix also included men from Ireland, Wales, Scotland, America and Germany. One name missing was Richard Pickersgill, whom Cook had enthusiastically supported in his two voyages. This time the Admiralty, for some unknown reason, sent him elsewhere.

As his three lieutenants, Cook had John Gore, James King and John Williamson. But it was his choice of sailing master that history would recognise as being most significant – a 21-year-old by the name of William Bligh, who was already making a bold impression on his superiors. Bligh came aboard on the strong recommendation of Lord Sandwich.

It was not until 30 May that *Resolution* was finally ready to depart from Deptford. On that day she worked the tide down the Thames to Long Reach where, as the commander noted, they 'took on board our artillery, Powder Shot and other Ordnance stores'. A journal entry a few days later told of another important cargo: 'Took on board a Bull, 2 Cows with their Calves & some sheep to carry to Otaheite with a quantity of Hay and Corn for their subsistence. These Cattle were put on board at His Majesty's Command and expense with a view of stocking Otaheite and the Neighbouring Islands with these useful animals ...' The very important instruments for the voyage also arrived: 'Received on board several Astronomical & Nautical Instruments which the Board of Longitude intrusted to me and Mr King my second Lieutenant ... They also put on board the same Watch Machine that was out with me last voyage ...'

Resolution was then moved to the anchorage at The Nore, at the entrance to the Thames, while Cook returned to London to farewell his family, and, no doubt, make a final visit to the Admiralty. His journal entry for 24 June read: 'At 6 o'clock in the Morning I set out from London in company with Omai, we got to Chatham between 10 & 11 and after dining with Commissioner Proby he very obligingly ordered his yacht to convey us to Sheerness where my boat was waiting to carry us on board ...'

Suitable weather conditions prevailed on 25 June, so *Resolution*'s anchor was weighed soon after midday and the sails set. After a brief stop off the coast at Deal, where two special small boats had been built for the ship, the voyage continued on to Devon. On 30 June, Cook wrote: 'At 3 PM Anchored in Plymouth Sound where the *Discovery* had arrived three days before.'

After a wait of almost two weeks, *Resolution* put to sea on 12 July 1776. It was a grey, cool summer morning when the call came from young Bligh to release the clew lines and buntlines so that the sails could fall freely from the solid timber yards and be set to suit the light breeze. At the same time, the men at the windlass weighed anchor, raising the bower to the point where it was supported at the cathead, then lashed securely into place against the topsides forward. With that done, the swishing sound of the bow wave confirmed for all that another history-making odyssey was underway for Captain James Cook. While the ship slowly gained speed, those on deck watched the coast of England fade into the mist. Despite the inevitable dangers they would face, who among them could have contemplated that this was to be the last time that their captain would see home shores?

The departure date was two months later than planned, but as *Resolution* sailed away, her consort was still riding at anchor. There *Discovery* would remain until Captain Clerke had successfully negotiated his freedom in London to be able to undertake the voyage. This came on 29 July, and he immediately headed to Plymouth to board his ship and put to sea as quickly as possible.

Cook was pleased to realise the value that came with having Bligh as his sailing master. As well as being a very capable presence on deck, the young Cornishman's talents were such that he would provide considerable assistance to the captain when it came to navigation, cartography and the surveying of some of their destinations. He wrote of Bligh: 'under my direction [he] could be easily employed in constructing charts, in taking views of the coasts and headlands near which we would pass, and in drawing plans of the bays and harbours in which we should anchor.' This, Cook said, was 'wholly requisite if we should render our discoveries profitable for future navigators'.

After making a slow exit from the Channel, *Resolution* soon harnessed a weather system that brought strong northerlies, and from that moment she began a charge to the south towards her first stop, the island of Tenerife. However, while the winds provided ideal sailing conditions, the large seas that accompanied this front meant that she was already taking an exceptionally large volume of water below through the poorly caulked decks and topsides, all the way from the waterline to the deck.

At Tenerife, when Cook manoeuvred *Resolution* into a position where she could be safely anchored, he noticed that all ships in the anchorage 'had four anchors out … and their Cables buoyed up with Casks'. This was done in order to suspend their thick hemp bower cables off the rocky ocean floor, so that they would not chafe and come apart. With *Resolution*'s anchors already set, Cook decided not to follow suit, but when they were raised, he was concerned to note the level of abrasion on the cables.

Continuing south from Tenerife, *Resolution* sailed towards the Cape Verde Islands, 800 nautical miles away. At this stage, the circumnavigation was only a month old, but it came horribly close to meeting an abrupt end in the middle of one pitch-dark night. The ship's surgeon, William Anderson, who happened to be on deck at the time, explained how the incident started when he saw waves breaking on a reef at a frighteningly close distance to leeward. Initially, he thought his eyes might be deceiving him, so he didn't raise the alarm.

> Fortunately, at this instant the Captain came over to the same place and just as I was going to mention my suspicions he observed something of the same sort and

ordered them to starboard the helm. In less than a minute
the cry of hard-a-starboard became general & we could
now see a range of breakers at a very small distance: upon
which we were steering a direct course. Orders were
given to brace the yards sharp up; but I who could only
be an idle spectator in this scene of confusion went abaft
and had a clear prospect of our impending danger. For
the space of ten minutes I thought it utterly impossible
we should avoid striking on the rocks: but the
manoeuvre with the sails being pretty quick I had the
pleasure to see the ship lie parallel to them.

It was a remarkably narrow escape. Not for the first time,
disaster had been averted only through the prompt response by
the captain, and the ability of the men on watch to appreciate
the magnitude of the danger and respond accordingly, by
manning the braces and sheets.

CHAPTER TWENTY

Islands, Ice and the Captain's Ire

As *Resolution* closed on the Equator, the water torture for those men below worsened with the caulking continuing to fail. Cook wrote in his journal:

> We had ... the Mortification to find the Ship exceeding leaky in all her upper works, the hot and dry weather we had just passed through had opened up her Seams, which had been badly Caulked at first, so wide that they admitted the rain Water through as it fell and there was hardly a Man that could lie dry in his bed; the officers in the gun room were all driven out of their cabins by the Water that came through the sides.

On 18 October, *Resolution* was anchored in Cape Town's Table Bay after a passage of more than fifty days from Plymouth. Three weeks later, during a period when Cook had his crew busy replacing the ship's caulking and carrying out general maintenance, he was pleased to see *Discovery* come into view on the distant horizon, then enter port.

The constant thump of caulking hammers was heard day after day aboard *Resolution* as a team of men worked relentlessly in the hope of making the ship watertight. Some plugged the gaps in the deck planks while others were suspended on ropes over the bulwarks so they could tend the topsides. When the job was complete, Cook sent his men across to *Discovery* to assist with the same task there.

By the end of November, it was time to sail. The animals that had been put ashore to graze were back aboard, and Cook remarked that under his orders the men had taken on a substantial supply of provisions, '[enough] for two years and upwards and every other necessary thing we could think of for such a Voyage, neither knowing when nor where we should come to a place where we could supply ourselves so well'. During these preparations, Cook also gave Clerke instructions regarding rendezvousing in New Zealand, should the two ships become separated while sailing through the Southern Ocean.

Everyone and everything was aboard by the morning of 30 November, and that afternoon, when a slight breeze developed out of the south-east, the sails were set and anchors weighed. Before long, *Resolution* and her support ship were clear of the confines of the bay and sailing close-hauled towards the Cape of Good Hope, 30 nautical miles south of Cape Town, the promontory that defines the boundary between the Atlantic and Indian oceans. From there it was another 80 nautical miles to the southernmost tip of the African continent, Cape Agulhas, the point from which Cook intended to sail to the south-east in the hope of finding the Kerguelen Islands.

Discovered by Yves-Joseph de Kerguelen de Trémarec in 1772, when the French explorer was conducting his own search for the great southern continent, this cluster of more than 300 small islets and one large island was believed to be around 2400 nautical miles from Cape Agulhas, at about 49 degrees south latitude. Apart from doing whatever survey work was possible in the time available, Cook wanted to place their position on the world map with greater accuracy. To find the islands, he sailed to a point where both ships could run directly downwind towards their position as shown on the chart. Then, when in close proximity to that point, a zigzag approach was adopted, with *Resolution* and *Discovery* sailing from horizon to horizon so that the chance of missing each other was minimised. It was a successful procedure; the target appeared through the fog at six o'clock in the morning on 24 December. Cook noted:

> ... as we were steering to the Eastward, the fog clearing away a little, we saw land, bearing South South East, which upon nearer approach we found to be an island of considerable height ... Soon after, we saw another of the same magnitude, one league to the Eastward; and between them, in the direction of South East, some smaller ones ... A third high island was seen ... a high round rock, which was named Bligh's Cap. Perhaps it is the same that Monsieur de Kerguelen called the Isle of Rendezvous; but I know nothing that can rendezvous at it, but fowls of the air; for it is certainly inaccessible to every other animal.

Come Christmas Day, both *Resolution* and *Discovery* were anchored in a well-protected inlet on the eastern side of the main island's northern tip. The boats were hoisted out and the captain taken to the shore, which he soon found to be 'in a manner covered with Penguins and other birds and Seals, but these were not numerous, but so fearless that we killed as ma[n] y as we chose for the sake of their fat or blubber to make Oil for our lamps and other uses'.

Two days later, the men were allowed a day of rest to belatedly celebrate Christmas, which led to some going ashore. One crewman returned to the ship with a sealed bottle he had found that had obviously been placed purposely on the shore. It contained a note written in Latin, recording the visit there of French expeditions in 1772 and 1774. Cook decided to leave his own message on the reverse side of the parchment, before inserting it in the bottle along with a silver twopenny coin. He then went ashore, placed the bottle atop a stone cairn built by his men, called for the Union flag to be raised, and named the inlet Christmas Harbour. Over the next few days, he had this inlet surveyed by Bligh while other exploration activities were conducted. Following these activities, and taking into consideration the inhospitable, remote and desolate nature of this main island, he chose to name it Island of Desolation.

On New Year's Eve, Cook decided to continue their voyage to the east. By now, the expedition was lagging well behind its original schedule, so the captain insisted that the maximum amount of sail be carried at all times in the hope that some lost days could be recovered. This proved to be a costly call, as he recorded in his journal almost three weeks later: '[Nothing] worthy of note till 4 oclock in the Morning of the 19th when in a sudden squall of wind the Fore Topmast went by the board and carried the Main Topgallant mast with it ...'

The squall had arrived with such suddenness and violence that it caught the crew unawares. There was not even time to ease the sheets or furl the sails to take the enormous pressure off the rig. Instead, they could only watch in horror as the two mast sections literally exploded overhead. In a flash, crewmen were confronted by a scene of utter destruction: spars, sails and rigging were thrashing through the air as the ship rolled heavily in the large Southern Ocean swells, and the wind continued to howl.

To contain the problem, they needed to lower everything to the deck – an action that called for masterly work from all hands. But still, it was an entire day before the vessel was able to get underway again with a new fore topmast in place. Unfortunately, the main topgallant could not be replaced, as there was no spare on board and not enough timber for the carpenters to make one.

During the twenty-four hours it took to jury-rig *Resolution*, the captain had the time to reconsider his immediate plans for the voyage, mainly because the ship would now be sailing at a slower rate of knots due to a reduced sail area. Also, many of the animals on board were dying because of the sub-Antarctic cold and a lack of fresh fodder. Then there was a need for wood for the ship's fireplaces. Only one solution could be adopted: to set a course for Van Diemen's Land.

It was 3 am on 24 January 1777 when the southern coast was sighted, and two days later, *Resolution* and *Discovery* were lying lazily at anchor in Adventure Bay, the haven that Tobias Furneaux had discovered and named during the previous voyage. Parties from both ships were now sent ashore to collect wood, water and feed, accompanied by marines for purposes of protection. However, it turned out that the marines from *Discovery* took stolen liquor with them and proceeded to stage what was possibly Australia's first-ever beach party. *Discovery*'s master, Thomas Edgar, noted that the revellers 'made themselves so Beastly Drunk that they were put motionless in the Boat, and when brought on board were obliged to be hoisted into the Ship'.

There was a surprisingly cordial level of contact with the natives during this stop – until the visitors put on a display of the power and accuracy of their weaponry. The sound of musket-fire and the sight of a ball hitting a distant target frightened the locals so much that they ran as fast as they could, disappearing into the forest.

The stay here was brief, but Cook still ensured that Bligh and others surveyed the surrounds as much as time would allow. By 30 January the boats were back aboard and secured, and everything was ready for the 2000-nautical-mile passage across the wilderness of what is now known as the Tasman Sea, to Queen Charlotte Sound in New Zealand. Before departing, Cook diarised his theory on Van Diemen's Land and its likely relationship to New Holland: 'I hardly need say it is the Southern point of New Holland, which if not a Continent, is one of the largest islands in the World …' It would be another twenty-one years before Matthew Flinders and George Bass circumnavigated Van Diemen's Land aboard HMS *Norfolk*, thus proving that it was an island.

Even with the assistance of what the commander described as a 'perfect storm' on the first day at sea, the two ships averaged only 4 knots for the eleven-day crossing to New Zealand. The only drama during the passage came aboard *Discovery* on the night of 6 February, when a marine fell overboard and was not recovered.

Resolution and *Discovery* anchored in Ship Cove on the morning of 12 February, and a few hours later several canoes laden with Maoris made a tentative approach to the visitors. 'It appeared to me that they were apprehensive we were come to revenge the death of Captain Furneaux's people,' wrote Cook, adding that while he wanted to extend friendship towards them, he also needed for them to know he was 'no longer a stranger to that unhappy affair'. Friendship or not, the captain still treated every Maori with extreme caution, and each time he sent his men to shore by boat to collect wood and water, every one of them was armed, each team supported by a complement of ten marines.

The two ships sheltered in the cove for fourteen days. During that time, worn rigging and any suspect spars were replaced, a move designed to minimise the risk of equipment failure during what was sure to be a torrid test while sailing towards the region of the Northwest Passage. When the time came to put to sea, Cook gave some of his livestock to the natives and set two pairs of rabbits free in the bushland.

The commander's initial plan was to reach Otaheite as soon as possible, benefiting from the anticipated fresh south-easterly trade wind for much of the time. He also hoped he might discover some unknown islands en route. Frustratingly though, his strategy was soon ruined by external forces: 'we were persecuted with a Wind in our teeth which every way we directed our course, and the farther Mortification to find here those very winds we had reason to expect ... farther South.' On the positive side, islands were discovered in the region of the Cook Islands, but he had to accept that his intention to explore the Northwest Passage as scheduled was no longer viable, with 'the summer of the northern Hemisphere already too far advanced for me to do anything there this year'. He would therefore 'persecute the Discoveries in the higher northern latitudes the ensuing summer'.

This decision was also influenced by the dire need, once again, for fodder for the cattle. Cook opted to change course, arcing back towards the Friendly Islands, as he had christened the Tongan archipelago, a destination that held happy memories for him from the visit there in 1773. There was an additional problem emerging, with water running low on board, so he ordered for the still to be set up in the galley – an apparatus that could supply up to 16 gallons of fresh water in ten hours. Supplies were further replenished on 10 April, when thunder squalls resulted in 5 puncheons of water, equivalent to 350 gallons, being collected via a catchment canopy set above the deck.

After their arrival at the Friendly Islands, Cook went ashore and revelled in the hospitality shown by the islanders, so much so that the ships spent an entire month at Tongatapu, the main island in the group. It was here that senior members of *Resolution*'s crew became concerned about an apparent change in their captain's persona: despite the affability of their surroundings, the officer recognised for his consideration towards his men was at times becoming agitated and angry. When those who had stolen some of the ship's food refused to identify themselves, Cook halved the meat ration for all on board in the hope that the culprits would be flushed out. Instead, the majority of men reacted by refusing to take any meat. It was a showdown, and Cook's temper erupted. He declared their actions to be in breach of the Articles of War. He dealt out floggings where the cat-o'-nine-tails was used to an unprecedented degree: men received twice or three times the number of lashes that would otherwise have been expected.

This alarming development in his character was evident again when natives who were aboard *Resolution* tried to steal everything possible. Cook's frustration with the thieving quickly turned to desperation, then near brutality when the guilty were presented to him. He called for one islander to be dealt an unheard-of sixty lashes; at other times he called for levels of punishment that were similarly almost beyond belief.

There was consternation among his senior officers, and although none dared question his behaviour, it was apparent in a note written by Midshipman George Gilbert:

> This [thieving], which is very prevalent here, Captain Cook punished in a manner rather unbecoming of a European, viz by cutting off their ears, firing at them with small shot, or ball, as they were swimming or paddling to the shore; and suffering the people as he rowed after them to beat them with the oars, and stick the boat hook into them ...

Inevitably, questions were raised regarding the captain's sanity. Was the heat of the tropics getting to him? Had he contracted some form of disease?

There was certainly evidence of mental instability. One moment he was dealing out the most severe form of punishment; the next, he was entertaining the natives with a concert by the ship's marine band – an act that confounded the local population. Even Bligh was confused. He described the captain's inconsistent behaviour as 'a most ludicrous performance'. Further cause for concern resulted from Cook's failure to undertake any exploration during this time, even though the natives had told him that a cluster of islands unknown to Europeans, and which they referred to as 'Fidgee', was a three-day sail to the north-west of the Tongan group. Cook had narrowly missed them on his last voyage in July 1774. Gilbert observed: 'it is somewhat surprising that Captain Cook did not go in search of it according to His usual practice. His reasons for not doing it I can't account for; as we certainly had time while we were lying at Tongatapu.' Ironically, Bligh would discover many of these islands a decade later, following the infamous mutiny he experienced. Initially they were named Bligh's Islands, and later Fiji.

Resolution and *Discovery* cruised through the Tongan group of islands for around ten weeks. Tellingly, perhaps, the captain's notes in his journal contradicted his actions when it came to punishing the pilfering islanders: 'Thus we took leave of these Friendly Islands and their Inhabitants after a stay of between two and three Months, during which time we lived together in the most cordial friendship, some accidental differences it is true now and then happened owing to their great propensity to thieving, but too often encouraged by the negligence of our own people ...'

In more recent times, Sir James Watt, medical director-general of the Royal Navy during the 1970s, stated that the symptoms shown by Cook – including fatigue, failing health, loss of interest, and depression – indicated that he was suffering from a parasitic infection of the lower intestine.

It was a 23-day passage to Otaheite from the time the two ships departed Tongatapu. The course was in the form of a loop so that the maximum benefit possible could be harnessed from the south-east trade wind – near perfect sailing conditions, where a full spread of sail was carried more often than not.

They anchored in Matavai Bay on 12 August, and while there was considerable celebration relating to Cook's return, this was also the homecoming of Omai after his sojourn to the land of the Englishmen. Yet, to everyone's amazement, the islanders gave him a most subdued reception. Not even his brother was excited ... until Omai produced some highly treasured red feathers as gifts.

Cook again thrived on the adulation he received, this time from a throng of islanders in canoes and others gathered on the black sand beach to welcome him. It was a very different situation for the crew: the irrational outbursts from their captain continued, becoming more frequent. A powerful example came when two of the ship's goats, which had been tethered on the beach, were stolen. Cook's immediate reaction was to order his men to torch canoes and native huts in the village. The crew feared that any response on their part to his actions might only exacerbate the situation, and cause him to become even more explosive.

To the surprise of many, the stay in Tahiti also led to an onshore pistol duel between *Resolution*'s third lieutenant, John Williamson, and the lieutenant of the marines, Molesworth Phillips. A seaman named Griffin told of the affair: 'when, after one or two rounds, neither being wounded, the Seconds interfered & ended the affair. Many persons would have rejoiced if Mr Williamson our third Lieutenant had fell, as he was a very bad man & a great Tyrant.'

During the six-week hiatus in Matavai Bay, Cook renewed many old acquaintances and gathered what provisions were available. Simultaneously, he presented the king with the cattle, horses and poultry (including peacocks and turkeys) that he had brought with him from England and Cape Town.

By 22 September, the maintenance schedule for *Resolution* – including re-caulking, replacing rigging, and bending on new sails – was complete, and a week later crewmen and equipment were aboard and ready to sail. At this stage, the men of the lower deck were still uncertain as to where they would be heading next. When Cook finally addressed them on the subject, Anderson, the surgeon, recorded the moment: 'The Captain intimated his intention to the ship's company of searching for a passage from the south into the Atlantic Sea by navigating to the northward of America, and if that should fail to attempt the same by sailing round the northern parts of Asia and Europe.'

This declaration had a direct impact on all of the men. During the stay in Otaheite, it became evident that, having lost a season due to the late departure from England, and then having to contend with light winds in the South Pacific, it was highly likely that both ships would run out of grog during the next stage of the expedition. However, as Cook noted in his journal, there was a solution of sorts: both he and Clerke had their crews agree that they would only consume grog 'on

Saturday nights when they had full allowance to drink to their female friends in England, lest amongst the pretty girls of Otaheite they should be wholly forgotten'.

The two captains also came together to view an event that took place some miles into the interior of the island, one they must surely have regretted attending. After being led to the site by their hosts, Cook and Clerke witnessed a human sacrifice – an offering to the gods as the natives prepared to attack a neighbouring island. The entire ceremony spanned two days.

Up to this point, Cook's three expeditions had seen him concentrate his exploration south of the Equator, but on departing from Matavai Bay on 29 September, to the booming sound of seven rounds of cannon-fire, *Resolution* and *Discovery* started out on the 5000-nautical-mile venture into the North Pacific.

Almost sixty days passed until, soon after sun-up on Christmas Eve 1777 – by which time they were a mere 140 nautical miles into the northern hemisphere – their next discovery appeared above the horizon. It was a low-profile, 300-square-mile uninhabited coral island, with a large, shallow lagoon on its north-east coast and countless sand cays adorning its coastline. This find was so impressive that Cook called for a stop to allow for a period of exploration. The two ships were there for a week, and at the end of the stay, the captain's not-infrequent lack of inspiration regarding place names resurfaced: he named it Christmas Island. It would later become known as Kiritimati Island – the largest coral atoll in the world and now part of the Republic of Kiribati.

A more significant discovery occurred two weeks later, on the morning of Sunday, 18 January 1778, when a shout from the man standing on *Resolution*'s lookout platform, 60 feet above the deck, announced the outline of another island. Soon afterwards, there was a second sighting. They had discovered Hawaii.

A day later they were in close proximity to the islands, which, much to Cook's delight, were obviously inhabited:

natives came off the shore in their canoes to investigate these two strange-looking vessels. Cook wrote of the historic moment when Europeans came face to face with these people for the first time: 'we were agreeably surprised to find them of the same Nation as the people of Otaheite and other islands we had lately visited.'

Within twenty-four hours, Cook had *Resolution* close on the coast so that she could anchor off the shore of what is now Kauai, one of the western islands in the group. Once there, a number of the thoroughly mystified islanders clambered up the steps on the side of the ship and onto her deck. The captain's journal recorded: 'I never saw Indians so much astonished at entering a ship before, their eyes were continually flying from object to object, the wildness of their looks and actions fully expressed their surprise and astonishment at the several new objects before them ...'

Pilfering was rampant from the outset. The first man aboard showed he was as light-fingered as his tribal cousins on other islands that *Resolution* had visited: he saw the lead-line, took a liking to it, and claimed it as his own. He only returned it after other islanders berated him for his actions.

As a mark of honour for his close friend and supporter Lord Sandwich, the captain soon declared that this island chain was to be known as 'the Sandwich Islands'. However, when creating their charts of the region, Cook, Bligh and others used the English phonetic spelling of a word that the natives applied to their homeland: 'O'why'he'. They became known as the Hawaiian Islands in the 1840s.

For the next five weeks, *Resolution* and *Discovery* cruised along the coastlines of some of the eight islands in the chain, situated 1200 nautical miles north of the Equator, and stretching in a gentle arc from the north-west to the south-east for 300 nautical miles. Everything was charted and logged in fine detail, and whenever possible, Cook would go ashore to explore the land and learn more about the people. He was intrigued to find that some of the islanders had objects made from iron; his only conclusion was that they must have originated from a shipwreck – probably a Spanish vessel from long before. It was a sombre reminder of just how vulnerable expeditions such as this really were. The line between success and tragedy was wafer-thin.

With the season for exploration in the north looming, it was time to sail on towards the ultimate goal of this voyage of discovery. Cook was once again about to lead his crew to the end of the Earth. In doing so, he and all those who were part of the circumnavigation of 1772–75 would become the first men to sail beyond both the Antarctic and Arctic circles.

When the bosun bellowed '*Anchor's aweigh!*' for the benefit of the officers on the quarterdeck, and with the master ordering the desired trim of the sails, *Resolution* and her consort were set on a course for the wide expanse of the North Pacific, and the far north coast of North America beyond. The two ships were pressed hard, so that maximum speed was maintained on what was an uneventful passage.

The weather was murky and foul when land was sighted on 7 March 1778, at a point south-west of where Portland, Oregon, is sited today. The captain then adopted the usual procedure of sailing a course that matched the coastline while continuing to head north, again charting as much of what they were observing, and naming as many of its features, as time and weather would allow. They sailed along the western coast of Vancouver Island (not realising it was an island), then continued on to Nootka Sound, where they came into contact with welcoming natives.

While the ship was in the sound, time was lost after the men discovered rot in *Resolution*'s fore and mizzen masts. It was a problem that could bring disaster to the expedition unless the masts were replaced, especially with the tough sailing conditions that undoubtedly lay ahead. Both ships came to anchor while Cook and his carpenters went into the dense pine forest onshore and selected two towering conifers that would serve as suitable replacements. The work involved in shaping and preparing the new masts took more than a week. Once the foremast was ready, it was floated out to the ship and re-stepped using large scissor-like sheers, but when the mizzenmast was half complete, it was realised that the chosen tree was flawed. The carpenters then had to find another tree and start all over again.

Having experienced the tropics for so long, the men were 'shivering with cold' as they tried to acclimatise themselves to this part of the world. The cold-weather clothing that Cook had ordered from the Navy Board was now being appreciated by every man.

Whenever the captain observed an inlet or sound that offered the potential for a passage to the east, he had it explored. One such probe took the ships 100 nautical miles up an inlet only for the beleaguered crew to discover that it ended as a river mouth. Another fruitless exploration gave Midshipman James Trevenen the opportunity to see his commander in a new light:

> … with several other of our Midshipmen [we] attended Captain Cook in this expedition, in which we rowed him not less than 30 miles during the day. We were fond of such excursions, although the labour of them was very great, as, not only this kind of duty, was more agreeable than the humdrum routine on board the Ships, but as it gave us an opportunity of viewing the different people & countries, and as another very principal consideration we were sure of having plenty to eat & drink, which was not always the case on board the Ship on our usual allowance. Capt Cook also on these occasions, would sometimes relax from his almost constant severity of disposition, and condescend now and then, to converse familiarly with us. But it was only for the time, as soon as we entered the ships, he became again the despot.

While in this region, Cook recorded that an unidentified crewman had a miraculous escape from death:

… we secured the Ship with the small Anchor; in
carrying this out in the Launch one of the Sailors was so
unfortunate as to get his Leg entangled in the Buoy rope
which carried him down with the Anchor, however he
disengaged himself when he got to the bottom & came
up again & saved his Life though he had his Leg broke in
a very dangerous Manner.

The exploration continued north towards the Alaskan
Peninsula, while Cook persisted in his attempts to find a passage
through the continent. When these efforts proved unsuccessful,
he decided to sail onwards and into the Bering Sea – the stretch
of water defined by the Alaskan Peninsula in the south, and
named after Danish navigator Vitus Bering's exploration of
1728. Off Unalaska Island, which forms part of the peninsula,
Resolution came remarkably close to being wrecked on a reef. It
was a very foggy day and, yet again, the alertness of the lookout
above deck led to the rapid deployment of the anchor and
ultimately the ship being saved. *Resolution*'s speed at the time
and the shallowness of the reef could easily have resulted in her
hull being ripped open.

On 3 August, the captain was deeply saddened to record
the death of William Anderson, from consumption, which the
popular surgeon had contracted some twelve months earlier.
Cook described him as 'a Sensible Young Man, an agreeable
companion, well skilled in his profession'. He named a nearby
island in Anderson's honour that same day.

Meanwhile, the captain's problems with his ship were
compounding. As well as the masts and spars suffering through
wear and tear, the hull was now leaking to a disturbing degree.
The gravity of this situation forced him to enter an inlet in thick
fog, in a bid to find an anchorage where repairs could be made.
Eventually, once they'd found a suitable location, the vessel was
heavily heeled using lines attached to objects on the shore, and
the men on caulking detail got down to work. All were alarmed
to see the width of the gap that had opened up between some

of the planks. Instead of employing finger-thin strands of caulking fibre, the men hammered a 'two and a half inch rope along the seams' to repair the leak. For the crew aboard *Discovery*, there was a different problem when it came to the ingress of water: rats had eaten a hole through her quarterdeck.

For much of August and September, the search took *Resolution* and *Discovery* across the Bering Sea, through the Bering Strait and into the Arctic Ocean. Cook noted: 'On the 18th [of August] at noon our latitude was 70° 44' ...' This was the highest latitude the ships reached. They were now well inside the Arctic Circle.

This region posed their most serious challenges, in the form of snow, ice and howling Arctic storms, but such conditions had to be confronted if the mission was to succeed. It continued to be a frustrating exercise, with the two ships at one stage heading west towards the coast of Russia. At this point, according to John Rickman, Clerke's second lieutenant:

> The frost set in and froze so hard, that the running
> rigging was soon loaded with ice, and rendered almost
> impossible to make the sheaves or blocks traverse
> without the assistance of six men to do the work of one.
> The ice was seen hanging at our hair, our noses and even
> the men's fingers' ends, if they did but expose them to
> the air for five or six minutes.

The magnitude of the challenge faced by the 180-odd men of this expedition was brought into sharp relief in late August. There, ahead of them and stretching as far as the eye could see, from horizon to horizon, was an impenetrable wall of ice some 12 feet high. Cook had no option but to turn back and try to find an alternative route. In early October, however, he realised that it was too late in the season to continue, with the threat of the ships becoming trapped by ice increasing each day. He therefore informed his ship's company of this fact – nothing more could be done this year.

Resolution and *Discovery* then retreated temporarily to Unalaska Island, among the Aleutian group, to the west of the Alaskan Peninsula. After putting to sea again on 26 October, he wrote of his plans for the northern hemisphere winter: 'My intention was now to proceed to Sandwich Islands to spend a few months of the Winter Months provided we met with the necessary refreshments there, and then proceed to Kamchatka [Peninsula, in Russia], endeavouring to be there by the Middle of May next.'

Should he reach Kamchatka Peninsula in the spring as planned, the captain intended to sail to regions not explored during this first attempt to find the passage. Cook's determination to return to the Arctic Circle in 1779 impressed many of the crew, as was apparent in a note written by one of *Resolution*'s midshipmen, James Trevenen: 'This indefatigability was a leading feature of his Character. If he failed in, or could no longer pursue, his first great object, he immediately began to consider how he might be most useful in prosecuting some inferior one. Procrastination & irresolution he was a stranger to. Action was life to him & repose a sort of death.'

Among Cook's officers, though, there was a degree of confusion regarding his decision to sail more than 2000 nautical miles back to the Sandwich Islands. To them, it made more sense to pass the winter on the west coast of North America, and that way be able to recommence the search at an earlier date in the new season. But it was the captain's choice. And it would prove to be a fatal one.

CHAPTER TWENTY-ONE

A Brutal End

It had been a month since *Resolution* and *Discovery* had parted company with the coast of North America, and by Cook's calculations, through sun sights and dead-reckoning, they would soon be entering the region in which he had discovered the Sandwich Islands almost a year earlier. To ensure that he and Clerke had every chance of finding the islands this time around, he signalled for *Discovery* to move to a point barely visible from his ship, thereby establishing the widest possible scope of vision. The first call of a sighting came at sunrise on 26 November 1778, when the 10,000-foot-high profile of a volcano, on the previously undiscovered island of Maui, was clearly evident in the distance, off *Resolution*'s bow. It would prove to be one of the southern islands in the group.

The voyage south had not been without incident. On 27 October – Cook's fiftieth birthday – an icy Arctic storm hammered the two ships with howling winds, snow and grotesque seas. *Resolution* and *Discovery* were battered mercilessly by the maelstrom, in what was possibly the worst storm encountered on the entire voyage. The motion aboard the vessels was so violent that men were being injured as they were dispersed across the decks like scattering ninepins. The worst incidents took place aboard *Discovery*. The coxswain there, Heinrich Zimmermann, came within feet of being hurled overboard when an unexpected squall tossed the ship onto her beam-ends, but less fortunate was Clerke's servant, John Mackintosh, who died instantly after being thrown down the main companionway.

Now they were in much calmer waters, crossing a glistening cobalt-blue tropical sea and feeling the excitement that every explorer experiences when something new comes into view. No suitable anchorage could be found upon reaching the island, but fortunately the natives came out to the ship in canoes laden with a wide variety of foodstuffs, including hogs. Four days later, while holding station on the southern side of this new find, crewmen noticed another large island some 8 leagues to the south. Cook then made the decision to head there in the hope of coming upon a sheltered bay where they could stop, make repairs to the ships and source more fresh provisions. This latter pursuit was always important to Cook, who wrote with pride that through the application of a good diet he had 'always kept my people generally speaking free from that dreadful distemper the Scurvy'.

It was an arduous, tedious passage upwind to the second island, where Cook began a slow cruise along the shore. This island, they were told, was the largest in the group and, for an unknown reason, took the same name as the group – O'why'he. To everyone's great surprise, its highest peaks were blanketed in deep snow – something not expected here in the tropics.

Initially, there was no safe haven to be found, so the trade in supplies continued to come via locals in canoes. Cook viewed this trading as beneficial to his situation, as the two crews were always receiving fresh foods rather than drawing on the provisions they had on board; in addition, it took just four or five hours to barter with the islanders and purchase supplies that would last for several days. With a regular source of food, therefore, and no shortage of fresh water as yet, Cook declared that there would be no rush to go ashore. This decision led to considerable disappointment among the crew, as noted by a marine, John Ledyard:

[The men] very naturally supposed, that Cook's first object now would be to find a harbour, where our weather beaten ships might be repaired, and our fatigued crews receive the rewards due to their perseverance and toil through so great a piece of navigation as we had performed the last nine or ten months, but it was not so, and we continued laying off and on the north side of Maui, and particularly Owyhee until the 7th of December without any other supplies than what was brought off to us by the natives in their canoes some leagues from the shore. This conduct of the commander in chief was highly reprobated and at last remonstrated against by the people on board both ships, as it appeared very manifest that Cook's conduct was wholly influenced by motives of interest, to which he was evidently sacrificing not only the ships, but the healths and happiness of the brave men ...

The situation was inflamed when Cook did not, as he had promised in Otaheite, release grog provisions to the men. Instead, the captain insisted that they consume 'a very palatable beer' that he'd brewed on board using sugar cane. The crew rebelled, refusing to consume any of the beer, because they saw it as being detrimental to their health, and complained to the captain via a letter about this and the 'scanty Allowance of Provisions served them'. Cook deemed this to be a 'mutinous' act. Midshipman John Watts wrote that the captain then 'ordered the Hands aft, & told them it was the first time He had heard anything relative to ye shortness of ye Allowance ... & that had He known it sooner, it should have been rectified'. Cook would not release the grog, since he viewed it as being a necessity for the planned second venture into the icy wastelands of the north. With this explanation, the men were satisfied and the matter was put to rest.

While the ships remained in the lee of this 4000-square-mile island, the crew were always on full alert for the sudden squalls that all too often descended unannounced from the high hills. They were a potent force, capable of blowing sails apart and damaging the masts and spars. On 19 December, Cook logged that the cover of darkness had concealed a very dangerous situation for *Resolution* as she plied along the coast: 'At day-break the coast was seen ... a dreadful surf broke upon the shore which was not more than half a league distant, it was evident we had been in the most imminent danger, nor were we yet out of danger; the wind veering more easterly so that for some time we did but just keep our distance from the coast.'

The New Year of 1779 was ushered in with what Cook described as 'very hard rain'. At the time, *Resolution* and *Discovery* were trying to round the easternmost point of the island of O'why'he.

When Cook finally decided it was time to continue the search for an anchorage, he had the two ships sail closer to the coast, and then directed Bligh to lead a party comprising a boat from each vessel and go in search of a bay where they could gain refuge. At the same time, the captain and his men were amazed at the number of natives who had come from the shore to see them. Some of these, the females, had a specific intention in mind, one that would be in breach of a rule that Cook had already laid down for his men: no island women were allowed aboard the ships. This made for a tormenting time for the women, who had deliberately come offshore with the intention of pleasing the visitors, and the crewmen, who hadn't seen such beauty for over a year. *Discovery*'s surgeon, David Samwell, described the situation: 'Many young Women came along side & wanted much to come on board, making many lascivious Motions & Gestures, but as we lay under the forementioned restrictions in respect to our intercourse with them we could not as yet conveniently admit them into the Ships, for which they scolded us very smartly.' Eventually the captain relented, as he later admitted in his journal: 'It was not possible to keep the [women] out of the Ship and no women I ever met with were more ready to bestow their favours, indeed it appeared to me that they came with no other view.'

The captain then described the amazing welcome they received when *Resolution* and *Discovery* cruised slowly along the coast, while waiting for Bligh to return:

> Canoes now began to come off all parts, so that before 10 o'clock there were not less than a thousand about the two Ships, most crowded with people, hogs and other productions of the Island. Not a man had with him a Weapon of any sort, Trade and curiosity alone brought them off. Among such numbers as we had at times on board, it is no wonder that some betrayed a thievish disposition, one man took out of the Ship a boats rudder, he was discovered, but too late to recover it. I thought this a good opportunity to show them the use of firearms, two or three muskets and as many four-pound shot were fired over the Canoe which carried off the rudder. As it was not intended that any of the Shot should take effect, the Indians seemed rather more surprised than frightened.

When Cook sat at his desk in the great cabin to update the ship's log, these words for Sunday, 17 January, would be among his last. Sadly for history, anything that he may have written between this date and his death has disappeared. The last known entry in his journal was on Wednesday, 6 January. He recorded that Bligh had brought good news the previous evening: 'Mr Bligh returned [to the ship] and reported that he had found a bay in which was good anchorage and fresh water tolerable easy to come at, into this bay I resolved to go to refit the ships and take in water ...'

When describing the reception afforded by the islanders after *Resolution* and *Discovery* had anchored in the bay, he wrote: 'The ships very much crowded with Indians and surrounded by a multitude of canoes. I have nowhere in this sea seen such a number of people assembled at one place, besides those in the canoes all the shore of the bay was covered with people and hundreds were swimming about the ships like shoals of fish.'

The name the natives used for the anchorage that Bligh had found was Kealakekua. Today, it is recognised as the best place for vessels to shelter on the western side of the island of Hawaii. Incredibly for the men on Cook's mission, it had taken seven long weeks, from the time land was first seen to when they anchored here and could go ashore.

Cook was welcomed in a most formal manner aboard his ship. 'Among our numerous visitors was a man named Tou-ah-ah,' he recorded, 'who we soon found belonged to the local Church, he introduced himself with much ceremony.' They then proceeded to the shore, where the commander and his officers were lauded by the islanders.

Back aboard the ships, crewmen were preparing to take ashore all the equipment that needed to be repaired, including spars and sails. The work took three weeks to complete, and during that period, Cook was treated as a god each time he went ashore. According to Samwell, 'a Herald walked before him repeating some Words & the Indians cleared the way & prostrated themselves on their Faces before Captain Cook.' James Burney, another of Clerke's lieutenants, added: 'All the people, except those of the Priesthood, laying prostrate or rather on their Hands and Knees with their Heads bowed down to the Ground ...'

The captain eventually met the island's high priest, Koa, who presented him with a piglet and two coconuts before draping a red cloak over his shoulders. There was a level of puzzlement for the visitors as the word 'Lono' was continually uttered any time the islanders were in Cook's presence. The crew came to realise that Captain Cook was seen as the god Lono – the god of abundant seasons – who had now returned, just as legend had foretold. The natives believed that Lono would one day appear off their shores in an extremely large canoe. Incredibly, the arrival of *Resolution* and *Discovery* coincided with the time of the year when Lono was celebrated, and for the islanders, this further reinforced the belief that their god was in their midst. Of equal significance to them was the fact that Lono had arrived in a bay whose name meant 'the path of the gods'.

The coincidences were overwhelming for the islanders: Cook could be none other than their god. They even saw the ships' navigational equipment, including telescopes and quadrants, as being indicative of the presence of a holy man.

Meanwhile, the crew, when not working on the maintenance of the ships, took time to enjoy being on land and observing the casual lifestyle of the islanders. During one such excursion, Samwell and his crewmates from *Discovery* became the first Europeans to see a Hawaiian pastime that, more than a century later, would become an international recreational activity – surf board riding.

> … two or three of us were walking along shore today
> we saw a number of boys & young Girls playing in the
> Surf, which broke very high on the Beach as there was a
> great swell rolling into the Bay. In the first place they
> provide themselves with a thin board about six or seven
> foot long & about 2 broad, on these they swim off shore
> to meet the Surf, as soon as they see one coming they
> get themselves in readiness & turn their sides to it, they
> suffer themselves to be involved in it … laying hold of
> the fore part of the board … & by that means keeps
> before the wave which drives it along with an incredible
> Swiftness to the shore.

Samwell also recorded that the islanders' hospitality was reciprocated by Cook: 'These People pay their greatest attention to Captain Cook, having a very high opinion of his Station & Quality, which he everywhere maintains by his happy method of managing Indians which never fails of obtaining their Friendship and Esteem.'

*

As the repair work on the ships was completed by early February, Cook called for a departure so that he could continue to explore this archipelago. In the preceding days, the natives had overwhelmed the visitors with supplies of fresh food and other gifts in the hope that Lono would continue to bless them with seasons of abundant crops.

With considerable reluctance, after their nineteen-day stay, the captains and crew of both ships farewelled Kealakekua and its wonderfully hospitable inhabitants. A small armada of canoes was on the water to escort them towards the open sea where, once *Resolution* and *Discovery* were experiencing fair winds, the ships turned north. On 8 February, however, when they were almost abeam of the northernmost tip of O'why'he, the vessels were confronted by a powerful storm, which they could not avoid. It arrived with such force that it was impossible for the crew of *Resolution* to ease the pressure the fore sails exerted on the foremast and, consequently, the mast suffered severe damage to the point where it almost broke. Cook knew there was only one solution: to return to Kealakekua and make repairs in an environment they knew to be friendly and welcoming.

Yet once they had arrived there, and *Resolution*'s best bower had hit the bottom of the bay and taken hold, the crew immediately noticed a difference in the islanders' reception compared to before. It was cool, to say the least, and the visitors could not understand why. Samwell wrote in his journal: 'We had but few Canoes about us in Comparison to the great number we had about us on our first coming into this Bay ...' There was some good news at least, for him and others, since 'Most of our old sweethearts came to see us'.

The theories on this change of attitude vary widely across a range of authoritative publications. It appears that the islanders believed that the return of Lono could only mean that they were now destined for crop failures and a further drain on their limited food resources, much of which they had already given to the ships, to please their god. They might also have thought that Lono was not the god they had believed him to be.

Two days after their return on 11 February, despite the tense atmosphere, Cook had his crew take the damaged mast ashore along with other equipment, so that repairs could be made. The ill feeling was heightened when, during the day, an islander who had stolen the armourer's tongs was captured, taken aboard *Discovery* and dealt forty lashes while tied to the main shrouds – the stays supporting the mainmast. He was released once the tongs were recovered.

The situation between the two sides continued to deteriorate throughout that day. George Gilbert wrote of a confrontation involving the master and midshipman of *Discovery* and an island chief whose canoe the two sailors, for some unknown reason, wanted to confiscate:

> The Chief laid hold of them and gave them a severe
> beating with his hands, which the two men, who
> remained in the Jolly boat perceiving, they rowed off to
> a little distance and got clear. Our pinnace, that was lying
> not far off waiting for Capt Cook with only the crew in
> her ... went without any orders to their assistance; but as
> soon as they came near the shore the Natives lay hold of
> the Boat and hauled her up high and dry upon the beach,
> and broke some of the oars, which obliged the crew to
> take to the water and swim to the Jolly boat, the Indians
> at the same time pelting them with stones.

That night, in what could have been seen as an act of retribution, *Discovery*'s cutter was stolen. At the time, it was attached to the bower buoy off the bow and flooded with water so that the hull planks would not open up in the heat of the day. Cook was made aware of the theft soon after daybreak on 14 February, and in response, as Coxswain Zimmermann later reported, the commander proposed that the remaining boats from both ships, under the command of *Resolution*'s master, should blockade the bay until the stolen craft was recovered. Bligh's first direction to those under his authority was, as a precaution against whatever situation might develop, to load their muskets with ball and not shot.

As these boats took up their position, it was clear to Bligh that a showdown was imminent: an increasing number of agitated islanders were gathering onshore and canoes were being launched. His immediate reaction was to try to intercept the canoes, and when some of them did not respond to his directions, he had no option but to have his men fire upon the occupants, killing some.

While this was happening, Cook had gone to the island to visit the king, Terre'oboo, to register his anger at the hostility being shown towards his crewmen. An accurate account of the sequence of events that took place as a consequence of this visit does not exist, but it is known that confusion and misunderstanding contributed to what followed. On realising that any effort to discuss the deteriorating situation with the king at his residence would be futile, since they were surrounded by potentially aggressive islanders, Cook apparently suggested that he and Terre'oboo retire to *Resolution*, so that matters could be discussed in a calmer environment. For this reason, it seems, the two men proceeded towards the beach, where Cook's pinnace, with crew and marines stationed on board, was waiting in the shallows.

It was 9 am when the English captain and the islander chief prepared to wade towards the boat, all the while shadowed by Terre'oboo's followers, and it appears that a belief spread among the islanders that the king was being taken hostage, and that if he went to the ship he would be killed. It is suggested that on hearing this assumption being shouted towards him by his people, Terre'oboo became reluctant to go to *Resolution*. Cook, knowing he could not compel the king to join him, immediately abandoned his plan.

Simultaneously, hatred towards the visitors became increasingly apparent as the large chanting mob began to arm themselves with spears and rocks. Marine Molesworth Phillips, who was standing with Cook, observed the developments: 'an artful Rascal of a Priest was singing & making a ceremonious offering of a coco Nut to the Captain and Terre'oboo to divert their attention from the Manoeuvres of the surrounding multitude.'

Escape to the ship was now paramount, but as Cook stepped into the shallow water and began making his way towards the pinnace, a man armed with a dagger and a rock came up behind him with the obvious intention of attacking him. Cook is said to have turned and fired one round of shot from his musket towards the man, who was protected from the pellets by the heavy matting he was wearing as clothing. This act enraged the islanders even more. They then began an all-out attack on the visitors.

Cook fired in self-defence once more, now with ball, and killed a man. He is then said to have shouted to his men: 'Take to the boats!' But confusion and mayhem were the by-products. What is known is that there were hand signals misunderstood between the men in the pinnace and others onshore as to what was occurring and what response was required. Samwell, the surgeon, described the horrid scene that followed:

> An Indian came running behind him, stopping once or twice as he advanced, as if he was afraid that he [Cook] should turn round. Then, taking him unaware, he sprung to him, knocked him on the back of his head with a large club taken out of a fence, and instantly fled with the greatest precipitation. The blow made Captain Cook stagger two or three paces. He then fell on his hand and one knee and dropped his musket. As he was rising another Indian came running at him, and before he could recover himself from the fall, drew out an iron dagger he concealed under his feathered cloak and stuck it with all his force into the back of his neck, which made Captain Cook tumble into the water ... [which was] about knee deep.

> Here he was followed by a crowd of people who
> endeavoured to keep him under water, but struggling
> very strong with them he got his head up, and, looking
> towards the pinnace which was not above a boat hook's
> length from him, waved his hands to them for assistance,
> which it seems ... was not in their power to give.

A powerful blow to the head from another club-wielding islander ended James Cook's life that day – 14 February 1779.

In an effort to protect their captain against the warlike islanders filling the beachfront, four marines – John Allen, Thomas Fatchett, Theophilus Hinks and James Thomas – had fired a volley of shots from their muskets. From that moment, they were defenceless. To reload the weapons would have taken around thirty seconds, time that the troopers simply did not have. All four were then speared and stoned to death by their assailants.

As if this dreadful scene wasn't enough for the other Englishmen who had observed it, what followed Cook's brutal slaughter was appalling. His body was dragged from the water and onto the rocky shore by a frenzied mob, who then carried out a heinous attack on the corpse.

As the first of the ships' boats made a frantic dash from the shallows and out towards the two ships, anxious shouts to Captain Clerke alerted him to the fact that his commander had been murdered in the fracas. Now the most senior officer on the expedition, Clerke immediately took charge of the situation and went aboard *Resolution*. He directed Bligh, who had returned to his ship, and others to go to shore and defend the men there, and try to establish some level of authority. The moment they arrived at the beach, Bligh's group came under a fusillade of rocks and spears, to which they returned fire with their muskets. According to witnesses, twenty-five natives were killed and fifteen wounded in the affray.

The bodies of the marines would never be recovered, but Clerke was determined to retrieve the captain's remains. This message was duly conveyed to the island's elders, including Terre'oboo.

The atmosphere between the two sides remained volatile overnight, but by morning, while still tense, all signs of aggression from the natives had disappeared. The situation surrounding Cook's death then went from macabre to ghoulish when an islander priest ventured out to *Resolution* on a canoe bearing a parcel, probably made from palm fronds, and covered in red and black feathers, which he delivered to Clerke. The latter opened it in his cabin – and was immediately confronted by part of Cook's dismembered and burnt corpse. Hatred for the islanders was ignited among the sailors from that moment.

In response to taunting behaviour from a large group assembled on the beach, cannons blasted out from the ships, the thundering sound echoing across the bay. In no time, these islanders had been scattered by a salvo of 4-pounder balls, but not before many had been killed or wounded. Another bitter confrontation followed when a watering party from the ships went ashore and came under attack. The response from the Englishmen was immediate and without restraint. They shot dead almost every native who came within range, then razed the nearby village.

If it had been possible, *Resolution* and *Discovery* would have quit Kealakekua that day. But because so much equipment remained onshore, including *Resolution*'s damaged foremast, they were forced to stay for another six days.

On 19 February, there was another grisly twist when Clerke demanded that Cook's missing remains be returned to the ship for burial. He stressed that there would be no peace until this occurred. The king sent a return message to Clerke, explaining that because Cook had been held in such high esteem by the islanders, his bones had been distributed to the most important chiefs. As a result, it would take some time to gather what remained of the captain.

Lieutenant James King, who had taken up the responsibility for continuing Cook's journal, described in detail what followed. It had been arranged that the island's chief priest, Koa, would personally carry out the handover. He also offered gifts of peace.

> To show them that we accepted the peace, Captain Clerke went in the pinnace and desired me to go in the cutter, to bring him [the chief priest] and the presents as was desired. We refused landing which was not much insisted upon, [Koa] coming with great composure into the pinnace and he and several others came on board. He gave us a bundle wrapped very decently, and covered with a spotted cloak of black and white feathers, which we understood to be a mourning colour. On opening it we found the Captain's hands, which were well known from a remarkable cut, the scalp, the skull, wanting thigh bones and arm bones. The hands only had flesh on them, & were cut in holes, and salt crammed in them; the leg bones, lower jaw, and feet which were all that remained & had escaped the fire ...

In the evening of 22 February, Cook's remains were placed in a shroud made from sail canvas and weighted with cannonballs, before being lowered over the side of *Resolution*. Then, as the shroud slipped beneath the surface of the sea that had been the great explorer's realm for so long, a bell tolled and ten rounds of cannon-fire boomed forth at thirty-second intervals.

Clerke wrote of the moment: 'I had the remains of Captain Cook committed to the deep, with all the attention and honour we could possibly pay it in this part of the world.'

Mourning the Master

It was a solemn departure from Kealakekua on 23 February 1779. After the anchors were weighed and sails set, *Resolution* and *Discovery* were eased slowly out of the bay on a gentle evening breeze. The crowd of islanders standing along the rugged and rocky shoreline, and the crew of both ships, were still grieving over what had occurred in those horrifying few minutes nine days earlier. Some of those onshore were wailing; the seamen were mourning in silence. The only sound of any significance was the screeching of the sheaves in the pulley blocks, as the men hauled away in unison on the lines that needed tending to get the vessels underway. The occasional order shouted from the quarterdeck could also be heard by those onshore.

Clerke, the popular new commander of the expedition, was suffering in his own right through illness – consumption – but he remained determined to prosecute Cook's plan to explore the Sandwich Islands, then return to the Arctic Circle during the approaching northern hemisphere summer. The search for the Northwest Passage would continue. It was not his intention to spend an excessive amount of time among the Sandwich Islands, however, for fear that news of the battle at Kealakekua, and Cook's death, should precede their arrival and cause another confrontation.

By early March, that part of the expedition had been completed without mishap. The ships then headed north, away from the tropics and towards the Arctic Circle. Four weeks later, their decks were covered by a thick spread of snow, and icicles were hanging through the rigging like Christmas decorations.

Clerke noted in his journal that they were experiencing 'very heavy snow & severe Frost, with fresh Gales & squally Weather'. He also mentioned how tough it was on the tars: 'The poor fellows after broiling as they have lately done several Months on the Torrid Zone are now miserably pinched with the Cold.' Some of the men felt the frigid temperature more than others, and the reason was simple enough: they had traded much of their clothing for favours from the honey-skinned maidens of Hawaii.

The captain decided that the only harbour on the eastern side of the Kamchatka Peninsula, Avacha Bay, would be their first destination. They would stop there and make final preparations for the passage through Bering Strait and into the ice-laden seas beyond. It was on 29 April, after the winter ice covering the wide, 15-mile-long bay had started to break up, that *Resolution* and *Discovery* commenced a slow and careful entry into this remote and sparsely populated Russian port.

Soon after their arrival, the governor of the region, a Major Behm, visited *Resolution* and established a strong rapport with Clerke. During their discussions, the captain learned that the major's presence created an opportunity for news of Cook's death to reach the Admiralty much sooner than would otherwise have been possible. Behm could arrange for a package to be transported almost 5000 miles across the Asian continent, to the British ambassador in St Petersburg, who could then forward it to London. It was estimated that this would take about six months, whereas *Resolution* would not be in home waters for more than a year. Lieutenant King wrote that another influence on Clerke's decision was the danger of one or both ships encountering a disaster, as they 'had a very hazardous part of the Voyage yet to go through'.

Behm's offer led to Clerke addressing a letter to the Secretary of the Admiralty before the ships' departure in June. It delivered the devastating news of Cook's death, and confirmed that his wishes would be followed: the search for the Northwest Passage would continue that summer. The package for Behm contained that letter, Cook's journal up to the time of his death, Clerke's most recent journal, and a chart.

The Russian officer was honoured to be entrusted with such an important undertaking, and seven months later, Sir Philip Stephens received the well-travelled package in his high-ceilinged office in London's Whitehall. When he read Clerke's letter, his eyes absorbed the tragic words that would shock King and country: Britain's legendary explorer, fifty-year-old Lieutenant James Cook, had been murdered by islanders in the Pacific.

It would most likely have been Stephens' duty to then visit Cook's wife at home, just 3 miles away, and share with her the crushing news of her husband's demise. After having spent only four and a half of their sixteen years of marriage in each other's company, a distraught Elizabeth Cook, at the age of thirty-eight, was a seafarer's widow, like so many women of her era.

King George III is said to have shed tears on receiving the news. Sir Joseph Banks was advised of the death in a letter from Lord Sandwich, dated 10 January 1780. 'Dear Sir,' it read, 'what is uppermost in our mind always must come out first, poor captain Cook is no more …'

The *London Gazette* published this announcement on 11 January:

> Captain Clerke of His Majesty's Sloop *Resolution*, in a letter to Mr Stephens, dated the 8th of June 1779, in the Harbour of St Peter and St Paul, Kamchatka, which was received yesterday, gives the melancholy account of the celebrated Captain Cook, late commander of that Sloop, with four of his private Marines having been killed on the 14th of February last at the island of O'Why'he, one of a

group of new discovered Islands in the 22nd Degree of
North Latitude, in an affray with a numerous and
tumultuous Body of the Natives.

A subsequent obituary read:

This untimely and ever to be lamented Fate of so
Intrepid, so able, and so intelligent a Sea-Officer, may
justly be considered as an irreparable Loss to the Public, as
well as to his Family, for in him were united every
successful and amiable quality that could adorn his
Profession; nor was his singular Modesty less conspicuous
than his other Virtues. His successful Experiments to
preserve the Healths of his Crews are well known, and his
Discoveries will be an everlasting Honour to his Country.

Thousands of miles away to the east of their homeland, the
crews of *Resolution* and *Discovery* remained determined to do
what they could to honour their late commander, by finding
the Northwest Passage. They sailed from Avacha Bay in mid
June, under an enormous cloud of ash from the erupting
Avachinsky volcano, which was just 20 miles to the north-east
of their anchorage.

Initially, the ships' progress was slowed due to it being too
early in the season for the majority of ice to have melted. Three
weeks later, after averaging less than 3 knots during that period,
the ships cruised through Bering Strait – only to be confronted
by large clusters of drift ice. In a bid to find a way around this
obstacle, Clerke took up a course to the north-east, towards the
coast of North America, crossing 70 degrees north latitude on
the way. This path was also dogged by huge ice floes, so much
so that on 19 July, Clerke was forced to turn back. He explained
why: 'this Sea is now so Choked with Ice that a passage I fear is
totally out of the question.' They were then only a few miles
south of the point that Cook had reached with *Resolution* the
previous summer.

Clerke's health continued to decline. By early August he was confined to his cabin, and, on accepting that death could come at any time, he advised his officers of the new chain of command. John Gore, the American-born seafarer who had already completed two circumnavigations, would become the new expedition commander, and captain of *Resolution*. Lieutenant King was appointed captain of *Discovery*, and 24-year-old Lieutenant Bligh became the full-time navigator for the remainder of the voyage. On 15 August, Clerke accepted he could no longer capably captain the ship, so he relinquished his command to Gore. A week later, Charles Clerke, aged thirty-eight, passed away.

The mission continued under the new regime, only to be beaten by impenetrable walls of ice no matter where they searched. Eventually, they gave up all hope of success, and with another winter approaching, Gore accepted that it was time to head home. Had the Northwest Passage been discovered during this expedition, then *Resolution* and *Discovery* would have needed to sail less than 5000 nautical miles to be back in English waters. Instead, they had to endure a fourteen-month, 18,000-nautical-mile passage – three-quarters of the way around the world – back to England, via the coast of Siberia, Japan and the Cape of Good Hope. The two ships anchored off The Nore on 4 October 1780, four years and three months after they had set sail from Plymouth. It would be another 125 years before the Northwest Passage was discovered and navigated by Norwegian polar explorer Roald Amundsen.

With news of Cook's death having preceded the arrival of the ships by some ten months, the homecoming was a sombre affair. There were no celebrations, and no bounty to be shared by the crews as their search for the passage had not borne results.

At this time, Elizabeth Cook continued to live at the family home in Mile End, tending her youngest child, four-year-old Hugh. Sadly, having endured the deaths of three infant children while her husband was away on the high seas, and after then suffering the loss of the great man himself, tragedy would continue to haunt her life. The Cooks' two eldest sons, James and Nathaniel, aged seventeen and fifteen respectively in October 1780, had proudly followed their father into the Royal Navy and both would mature into active service. In the same month as *Resolution* and *Discovery*'s muted return, Nathaniel was serving as a midshipman aboard HMS *Thunderer* when she foundered with the loss of all hands. In what was described as the greatest of all hurricanes ever to hit the West Indies, it claimed 20,000 lives and sank nearly fifty ships, primarily British and French ships of war.

In 1784, there was a heart-warming moment for Elizabeth when she was shown the proposed design for a medal that would be struck in honour of her husband. This tribute had been initiated by Banks, as president of the Royal Society since 1778. Deeply touched by the gesture, Elizabeth wrote to him: 'My greatest pleasure now remaining is in my sons, who, I hope, will ever strive to copy after so good an example, and, animated by the honours bestowed on their Father's memory, be ambitious of attaining by their own merits your notice and approbation.'

Thirteen years later, there was more heartbreak for the widow. Hugh, then a student in residence at Christ's College in Cambridge, fell victim to scarlet fever and died four days before Christmas 1793.

This was the most dreadful period in Elizabeth Cook's life. Just five weeks after Hugh's death, she learned that her only surviving child, thirty-year-old James, who had recently been promoted to the position of commander in the Royal Navy, had perished in a tragic accident on the Solent. He was aboard a small navy boat sailing from Poole to Portsmouth, so he could take up the command of HMS *Spitfire*, when it was apparently overwhelmed by bad weather. His body was found washed ashore on the Isle of Wight, stripped of all valuables and with a wound to his head. The wreck of the boat was nearby, but no other members of the crew were ever found.

No doubt Elizabeth had looked forward to the days when she and her husband would enjoy their retirement, surrounded by their children and grandchildren. But that wasn't to be. This was the final, grief-laden chapter in the story of Elizabeth and James Cook's family, a family she had so doggedly and determinedly nurtured, more often than not alone. Elizabeth was to remain a widow until her death, in 1830, at the age of ninety-three.

James Cook left an extraordinary legacy: expanding the outline of the world map like no other, and naming around 300 landmarks across the Pacific, from South America to Australia and New Zealand, and from the Antarctic Circle to the Arctic Circle. He was, without doubt, the world's greatest maritime explorer.

The famous John Webber portrait of the great mariner Captain James Cook, in full regalia with his right hand ungloved. National Portrait Gallery, Accession No: 2000.25.

abaft Towards the stern of a ship. 'Abaft the beam' means aft of abeam.

abeam A point 90 degrees out from anywhere along the centre-line of a ship.

anchor Bower, the biggest anchor; stream, the next largest anchor; kedge, a smaller anchor for special purposes, usually stored below decks.

anchor stock The heavy timber crossbar at the top of an anchor.

arrack A distilled alcoholic drink usually made from fermented coconut-palm sap.

athwartships Directly across the ship, from side to side.

baffling winds An erratic wind that frequently changes direction.

ballast Any heavy material (such as gravel, iron, lead, sand or stones) placed in the hold of a ship to provide stability.

beam ends The sides of a ship. 'On her beam ends' is used to describe the rolling effect of very rough seas on a vessel: the ship is almost on her side and possibly about to capsize.

beat, to To sail upwind.

belaying pin Wooden pins found around the mast at deck level, or at the side of a ship, that are used to secure a rope.

bend/unbend sails To attach or remove sails from their yards.

best bower The starboard of the two anchors carried at the bow of the ship. That on the port side was known as the smaller bower, even though the two were identical in weight.

bilge The curved part of a ship's hull immediately above the keel.

block A single- or multiple-sheaved pulley.

bosun/boatswain Warrant or non-commissioned officer responsible for the maintenance of the ship's rigging, anchors and cables.

bower Bow anchor or cable.

bowsprit A pole extending forward from a vessel's bow.

brace A rope or line attached to the end of a yard which is either eased or hauled in, so that the sail is trimmed to suit the wind direction.

brig A two-masted square-rigger.

bulwarks The planking along the sides of a ship above the upper deck that acts as a railing to prevent crew and passengers from going overboard.

buntlines Ropes tied to the foot of a square sail that keep it from opening or bellying when it is being hauled up for furling to the yard.

burthen Displacement.

cable 1. A long, thick and heavy rope attached to the ship's anchor. 2. A naval unit of distance – 10 cables is 1 nautical mile.

capstan A large waist-high vertical winch turned by crewmen manning the capstan bars, which lock into the head of the winch. The crew then walk in a circle to work the winch. Used to raise the anchor and other heavy objects.

careen To heel a ship over on one side for cleaning, caulking or repairing.

carronade A short-barrelled, limited-range gun, used for close-quarter action, that was enormously destructive to an enemy ship's timbers.

carvel planking A method of shipbuilding whereby the planks are laid flush and edge to edge.

cat-built Defines a ship's shape: usually a hull with round, bluff bows, a wide deep waist, and lines that taper towards the stern. The name was derived from the Norwegian '*kati*', meaning a ship.

cathead A sturdy timber projection near the bow to hold the anchor.

cat–o'–nine–tails A lash used as a form of punishment aboard a naval ship.

caulking Material making the ship watertight (such as cotton fibres or oakum) that is forced between the planks to stop leaks.

cay A low bank or reef of coral, rock or sand.

chains The area outside the ship where the dead-eyes, rigging and other hardware come together to support the mast.

clew The bottom corners of the square sail, or the lower back corner of a triangular sail.

clinker A construction method for ships and boats where the external planks overlap each other and are fastened together with clenched copper nails.

close–hauled Sailing with the sails trimmed in as close as possible to the centre-line. This allows the ship to sail as close as possible to the direction of the wind.

collier A cargo ship that hauled coal.

commander The next rank above lieutenant in the Royal Navy prior to the introduction of the rank of lieutenant-commander in the early twentieth century.

coxon/coxswain The helmsman of a ship's boat.

cutter A fast sailboat with one mast that carries several headsails.

dead reckoning A method for estimating a vessel's current position, based on its previously determined position and advanced by estimating speed and course over an elapsed time.

deck beams Timbers running from side to side of a ship to support the deck.

Doldrums A region of the ocean near the Equator, characterised by calms, faint breezes or squalls.

Downs, The An anchorage off the coast of England at Kent, between Dover and Deal.

draught The measurement from the waterline to the deepest point of the vessel in the water.

dreadnought A person who fears nothing – hence the adoption of the name as a generic term for battleships of the early twentieth century.

driver boom The yard carrying the driver, which is a square sail set from the peak of the gaff on the mizzenmast.

fathom A unit of measurement for depth – 1 fathom is 1.83 metres or 6 feet.

fire-ship A vessel filled with combustibles and explosives, which, having been set aflame, is released to drift among enemy ships.

forecastle/foc'sle/fo'c's'le The living quarters in the bow of the ship where crew are accommodated.

foremast The first mast, or the mast fore of the mainmast.

fothering To seal a leak by lowering a sail over the side of the ship and positioning it to be sucked into the hole by the rushing sea.

frigate A three-masted sailing warship with two full decks, with only one gun deck. Usually armed with 30–44 guns, located on the gun deck.

futtock An iron plate in the ship's topmast for securing the rigging.

great cabin An interior, windowed area of the ship spanning the width of the stern. Traditionally, this was the captain's private quarters, subdivided by partitions at his discretion.

grog A mixture of rum and water served to a ship's crew.

guinea An English gold coin worth £1 1 shilling.

gunwale/gunnel The top edge of the planking at the sides of a ship – named for the place where a crewman rested his gun to take aim.

halyard A rope used for raising or lowering a sail, yard, spar or flag.

haul up/haul onto the wind To change a ship's course so that it is sailing closer to the direction from which the wind is blowing. At the same time, the ship's sails are trimmed to suit the new course.

hawsehole A cylindrical hole in the bow of a vessel for the anchor cable to run through.

headed When the wind changes direction so that it is coming from a point closer to the ship's bow, causing the vessel to change course to leeward, so that it can continue sailing effectively.

heel To tilt to one side.

helm The apparatus used to steer a vessel by moving the angle of the rudder.

HMS His/Her Majesty's Ship.

hove Raised or lifted with effort or force, particularly the anchor.

hove to Slowing a ship's forward progress by fixing the helm and fore sail so that the vessel does not need to be steered – a procedure usually applied in very rough weather.

jib A triangular headsail set from the foremast which is the foremost sail.

junk A name given to any remnants or pieces of old cable, which is usually cut into small portions for the purpose of caulking seams in wooden ships, creating padding, etc.

jury rig A temporary rig put up in place of a mast that has broken or been carried away.

kedge A small anchor used to keep a ship steady and clear from her bower anchor.

knot A unit of speed equal to 1 nautical mile per hour, or 1.151 miles (1.852 kilometres) an hour.

larboard The old name for port, the left-hand side of a ship. The term 'fine on the larboard bow' refers to an area just off the vessel's centre-line, looking forward on the port side.

lay-to/lying-to Waiting out a storm by lowering all sails and letting the vessel drift.

lead-line A sounding line with a lead weight at one end, used to record the depth of water under the ship.

leadsman The man who, standing in the chains, heaves the lead to take soundings.

league A unit of distance in the eighteenth century equal to 3 nautical miles.

lee The sheltered side.

leeward The direction away from the wind; the opposite of windward.

lieutenant The lowest rank of commissioned officer in the Royal Navy, prior to the introduction of the rank of sub-lieutenant in the twentieth century.

log 1. A device for measuring a ship's speed. 2. A record of a ship's movements, the weather for navigational purposes, and general and pertinent information regarding incidents, observations and shipboard routine. Usually kept by the captain, masters and lieutenants.

luff 1. The leading edge of a fore-and-aft sail. 2. To change course into the wind so that the sails flap.

mainmast The tallest mast on a vessel.

make fast To secure a line.

mal de mer Seasickness (French).

marines Seaborne contingent of soldiers.

master The most senior non-commissioned officer or warrant officer in the Royal Navy at the time, responsible for the navigation of the ship, subject to the command of its officers.

masthead The very top part of a mast.

mate Assistant warrant officer to a senior warrant officer – hence bosun's mate and master's mate.

mizzenmast On a ship with three masts, this is the one nearest the stern.

nautical mile A mathematical calculation based on the circumference of the Earth at the Equator.

Nore, The A sandbank that marks the official meeting point between the River Thames and the North Sea. It is roughly 6 miles to the north-east of Sheerness, in Kent, and some 4 miles south-east of Shoeburyness, on the Essex coast.

oakum Old pieces of rope picked to shreds and tarred for use as caulking. Known as rope junk.

offing Distance from shore, land or other navigational hazards.

pawl A hinged or pivoted catch on a ratchet wheel that prevents the wheel from slipping back.

pig iron/pigs of iron An oblong block of metal, usually iron or lead, used for ballast.

pinnace A small vessel with two fore-and-aft rigged masts; it can be rowed or sailed and usually carried men between shore and ship.

poop deck The short deck towards the stern above the quarterdeck of a ship. Similarly, 'pooped' is the term for when a wave breaks over the stern and onto the deck.

port The left-hand side of a vessel.

post-captain An alternative form of the rank of captain. It distinguished those who were captains by rank from officers in command of a naval vessel who were recognised as captain regardless of rank, and commanders who received the title of captain regardless of them being in command or not.

pounds, shillings, pence English currency.

put the wheel/helm down To turn the steering wheel in a particular direction.

quadrant A very simple instrument used to determine the altitude of a heavenly body.

quarterdeck The upper exposed deck at the stern of a vessel from the mainmast to the back, usually the territory of the ship's officers.

quitted the chains Whereby the crewman heaving the lead to check water depth leaves his post in the chains and returns to the deck.

ratlines Bands of ropes lashed across the shrouds like steps, allowing crew to easily climb aloft.

reciprocal course/track To return along the course from whence you came.

reef/reefed To take in or reduce the area of a sail without furling it.

refit Repair or restore a vessel.

rigging All ropes, wires and chains used to support the masts and yards.

schooner A fore-and-aft rigged vessel, originally with two masts, but later with three or more. Designed for blockade running and as a fast naval vessel.

seine net A fishing net weighted so that it trawls along the seabed.

sextant A navigational instrument used to measure the angle of elevation of an object above the horizon.

Sheerness (dockyard) An important naval dockyard at Sheerness, on the Isle of Sheppey, in the Thames Estuary.

sheet anchor Traditionally, the largest of a ship's anchors, carried so that they can be dropped quickly in the event of an emergency.

ship-of-the-line A sailing warship built to fight in the line of battle – the traditional form of battle in the late eighteenth and early nineteenth century, where the ships formed a line so that they could fire broadsides at the enemy.

shroud The standing rigging on a ship that provides lateral support to the mast.

slatted A sail flopping backwards and forwards in near windless conditions.

sloop A single-masted sailing ship usually carrying a mainsail and a single jib or headsail.

slops Ready-made clothing from the ship's stores that was sold to the seamen.

spanker A large fore-and-aft sail set from the mizzenmast using a gaff – a wooden spar that supports the top of the sail.

spars A general term relating to all the poles in a vessel's rig, such as masts, yards, booms and gaffs.

Spithead A stretch of water at the eastern end of the Solent, located between Portsmouth and the Isle of Wight.

spritsail A four-sided sail set from a sprit which usually extends beyond the end of the yards.

square-rigger A ship using square sails as its principal form of sail.

starboard The right-hand side of a vessel.

stay A large long rope that acts as a piece of standing rigging to support the mast either athwartships or fore-and-aft.

strake A line of planking on the side of a vessel.

taffrail The railing around a ship's stern.

tar A nickname for a lower-deck sailor. Derived from their canvas coats and hats being waterproofed with tar.

tender A small vessel that attends a man-of-war, primarily in harbour. Usually used to carry munitions, provisions, mail and despatches to and from the ship.

timoneer An alternative term for the helmsman.

topgallant In a square-rigged ship, the spars and rigging at the very top of the masts, above the topsails.

trestletree Framing comprising two short strong parallel timbers fixed fore-and-aft on the opposite side of the lower masthead to support the topmast, or at the top of the topmast to support the topgallant mast.

uncleat To untie from a cleat – a T-shaped low-profile anchor point for securing lines.

waist In a nautical context, the middle part of a ship's upper deck, between the quarterdeck and the forecastle.

warp A rope attached to a ship, used to move her from one place to another by men pulling on it when the ship is in harbour; hence, 'warping' means to move or reposition a ship by hauling on a line or anchor line.

wear ship, to A manoeuvre in which a square-rigger changed course by the ship's stern being turned through the wind, so that the direction of the wind came onto the opposite side of the ship. Today it is referred to as a gybe.

weather helm A term for when a sailing vessel has a tendency to turn towards the direction of wind, an action that is countered by turning the helm.

windage The exposed part of a ship's hull and rig that causes wind resistance.

windlass A horizontal and cylindrical barrel used as a lifting device for a rope or anchor cable. It was turned by rods called handspikes.

yard A slender wooden spar slung at its centre on the forward side of a mast on a square-rigged ship.

yardarm The outer end of each yard, from where, on a square-rigger, signal flags were flown and men sentenced to death following a court martial were hanged.

SOURCES

Lieutenant James Cook having been the focus for scores of authors and researchers for more than two centuries, it's little wonder that the material relating to his life and exploits is both abundant and readily available. When it came to writing this book, however, the challenge was to source information that would allow me to bring new light to the legacy of the famous seafarer, and I am confident this has been achieved.

My intention was also to enlighten those readers who already had an interest in Cook's exploits and in maritime history, especially that of Australia and New Zealand. In fact, the sources I used for my research provided a plethora of information about almost every aspect of the great man's fifty years on earth (and water). Sadly, one thing is missing: details of his personal life, in particular his family life. As mentioned previously, the reason for this is that Elizabeth Cook chose to destroy every letter she and her husband had exchanged, because she believed they were too private to be shared with others.

I have deliberately not provided the finer detail regarding sources. It is safe to say that those sources given in the text and below will provide that information, should it be required by researchers or academics.

I must mention two publications in particular. *The Life of Captain James Cook*, written by acclaimed Cook biographer John Cawte Beaglehole, and first published by Stanford University Press in 1974, furnished me with invaluable, extensive material. In the quest for specifics on ships of the eighteenth century, and the lifestyle that those on board were forced to endure, I hardly needed to look further than Ray Parkin's *H.M. Bark Endeavour*, published by The Miegunyah Press in 1997. This superb publication took Parkin twenty years to research and write – I have no doubt that there is no other to match it when it comes to specific detail, presented in words and magnificent fine-pen drawings. Parkin concentrated his research on *Endeavour*, but so much of it can be applied to other vessels of the era. *H.M. Bark Endeavour* is an enthralling read for anyone with salt in their veins.

Most importantly, it was the captain's journals relating to his three voyages of discovery that laid the foundation for much of my book. Here, a single publication – *James Cook, The Journals*, published by Penguin Classics (2000) – served as the primary source for my research.

There were several other books that I found to be insightful and beneficial:

- *Resolution: Captain Cook's Second Voyage of Discovery*, written by Peter Aughton and published by Phoenix (2005);
- *Captain James Cook: A Biography*, from the pen of Richard Hough and published by Coronet Books (1994);
- Tony Horwitz's witty and informative *Blue Latitudes*, published by Picador USA (2002);
- *The Life of Captain James Cook, the Circumnavigator* by Arthur Kitson, published by John Murray (1912; first published 1907);
- Andrew Kippis' *A Narrative of the Voyages around the World, Performed by Captain James Cook*, published by Porter & Coates (1850; first published 1783); and
- *Ship: 5,000 Years of Maritime Adventure* by Brian Lavery, published by Dorling Kindersley (2010).

In today's world of instant communications, the internet makes life so much easier when researching a new book. Yet the amount of information that is available calls for greater scrutiny when it comes to gauging the accuracy of what instantly appears on one's computer screen. Among the websites I accessed for information or confirmation were the following:

- http://science.nasa.gov/science-news/science-at-nasa/2004/28may_cook (The Transit of Venus – NASA Science – Science News)
- http://gutenberg.net.au (The *Endeavour* Journal of Sir Joseph Banks)
- www.captaincooksociety.com (General research)
- www.britishbattles.com/battle-of-quebec.htm (The Battle of Quebec)
- www.historyofwar.org/articles/wars_sevenyears.html (The Seven Years War)
- www.hollandcollege.com/about_holland_college/why_holland.php (Surveyor, Samuel Holland)
- www.antiquetelescopes.org/cook.html (Transit of Venus – Astronomical Instruments)
- www.adsb.co.uk/date_and_time/calendar_reform 1752 (Calendar change in England 1752)

From his humble beginnings in Marton-in-Cleveland in North Yorkshire, James Cook went on to cover some 220,000 nautical miles during his life under sail, literally travelling to the ends of the Earth. Two-and-a-half centuries later, Google Earth and Google Images provided me with the opportunity to 'visit' anywhere in the world. In a matter of seconds, I could be transported from an idyllic situation on a tropical island to a bleak, barren, snow-covered coastline within the Arctic Circle. With each 'trip' I was able to appreciate much of what Cook saw and experienced when he was there. And it afforded me an opportunity to wonder yet again at his much-lauded navigational charts, the accuracy of which fails to diminish alongside advances such as satellite imagery, given the limitations of that long-gone era.

ACKNOWLEDGEMENTS

It takes a talented team and considerable dedication to get a highly detailed book such as this completed and onto the shelves in bookshops on schedule – and that was my experience in creating *Cook*.

It began with the enthusiastic support of Helen Littleton, Associate Publisher, ABC Books, a woman whose approach to publishing I much admire. It was Helen who first convinced me that I should dip my oar into writing maritime history, and advanced the idea of me penning this book, seen as a refreshing new look at the life of the remarkable seafarer and explorer, Captain James Cook. It would be the third book in a trilogy of maritime heroes, my two previous books having dealt with the lives of Captain William Bligh and the man to first circumnavigate Australia, Lieutenant Matthew Flinders. The link comes from the fact that Bligh sailed with Cook, and Flinders sailed with Bligh.

This project also saw me return to the fold at HarperCollins Publishers and, through that move, establish a very satisfying link with ABC Books.

Along with Helen on the publishing side, I want to recognise the people who contributed so ably and directly to this book from start to finish. Special mention must be made of the Senior Editor, Mary Rennie, as well as Linda Brainwood and Denise O'Dea.

There are two people outside that organisation who most certainly deserve meritorious mention: Paul Brunton, Emeritus Curator at the Mitchell Library, State Library of NSW, and Jon

Gibbs, the editor. Paul did a superb job when cross-checking facts; and I can't speak highly enough of the effort Jon put into the editing. It seemed the greater the pressure, the greater his effort.

My approach to writing is very much hands-on: once I have the storyline in place I prefer to do the vast majority of the research myself, rather than farm it out. Even so, I would have struggled to get this project completed on time were it not for the selfless dedication of my assistant, Liz Christmas. She has worked untiringly with me on each book in this trilogy, and for that I am infinitely thankful.

On a personal note, there was one person who stood steadfastly by me from the start to the finish – my partner, Prue. My having to spend weekends and nights writing only brought complete understanding from her. She was my support team.

Finally, I want to acknowledge the remarkable encouragement I have received in recent years from the all-important booksellers. Their enthusiasm and support for this book, and my previous publications, make my endeavours all the more worthwhile.

Rob Mundle

ROB MUNDLE O.A.M. is a bestselling author, journalist and competitive sailor whose family heritage is with the sea, dating back to his great-great-grandfather, who was the master of square-riggers.

For over forty years, Rob has combined his passions for sailing and writing. He has written twelve books – including the international bestseller *Fatal Storm* – reported on more than thirty-five Sydney-to-Hobart yacht races (and competed in three), and covered seven America's Cups, four Olympics and numerous international events.

He is the winner of many sailing championships, has been a competitor in local and international contests, and has sailed everything from sailboards and 18-foot skiffs through to supermaxi yachts and offshore multihulls.

He was awarded an Order of Australia Medal in the Queen's Birthday Honours List 2013 for services to sailing and journalism.

His most recent book is *Flinders: The Man Who Mapped Australia*.